Sovereign Immunity Law

SOVEREIGN IMMUNITY LAW

Marilyn E. Phelan, Kimberly Mayfield
& Judge Jay M. Pat Phelan

SOVEREIGN IMMUNITY LAW

Marilyn E. Phelan, Kimberly Mayfield & Judge Jay M. Pat Phelan

Published by:

Vandeplas Publishing, LLC – February 2019

801 International Parkway, 5th Floor
Lake Mary, FL. 32746
USA

www.vandeplaspublishing.com

ISBN 978-1-60042-301-7

Preface

This book represents a first time and the only comprehensive coverage of the doctrine of sovereign immunity; one chapter provides a summary of the sovereign immunity laws in all of the states. Our objective in preparing this text is to provide the reader with a knowledge and understanding of the sovereign immunity doctrine and a realization of how Congress, state legislatures, and courts in the United States have incorporated into the "fabric" of our jurisprudence an antiquated doctrine that unfairly leaves victims of governmental wrongdoing without any remedy for their injuries or damages but also to provide the reader with an awareness and understanding of the important legal problems and road blocks that confront attorneys who represent victims of improvident government actions. The book provides crucial guidance and serves as an invaluable reference work for attorneys who may represent victims of governmental misconduct. Attorneys should read this book in advance to filing a lawsuit against the government in any context for, unfortunately, attorneys who have filed lawsuits against the government undoubtedly have found to their dismay that any actions they have brought either against the Federal government, most of the states, governmental agencies, as well as their officials and employees, were summarily dismissed based on the sovereign or governmental immunity doctrine.

The book critically reviews Federal and state tort claims and whistleblower acts as well as the difficulties victims encounter when they seek redress through these acts. Chapters address the applicability of the sovereign immunity doctrine to tribal nations, to municipalities and lesser governmental agencies, in bankruptcy proceedings, to civil rights proceedings, and to breach of contract claims against the government. One chapter reviews actions against state officials under 42 U.S. C. §1983 and similar actions against federal officials in what has been termed *Bivens* actions. A chapter also provides insights into the immunity of foreign States regarding claims filed against foreign governments in United States courts and when and how a claim can be brought successfully against a foreign State in a court in the United States for violations, among others, of international law. A summary chapter reviews briefly the sovereign immunity principles set out in more detail in the chapters and includes suggested, summarized steps in filing legal actions against the government.

Additionally, although the book not only defines the sovereign immunity doctrine and analyzes its statutory and judicial interpretations, it also presents important questions regarding the expansive and harsh application of the doctrine by both the federal government and by some of the states in a mission to assure the "absolute sovereignty" of the government when in our democratic system, the people should be the sovereign. One chapter traces the origin of the sovereign immunity doctrine back to the drafting of the United States Constitution and points out that the doctrine is a carryover from the then near-absolute power of the English kings. While the colonists rejected English political theory, the doctrine that a sovereign could not be sued without its consent was approved and, since that time, has been consistently upheld. In reviewing tenets of the doctrine, as well as its history, the reader should resolve why the rights of the people of the United States, who are in fact the sovereign, should give way to a loyalty and absolute power in the government. Moreover, because in granting immunity to governmental officials and employees, courts can cause them to become a privileged class who are above the law and free from liability for wrongs they inflict, the reader should consider whether the doctrine has not only limited, but also impeded and perhaps obviated, accountability and responsibility for governmental officials and employees. The reader should debate whether a harsh and rigid application of the sovereign immunity doctrine that exists in some states runs counter to democratic notion of the moral responsibility of the State.

In abrogating the state's immunity, the North Dakota Supreme Court[1] decided that "whatever justifications initially existed for sovereign immunity, they are no longer valid in today's society" and noted that few principles of modern law have been so uniformly and soundly criticized. Still, the opinion of the North Dakota Supreme Court must be compared with earlier reasoning of the Virginia Supreme Court[2] that the sovereign immunity doctrine "serves a multitude of purposes, including but not limited to protecting the public purse, providing for smooth operation of government, eliminating public inconvenience and danger

1 *Bulman v. Hulstrand Constr. Co., Inc.*, 521 N.W. 2d 632, 638 (N.D. 1994).

2 *Messina v. Burden*, 321 S.E.2d 657 (Va. 1984).

that might spring from officials being fearful to act, assuring that citizens will be willing to take public jobs, and preventing citizens from improperly influencing the conduct of governmental affairs through the threat or use of vexatious litigation." The Virginia Court referred to the doctrine "as a rule of social policy, which protects the state from burdensome interference with the performance of its governmental functions and preserves its control over state funds, property and instrumentalities."

The reader must decide which position, that of the Supreme Court of North Dakota or that of the Virginia Supreme Court, is most accurate and preferable or whether, in the alternative, there should be an intermediate and limited application of the doctrine as evidenced by the sovereign immunity law in some of the other states. Sovereign immunity provisions in each of the states are summarized in Chapter 6 to provide the reader with a valuable starting point in determining each state's sovereign immunity law.

The reader is cautioned that while even many jurists concede that the sovereign immunity doctrine is a persistent threat to the impartial administration of justice, it indeed has become a "fabric" of our law and attorneys representing victims of governmental wrongdoing must be fully aware of the far-reaching application of the doctrine and the means, if any, to counter its adverse consequences. The authors expect to provide the reader that awareness as well as helpful advice and easy reference to provide solutions to, and hopefully to prevent, courts' negative responses to their attempts to find redress for victims of wrongful governmental conduct.

We welcome readers' comments, questions, and feedback and encourage readers to contact us at marilyn.phelan@mail.com, kimberlymayfieldlaw@gmail.com, or patp922@aol.com.

Marilyn E. Phelan
Kimberly Mayfield
Jay M. (Pat) Phelan

Table of Contents

CHAPTER 1. SOVEREIGN IMMUNITY DOCTRINE IN THE UNITED STATES 1

A. Origin of the Sovereign Immunity Doctrine 2

B. Preservation of the Doctrine through *Stare Decisis* 8

C. Sovereign Immunity Deprives Courts of Jurisdiction 12

D. Eleventh Amendment Immunity 13

CHAPTER 2. IMMUNITY FOR GOVERNMENTAL OFFICIALS 19

A. Qualified Immunity 20

B. *Ex Parte Young* and Injunctive Relief 24

C. Suits in a Governmental Official's Individual Capacity 26

D. Suits against State Officials under 42 U.S.C. §1983 27

E. Suits against Federal Officials in a *Bivens* Action 30

CHAPTER 3. ABROGATION OF SOVEREIGN IMMUNITY 35

A. Section Five of the Fourteenth Amendment 36

B. Copyright Infringement 40

C. Jones Act 42

D. Federal Civil Rights Acts 45

1. Title VII, the Civil Rights Act of 1964 45
2. Equal Pay Act 49
3. Age Discrimination in Employment Act 51
4. Americans with Disabilities Act 53

E. Bankruptcy Proceedings 57

CHAPTER 4. EXCEPTIONS TO SOVEREIGN OR GOVERNMENTAL IMMUNITY 61

A. Takings Clauses and Inverse Condemnation Suits 62

B. Immovable Property 65

C. Governmental/Proprietary and Discretionary/Ministerial Dichotomies 65

D. Waiver of Sovereign Immunity 73

1. Breach of Contract Claims 77
2. Tort Claims Acts 84
3. Whistleblowers' Acts 98

E. Open Court Restrictions 117

CHAPTER 5. TRIBAL NATIONS AND FOREIGN STATES SOVEREIGN IMMUNITY 120

A. Tribal Nation Immunity 120

B. Sovereign Immunity as a Doctrine of International Law 122

C. Alien Tort Claims Act 127

D. Foreign Sovereign Immunities Act 132

E. Waiver of Immunity for Foreign Officials 147

CHAPTER 6. STATE SOVEREIGN IMMUNITY PROVISIONS 153

A. Alabama 156

B. Alaska 161

C. Arizona 162

D. Arkansas 163

E. California 164

F. Colorado 168

G. Connecticut 169

H. Delaware 171

I. District of Columbia 172

J. Florida 173

K. Georgia 175

L. Hawaii 176

M. Idaho 177

N. Illinois 178

O. Indiana 180

P. Iowa 182

Q. Kansas 182

R. Kentucky 183

S. Louisiana 184

T. Maine 186

U. Maryland 187

V. Massachusetts 190

W. Michigan 191

X. Minnesota 193

Y. Mississippi 195

Z. Missouri 196

AA. Montana 197

BB. Nebraska 198

CC. Nevada 199

DD. New Hampshire 200

EE. New Jersey 201

FF. New Mexico 202

GG. New York 204

HH. North Carolina 206

II. North Dakota 207

JJ. Ohio 209

KK. Oklahoma 210

LL. Oregon 211

MM. Pennsylvania 212

NN. Rhode Island 213

OO. South Carolina 215

PP. South Dakota 216

QQ. Tennessee 217

RR. Texas 217

SS. Utah 234

TT. Vermont 235

UU. Virginia 236

VV. Washington 238

WW. West Virginia 240

XX. Wisconsin 241

YY. Wyoming 243

CHAPTER 7. A SUMMATION OF SOVEREIGN IMMUNITY PRINCIPLES WITH A CHECKLIST OF PROCEDURAL GUIDELINES FOR SUITS AGAINST THE STATE 245

A. Review of Sovereign Immunity Principles 245

B. Summary Critique of Sovereign Immunity Doctrine 249

C. Steps in Filing Legal Actions Against the Government 251

CHAPTER 1.
SOVEREIGN IMMUNITY DOCTRINE IN THE UNITED STATES

The long-standing judicial doctrine of sovereign immunity prevents citizens from suing the government for money damages unless the government gives its consent to such suits. This chapter reviews the doctrine in its historical context to demonstrate that despite the questionable origins of the doctrine, it nonetheless has become a "fabric of the law" that sustains a perceived right of both federal and state governments to deprive its citizens of a remedy to challenge improvident, even illegal, governmental actions. The philosophy questionable historical roots have initiated and sustained a judicial philosophy that often places governmental officials and employees above the law. Because victims of governmental misconduct have no redress against the government when courts apply a strict construction of the doctrine and thus summarily dismiss claims against the government, it becomes clear that jurists, scholars, as well as the general public, should revisit the doctrine, consider its history, and then determine whether the doctrine has any continuing merit and, if so, which principles underlying the doctrine should be retained, and in what context.

Sovereign immunity is a common-law doctrine that developed without legislative or constitutional enactment[1] and while scholars and some courts have recognized the lack of justification for, and what some have termed inequities caused by, the judicially created sovereign immunity doctrine, the doctrine has evolved into an inviolable principle of American jurisprudence.[2] As such, attor-

1 See *Cohens v. Virginia,* 6 Wheat. 246, 19 U.S. 264, 293, 5 L. Ed. 257 (1821) and *Hosner v. De Young*, 1 Tex. 764,769 (1946) (discussed in *Reata Const. Corp. v. City of Dallas*, 197 S.W.3d 371 (Tex. 2006) and recognizing the doctrine as without constitutional or statutory authority.)

2 Discussion in *Indian Towing Co. v. United States,* 350 U.S. 61, 69, 76 S.Ct. 122, 100 L.Ed.21d 48 (1955). *See Hans v. Louisiana,* 134 U.S. 1, 16, 10 S. Ct. 504, 33 L. Ed. 842 (1890) ("The suability of a State, without its consent, was a thing unknown to the law. This has been so often laid down and acknowl-

neys must not only be aware of the long reaching effects of the doctrine that most often will deny their clients redress for governmental misconduct, they also must be knowledgeable of the instances in which Congress has abrogated sovereign immunity as well as federal and state statutes that have waived the doctrine in certain cases. Still, attorneys must also be aware of governmental road blocks limiting any such waivers in a definite purpose to broaden governmental power under the general guise of protecting the public fisc.[3]

A. ORIGIN OF THE SOVEREIGN IMMUNITY DOCTRINE

The sovereign immunity doctrine is a "carryover from the days of the near-absolute power of the English kings and is based on the philosophy that a sovereign cannot commit a legal wrong and should be immune from civil suit."[4]

edged by courts and jurists that it is hardly necessary to be formally asserted.") The Supreme Court stated in *Pennhurst State School and Hospital v. Halderman,* 465 U.S. 89, 105, 104 S.Ct. 900, 79 L.Ed.2d 67 (1984): "The principle of sovereign immunity as reflected in our jurisprudence strikes the proper balance between the supremacy of federal law and the separate sovereignty of the States."

3 These roadblocks are evident in amendments to the Texas Tort Claims Act that have eliminated for the most part the waiver of governmental immunity provisions in that statute. Discussion in Chapters 4 and 6.

4 Discussion in *Humane Society of the United States v. Clinton,* 236 F.3d 1320, 1326 (Fed. Cir. 2001). *See also Alden v. Maine,* 527 U.S. 706, 715, 119 S. Ct. 2240, 144 L. Ed. 2d 636 (1999) (stating "generations that designed and adopted our federal system considered immunity from private suits central to sovereign dignity"). The Supreme Court discussed the origin of the sovereign immunity doctrine in *Alden,* noting that the "leading advocates of the Constitution assured the people in no uncertain terms that the Constitution would not strip the States of sovereign immunity." *Id.* at 716. In *Alden,* the Court referred to *Chisholm v. Georgia,* 2 Dall. 419, 1 L. Ed. 440 (1793), wherein, just five years after the Constitution was adopted, the Court had ruled that Article III of the Constitution authorized a private citizen of another State to sue the State of Georgia without its consent. (Article III grants jurisdiction to federal courts over controversies to which the United States is a party.) Two Justices in *Chisholm* had argued that sovereign immunity was inconsistent with the principle of popular sovereignty established by the Constitution, *id.* at 454-458 (Wilson, Jr.); *id.* at 470-472 (Jay, C.J.). Other justices contended the text of Article III evidenced the States' surrender of sovereign immunity as to provisions extending jurisdiction over suits to which States were parties, *id.* at 452 (Blair, J.); *id.,* at 468 (Cushing, J.) Discussion in *Alden,* 527 U.S. at 719-20 ("The Court's decision [in *Chisholm*] 'fell upon the country with a profound shock" (citing 1 C. Warren, The Supreme Court in United States History 96 (rev. ed. 1926) and *Hans,* 134 U.S. at 11)) and noting: "The States, in particular, responded with outrage to the decision." The result of this concern about the States' sovereignty was the adoption of the Eleventh Amendment, discussed *infra.* Still, the Supreme Court has upheld state assertions of sovereign immunity in contexts outside the text of the Eleventh Amendment. In *Alden,* 527 U.S. at 728, the Court noted that subsequent Supreme Court decisions reflected "a settled doctrinal understanding, consistent with the views of the leading advocates of the Constitution's ratification, that sovereign immunity derives not from the Eleventh Amendment but from the structure of the original Constitution itself." The Court stated in *Alden:* "The Eleventh Amendment

Strangely, as some jurists have noted, the sovereign immunity doctrine evolved from the theory of absolute sovereignty despite the fact that the Declaration of Independence recorded the many wrongs of the King and that the colonists rejected the fiction that the king could do no wrong when they declared their independence from the Crown.[5] In a 1979 case,[6] the Supreme Court supported this proposition by quoting the Declaration of Independence as follows:

> [T]hat whenever any form of government becomes destructive of these ends, it is the right of the People to alter or to abolish it, and to institute new government...and such is now the necessity which constrains them to alter their former systems of government. The history of the present King of Great Britain is a history of repeated injuries and usurpations, all having its direct objective the establishment of an absolute tyranny over these states.

Further, the Supreme Court[7] very early stated:

> We do not understand that, either in reference to the government of the United States, or of the several States, or of any of their officers, the English maxim [that the king can do no wrong] has an existence in this country.

Still, Supreme Court justices also have acknowledged that while "the American people had rejected other aspects of English political theory, the doctrine that a sovereign could not be sued without its consent was universal in the states when the Constitution was drafted and ratified."[8] Further, despite its ancient lineage, a Supreme Court justice described the doctrine of sovereign immunity as a judge-made rule that "rests on considerations of policy given legal sanctions" by the Supreme Court.[9]

---

confirmed, rather than established, sovereign immunity as a constitutional principle; it follows that the scope of the States' immunity from suit is demarcated not by the text of the amendment alone but by fundamental postulates implicit in the Constitutional design." *Id.* at 728-29.

5 See, e.g., *Nevada v. Hall*, 440 U.S. 410, 414-15, 99 S. Ct. 1182, 59 L. Ed. 2d 416 (1979) wherein the Supreme Court discussed the origins of the sovereign immunity doctrine.

6 Id.

7 *Langford v. United States*, 101 U.S. 341, 343, 25 L. Ed. 1010 (1879).

8 Discussion in *Alden*, 527 U.S. at 715-16.

9 Justice Frankfurter in *National City Bank of New York v. Republic of China*, 348 U.S. 356, 358, 75 S.Ct. 423, 99 L.Ed. 389 (1955). Justice Frankfurter stated that the doctrine "has become solely through

Some legal theorists have agreed that the courts' original reliance on the notion that a divinely ordained monarch "can do no wrong" has been "thoroughly discredited."[10] A dissenting Michigan justice declared in a 1961 case that the only argument supporting the doctrine of governmental immunity was that "age has lent weight to the unjust whim of long-dead Kings." This justice postulated:[11]

> It is hard to say why the courts of America have adhered to this relic of absolutism so long a time after America overthrew monarchy itself!

One Justice of the Supreme Court conceded that the doctrine's "persistent threat to the impartial administration of justice has been repeatedly acknowledged and recognized."[12]

Although the concept of sovereign immunity was adopted initially by the first courts in the United States, some jurists did disapprove of the doctrine early in its employment. In 1882, one Supreme Court justice concluded that the doctrine clearly had no justification in our system of jurisprudence.[13] In pointing out that the principle of sovereign immunity "is derived from the laws and practices of our English ancestors," this justice traced the doctrine that the king of England was "not suable in the courts of that country" from the time of Edward the First.[14] An interesting quirk of legal history is that while the United Kingdom retains a vestigial monarchy, English courts have permitted actions against the government since the early 1900s.[15]

In questioning whether the king was suable "in his kingly character as other persons" prior to the establishment of the petition of right, a king apparently was

adjudications of this Court." See also *United States v. Nordic Village*, 503 U.S. 30, 42, 112 S. Ct. 1011, 117 L. Ed. 2d 181 (1992).

10 Justice Stevens, in *Nordic Village*, 503 U.S. at 42.

11 Justice Edwards, dissenting opinion in *Williams v. City of Detroit*, 111 N.W. 2d 1, 24 (Mich. 1961).

12 Justice Stevens, *Nordic Village*, 503 U.S. at 43.

13 Justice Miller in the 5-4 decision in *United States v. Lee*, 106 U.S. 196, 205, 15 S.Ct. 240, 27 L. Ed. 171 (1882).

14 *Id.*

15 See *generally, Shrimpton v. Hertfordshire County Council*, 104 Law Times Rep. 145, 2 N.C.C.A. 238 (1911); *Ching v. Surrey County Council*, 1 K.B. 736, 2 N.C.C.A. 229 (1910); and *Smith v. Martin and the Corporation of Kingston-Upon-Hull*, 2 K.B. 775, 2 N.C.C.A. 215 (1911).

never suable of common right.[16] However, during the reign of Edward the First, one could sue the king in his own courts if the king gave consent in a "petition of right." Evidently the purpose of the petition of right, as it was used in England, was to secure rights of suitors against the crown in the same manner as did legal controversies between subjects of the king among themselves. However, after the "petition of right" was instituted, one could sue the king in any court only as permitted in the petition.[17]

The English remedy of petition of right was never introduced into the United States. As the Supreme Court recognized in 1882, "there is in this country...no such thing as the petition of right, [just] as there is no such thing as a kingly head to the nation, or to any of the States which compose it."[18] The Court then questioned the reasons that would forbid one to sue the king in the king's own court and how those reasons apply to the "political body corporate which we call the United States of America."[19] As the Court noted, "the absurdity of the king's sending a writ to himself to command the king to appear in the king's court," does not exist in our government because in the United States, "process runs in the name of the president and may be served on the attorney general." The Court further explained that "the dignity of the government is [not] degraded by its appearing as a defendant in the courts of its own creation, because it is constantly appearing as a party in such courts and submitting its rights as against the citizens."[20] Another reason the Court considered in support of the doctrine of sovereign immunity, as it originated in England, was that

> it would be inconsistent with the very idea of supreme executive power and would endanger the performance of the public duties of the sovereign, to subject the king to repeated suits as a matter of right, at the will of any citizen, and to submit to the judicial tribunals the control and disposition of his public property.[21]

16 *United States v. Lee,* 106 U.S. at 205.

17 *Id.*

18 *Id.* at 205-6.

19 *Id.* at 206.

20 *Id.*

21 *Id.*

The Court countered this notion by observing that, because "we have no person in this government who exercises supreme executive power or performs the public duties of a sovereign, it is difficult to see on what solid foundation of principle the exemption from liability to suit rests."[22] The Court gave great weight to "the vast difference in the essential character of the two governments as regards the source and the depositaries of power and, despite progress made to strip the crown of its powers, the public's undoubted reverence for the English monarchy to not subject it to the same legal demands as ordinary citizens."[23] In considering these differences, one might question, as the Court did, why the rights of the people of the United States-- who are in fact the sovereign-- should give way to a "sentiment of loyalty" to the government. As the Court stated:[24]

> Under our system the *people*...are the sovereign. Their rights...are not bound to give way to a sentiment of loyalty to the person of the monarch. The citizen here knows no person, however near to those in power, or however powerful himself, to whom he need yield the rights which the law secures to him when it is well administered. When he, in one of the courts of competent jurisdiction, has established the right to property, there is no reason why deference to any person, natural or artificial, not even the United States, should prevent him from using the means which the law gives him for the protection and enforcement of that right.

The old form of bringing a claim against the English monarchy by petition of right was tedious and expensive and, thus, fell into disuse.[25] Eventually, however, royal consent later was granted as a matter of course.[26] The Secretary of State would bring a petition before the monarch for the monarch's consideration. Still, if the monarch refused to grant his fiat, the claimant was without a remedy.[27] However, in 1947, the United Kingdom granted suits against

22 *Id.*

23 *Id.*

24 *Id.* at 208-09.

25 *Id.* at 238. (Gray, J., dissenting).

26 *Lee,* 106 U.S. at 238 (Gray, J., dissenting) (citing *E. Archipelago Co. v. Queen,* (1856) 118 Eng. Rep. 988 (Q.B.) 1009, 2 El & Bl. 856, 914-15).

27 T*obin v. Queen,* 14 C.B. (N.S.) 505, 521.

the government in tort and contract by the Crown Proceedings Act of 1947.[28] This Act permits claims against the government if the claims can be brought against any other defendant. Civil proceedings against the Crown must be instituted against the appropriate authorized governmental department or, if none is appropriate or there is doubt as to whether any is appropriate, against the Attorney General.[29] All documents required to be served on the Crown must be served on the solicitor for the appropriate department or if there is no such solicitor upon the solicitor of the monarch's treasury.[30]

Although English courts for the most part have repudiated the doctrine of sovereign immunity, it continues as a "fabric of our law."[31] Some jurists early rationalized that the public would be harmed, public service would be hindered, and public safety endangered if the government was subjected to suit at the instance of every citizen.[32] A Supreme Court justice later disagreed, however, stating in a dissenting opinion that "changes in our social fabric favor limitation rather than expansion of sovereign immunity."[33] This justice thought the concept of sovereign immunity, which he believed dictates that "citizens should be remediless in the face of its abuses," was more "a relic of medieval thought than anything else."[34] He further remarked:

> Whether this immunity is an absolute survival of the monarchial privilege, or is a manifestation merely of power, or rests on abstract logical grounds, it undoubtedly runs counter to modern democratic notions of the moral responsibility of the State.[35]

28 Crown Proceedings Act, 1947, 10 & 11 Geo.6, c. 44, § 1.

29 *Id.* Sections 17(3) and 18 of the Crown Proceedings Act of 1947.

30 *Id.* In Scotland civil proceedings against the Crown are directed against the Advocate General for Scotland.

31 See *National City Bank of New York v. Republic of China*, 348 U.S. at 358. The Court compared the sovereign immunity of foreign nations as solely recognized under adjudications of the Court with "the nonsuability of the United States...[which is also] derived from considerations of policy." (Discussion of sovereign immunity of foreign nations in Chapter 6.)

32 Discussion in *United States v. Lee*, 106 U.S. at 247.

33 *Pennhurst State School & Hospital v. Halderman*, 465 U.S. at 166, Stevens, J.

34 *Id.*

35 *Id.*

Another Supreme Court justice early referred to a statement by Frederick William Maitland that "it is a wholesome sight to see 'the Crown' sued and answering for its torts."[36]

B. PRESERVATION OF THE DOCTRINE THROUGH *STARE DECISIS*

The continuing adherence of courts to the sovereign immunity doctrine is intertwined with, and preserved by, another long-established doctrine, the principle of *stare decisis*. The Supreme Court has stated that *stare decisis* "promotes the evenhanded, predictable, and consistent development of legal principles, fosters reliance on judicial decisions, and contributes to the actual and perceived integrity of the process."[37] Based on this principle, the Supreme Court has treated the tenet--that citizens cannot sue their government--as a fabric of our

---

36 Chief Justice Reed in *Great Northern Life Ins. Co. v. Read,* 322 U.S. 47, 59, 64 S.Ct. 873, 88 L.Ed. 1121 (1944), citing 3 Maitland, Collected Papers, 263 (1911).

Courts have not granted foreign governments immunity from suit in federal courts in like manner as it has provided immunity for the federal and state governments. In 1812 in *Schooner Exchange v. McFaddon,* 7 Cranch 116, 3 L.Ed. 287 (1812), then Chief Justice Marshall ruled that foreign sovereigns had no right to immunity in our courts. However, Chief Justice Marshall explained that, as a matter of comity, members of the international community had implicitly agreed to waive the exercise of jurisdiction over other sovereigns in certain classes of cases. As a result, the U.S. Supreme Court had "consistently...deferred to the decisions of the political branches–in particular, those of the Executive Branch–on whether to take jurisdiction" over particular actions against foreign sovereigns. See *Verlinden B.V. v. Central Bank of Nigeria,* 461 U.S. 480, 486, 103 S.Ct. 1962, 76 L.Ed.2d 81 (1983). Until 1952, the Executive Branch followed a policy of requesting immunity in all actions against friendly sovereigns. However, in that year the State Department concluded immunity should no longer be granted in certain types of cases. Foreign nations often placed diplomatic pressure on the State Department, and political considerations led to the Department filing "suggestions of immunity" where immunity otherwise would not have been available. Responsibility fell to the courts to determine whether sovereign immunity existed. *See* discussion in *Austria v. Altmann,* 541 U.S. 677, 690, 124 S.Ct. 2240, 159 L.Ed.2d 1 (2004) and a review of the Federal Sovereign Immunities Act in Chapter 5.

In *National City Bank of New York v. Republic of China,* 348 U.S. at 423, Justice Frankfurter reasoned that the limitation of immunity for foreign governments was justified because, according to Justice Frankfurter: "Unlike the special position accorded our States as party defendants by the Eleventh Amendment, the privileged position of a foreign state is not an explicit command of our Constitution." (In 1976, Congress sought to remedy problems relating to immunity for foreign governments by enacting the Foreign Sovereign Immunities Act, 28 U.S.C. §§1601-11. In that Act, Congress provided foreign states with immunity from suit in federal courts but set out certain specified exceptions, one being an action based upon a commercial activity carried on in the United States by the foreign state. The Foreign Sovereign Immunities Act and immunity for foreign states, with limitations on immunity, are discussed in Chapter 5.)

37 *Pearson v. Callahan,* 555 U.S. 223, 129 S. Ct. 808, 816, 172 L.Ed.2d 565 (2009) (quoting *Payne v. Tennessee,* 501 U.S. 808, 827, 111 S.Ct.2597, 115 L.Ed 2d 720 (1991)).

jurisprudence since the Constitution was drafted and ratified and the first courts were instituted.[38]

Although the rule of *stare decisis* advances "consistency and uniformity of decision," the Court early recognized the doctrine is flexible.[39] Because the Supreme Court bears the ultimate obligation for development of the law as institutions develop,[40] the Court has chosen on occasion to ignore the principle of *stare decisis* and to overrule or modify significantly its prior decisions.[41] Depending on the subject matter in a particular case, a majority of the Court has occasionally disregarded *stare decisis* with respect to previous decisions they disapprove. In 2009, the Court rejected a two-step rule (that the precedent was not well reasoned and produced erroneous results) and announced it must consider many factors before overruling a past decision.[42] Specifically, the Court focuses on four considerations: the reasoning of the decision, the workability of the rule, the reliance interests at stake, and the antiquity of the precedent.[43] The Court then overruled two prior decisions in 2009, one of which had been the

---

38 Discussion in the 1882 decision, rendered 5-4, in *United States v. Lee*, 106 U.S. at 205. In 1999, in *Alden v. Maine*, 527 U.S. at 714, a majority of the justices of the Supreme Court, in tracing the history of the sovereign immunity doctrine, asserted that when the Constitution was ratified it was well established in English law the Crown could not be sued without consent in its own courts. Over two hundred years prior to the *Alden* decision and just five years after the Constitution was adopted, in *Chisholm v. Georgia*, 2 U.S. 419, 425, 2 Dal. 419, 1 L. Ed 440 (1793), the newly constituted Supreme Court, in four separate opinions, acknowledged that the United States could not be sued. The Court sustained the right of a South Carolina citizen to bring a lawsuit against the State of Georgia. In the four separate opinions, members of the Court generally reasoned that a state's immunity was qualified by the general provisions of Article III of the United States Constitution and, more specifically, by the provision in Article III, §2, which extended the federal judicial power to controversies between a state and citizens of another state. Id. at 454-8. Later, as noted *infra*, the adoption of the Eleventh Amendment eliminated the right of a citizen of one state to bring a suit in federal court against another state. *Alden*, 527 U.S. at 713. Further, the Supreme Court subsequently decided, in the 1890 landmark case of *Hans v. Louisiana*, 134 U.S. 1, 9-10, 14-15, 10 S.Ct. 504, 33 L.Ed. 842 (1890), that a citizen also may not sue the state of her residence in a federal court even though the Eleventh Amendment does not so state. Thus, as discussed *infra*, the Supreme Court since 1890 has sanctioned dual sovereign immunity. *Stare decisis* has sustained the doctrine.

39 *Hertz v. Woodman*, 218 U.S.205, 212, 30 C. Ct. 621, 54 L.Ed. 1001 (1910).

40 See generally *Smith v. All-wright*, 321 U.S. 649, 665-66, 64 S. Ct. 757, 88 L. Ed 987 (1944) (discussing the Court's ability to reexamine its decisions and not be bound by *stare decisis*).

41 In *Pearson v. Callahan*, 555 U. S. at 234-35, the Court softened the perceived hard line laid out by *Saucier v. Katz*, 533 U.S. 194, 121 S.Ct. 2151, 150 L.Ed.2d 272 (2001) and recognized the discretion of lower courts to decide whether to apply the precedent of *Saucier* in certain cases.

42 *Montejo v. Louisiana*, 556 U.S. 778, 129 S. Ct. 2079, 173 L. Ed.2d 955 (2009).

43 *Id.*

law for twenty-eight years.[44] Further, the Court overruled one prior Supreme Court decision as well as part of another in 2010, in *Citizens United v. Federal Election Commission*.[45] In 2015, the Court affirmed that "continued adherence" to some decisions "would undermine, rather than promote, the goals of evenhandedness, predictability, and consistency served by *stare decisis*."[46] The Court declared: "[T]he doctrine of *stare decisis* allows us to revisit an earlier decision where experience with its application reveals that it is unworkable."[47] In 2016, the Supreme Court restated a prior position that its precedents "are not sacrosanct" and acknowledged it had overruled prior decisions "where the necessity and propriety of doing so has been established."[48] Thus, the Supreme Court has acknowledged it will discount *stare decisis* concerns if "the precedent was badly reasoned and produces erroneous results"[49] and has ruled that revisiting precedent is particularly appropriate where a departure will not upset settled expectations.[50]

Notwithstanding that depending upon the subject matter of a particular decision, a majority of members of the Court have dismissed the doctrine with respect to previous decisions they disapprove,[51] the Court continues to recog-

---

44 In *Arizona v. Gant*, 556 U.S.332, 129 S. Ct. 1710, 173 L.Ed.2d 485 (2009), the Supreme Court overruled *New York v. Belton*, 453 U.S. 454, 101 S.Ct.2860, 69 L.Ed.2d 768 (1981) even though that case had been the law for twenty-eight years. In addition, in *Montejo v. Louisiana*, 556 U. S. at 797, the Court overruled *Michigan v. Jackson*, 475 U.S. 625, 106 S.Ct.1404, 89 L.Ed.2d 631 (1986).

45 *Citizens United*, 558 U. S 310, 130 S.Ct 876, 175 L.Ed. 2d 753 (2010). The Supreme Court overruled *Austin v. Michigan Chamber of Commerce*, 494 U.S. 652, 110 S.Ct. 1391, 108 L.Ed.2d 652 (1990) and part of *McConnell v. F.E.C.*, 540 U.S. 93, 124 S.Ct. 619, 157 L.Ed.2d 491 (2003).

46 See *Johnson v. United States*, 135 S. Ct. 2551, 2553-4, 192 L. Ed. 2d 59 (2015)

47 *Id.*

48 *Hurst v. Florida*, 136 S.Ct. 616, 623, 193 L. Ed.2d 504 (2016) (expressly overruling in relevant part *Hildwin v. Florida*, 490 U.S. 638, 109 S. Ct. 2055, 104 L.Ed. 2d 728 (1989) and *Spaziano v. Florida*, 468 U.S. 447, 104 S. Ct. 3154, 82 L. Ed. 2d 340 (1984). The Court stated "[T]ime and subsequent cases have washed away the logic of *Spaziano and Hildwin*. 136 S. Ct. at 624.)

49 See *Gant*, 556 U. S. at 353-54. The Court noted the "narrow view of *stare decisis*" provided "the only principle on which the decision in Gant can be justified." *Id.*

50 *Pearson v. Callahan*, 553 U.S. at 232-33.

51 See, e.g. *College Savings Bank v. Florida Prepaid Postsecondary Education Expense Board*, 527 U.S. 666, 680, 199 S.Ct. 2219, 144 L.Ed.2d 605 (1999) (presenting Justice Scalia's discourse on the effect of *stare decisis* on decisions relating to sovereign immunity). Notwithstanding the principle of stare decisis, the majority of the Court in *College Savings Bank* overruled a decision of the Court that was rendered in a unanimous opinion thirty-five years previously. Justice Scalia referred to the prior decision, *Parden v. Terminal R. of Ala. Docks Dept.*, 377 U.S. 184, 84 S.Ct.1207, 12 L.Ed. 2d 233 (1964), as "an elliptical opinion that stands at the nadir of our waiver (and, for that matter,

nize *stare decisis* as "a foundation stone of the rule of law."[52] The Court recently stated: "[T]he doctrine of *stare decisis* provides that today's Court should stand by yesterday's decisions" and that application of the doctrine is the "preferred course."[53] Nonetheless, the Court recently recognized that "respecting *stare decisis* means sticking to some wrong decisions," but conceded that "*stare decisis* carries enhanced force when a decision...interprets a statute."[54]

As noted *supra*, the sovereign immunity doctrine was adopted by the first courts in the United States based on laws and practices of England; it is not based on statute. Further, while the doctrine of *stare decisis* treats as general law prior court opinions, specifically those of the Supreme Court, some have questioned whether this treatment provides for judicial usurpation of the legislative power granted Congress by Article I of the Constitution, which provides that Congress alone can make the laws.[55] In addition, if governing decisions can have less value

sovereign-immunity) jurisprudence." 527 at 676. In *Parden*, the Supreme Court ruled that employees of a railroad owned and operated by Alabama could bring an action against their employer under the Federal Employers' Liability Act, 45 U.S.C. § 51. The Court decided that, despite the absence of any provision in that statute specifically referring to the states, the Act authorized suits against the states by virtue of the Act's general provision subjecting to suit "[e]very common carrier by railroad...engaging in commerce between...the several states." Twenty-three years later in *Welch v. Texas Dept. of Highways and Public Transp*, 483 U.S. 468, 478, 107 S.Ct. 2941, 97 L.Ed.2d 389 (1987), the Supreme Court overruled *Parden* "to the extent it was inconsistent with the requirement that an abrogation of Eleventh Amendment immunity by Congress must be expressed in unmistakably clear language." Thirty-five years after *Parden*, the Supreme Court, in *College Savings Bank*, 527 U.S. at 680, expressly overruled "whatever may remain of our decision in *Parden*." The majority of the Court in *College Savings Bank* decided that "the constructive-waiver experiment of *Parden* was ill conceived," and stated that there was "no merit in attempting to salvage any remnant of it." *Id.* The Court commented that "the very cornerstone of the *Parden* opinion was the notion that state sovereign immunity is not constitutionally grounded." *Id.* at 682. In *College Savings Bank*, 527 U.S. at 687, Justice Scalia, writing for the majority of the Court, referred to what he termed "the still-warm precedent of *Seminole Tribe* and to the 110-year old decision in *Hans* that supports it." [In *Seminole Tribe of Fla. v. Florida*, 517 U.S. 44, 54, 66-68, 116 S.Ct. 1114, 134 L.Ed.2d 252 (1996), the Supreme Court reaffirmed its ruling in *Hans*, which had repudiated its earlier decision in *Chisholm v. Georgia*, that Article III of the Constitution superseded sovereign immunity of the states.] Justice Scalia then referred to the dissenters in *College Savings Bank* as having "adopted a decidedly perverse theory of *stare decisis*." 527 U.S. at 689.

52 See *Kimble v. Marvel Entertainment*, LLC, 135 S. Ct. 2401, 2409, 192 L. Ed. 2d 463 (2015), quoting *Michigan v. Bay Mills Indian Community*, 134 S. Ct. 2024, 2036, 188 L. Ed. 2d 1071 (2014).

53 *Kimble*, 135 S. Ct. at 2404, quoting *Payne v. Tennessee*, 501 U.S. 808, 828, 827, 111 S. Ct. 2597, 115 L. Ed. 2d 720 (1991).

54 *Kimble*, 135 S. Ct. at 2409.

55 See United States Constitution, Article I, §1 ("All legislative Powers herein granted shall be vested in a Congress of the United States....") Interestingly, in *College Savings Bank*, 527 U.S. at 683, Justice Scalia decided that recognizing "a congressional power to exact constructive waivers of sovereign immunity through the exercise of Article I powers would also, as a practical matter, permit Congress

in our system of jurisprudence and can be overruled when they no longer meet the requirements for good law, courts should revisit the reasoning, workability, reliance, interest, and antiquity of the sovereign immunity doctrine in light of an increasing need for governmental accountability and transparency.[56]

C. SOVEREIGN IMMUNITY DEPRIVES COURTS OF JURISDICTION

Courts have applied the sovereign immunity doctrine consistently to continue the judicial notion that citizens cannot bring suits against the government. Sovereign immunity deprives a trial court of subject-matter jurisdiction in a suit against the government unless the government consents to suit.[57] The Supreme Court has referred to suits for money damages against states as possibly threatening "the financial integrity of the States" and has concluded that "at the time of the founding, many of the States could have been forced into insolvency but for their immunity from private suits for money damages."[58] Thus, sovereign immunity protects state governments, as well as the federal government, from money judgments even if the government's liability is undisputed. Further, political subdivisions of the state, including cities, also are entitled to immunity–referred to as governmental immunity.[59]

---

to circumvent the anti-abrogation holding of *Seminole Tribe*." (In *Seminole Tribe*, 517 U.S. at 68, the Supreme Court ruled that Congress lacks authority to abrogate the States' Eleventh Amendment immunity.) In a dissenting opinion in that case, Justice Breyer concluded the Supreme Court had made the sovereign immunity doctrine immune from congressional Article I modification, and, thus, had made "it more difficult for Congress to decentralize governmental decision making and to provide individual citizens, or local communities, with a variety of enforcement powers." *College Savings Bank*, 527 U.S. at 705. Justice Breyer opined that by diminishing congressional flexibility, the Supreme Court made it "more difficult to satisfy modern federalism's more important liberty-protecting needs." *Id.* Thus, Justice Breyer concluded that the doctrine of sovereign immunity is "counterproductive." *Id.* In *Alden v. Maines*, 527 U.S. at 711, the Court ruled that powers delegated to Congress under Article I of the United States Constitution do not include the power to subject nonconsenting states to private suits for damages in state courts.

56 See *Montejo*, 556 U.S. at 791-93 (enumerating the factors the court must consider before overruling a prior decision.)

57 See, e.g., *Tex. Dep't of Parks & Wildlife v. Miranda*, 133 S.W.3d 217, 224 (Tex. 2004). Discussion of consent to suit through waiver of sovereign immunity in Chapter 4. Whether a court has subject matter jurisdiction is a question of law for a court to decide. See *Williamson v. Tucker*, 645 F.2d 404, 413 n. 6, 416 n. 10 (5th Cir. 1981).

58 *Alden v. Maine*, 527 U.S. at 750.

59 See *Wichita Falls State Hosp. v. Taylor*, 106 S.W.3d 692, 694 n. 3 (Tex. 2003)

Despite the problem that the sovereign immunity doctrine can, and often does, protect wrongful governmental conduct[60] and it did fall into some disfavor in the past, courts have decided they must be "self-constituted" guardians of the Treasury. The Supreme Court[61] has stated that a "general federal power to authorize private suits for money damages would place unwarranted strain on the State's ability to govern in accordance with the will of their citizens." The Court decided that while a judgment creditor of a state could have a legitimate claim for compensation, "other important needs and worthwhile ends compete for access to the public fisc."[62]

D. ELEVENTH AMENDMENT IMMUNITY

The Supreme Court's interpretation of the Eleventh Amendment provides the authority for sovereign immunity for the states when they are sued in federal courts. Article III of the Constitution, which created the courts, extends federal judicial power to controversies "between a State and Citizens of another State."[63] Relying on this language, the Supreme Court in 1793 assumed original jurisdiction over a suit brought by a citizen of South Carolina against the State of Georgia.[64] The decision created great concern as to the reach of federal judicial power and led immediately to the proposal and enactment of the Eleventh Amendment in 1795 to prevent a citizen of one state from bringing a suit in federal courts against another state.[65] The Eleventh Amendment reads:

> The Judicial power of the United States shall not be construed to extend to any suit in law or equity, commenced or prosecuted against one of the United States

60 See discussion of many of these cases in Chapter 4 in the discussion of Texas law relating to torts claims act and whistleblowers acts.

61 *Alden v. Maine*, 527 U.S. at 750.

62 *Id.* According to the Court, because "all cannot be satisfied in full," difficult decisions must be made. *Id.*

63 Article III courts are law courts, equity courts, and admiralty courts all of which are specifically named in Article III. They sit to determine "cases" or "controversies."

64 *Chisholm v. Georgia*, 2 U.S. at 430, 452.

65 Discussion in *Monaco v Mississippi*, 292 U.S. 313, 325, 54 S.Ct.745, 78 L.Ed. 1282 (1934).

by Citizens of *another* State, or by Citizens or Subjects of any Foreign State. (Emphasis added.)

Courts now postulate that the principle of sovereign immunity was incorporated into the Constitution through the Eleventh Amendment as a constitutional limitation on federal judicial power established in Article III of the Constitution.[66]

Although the Eleventh Amendment only bars actions by non-citizens against a state, in an 1890 decision, *Hans v. Louisiana*,[67] the Supreme Court ruled that, despite limited terms of the Eleventh Amendment, a federal court also cannot entertain a suit brought by a citizen against her own state. After reviewing constitutional debates concerning the scope of Article III, the Court decided framers of the Constitution did not contemplate federal jurisdiction over suits against nonconsenting state when they established through the Constitution the judicial power of the United States.[68] Since that decision, the Supreme Court has ruled consistently that a state may not be sued without its consent.[69] As the Supreme Court has stated, its "repeated decisions" have established as "a fundamental rule of jurisprudence" the principle that a state cannot be sued without its consent.[70]

The Supreme Court has ruled that "neither substantive federal law nor attempted congressional abrogation under Article I bars a State from raising a constitutional defense of sovereign immunity in federal court."[71] Further, according to the Supreme Court, the states "retain an analogous constitu-

66 Discussion in *Pennhurst State School & Hospital v. Halderman*, 465 U.S. at 98.

67 *Hans*, cited in note 2, 134 U.S. at 9-10.

68 *Id.* at 15.

69 In *Alden v. Maine*, 527 U.S. at 716-7, the Supreme Court commented that the principle of sovereign immunity was applicable to state governments as early as the ratification of the Constitution. The court referred to Alexander Hamilton's assurance to the states in Federalist No. 81 when he stated: "It is inherent in the nature of sovereignty not to be amenable to the suit of an individual without its consent. This is the general sense and the general practice of mankind; and the exemption, as one of the attributes of sovereignty, is now enjoyed by the government of every state in the Union." *Id.* The Court noted James Madison's statement at the Virginia ratifying convention: "It is not in the power of individuals to call any state into court." *Id.* In *Board of Trustees of Univ. of Alabama v. Garrett*, 531 U.S. 356, 363,121 S.Ct.955, 148 L. Ed. 2d 866 (2001), the Supreme Court noted that the "ultimate guarantee of the Eleventh Amendment is that nonconsenting States may not be sued by private individuals in federal court."

70 *Pennhurst State School & Hospital*, 465 U.S. at 98.

71 *Alden v. Maine*, 527 U.S. at 748.

tional immunity from private suits in their own courts."[72] Thus, the Supreme Court, in taking the position the Eleventh Amendment has incorporated into the Constitution a common law doctrine of sovereign immunity, has ruled that while "the Constitution grants broad powers to Congress, our federalism requires that Congress treat the state in a manner consistent with their status as residuary sovereigns and joint participants in the governance of the Nation."[73] The Court referred to the "founding generation thought" that the several states of the Union should not be summoned to answer as defendants "the complaints of private persons."[74]

By viewing the Eleventh Amendment as being consonant with principles of federalism, the Supreme Court has referred to sovereign immunity as "a guarantee that is implied as an essential component of federalism" and "sufficiently fundamental to our federal structure to have implicit constitutional dimension."[75] Thus, the Court has insisted a state must consent to suit against it in federal court, and its consent must be "unequivocally expressed."[76] The Supreme Court also has ruled that a state's waiver of sovereign immunity in its own courts is not a waiver of the Eleventh Amendment immunity in the federal courts.[77]

Although the Supreme Court has interpreted the Eleventh Amendment to provide States with immunity, the Court announced a state can waive immunity in *Lapides v. Board of Regents of the University System of Georgia*,[78] wherein the Court referred to its many rulings that "established the general principle that a State's voluntary appearance in federal court amounts to a waiver of its Eleventh Amendment immunity." The Court announced in *Lapides*:[79]

---

72 *Id.*

73 *Id.*

74 *Id.*

75 See *Nevada v. Hall*, 440 U.S. at 418-419. See also *Hutto v. Finney*, 437 U.S. 678, 691, 98 S.Ct. 2565, 57 L.Ed.2d 522 (1978).

76 *Edelman v. Jordan*, 415 U.S. 651, 673, 94 S.Ct. 1347, 39 L.Ed.2d 662 (1974). In *Great Northern Life Ins. Co. v. Read*, 322 U.S. at 54, the Supreme Court ruled that it will find a waiver of immunity "if the State makes a 'clear declaration' that it intends to submit itself to our jurisdiction." *Id.*

77 *Florida Department of Health v. Florida Nursing Home Assn.*, 450 U.S.147, 150, 101S.Ct. 1032, 67 L.Ed.2d 132 (1981).

78 *Lapides*, 535 U.S.613, 620-23, 122 S.Ct. 1640, 152 L.Ed.2d 806 (2002).

79 *Id.* at 619.

> [I]t "would seem anomalous or inconsistent for a State both (1) to invoke federal jurisdiction, thereby contending that the "Judicial power of the United States" extends to the case at hand, and (2) to claim Eleventh Amendment immunity, thereby denying that the "Judicial power of the United States" extends to the case at hand."[80]

The Constitution was amended in 1868 to add the Fourteenth Amendment to protect certain civil rights of private parties. Pursuant to Section Five of the Fourteenth Amendment, discussed in Chapter 3, Congress can abrogate Eleventh Amendment immunity if it does so specifically in legislation enacted under the protections of the Fourteenth Amendment.[81] However, the Supreme Court has stated that because "in light of history, practice, precedent, and the structure of the Constitution" the states retain immunity from private suit in their own courts, state immunity is "beyond the congressional power to abrogate by Article I legislation."[82] Further, in *Seminole Tribe of Florida v. Florida*,[83] the Court ruled Congress cannot abrogate sovereign immunity of the states when acting pursuant to its plenary power to regulate commerce under Article

80 The Court reasoned that "an interpretation of the Eleventh Amendment that finds waiver in the litigation context rests upon the Amendment's presumed recognition of the judicial need to avoid inconsistency, anomaly, and unfairness, and not upon a State's actual preference or desire, which might, after all, favor selective use of 'immunity' to achieve litigation advantages." *Id.* at 620. The State contended in *Lapides*, 535 U.S. at 620-23, it had a benign motive for moving the case to federal court; it wanted to provide the state's codefendant, the officials sued in their personal capacities, with the generous interlocutory appeal provisions available in federal courts that were not available in state court. However, the Court determined that motives are difficult to evaluate and that jurisdictional rules should be clear. The Court decided that if it adopted the State's Eleventh Amendment position, it would permit States to achieve unfair tactical advantages, "if not in this case, in others." *Id.* at 621. The Court noted that it had 'consistently" found a waiver when a State's attorney general "has voluntarily invoked that court's jurisdiction." *Id.* The Court ruled that whether a particular set of state laws, rules, or activities amounts to a waiver of the State's Eleventh Amendment immunity is a question of federal law." It then stated that a rule of federal law, which finds waiver through a state attorney general's invocation of federal-court jurisdiction, avoids inconsistency and unfairness. *Id.* The Court commented that its "rule is a clear one easily applied by both federal courts and the States themselves." *Id.* at 623-4. That rule provides that "removal is a form of voluntary invocation of a federal court's jurisdiction sufficient to waive the State's otherwise valid objection to litigation of a matter...in a federal forum." *Id.* at 624.

81 *Atascadero State Hospital v. Scanlon*, 473 U.S. 234, 105 S.Ct. 3142, 87 L.Ed.2d 171 (1985). The Supreme Court ruled that Congress may abrogate a state's sovereign immunity pursuant to Section Five of the Fourteenth Amendment only by doing so unequivocally and pursuant to a valid grant of constitutional authority. See *Kimel v. Florida Board of Regents*, 528 U.S. 62, 120 S.Ct. 631, 145 L.Ed.2d 522 (2000).

82 *Alden v. Maine*, 527 U.S. at 754.

83 *Seminole Tribe*, 517 U.S. at 72-73.

I of the Constitution. Still, the Supreme Court has ruled that Congress can abrogate immunity under the Eleventh Amendment from suits by recipients of federal financial assistance,[84] and, as a result, Congress has enacted provisions abrogating Eleventh Amendment immunity in these instances.[85]

Although there is copious argument that sovereign immunity and Eleventh Amendment principles run counter to modern democratic notions of the moral responsibility of the states, decisions of the Supreme Court have reflected an insistence this "argument has not been adopted" by the courts.[86] Nonetheless, some justices of the Supreme Court have recognized that the Court's termed "necessity" that "a sovereign...be free from judicial compulsion in the carrying out of its policies within the limits of the Constitution," can collide with the need to bring suits against the government and its officials.[87] Moreover, the Supreme Court has stated that the "constitutional privilege of a State to assert its sovereign immunity in its own courts does not confer upon the State a concomitant right to disregard the Constitution or valid federal law."[88] Unfortunately, how-

---

84 See *Atascadero State Hospita,* 473 U.S. 234 *Dellmuth v. Muth,* 491 U.S. 223, 109 S. Ct. 2397, 105 L.Ed. 2d 81 (1989); and *Kimel v. Florida Board of Regents,* 528 U.S. at 80-81.

85 See, e.g., 42 U.S.C. §2000d-7, 42 U.S.C. §2000e, and 20 U.S.C. §1403 and discussion in Chapter 3. In 17 U.S.C. §511 (Copyright Clarification Act), Congress abrogated Eleventh Amendment immunity for copyright infringement and made the states and state officials liable in damages for copyright violations. The Supreme Court has not ruled on whether Congress can abrogate Eleventh Amendment immunity in this context. However, the Fifth Circuit Court of Appeals decided, in *Rodriquez v. Tex. Comm'n on the Arts,* 199 F.3d 279, 281 (5th Cir. 2000), that the Copyright Clarification Act (17 U.S.C. § 511) does not abrogate a state's Eleventh Amendment immunity pursuant to a valid exercise of congressional power. The Court of Appeals for the Fourth and Eleventh Circuits are in agreement. See *National Association of Boards of Pharmacy v. Board. of Regents of Georgia.,* 633 F.3d 1297 (11th Cir. 2011) and *Allen v. Cooper,* 895 F.3d 337 (4th Cir. 2018). (Discussion of abrogation of sovereign immunity for copyright violations in Chapter 3.)

86 *Pennhurst State School,* 465 U.S. at 116. In *College Savings Bank v. Florida Prepaid Postsecondary Education Expense Board,* 527 U.S. at 686, a majority of Supreme Court Justices rejected Justice Breyer's suggestion that the Court limit state sovereign immunity to noncommercial state activities like Congress had done with respect to foreign sovereign immunity. (Discussion of foreign sovereign immunity in Chapter 5.) Justice Breyer referred to such a limitation as "the modern trend." *Id.* However, a majority of the court decided that "state sovereign immunity, unlike foreign sovereign immunity, is a constitutional doctrine that is meant to be both immutable by Congress and resistant to trends." *Id.* The majority noted the text of the Eleventh Amendment made no distinction between commercial and noncommercial state activities.

87 Discussion in *Pennhurst,* 465 U.S. at 117.

88 *Alden v. Maine,* 527 U.S. at 754-5. Earlier in *Butz v. Economou,* 438 U.S. 478, 503, 98 S.Ct. 2894, 57 L Ed. 2d 895 (1978), the Court, in recognizing that Congress relied on state courts to vindicate essential rights arising under the Constitution and federal laws, declared: "[W]ith the growing awareness that this reliance had been misplaced, however, Congress recognized the need for original federal court jurisdiction as a means to provide at least indirect federal control over the unconstitutional

ever, the Court also has decided "good faith of the States" provides "an important assurance" that states will follow the Constitution and federal laws and has expressed an unwillingness "to assume the States will refuse to honor the Constitution or obey the binding laws of the United States."[89] With that "important assurance," the Court continues its strict application of sovereign immunity principles. Members of the public clearly harmed by improvident governmental conduct might question the Court's assurance.

Because the Eleventh Amendment precludes monetary damages against the State and because the Supreme Court has ruled that a claim for monetary damages brought against state officers in their official capacity would actually be a suit against the state, thus depriving the state of its sovereign immunity, parties cannot sue state officers in their official capacity for monetary damages.[90] Therefore, parties seeking monetary damages against state officers must bring a federal claim against them in their individual capacities.[91]

---

actions of state officials." The Court was referring to 42 U.S.C. §1983, discussed in Chapter 2.

89 *Alden v. Maine,* 527 U.S. at 754-5.

90 *Pennhurst,* 465 U.S. at 102-03, 117 (echoing *Edelman's* holding that a federal court cannot award monetary relief and declaring that the Eleventh Amendment is violated when the relief sought "has an impact directly on the State itself").

91 In *Butz v. Economou,* 438 U.S. at 504, the Court explained that "a citizen suffering a compensable injury to a constitutionally protected interest could invoke the general federal-question jurisdiction of the district courts to obtain...monetary damages against the responsible federal official."

Discussion of bringing a suit against a governmental official in the official's individual capacity in Chapter 2.

CHAPTER 2. IMMUNITY FOR GOVERNMENTAL OFFICIALS

Courts have granted immunity to the sovereign's officials and have accordingly extended the sovereign immunity doctrine to protect those who carry out the sovereign's commands. There should be concern that this expansion of the doctrine in the United States has created "a privileged class free from liability from wrongs inflicted or injuries threatened."[1]

In applying the sovereign immunity doctrine, English courts "traditionally distinguished between the king and his agents [based] on the theory that the king would never authorize unlawful conduct and that therefore the unlawful acts of the king's officers ought not to be treated as acts of the sovereign."[2] The king's servants were liable for their unlawful acts since the fifteenth century.[3] Apparently the rule of law--that the king's officers could be liable for wrongful acts--was used "to curb the king's authority."[4] As one English court stated, although process would not issue against the sovereign, it could issue against the sovereign's officers.[5] By the eighteenth century, this rule of law was not

---

1 *Pennhurst State School and Hospital v. Halderman*, 465 U.S. 89, 133, 104 S. Ct. 900, 79 L.Ed.2d 67 (1984) (Stevens, J. dissenting) (quoting *Hopkins v. Clemson Agri. Coll.*, 221 U.S. 636, 646, 31 S. Ct. 654, 55 L. Ed. 890 (1911)).

2 *Id.* at 142; accord, 1 William Blackstone, Commentaries on the Laws of England 244 (J. Andrews ed., Callaghan & Com. 4th ed. 1899) (1765) (stating that the king's officers could be liable for their unlawful acts but the king himself was immune).

3 *Pennhurst*, 465 U.S. at 142 (Stevens, J. dissenting).

4 *Id;* accord VI William Holdsworth, A History of English Law 101 (2d ed. 1937 (recounting that the king's commands or instructions could not protect his officers if they committed wrongs).

5 *Pennhurst*, 465 U.S. at 142 (Stevens, J., dissenting) (citing and discussing *Sands v. Child,* (1698) 83 Eng. Rep. 725 (K.B.) 726; 3 Lev. 361, 361-62).

questioned, and it was so well-settled in the nineteenth century that citation of authority was not required.[6]

In 1883, the Supreme Court ruled that sovereign immunity is not a defense against a suit charging federal officials with unconstitutional conduct.[7] Later, however, the Supreme Court ruled that when a suit is brought against a state official but the State is the "real, substantial party in interest," sovereign immunity applies.[8] The Supreme Court further declared a suit against state officials that is in fact a suit against the state is barred regardless of whether it seeks damages or injunctive relief.[9]

A. QUALIFIED IMMUNITY

Sovereign immunity does not apply to the *individual* acts of federal governmental officials, but, nonetheless, these officials can have "qualified immunity" for their wrongful acts. Federal officials and employees are protected "from liability for civil damages insofar as their conduct does not violate clearly established statutory or constitutional rights of which a reasonable person would have known."[10]

The Supreme Court[11] has established that a "good faith" qualified immunity defense has both an "objective" and a "subjective" aspect. The objective element involves a presumptive knowledge of, and respect for, "basic, unquestioned

6 *Id.* at 142-43 (citing X William Holdsworth, A History of English Law 650-52 (1938) and *Feather v. The Queen* (1865) 122 Eng. Rep. 1191 (Q.B), 1205-1206; 6 B. & S. 257, 291-97).

7 *United States v. Lee*, 106 U.S. 196, 219-222, 1 S. Ct. 24, 27 L. Ed. 171 (1882) (declaring the judiciary has a right to enforce the provisions of the Constitution against officers of the executive).

8 *Ford Motor Co. v. Department of Treasury*, 323 U.S. 459, 464, 65 S.Ct. 347, 89 L.Ed. 389 (1945), *overruled on other grounds by Lapides v. Bd. of Regents of the Univ. Sys. of Ga.*, 535 U.S. 613, 122 S. Ct. 1640, 152 L. Ed. 2d 806 (2002); *accord Pennhurst State Sch. & Hosp. v. Halderman*, 465 U.S. at 102-03 (acknowledging that, although precedent was inconsistent, the Eleventh Amendment principle is applicable when a suit against a state official is substantially against the State).

9 *Cory v. White*, 457 U.S. 85, 91, 102 S.Ct. 2325, 72 L.Ed.2d 694 (1982) (holding the type of relief sought does not affect the applicability of the Eleventh Amendment to state officials when the State is a substantial party). Refer, however, to the discussion infra regarding a claimant seeking injunctive relief against a governmental official.

10 *Pearson v. Callahan*, 555 U.S. 223, 231, 129 S. Ct. 80-8, 172 L. Ed. 2d 565 (2009).

11 *Wood v. Strickland*, 420 U.S. 308, 95 S.Ct. 992, 43 L.Ed.2d 214 (1975).

constitutional rights;" the subjective component refers to "permissible intentions."[12] In referring both to the objective and subjective elements, the Supreme Court stated that qualified immunity is defeated if an official "knew or reasonably should have known that the action he took within his sphere of official responsibility would violate the constitutional rights of the plaintiff, or if he took the action with the malicious intention to cause a deprivation of constitutional rights or other injury."[13]

In *Butz v. Economou*,[14] the Supreme Court compared immunity for federal officials to their counterparts in state government under 42 U.S.C. §1983.[15] The Supreme Court considered the government's position in *Butz*--that federal officials have a higher immunity than state officials--and began its comparison of immunity for federal officials to that for state governmental officials with the recognized premise that state officials earlier had only qualified immunity.[16] The Court stated:

> We agree with the perception of these courts that, in the absence of congressional direction to the contrary, there is no basis for according to federal officials a higher degree of immunity from liability when sued for a constitutional infringement...than is accorded state officials when sued for the identical violations under §1983.

The Supreme Court pointed to the general rule, which it noted has "long prevailed," that "a federal official may not with impunity ignore the limitations which the controlling law has placed on his powers."[17] The Court explained that a governmental official will "not be excused from liability if he failed to observe

12 *Wood*, 420 U.S. at 321-22, (establishing the qualified immunity defense has both an objective and subjective component and stating that, to be entitled to qualified immunity, a school board member "must be held to a standard of conduct based not only on permissible intentions, but also on knowledge of the basic unquestioned constitutional rights of his charges," reasoning that qualified immunity for a school board member requires, in part, "permissible intentions").

13 *Id.* at 322.

14 *Butz*, 438 U.S. 478, 500, 98 S.Ct. 2894, 57 L. Ed. 2d 895 (1978).

15 See discussion *infra* regarding immunity of state officials under 42 U.S.C. §1983.

16 *Butz*. 438 U.S. at 484-501 (discussing different immunity standards in actions against state officials under §1983 and suits against federal officers under the Constitution). Discussion of §1983 *infra*.

17 *Id.* at 490.

obvious statutory or constitutional limitations on his powers or if his conduct was a manifestly erroneous application of [a] statute."[18]

The Supreme Court did acknowledge in *Butz* that judges and "heads of Executive Departments, when engaged in the discharge of duties imposed upon them by law," have absolute immunity.[19] However, the Supreme Court also stated that an executive officer nonetheless would be vulnerable if the officer took action "manifestly or palpably" beyond his authority or ignored a clear limitation on his enforcement powers. According to the Court in *Butz*:[20]

> Whatever level of protection from state interference is appropriate for federal officials executing their duties under federal law, it cannot be doubted that these officials, even when acting pursuant to congressional authorization, are subject to the restraints imposed by the Federal Constitution.

The Court then commented "it would be incongruous" to hold that federal officers could willfully or knowingly violate constitutional rights without fear of liability.[21]

More recently, the Supreme Court ruled that an initial inquiry regarding an official's immunity requires consideration of a threshold question: "Taken in the light most favorable to the party asserting the injury, do the facts alleged show the officer's conduct violated a constitutional right?"[22] The Court has defined a "clearly established right" as "one that is 'sufficiently clear that every reasonable official would have understood...what he is doing violates that right.'"[23] Additionally, the Supreme Court has explained: "The qualified immunity rule seeks a proper balance between two competing interests. On one hand, a dam-

---

18 *Id.* at 493-94.

19 *Id.* at 495.

20 *Id.* at 493, n. 18, 495.

21 *Id.*

22 *Brosseau v. Haugen*, 543 U.S.194, 197, 125 S. Ct. 596, 160 L. Ed. 2d 583 (2004); *accord Siegert v. Gilley*, 500 U.S. 226, 232, 111 S.Ct.1789, 114 L.Ed.2d 277 (1991) (stressing that, as an additional inquiry, the plaintiff needs to establish a violation of a constitutional right").

23 *Mullenix v. Luna*, 136 S. Ct. 305, 308, 193 L. Ed.2d 255 (2015) (quoting *Reichle v. Howards*, 566 U.S. 658, 132 S. Ct. 2088, 2093, 183 L. Ed. 2d 985 (2012)). In *Vos v. City of Newport Beach*, 892 F.3d 1024, 1035 (9th Cir. 2018), the court stated: "The dispositive question is...whether the violative nature of *particular* conduct is clearly established in the specific context of the case," quoting *Ashcroft v. Al-Kidd*, 536 U.S. 731, 742, 131 S. Ct. 2074, 179 L. Ed. 2d 1149 (2011), and stating that the plaintiff bears the burden of showing that rights allegedly violated were clearly established.

ages suit 'may offer the only realistic avenue for vindication of constitutional guarantees.'"[24] "On the other hand, permitting damages suits against government officials can entail substantial social costs, including the risk that fear of personal monetary liability and harassing litigation will unduly inhibit officials in the discharge of their duties."[25] The Court decided: "As one means to accommodate these two objectives, the Court has held that Government officials are entitled to qualified immunity with respect to 'discretionary functions' performed in their official capacities" and reasoned that "[t]he doctrine of qualified immunity gives officials 'breathing room to make reasonable but mistaken judgments about open legal questions.'"[26] The Court further commented that "[w]hether qualified immunity can be invoked turns on the 'objective legal reasonableness' of the official's acts"[27] and stated that "reasonableness of official action, in turn, must be 'assessed in light of the legal rules that were clearly established at the time [the action] was taken.'"[28] In *Abbasi*,[29] the Supreme Court referred to an earlier ruling wherein it had "held that qualified immunity protects 'all but the plainly incompetent or those who knowingly violate the law.'"[30]

Qualified immunity is an affirmative defense that must be pleaded by the defendant official.[31] The Supreme Court has ruled that a qualified immunity defense must be considered in proper sequence and that a ruling should be made

24 *Ziglar v. Abbasi*, 137 S. Ct. 1843, 1866, 198 L. Ed. 2d 190 (2017) (quoting *Harlow v. Fitzgerald*, 457 U.S. 800, 814, 102 S. Ct. 2727, 73 L. Ed. 2d 396 (1982)).

25 *Abbasi*, 137 S. Ct. at 1866 (quoting *Anderson v. Creighton*, 483 U.S. 635, 638, 107 S. Ct. 3043, 97 L. Ed.2d 523 (1987)).

26 *Id.* quoting *Ashcroft v. al-Kidd*, 563 U.S. at 743. ("Discretionary function" discussed in Chapter 4.)

27 *Id.* quoting *Harlow*, 457 U.S. at 819.

28 I*d.* quoting *Anderson*, 483 U.S. at 639. The Court concluded in *Abbasi*, id., that the "requirement—that an official loses qualified immunity only for violating clearly established law–protects officials accused of violating 'extremely abstract rights,'" quoting *Anderson*, 483 U.S. at 639.

29 *Abbasi*, cited in note 24. 137 S. Ct. at 1867.

30 *Id.* citing *Malley v. Briggs*, 475 U.S. 335, 341, 106 S. Ct. 1092, 89 L. Ed. 2d 271 (1986). The Court stated: "To determine whether a given officer falls into either of those two categories, a court must ask whether it would have been clear to a reasonable officer that the alleged conduct 'was unlawful in the situation he confronted,'" citing *Saucier v. Katz*, 533 U.S. 194, 202, 121 S.Ct. 2151, 150 L. Ed. 2d 272 (2001)). "If so, then the defendant officer must have been either incompetent or else a knowing violator of the law, and thus not entitled to qualified immunity. If not, however–i.e., if a reasonable officer might not have known for certain that the conduct was unlawful–then the officer is immune from liability." *Abbasi*, 137 S. Ct. at 1867.

31 See *Gomez v. Toledo*, 446 U.S. 635, 640, 100 S.Ct. 1920, 64 L.Ed.2d 572 (1980) ("Since qualified immunity is a defense, the burden of pleading it rests with the defendant.")

early in the proceedings so that the cost and expenses of trial are avoided where the defense is dispositive.[32] The Court further ruled that "an order rejecting qualified immunity at the motion-to-dismiss stage is a 'final decision under 28 U.S.C. §1291,' which vests courts of appeals with 'jurisdiction of appeals from all final decisions of the district courts.'"[33] The Court stated: "This is so because qualified immunity–which shields Government officials 'from liability for civil damages insofar as their conduct does not violate clearly established statutory or constitutional rights,'–is both a defense to liability and a limited 'entitlement not to stand trial or face the other burdens of litigation.'"[34] Attorneys then must have obtained sufficient documents and other evidence to demonstrate a violation of a constitutional claim prior to filing a claim against a federal employee. Without such documentation, federal courts generally summarily dismiss such claims.

B. *EX PARTE YOUNG* AND INJUNCTIVE RELIEF

"Prospective relief requiring, or having the effect of requiring governmental officials to obey the law has long been available; sovereign immunity does not bar such relief."[35] In *Ex Parte Young*,[36] in permitting an injunction against the Attorney General of Minnesota despite the Eleventh Amendment, the Supreme Court decided that a suit challenging the constitutionality of a state official's action is not one against the state.[37] Further, if a state official acts contrary to laws of the state, the Court acknowledged in *Young* that the official should not have immunity because, a sovereign could not and would not authorize its officers to

32 *Mitchell v. Forsyth*, 472 U.S. 511, 526, 105 S.Ct. 2806, 86 L.Ed.2d 411 (1985) (explaining that qualified immunity may be "effectively lost if a case is erroneously permitted to go to trial").

33 *Ascroft v. Iqbal*, 556 U.S. 662, 665, 129 S. Ct. 1937, 173 L. Ed. 2d 868 (2009) (citing *Behrens v. Pelletier*, 526 U.S. 299, 307, 116 S. Ct. 834, 133 L. Ed. 2d 773 (1996)). The Court agreed that "[a] district-court decision denying a Government officer's claim of official immunity can fall within the narrow class of appealable orders despite 'the absence of a final judgment.'" *Id.* at 671, citing *Mitchell v. Forsyth*, 472 U.S. at 530.

34 *Iqbal*, 556 U.S. at 671, citing *Mitchell*, 472 U.S. at 530.

35 E.*E.O.C. v. Peabody Western Coal Co.*, 610 F.3d 1070 (9th Cir. 2010).

36 *Young*, 209 U.S. 123, 28 S.Ct. 441, 52 L.Ed. 714 (1908).

37 Y*oung*, 209 U.S. at 159-60. In *Verizon Maryland, Inc. v. Public Service Comm'n*, 535 U.S. 635, 122 S. Ct. 1753, 153 L. Ed. 2d 871 (2002), the Court permitted injunctive and declaratory relief against individual state officials despite the Eleventh Amendment.

violate its own laws.[38] Thus, a suit against a state official that seeks redress for conduct not permitted by state law is a suit against the officer, not the sovereign. Similarly, as the Court later stated, when a state official violates a state statute, the sovereign has not erected a shield against liability.[39] The Court permitted an exception to Eleventh Amendment immunity in *Young* so that a private party could bring suit against a state official in that officer's official capacity but only for injunctive relief.[40]

In 1976, the Administrative Procedure Act (APA)[41] "replaced the *Ex parte Young* fiction as the doctrinal basis for a claim for prospective relief."[42] Pursuant to the APA, waiver covers "all actions seeking relief from official misconduct except for money damages."[43] In *Muniz-Muniz v. U.S. Border Patrol*,[44] the Court of Appeals for the Sixth Circuit ruled that the waiver of sovereign immunity in the APA applies to all non-monetary claims against federal agencies.[45]

---

38 *Id.* at 159-60. The Court theorized that an unconstitutional enactment is void and does not impart immunity to a state official. Because the state cannot authorize the action, the officer is "stripped of his official or representative character" and is "subjected to the consequences of his official conduct." *Id.* at 160.

39 *Pennhurst*, 465 U.S. at 159 (Stevens, J., dissenting).

40 *Young*, 209 U.S. at 163 (establishing an exception to the immunity principle for parties seeking injunctive relief).

41 APA, 5 U.S.C. §702.

42 Discussion in *E.E.O.C. v. Peabody Western Coal Co.*, 610 F.3d 170 (9th Cir. 2010). The Court of Appeals for the Ninth Circuit declared that Congress amended the APA to eliminate the need to invoke the *Young* fiction.

43 *Presbyterian Church v. United States*, 870 F.2d 518, 525 (9th Cir. 1989).

44 *Muniz*, 741 F.3d 668 (6th Cir. 2013).

45 *Id.* at 673. In Muniz, the Sixth Circuit rejected a restrictive reading of the APA §702, which would have limited the §702 waiver only to complaints filed under the APA. The Sixth Circuit quoted *Trudeau v. Federal Trade Comm'n*, 456 F.3d 178, 187 (D.C. Cir. 2006) (stating section 702's waiver of sovereign immunity is not limited to APA cases) and *Red Lake Band of Chippewa Indians v. Barlow*, 846 F.2d 474, 476 (8th Cir. 1998) (ruling "waiver is not dependent on application of the procedures and review standards of APA, that it is only dependent on the suit against the government being one of non-monetary relief").

C. SUITS IN A GOVERNMENTAL OFFICIAL'S INDIVIDUAL CAPACITY

In *Edelman v. Jordan*,[46] the Court held that a federal court cannot award retroactive monetary damages when private parties bring suit against state officers in their official capacity. Thus, parties can only obtain injunctive relief against future conduct, and generally cannot, through a suit against state officials in their official capacity, obtain monetary damages against the state. Because the Eleventh Amendment precludes monetary damages against the state and because a claim for monetary damages brought against state officers in their official capacity would actually be a suit against the state, thus depriving the state of its sovereign immunity, the Supreme Court ruled that parties cannot sue state officers in their official capacity for monetary damages.[47] Therefore, parties seeking monetary damages must bring suit against governmental officers in their individual capacities.[48]

Bringing an action against a governmental official in that person's individual capacity does not implicate sovereignty.[49] Governmental officials can be liable in their individual capacities for their wrongful acts; however, governmental officials do have "qualified immunity" even in their individual capacities. The Supreme Court has ruled that immunity of state officials depends upon the responsibilities of the office and the scope of the official's discretion[50] and has

---

46 *Edelman*, 415 U.S. 651, 673, 775-7794 S. Ct. 1247, 39 L. Ed. 2d 662 (1974).

47 *Pennhurst*, 465 U.S. at 102-03, 117 (echoing Edelman's holding that a federal court cannot award monetary relief and declaring that the Eleventh Amendment is violated when the relief sought "has an impact directly on the State itself").

48 In *Butz v. Economou*, 438 U.S. at 504, the Court explained that "a citizen suffering a compensable injury to a constitutionally protected interest could invoke the general federal-question jurisdiction of the district courts to obtain...monetary damages against the responsible federal official."

49 In *Owen v. City of Independence*, 445 U.S. 622, 638 n. 18, 100 S. Ct. 1298, 63 L. Ed. 2d 673 (1980), the Court noted that previous decisions have allowed for qualified immunity for governmental officials in their individual capacities. In *Stoner v. Santa Clara Cnty. Office of Educ.*, 501 F.3d 1116, 1125 (9th Cir. 2007), the court asserted that the Eleventh Amendment does not protect state officials in their individual capacities from suit.

50 *Butz*, 438 U.S. at 500. The Supreme Court decided in *Butz* that some officials should have absolute immunity due to "the special nature of their responsibilities." The Court not only determined that some officials should have absolute immunity but also held that federal officials who seek absolute exemption from personal liability for unconstitutional conduct must bear the burden of showing that public policy requires an exemption of that scope. *Id.* at 507 (proclaiming that federal officials will generally be accorded qualified immunity unless there are "exceptional situations where it is demonstrated that absolute immunity is essential for the conduct of the public business").

recognized that the judicial, prosecutorial, and legislative functions may require absolute immunity in certain instances.[51] The Court also has explained that, for executive officials in general, qualified immunity represents the norm.[52] In *Scheuer v. Rhodes*,[53] the Court acknowledged high officials require greater protection, but ruled that those with less complex discretionary responsibilities are subject only to a qualified immunity defense.[54]

D. SUITS AGAINST STATE OFFICIALS UNDER 42 U.S.C. §1983

Most suits against state officials are brought pursuant to 42 U.S.C. §1983, which provides that a "person" who, under color of state statute, regulation, or custom, deprives another of any rights, privileges or immunities "secured by the Constitution and laws" shall be liable to the injured party. Section 1983 makes a deprivation of constitutional rights actionable independent of state law.[55] State

51 *Id.* According to the Court, these officials are: judges, grand jurors, public prosecutors, federal hearing examiners, and administrative law judges. *See id.* at 512-13 (stating that judges are absolutely immune due to the "special nature of their responsibilities" and their quasi-judicial nature). In *Gravel v. United States*, 408 U.S. 606, 625, 92 S.Ct. 2614, 33 L.Ed. 2d 583 (1972), the Court recognized absolute immunity for judicial and legislative governmental functions. In *Forrester v. White*, 484 U.S. 219, 229, 108 S.Ct. 538, 98 L.Ed.2d 555 (1988), the Court stated that it is "the nature of the function performed, not the identity of the actor who performs it, that informs our immunity analysis." Thus, as the Court pointed out in *Harlow v. Fitzgerald*, 457 U.S. 800, 807, 102 S. Ct. 2727, 73 L.Ed.2d 396 (1982), legislators have absolute immunity in their legislative functions as do judges in their judicial functions. Some officials of the Executive Branch, such as the President, have this absolute immunity. *See id.* (recognizing that absolute immunity has been extended to the President, prosecutors, and certain officials of the executive branch exercising adjudicative functions (citing *Nixon v. Fitzgerald*, 457 U.S. 731, 750, 102 S. Ct. 2690, 73 L. Ed. 2d 349 (1982)). In *Forrester*, the Court recognized that judicial prosecutorial and other quasi-judicial functions may require absolute immunity in certain instances. *Id.* at 225-26.

52 See *Butz*, 438 U.S. at 508 (opining that qualified immunity is the general rule for both federal and state executive officials) Scheuer *v. Rhodes*, 416 U.S. 232, 247-48, 94 S. Ct. 1683, 40 L Ed. 2d 90 (1982) (acknowledging that state executive officials generally have qualified immunity for constitutional violations).

53 *Scheuer*, 416 U.S. at 247-248.

54 *Id.* (explaining that officers with more responsibility have a greater range of discretion, making qualified immunity applicable to their position).

55 See *Monroe v. Pape*, 365 U.S. 167, 180, 81 S. Ct. 473, 5 L.Ed. 2d 492 (1961) (concluding that Congress clearly intended §1983 to provide "a federal right in federal courts because...state laws might not be enforced"), *overruled on other grounds by Monell v. Dep't of Soc. Servs. of N.Y.*, 436 U.S. 658, 98 S. Ct. 2018, 56 L. Ed. 2d 611 (1978). A *Bivens* action, discussed supra, is an action against federal officials that is analogous to a suit against state officials under §1983.

immunities are not applicable in these suits.[56] However, the Supreme Court later sustained sovereign immunity for the states despite the language in §1983 by ruling that neither States nor state officials acting in their official capacities are "persons" within the meaning of §1983.[57] Thus, to obtain damages, a plaintiff must bring the lawsuit against a state official in the official's individual capacity rather than the person's official capacity.[58]

Section 1983 was enacted originally as the Ku Klux Act of 1871.[59] This Act was "one of the means whereby Congress exercised power vested in it by [Section Five] of the Fourteenth Amendment to enforce the provisions of that Amendment."[60] The Supreme Court has ruled that §1983 was enacted to provide "a federal right in federal courts because, by reason of prejudice, passion, neglect, intolerance or otherwise, state laws might not be enforced and claims

56 In *Martinez v. California,* 444 U.S. 277, 284, 100 S.Ct.553, 62 L.Ed.2d 481 (1980), the Court ruled that conduct by persons acting under color of state law which is wrongful under 42 U.S.C. §1983 cannot be immunized by state law. The Court reasoned that a construction of the federal statute that permitted a state immunity defense to have controlling effect "would transmute a basic guarantee into an illusory promise." *Id.*

57 *Will v. Michigan Dep't of State Police,* 491 U.S. 58, 109 S.Ct. 2304, 105 L.Ed.2d 45 (1989). The Court concluded that if a State is a "person" within the meaning of §1983, the statute would be read as stating that "every person, including a State," falls within its purview. *Id.* at 60, 64. The Court opined that "in common usage" the term "person" does not include the sovereign. *Id.* at 65 (quoting *Willson v. Omaha Tribe,* 442 U.S. 653, 667, 99 S. Ct. 2529, 61 L. Ed. 2d 153 (1979). [However, the Court's statement is in direct contradiction of the "common usage" of the term "person" as defined in the Uniform Statute and Construction Act. See Unif. Statute 7 Constr. Act §3, 14 U.L.A. 483 (2005) (defining a "person" as "an individual, corporation, business trust, estate, trust, partnership, limited liability company, association, joint venture, public corporation, government or governmental subdivision, agency, or instrumentality, or any other legal or commercial entity.")] In *Will,* the Court recognized state officials are "persons" but ruled that because a suit against a state official in his or her official capacity is not a suit against the official but rather is a suit against the official's office, such a suit "is no different from a suit against the State itself." *Will,* 491 U.S. at 71. The Court did decide a state official could be sued under §1983 in his or her official capacity when sued for injunctive relief because "official-capacity actions for prospective relief are not treated as actions against the State." *Id.* at 71, n. 10 (quoting *Kentucky v. Graham* 473 U.S. 159, 167 n. 14, 105 S. Ct. 3099, 87 L. Ed. 2d 114 (1985)).

58 *See Hafer v. Melo,* 502 U.S. 21, 31, 112 S. Ct. 358, 116 L. Ed. 2d 301 (1990) (holding "that state officials, sued in their individual capacities are 'persons' within the meaning of §1983"). In *Monroe v. Pape,* 365 U.S. at 187, the Court ruled that municipalities were not "persons" to whom §1983 applied. However, the Court overruled this part of its decision in *Monell v. Dept. of Social Services,* 436 U.S. 658, 664, 98 S. Ct. 2018, 56 L. Ed. 2d 611 (1978) when it concluded that Congress intended to include municipalities or local governments as "persons" under §1983. Id. at 690.

59 Act of Apr. 20, 1871, ch. 122, 17 Stat. 13. *See also Monroe,* 356 U.S. at 170-82 (discussing the background of §1983).

60 *Monroe,* 365 U.S. at 171.

of citizens to the enjoyment of their rights... guaranteed by the Fourteenth Amendment might be denied by state agencies."[61]

As the Supreme Court stated in *Monroe v. Pape*,[62] an allegation of facts constituting a deprivation under color of state authority of a right guaranteed by the Fourteenth Amendment satisfies the requirements of §1983. The Supreme Court concluded in *Monroe* that, in enacting §1983, Congress intended to give a remedy to parties deprived of constitutional rights, privileges and immunities by a state official's abuse of the official's position.[63] Additionally, the Court recently acknowledged in *Ziglar v. Abbasi*,[64] that §1983 "entitles an injured person to money damages if a state official violates his or her constitutional rights."

The Eleventh Amendment does not bar Congress from authorizing suits in state courts to implement federal statutory rights.[65] The Supreme Court has ruled that suits under §1983 may be brought in state courts.[66] Moreover, state courts presumably must hear §1983 claims.[67]

---

61 *Id.* at 180.

62 *Id.* at 171.

63 *Id.* at 172. Pursuant to 42 U.S.C. §1988, in an action to enforce the provisions of 42 U.S.C. §1983, "a court, in its discretion, may allow the prevailing party, other than the United States, a reasonable attorney's fee as part of the costs."

64 *Abbasi,* 137 S. Ct. 1843, 1854, 198 L.Ed. 2d 290 (2017).

65 See *Maine v. Thiboutot,* 448 U.S. 1, 10-11, 100 S.Ct. 2502, 65 L.Ed.2d 555 (1980).

66 *Id.*

67 *Id. See also Martinez v. California,* 444 U.S. 277, 283 n. 7, 100 S. Ct. 553, 62 L. Ed. 2d 481 (1980) (noting that while it had never considered the question of whether a State *must* entertain a claim under §1983, where the same type of claim, if arising under state law, would be enforced in the state courts, the state courts are generally not free to refuse enforcement of the federal claim.) Nonetheless, a litigant should consider that in filing in a state court, a victim may be denied some of the rights the federal courts have afforded victims in §1983 cases and should elect the federal court, particularly in those states that adhere to absolute sovereign immunity. For example, in *Prairie View A & M University v. Chatha,* 381 S.W.3d 500 (Tex. 2012), the Texas Supreme Court dismissed a Title VII discriminatory action, which was based on salary differentials at a state university, by deciding a 180-day limitations period on time to file a complaint begins to run "when a discriminatory employment decision is made–not when the effects of that decision become manifest in later events" and that the government has not waived sovereign immunity with respect to notice requirements. The Texas Supreme Court's rigid interpretation of the notice requirements for bringing an EEOC complaint pursuant to Title VII, in conjunction with the court's strict application of the sovereign immunity doctrine, may preclude many discrimination claims brought in Texas courts. See further discussion of the *Chatha* decision in Chapter 3. Still, if suit is brought in federal court against a state employee, recall from discussion in Chapter 1 that the suit must be brought in the employee's individual capacity or a federal court will dismiss the suit based on Eleventh Amendment immunity.

In *Butz v. Economou*,[68] the Court earlier considered immunity of state officers when sued under 42 U.S.C. §1983 for violations of constitutional rights and commented that, under the common law high ranking state officials and police officers were never granted absolute and unqualified immunity.[69] The Supreme Court declared:[70]

> Our system of jurisprudence rests on the assumption that all individuals, whatever their position in government, are subject to federal law. No man in this country is so high that he is above the law. No officer of the law may set that law at defiance with impunity. All the officers of the government from the highest to the lowest, are creatures of the law, and are bound to obey it.

E. SUITS AGAINST FEDERAL OFFICIALS IN A *BIVENS* ACTION

The Supreme Court[71] pointed out that "[i]n 42 U.S.C. *§1983*, Congress provided a specific damages remedy for plaintiffs whose constitutional rights were violated by state officials, and stated that "[i]n 1971, and against this background" the court recognized...an implied damages action to compensate persons injured by federal officers..."[72] This remedy, called a *Bivens* action,[73] may provide a victim of a federal official unconstitutional conduct a special cause of action that would preclude sovereign immunity related to that conduct.[74] Still, as noted in cases cited *infra*, courts have denied most of the few *Bivens* actions that have been brought against federal officials.

---

68 *Butz*, 438 U.S. at 496-7.

69 *Id.* (citing *Scheuer v. Rhodes*, 416 U.S. 232, 246, 94 S. Ct. 1683, 40 L. Ed. 2d 90 (1974).

70 *Id.* at 506 (quoting *United States v. Lee*, 106 U.S. 196, 220, 1 S. Ct. 240, 27 L. Ed. 171 (1882).

71 *Ziglar v. Abbasi*, 137 S. Ct. at 1848.

72 *Id.*

73 Based on the Supreme Court decision in *Bivens v. Six Unknown Named Agents of Federal Bureau of Narcotics*, 403 U.S. 388, 389, 91 S.Ct. 1999, 29 L. Ed.2d 619 (1999). The Supreme Court commented in *Abbasi*, 137 S. Ct. at 1854, that "in the 100 years leading up to *Bivens*, Congress did not provide a specific damages remedy for plaintiffs whose constitutional rights were violated by agents of the Federal Government."

74 *Bivens*, 403 U.S. at 389 (pronouncing the existence of a cause of action, for damages resulting from a federal agent's unconstitutional conduct, that cannot be barred by immunity).

In *Bivens v. Six Unknown Named Agents of Federal Bureau of Narcotics*,[75] agents of the Federal Bureau of Narcotics, acting under color of federal authority, made a warrantless entry of the petitioner's apartment, searched the apartment, and arrested him on narcotics charges, all without probable cause. The Supreme Court ruled that the victim had a cause of action under the Fourth Amendment and that he was "entitled to recover money damages for any injuries...he suffered as a result of the agents' violation of the Amendment,"[76] recognizing "for the first time an implied private action for damages against federal officers alleged to have violated a citizen's constitutional rights.'"[77]

In reviewing the history of the *Bivens* action, the Supreme Court noted:[78] "In the decade that followed [the *Bivens* decision], the Court recognized what has come to be called an implied cause of action in two cases involving other constitutional violations...an administrative assistant sued a Congressman for firing her because she was a woman[79]...[and] a prisoner's estate sued federal jailers for failing to treat the prisoner's asthma."[80] The Court stated that only in *Bivens* and in these two cases has the Court "approved of an implied damages remedy under the Constitution itself."[81] The Court decided in *Ashcroft v. Iqbal*[82] that: "[b]ecause implied causes of action are disfavored, the Court has been reluctant to extend *Bivens* liability 'to any new context or new category of defendants.'"[83]

---

75 *Id.*

76 *Id.* at 397.

77 Discussion in *Ashcroft v. Iqbal,* 556 U.S. 661, 675, 129 S. Ct. 1937, 173 L. Ed. 2d 868 (2009), citing *Correctional Services Corp. v. Malesko,* 534 U.S. 61, 66, 122 S. Ct. 515, 151 L. Ed. 2d 456 (2001).

78 *Abbasi,* 137 S. Ct. at 1854-55.

79 *Id.* referring to *Davis v. Passman,* 442 U.S. 228, 99 S. Ct. 2264, 60 L. Ed. 2d 846 (1979). "The Court held that the Fifth Amendment Due Process Clause gave her a damages remedy for gender discrimination." *Id.* The Court noted in *Iqbal,* 556 U.S. at 675, that while it did permit "'a *Bivens* action to redress a violation of the equal protection component of the Due Process Clause of the Fifth Amendment'" in *Davis,* it "declined to extend *Bivens* to a claim sounding in the First Amendment." *Id.,* citing *Bush v. Lucas,* 462 U.S. 367, 103 S. Ct 2404, 76 L. Ed. 2d 648 (1983).

80 *Id.* at 1855, referring to *Carlson v. Green,* 446 U.S. 14, 100 S. Ct. 1468, 64 L.Ed. 2d 15 (1980). "The Court held that the Eighth Amendment Cruel and Unusual Punishments Clause gave him a damages remedy for failure to provide adequate medical treatment." *Id.*

81 *Abbasi,* 137 S. Ct. at 1855. The Court pointed out in *Abbasi* that after these cases "the arguments for recognizing implied causes of action for damages began to lose their force." *Id.*

82 *Iqbal,* 556 U.S. at 675.

83 *Id.* The Court stated in *Iqbal*: "Given the notable change in the Court's approach to recognizing implied causes of action..., the Court has made clear that expanding the *Bivens* remedy is now a 'disfavored' judicial activity." *Id.*

In *Iqbal*,[84] a muslim citizen of Pakistan, who was arrested in the wake of the September 11, 2001, terrorist attacks, contended he was deprived of various constitutional protections while in federal custody. The Supreme Court ruled that "[b]ecause vicarious liability is inapplicable to *Bivens*..., the plaintiff in a suit... must plead that each Government-official defendant, through his own individual actions, has violated the Constitution."[85] The Court stated: "Purposeful discrimination requires more than 'intent as volition or intent as awareness of consequences;' it involves a decisionmaker's undertaking a course of action 'because of,' not merely 'in spite of,' the action's adverse effects upon an identifiable group,"[86] and ruled the plaintiff did not plead sufficient facts to state a claim for purposeful and unlawful discrimination.

In *Hernandez v. Mesa*,[87] the parents of a fifteen-year-old Mexican boy, who was shot and killed while standing on Mexican soil by a United States Border Patrol Agent standing on United States soil, brought a *Bivens* action against the United States and various federal agencies, alleging the agent violated their son's rights under the Fourth and Fifth Amendments. After the lower courts dis-

---

In *Abbasi*, 137 S. Ct. at 1857, the Court set out cases in which it had declined to create an implied damages remedy. These are *Bush v. Lucas*, cited *supra* (a First Amendment suit against a federal employer); *Chappell v. Wallace*, 426 U.S. 296, 103 S. Ct. 2362, 76 L. Ed.2d 586 (1983) (a race-discrimination suit against military officers); *United States v. Stanley*, 483 U.S. 669, 107 S. Ct. 3054, 97 L. Ed. 2d 550 (1987) (a substantive due process suit against military officers); *Schweiker v. Chilicky*, 487 U.S. 412, 108 S. Ct. 2460, 101 L. Ed. 3d 370 (1988) (a procedural due process suit against Social Security officials); *FDIC v. Meyer*, 510 U.S. 471, 114 S. Ct. 996, 127 L. Ed. 2d 308 (1994) (a procedural due process suit against a federal agency for wrongful termination); *Malesko*, cited *supra* (an Eighth Amendment suit against a private prison operator); *Wilkie v. Robbins*, 551 U.S. 537, 127 S. Ct. 2588, 168 L. Ed. 2d 389 (2007) (alleged retaliation by federal employee); and *Minneci v. Pollard*, 565 U.S. 118, 132 S.Ct. 617, 181 L.Ed. 2d 606 (2012) (an Eighth Amendment suit against prison guards at a private prison).

In *Klay v. Panetta*, 758 F.3d 369, 370, 375 (D.C.Cir. 2014), the "D.C. Circuit rejected as "patently deficient' a *Bivens* claim pressed by current and former sailors and Marines who alleged they were the victims of sexual assault or harassment resulting from a military culture attributable to their superiors and stated: 'If adjudicating the case would require military leaders to defend their professional management choices–'to convince a civilian court of the wisdom of a wide range of military and disciplinary decisions'–then the claim is barred by the 'incident to service' test.'" Discussion in *Doe v Hagenbeck*, 870 F.3d 36, 46 (2nd Cir. 2017). In *Cioca v. Rumsfeld*, 720 F.3d 505, 512 (4th Cir. 2013), in addressing a similar claim as in *Klay*, the Court of Appeals for the Fourth Circuit stated: "*Bivens* suits are never permitted for constitutional violations arising from military service, no matter how severe the injury or how egregious the rights infringement." Additionally, in *Doe v. Hagenbeck*, the Court of Appeals for the Second Circuit rejected a *Biven's* action involving a female cadet's claim of sexual assault at a military academy brought against the United States, the academy's superintendent, and the academy's commandant of cadets.

84 *Iqbal*, 556 U.S. at 666.

85 *Id.* at 671.

86 *Id.*, citing *Personnel Admin. of Mass. v. Feeney*, 442 U.S. 256, 279, 99 S. Ct. 2282, 60 L. Ed. 2d 870 (1979).

87 *Hernandez*, 137 S. Ct. 2003, 198 L.Ed. 2d 625 (2017).

missed the claim, the Supreme Court granted *certiorari*, vacated and remanded the case, with instructions, for the court of appeals to address whether the claim could be asserted under *Bivens*.[88] The Supreme Court decided the appellate court "has not had the opportunity to consider how the reasoning and analysis in *Abbasi* may bear on this case."[89] On remand, the Court of Appeals for the Fifth Circuit[90] ruled that the claim "presents no 'new context' under *Bivens*."[91]

In *Vega v. United States*,[92] the Court of Appeals for the Ninth Circuit decided a former prisoner's claim against private defendants for allegedly violating his First Amendment right to access to courts, as well as his Fifth Amendment right to procedural due process, "arose in a context different from context previously recognized for claims under *Bivens*" and ruled that circumstances in that case, "a prisoner's First Amendment access to court or Fifth Amendment procedural due process claims arising out of a prison disciplinary process...against private defendants, plainly present[ed] a 'new context' under *Abbasi*."[93] The Ninth Circuit did decide, however, that "a new *Bivens* claim was not warranted" because the court decided the plaintiff "had alternative means for relief against the alleged violations of his First and Fifth Amendment rights by private defendants."[94] The Court of Appeal for the Ninth Circuit affirmed that *Bivens* is still good law,[95] and

88 *Id.* at 2008.

89 *Id.* at 2006. Additionally, the Court decided the parties had "not had the opportunity to brief and argue its significance." The Court decided that it was "appropriate for the Court of Appeals...to address the *Bivens* question in the first instance" because the Supreme Court "after all, is one 'of review, not of first view,'" citing *Expressions Hair Design v. Schneiderman*, 137 S. Ct. 1144, 1151, 197 L.Ed.2 d 442 (2017) (quoting *Nautilus, Inc. v. Biosig Instruments, Inc*, 134 S. Ct. 2120, 2131, 189 L. Ed. 2d 37 (2014)).

90 *Hernandez v. Mesa*, 885 F.3d 811 (5th Cir. 2018), pet. for certiorari filed.

91 *Id.* at 816. The Fifth Circuit stated: "Because Hernandez was a Mexican citizen with no ties to this country, and his death occurred on Mexican soil, the very existence of any 'constitutional' right benefitting him raises novel and disputed issues. There has been no direct judicial guidance concerning the extraterritorial scope of the Constitution and its potential application to foreign citizens on foreign soil." *Id.* at 817. The Fifth Circuit expressed concern that "extension of *Bivens* threatens the political branches' supervision of national security." *Id.* at 818. That court stated: "In particular, the threat of *Bivens* liability could undermine the Border Patrol's ability to perform duties essential to national security." *Id* at 819. It further stated: "Here, extending *Bivens* would interfere with the political branches' oversight of nation security and foreign affairs." *Id.* at 823.

92 *Vega*, 881 F.3d 1146, 724 Fed. Appx. 536 (9th Cir. 2018).

93 *Id.* at 1154.

94 *Id.* The court pointed to the plaintiff's administrative remedies and his right to appeal any adverse findings.

95 *Rodriguez v. Swartz*, 899 F.3d. 719, 738 (9th Cir. 2018), pet. for Cert. filed.

that a court's failure to provide a *Bivens* remedy for "an egregious constitutional violation would tempt others to do the same and would run afoul of [a court's] mandate to enforce the Constitution."[96]

The theory under a *Bivens* action is that federal officials lose their sovereign immunity shield when they are involved in constitutional torts.[97] Moreover, despite the reluctance of some courts to permit *Bivens* actions, a Federal statute specifically provides that such an action can be brought against federal officials or employees when they violate the United States Constitution.[98] A victim of a federal constitutional tort who can bring forward a claim for money damages in a *Bivens* action, must bring the action against the federal official or employee in that person's individual capacity, not in the person's official capacity.[99]

---

96 *Lanuza v. Love*, 899 F.3d 1019, 1034 (9th Cir. 2018).

97 The Court of Appeals for the Seventh Circuit acknowledged in *Okoro v. Callaghan*, 324 F.3d 488 (7th Cir. 2003), that *Bivens* creates "a right of action against individual federal officers for violation of constitutional rights." The Seventh Circuit stated: "Damages suits complaining about unconstitutional actions by federal law enforcement officers are governed by *Bivens* if suit is against the officers and by the Federal Tort Claims Act if it is against the United States." *Id.* at 490. (Discussion of the Federal Tort Claims Act in Chapter 4.)

A provision of the Federal Tort Claims Act, 28 U.S.C. §2679(b)(1), requires money actions against the United States "for injury or loss of property, or personal injury or death arising or resulting from the negligent or wrongful act or omission of any employee of the Government while acting with the scope of his office or employment" to be brought against the Government only, not against the governmental employee. However, §2679(b)(2) provides exceptions for "a civil action against an employee of the Government–(A) which is brought for a violation of the Constitution of the United States, or (B) which is brought for a violation of a statute of the United States under which such action against an individual is otherwise authorized." (Section 2679(b)(2)(A) is the *Bivens* action. Section 2679(b)(2)(B) is applicable, among others, to federal civil rights acts discussed in Chapter 3.)

98 28 U.S.C. §2679(b)(2)(A).

99 *Vega*, 882 F.3d at 1154 (reasoning that sovereign immunity disappears when officials violate an amendment of the Constitution).

CHAPTER 3. ABROGATION OF SOVEREIGN IMMUNITY

Although Congress has statutorily abrogated state immunity in some cases, the Supreme Court has ruled that Congress must make its intent to do so "unmistakably clear in the language of the statute."[1] Courts have ruled that to determine whether Congress abrogated a state's sovereign immunity, it must consider whether Congress unequivocally expressed its intent to abrogate immunity and whether Congress acted pursuant to a valid exercise of its power.[2] The Supreme Court originally ruled Congress could abrogate state immunity provided by the Eleventh Amendment[3] under its Article I powers.[4] However, the Court later decided Congress lacks power under Article I to abrogate a state's Eleventh Amendment immunity.[5] Conversely, courts have ruled that Congress has power to abrogate Eleventh Amendment immunity, as well as other privileges of the states, pursuant to its enforcement power in the Fourteenth Amendment.[6]

---

1 *Atascadero State Hospital v. Scanlon*, 473 U.S. 234, 242, 105 S. Ct. 3142, 87 L. Ed. 2d 171 (1985) (recognizing Congress' power to disregard state sovereign immunity under the Eleventh Amendment in certain circumstances).

2 *See Seminole Tribe v. Florida*, 517 U.S. 44, 55, 116 S. Ct. 1114, 134 L. Ed 2d 252 (1996) (concluding that Congress may not abrogate sovereign immunity unless it does so in accordance with a valid exercise of its powers).

3 Discussion of the Eleventh Amendment in Chapter 2.

4 *See e.g., Pennsylvania v. Union Gas Co.,*, 491 U.S. 1, 23, 109 S. Ct. 2273, 105 L. Ed. 2d 1 (1989) (holding that Congress has the power to abrogate Eleventh Amendment immunity under the Commerce Clause when it clearly expresses its intent to do so), *overruled by Seminole Tribe*, 517 U.S. at 72-73. In *Alden v. Maine*, 527 U.S. 706, 707, 755-56, 19 S. Ct. 2240, 2243, 2254-2266, 144 L. Ed. 2d 636 (1999), the Court ruled that the states' immunity from private suit in their own courts was beyond congressional power to abrogate by Article I legislation.

5 *See, e. g. Florida Prepaid Postsecondary Educ. Exp. Bd. v. College Savings Bank*, 527 U.S. 627, 637-40, 119 S.Ct. 2199, 2204, 144 L. Ed.2d 575 (1999) (quoting *Seminole Tribe* as having made it clear that Congress may not abrogate state sovereign immunity pursuant to its Article I powers).

6 Section Five of the Fourteenth Amendment states: "The Congress shall have the power to enforce by

A. SECTION FIVE OF THE FOURTEENTH AMENDMENT

The Fourteenth Amendment, which was adopted in 1868, long after the Eleventh Amendment, expanded federal power at the expense of state autonomy and "fundamentally altered the balance of state and federal power struck by the Constitution."[7] As the Supreme Court explained in *Katzenbach v. Morgan*,[8] Section Five of the Fourteenth Amendment, which gives Congress power to adopt legislation to enforce provisions of the Fourteenth Amendment, "is a positive grant of legislative power authorizing Congress to exercise its discretion in determining whether and what legislation is needed to secure the guarantees of the Fourteenth Amendment."[9] The Court has stated: "Indeed, whatever amount of sovereign immunity the states retained upon ratification of the Constitution was unmistakably reined in by the passage of the Fourteenth Amendment."[10] The Supreme Court commented that, although "state sovereign immunity does not yield to Congress' Article I powers, ...Congress retains the authority to abrogate

---

appropriate legislation, the provisions of this article." Thus, Congress has the power under Section Five to enforce the provisions of Section One of the Fourteenth Amendment which states: "No State shall make or enforce any law which shall abridge the privileges or immunities of citizens of the United States; nor shall any State deprive any person of life, liberty, or property without due process of law, or deny to any person within its jurisdiction the equal protection of the law."

See Fitzpatrick v. Bitzer, 427 U.S. 445, 456, 96 S. Ct. 2666, 49 L. Ed. 2d 614 (1976) (recognizing the congressional power to allow private suits against states for purposes of enforcing the Fourteenth Amendment); *See also Seminole Tribe,* 517 U.S. at 72 (acknowledging the congressional power established in *Fitzpatrick). See also Florida. Prepaid,* 527 U. S. at 670 and *Alden v. Maine,* 527 U.S. at 756 ("in adopting the Fourteenth Amendment, the people required the States to surrender a portion of the sovereignty that had been preserved to them by the original Constitution so that Congress may authorize private suits against nonconsenting States pursuant to its §5 enforcement power" (quoting *Fitzpatrick*).) In *Alden v. Maine,* 517 U.S. at 756, the Court acknowledged that, "by imposing explicit limits on the powers of the States and granting Congress the power to enforce them, the Amendment 'fundamentally altered the balance of state and federal power struck by the Constitution."(quoting *Seminole Tribe,* 517 U.S. at 59). In *Florida Prepaid,* 527 U.S. at 639, the Court reiterated that "for Congress to invoke §5, it must identify conduct transgressing the Fourteenth Amendment's substantive provisions, and must tailor its legislative scheme to remedying or preventing such conduct."

7 *Seminole Tribe,* 517 U.S. at 59. *See City of Boerne v. Flores,* 521 U.S. 507, 536, 117 S. Ct. 2157, 138 L.Ed.2d 624 (1997) ("Section 5 authorizes Congress the authority to enforce; 'the substantive guarantees contained in §1 of that Amendment [the due process guarantees] by enacting 'appropriate legislation'").

8 *Katzenbach,* 384 U.S. 641, 651, 86 S. Ct. 1717, 16 L. Ed.2d 828 (1966).

9 *Id.* (defining Section Five legislation as legislation that: (a) may be regarded as an enactment to enforce the equal protection clause; (b) is plainly adapted to that end; and (c) is not prohibited by, but is consistent with, the letter and spirit of the Constitution).

10 *Fitzpatrick,* 427 U.S. at 456 (quoting *Hans v. Louisiana, 134 U.S. 1, 10 S. Ct. 504, 33 L. Ed. 842 (1890)* and acknowledging "the Eleventh Amendment and the principle of state sovereignty which it embodies are necessarily limited by the enforcement provisions of §5 of the Fourteenth Amendment.).

state sovereign immunity pursuant to enforcement provisions of the Fourteenth Amendment."[11] Section Five of the Fourteenth Amendment thus renders state sovereign immunity inapplicable to legislation Congress enacts pursuant to its Section Five authority.[12]

Section Five of the Fourteenth Amendment empowers Congress to enforce substantive provisions of the Fourteenth Amendment by appropriate legislation.[13] More specifically, Section Five grants Congress the power to enforce legislatively the prohibitions in Section One of the Fourteenth Amendment, which prevents states from enforcing any law that would "abridge the privileges or immunities of citizens of the United States," that would "deprive any person of life, liberty, or property without due process of law," or that would deny any person within a state's jurisdiction "the equal protection of the law."[14] Section Five then authorizes Congress to create a cause of action through which a citizen may vindicate the citizens' Fourteenth Amendment rights.[15] This congressional enforcement power includes the power to abrogate state sovereign immunity by authorizing private suits for damages against the states.[16] If an official's conduct

---

11 *Florida. Prepaid,* 527 U.S. at 636-37.

12 In *Okruhlik v. Univ. of Ark.,* 255 F.3d 615, 625 (8th Cir. 2001), the court rejected an Eleventh Amendment challenge to Title VII, discussed *infra.* It compared the scope of the employer's responsibility under Title VII to its responsibility under the Equal Protection Clause and noted that "the elements of a claim of intentional discrimination are essentially the same under Title VII and the Constitution." *Id.* at 626. The court stated that "differences between the two protections, either by way of remedies or scope, were 'proportional and congruent' responses to a pattern of unconstitutional state action." *Id.*

13 United States Constitution. Amendment, XIV, §5; *see also, U.S. v. Georgia,* 546 U.S. 151, 126 S. Ct. 877, 163 L.Ed. 2d 650 (2006) (stating that no one doubts the enforcement powers conferred by Section Five of the Fourteenth Amendment).

14 *See Seminole Tribe,* 517 U.S. at 59 (recognizing the relationship between Sections One and Five of the Fourteenth Amendment as a fundamental alteration of the "balance of state and federal power") and *Ex parte Virginia,* 100 U.S. 339, 347-48, 25 L. Ed. 676 (1879) (determining that the states may not "disregard the limitations which the Federal Constitution has applied" through the Fourteenth Amendment).

15 *United States v. Georgia,* 546 U.S. 151,158, 126 S. Ct. 877, 163 L. Ed. 2d 750 (2006) (quoting *Tennessee v. Lane,* 541 U.S. 509, 559, 124 S. Ct. 1987, 158 L. Ed 2d 820 (2004); *see also City of Boerne v. Flores,* 521 U.S. at 524 (striking down the Religious Freedom Restoration Act in deciding it exceeded Congress' Section Five power; clarifying the extent of Congress' Section Five power; and identifying the "remedial and preventive nature of Congress' enforcement power").

16 *See Flores,* 521 U.S. at 524 (declaring that "the Fourteenth Amendment confers substantive rights against the States").

violates the Fourteenth Amendment, Section Five permits an action for monetary damage against that official.[17]

In addition to the enforcement of the specific rights outlined in Section One of the Fourteenth Amendment, Congress' authority to abrogate state immunity has been expanded to cover rights that have been incorporated into the Fourteenth Amendment via the Privileges and Immunities Clause of the Due Process Clause.[18] The Fourteenth Amendment is a clear limitation on authority of the states. The Supreme Court has commented that Congress' Section Five power to enforce the substantive provisions of the Fourteenth Amendment is "the solitary legislative tool" it will recognize "for abrogating the sovereign immunity of the states."[19] The Court affirmed: "[T]he Fourteenth Amendment confers substantive rights against the States [that] like the provisions of the Bill of Rights, are self-executing."[20]

Still, given the importance of the Eleventh Amendment's grant of sovereign immunity, the Supreme Court has cautioned that courts must not assume Congress intended to use its power to abrogate state immunity unless "evidence

17 The Supreme Court early ruled, in *Ex parte Virginia,* 100 U.S. 339, 25 L. Ed. 676 (1879) that Section Five of the Fourteenth Amendment granted Congress authority to enforce the substantive provisions of the Fourteenth Amendment by providing actions for money damages against the states. *See Virginia,* 100 U.S. at 347-48 (denying habeas corpus relief to a state judge imprisoned for violating the Fourteenth Amendment in his capacity as a state official).

18 *See Mapp v. Ohio,* 367 U.S. 643, 655, 81 S. Ct. 1684, 6 L. Ed. 2d 1081 (1961) (enforcing Fourth Amendment protection as guaranteed by the Fourteenth Amendment by applying the exclusionary rule to the States) and *Gitlow v. New York,* 268 U.S. 562, 666, 45 S. Ct. 625, 69 L. Ed. 1138 (1925) (identifying freedom of speech and freedom of press as fundamental liberties protected from state infringement by the Fourteenth Amendment). Thus, the states must meet certain procedural requirements before a state can deprive a person of life, liberty, or property. *See Duncan v. Louisiana,* 391 U.S. 145, 164, 88 S. Ct. 1444, 20 L. Ed. 2d 491 (1968) (outlining the doctrine of "Selective Incorporation" and identifying the following incorporated rights: the right to trial by jury in criminal cases, the right against self-incrimination, "the right to counsel, the right to compulsory process for witnesses, the right to confront witnesses, the right to a speedy and public trial, and the right to be free form unreasonable searches and seizures"). Since *Ex parte Virginia,* 100 U.S. 339 (1879), the Court has ruled that Congress may enforce "the Fourteenth Amendment against those who carry a badge of authority of a State and represent it in some capacity," even if they misuse their authority. *Monroe v. Pape,* 365 U.S. 167, 172 (1961) (citing *Home Tel. & Tel. Co. v. City of L.A.,* 227 U.S 278, 288, 33 S. Ct. 312, 57 L. Ed. 2d 520 (1913) , *overruled on other grounds by Monell v. Dep't of Soc. Servs. of N.Y.,* 436 U.S. 658, 98 S. Ct. 2018, 56 L. Ed. 2d 611 (1978).

19 *Florida Prepaid,* 527 U.S. at 628. In enforcing the Equal Protection Clause of the Fourteenth Amendment, the Supreme Court has prohibited unjustified discrimination, as noted *infra.* The Court also has read Section Five expansively to prohibit state actions wholly unrelated to discrimination. See e.g., *Barry v. Barchi,* 443 U.S. 55, 64, 99 S.Ct. 2642, 61 L.Ed.2d 365 (1979).

20 *Flores,* 521 U.S. at 524.

of congressional intent" to do so is "both unequivocal and textual."[21] The Court has maintained that Congress has identified conduct transgressing the Fourteenth Amendment's substantive provisions and has tailored its legislative scheme to remedying or preventing the conduct.[22] In *Board of Trustees of the University of Alabama v. Garrett,*[23] the Supreme Court noted that Congress may abrogate the States' Eleventh Amendment immunity when it both unequivocally intends to do so and acts pursuant to a valid grant of constitutional authority.[24] The remedy imposed by Congress must be "congruent" and "proportional to the targeted violation."[25] Thus, the Supreme Court reasoned that, while Congress clearly expressed its intent to abrogate state sovereign immunity for patent infringement suits brought in federal courts in the Patent Remedy Act,[26] the Fourteenth Amendment's authorization for "appropriate legislation" to protect against deprivations of property without due process of law did not provide Congress with authority to abrogate state sovereign immunity in that Act.[27] The Court

---

21 *Dellmuth v. Muth,* 491 U.S. 223, 230, 109 S. Ct. 2397, 105 L. Ed.2d 181 (1989), *superseded by statute,* Individuals with Disabilities Education Improvement Act of 2004, Pub. L. No. 104-446, sec. 101, §604, 118 Stat. 2647, 2659. *See also Atascadero State Hosp. v. Scanlon,* 473 U.S. at 242-43.

22 *Florida Prepaid,* 527 U.S. at 639. The Court stated in *Flores,* 521 U.S. at 518-19, that Congress power to abrogate state sovereign immunity pursuant to a valid exercise of its power under Section Five is not unlimited. *See also Tennessee v. Lane,* 541 U.S. 509, 520 (2004) (opining that, although Congress "must have a wide berth in devising appropriate remedial and preventative measures for unconstitutional actions, those measures may not work a 'substantive change in the governing law'" (quoting *Flores,* 521 U. S. at 519). In *Flores,* the Court set forth the test for distinguishing between permissible remedial legislation and unconstitutional substantive redefinitive: "Section Five legislation is valid if it exhibits a congruence and proportionality between the injury to be prevented or remedied and the means adopted to that end." *Lane,* 541 U. S. at 520 (quoting *Flores,* 521 U.S. at 520).

23 *Garrett,* 531 U.S. 356, 363, 121 S. Ct. 955, 148 L. Ed. 2d 866 (2001).

24 *Id.* (quoting *Kimel v. Fla. Bd. Of Regents,* 528 U.S. 63, 73, 120 S. Ct. 631, 145 L. Ed. 2d 522 (2000)); *see also Flores,* 521 U.S. at 519 (limiting Congress' enforcement power to remedial and preventive measures rather than substantive measures).

25 *Garrett,* 531 U.S. at 374; *see also Kimel,* 528 U.S. at 91-02 (holding that Congress did "not validly abrogate the States' sovereign immunity" in the Age Discrimination in Employment Act (ADEA) and that "the ADEA is not a valid exercise of Congress' power under [Section Five]" because of "the indiscriminate scope of the Act's substantive requirements").

Discussion of Age Discrimination in Employment Act *infra.*

26 Patent and Plant Variety Protection Remedy Clarification Act (Patent Remedy Act), 35 U.S.C. §§571 et. seq.

27 *Florida Prepaid,* 527 U.S. at 635 (ruling that neither the Commerce Clause nor the Patent Clause provided Congress with authority to abrogate state sovereign immunity). The Court noted the ruling in *Seminole Tribe* provided that Congress cannot use its Article I powers to abrogate state sovereign immunity. In *Seminole Tribe,* 517 U.S. 44 at 72-37, the Supreme Court held that Congress' vast power to regulate interstate commerce nevertheless was subordinate to the protection to states from fed-

ruled that a state's infringement of a patent violates the Fourteenth Amendment only where the state provides no remedy, or inadequate remedies, to injured patent owners for infringement of their patent.[28] However, in *Tennessee v. Lane*,[29] the Court ruled that Title II of the Americans with Disabilities Act[30] constitutes a valid exercise of Congress' enforcement power under the Fourteenth Amendment when applied to cases implicating the fundamental right of access to the courts. Further in *Boddie v. Connecticut*,[31] the Court noted that the Due Process Clause requires states to afford civil litigants a "meaningful opportunity to be heard" by removing obstacles to their full participation in judicial proceedings.[32]

B. COPYRIGHT INFRINGEMENT

The Copyright Remedy Clarification Act (CRCA),[33] abrogated a state's sovereign immunity from copyright infringement claims. Still, although the Supreme Court has not addressed the issue, several lower courts have reasoned that Congress exceeded its authority in enacting CRCA. Because CRCA was enacted pursuant to the Copyright Clause found in Article I, §8 of the U.S. Constitution, and its legislative history makes clear that "Congress intended to abrogate state sovereign immunity for copyright infringement under its Article I powers,"[34] courts have ruled that Congress was without authority in CRCA to abrogate a

eral suits granted to them by the Eleventh Amendment.

28 *Florida Prepaid*, 527 U.S. at 646-47. The Court decided that the Patent Remedy Act's purposes "to provide a uniform remedy for patent infringement and place States on the same footing as private parties" were proper Article I concerns, but that *Seminole Tribe* eliminated Congress' power to enact such legislation. *Id.* at 647-48.

29 *Lane*, 541 U.S. 509, 533-34, 124 S.Ct. 1978, 158 L.Ed.2d 820 (2004).

30 42 U.S.C. §12132. Americans with Disabilities Act is discussed *infra.*

31 *Boddie*, 401 U.S. 371, 91 S.Ct. 780, 28 L.Ed.2d 113 (1971)

32 *Id.* at 379 (ruling that a state may not deny a citizen access to the courts without infringing on the "Due Process Clause of the Fourteenth Amendment").

33 17 U.S.C. §511a.

34 See, e.g., *Nat'l Ass'n Boards of Pharmacy v. Bd. of Regents of the Univ. Sys. of Ga.*, 633 F.3d 1297, 1313 (11th Cir. 2011) (reasoning that "[i]t would be incongruous to hold that Congress may abrogate the State's sovereign immunity under" the same clause "for actions brought under CRCA").

state's sovereign immunity.[35] Nonetheless, there remains a question of whether Congress can abrogate sovereign immunity under Section Five of the Fourteenth Amendment. One district court that ruled Congress validly abrogated the state's Eleventh Amendment immunity under Section Five,[36] was reversed on appeal.[37] The district court pointed out that, in enacting CRCA, "Congress was clearly responding to a pattern of current and anticipated abuse by the states of the copyrights held by their citizens."[38] It then found it "appropriate...to note its disagreement" with standards that "spawned" Eleventh Amendment jurisprudence.[39] In referring to the founders writing "a Constitution founded upon the sovereignty of the people, not the states," the district court expressed concern that the doctrine of sovereign immunity "does not enhance constitutional protections or advance the ideals of our constitutional form of government in which the people are sovereign."[40] On appeal, the Court of Appeals for the Fourth Circuit stated that in exercising its Section Five powers under the Fourteenth Amendment, "Congress must both (1) make clear that it is relying on §5 of the Fourteenth Amendment as the source of its authority and (2) ensure that

35 *Rodriguez v. Texas Comm'n on the Arts*, 199 F. 3d 279 (5th Cir. 2000) and *Coyle v. University* of *Kentucky*, 2 F. Supp. 3d 1014, 1018-19 (E. D. Ken. 2014) (contending CRCA did not validly abrogate state sovereign immunity because it was enacted under Congress' Article I powers).

36 *Allen v. Cooper*, 244 F. Supp. 3d 525, 535 (E.D. N.C. 2017), (ruling Congress appropriately exercised its Section Five powers under the Fourteenth Amendment in passing the Copyright Remedy Clarification Act to abrogate state sovereign immunity to copyright claims), but reversed, *Allen v. Cooper*, 895 F.3d 337 (4th Cir. 2018); see also *Nettleman v. Fla. Atlantic Univ. Bd. of Trustees*, 228 F. Supp. 3d 1303 (S.D. Fla. 2017) (abrogation not valid); *Coyle*, 2 F. Supp. 3d at 1018 (stating court was not persuaded "that Section 5 is the means by which Congress passed the CRCA"); *Reiner v. Canale*, 301 F. Supp. 3d 727 (E.D. Mich. 2018) (ruled a professor had qualified immunity to the extent the professor was sued in his individual capacity and Eleventh Amendment immunity to the extent he was sued in his official capacity); *Chavez v. Arte Publico Press*, 204 F.3d 601, 604 (5th Cir. 2000) (ruling CRCA was an invalid exercise of Article I legislative power and reasoning that upholding CRCA as valid exercise of legislative power "pursuant to section 5 of the Fourteenth Amendment would be an impermissible end-run around *Seminole*"); *InfoMath, Inc. v. Univ. of Arkansas*, 633 F. Supp. 2d 674, 680 (E.D. Ark. 2007) (agreeing with the Fifth Circuit "that the CRCA was an improper exercise of Congressional legislative powers"); *National Association of Boards of Pharmacy v. Board. of Regents of Georgia.*, 633 F.3d 1297 (11th Cir. 2011) ("Fourteenth Amendment does not itself justify the CRCA's abrogation of state sovereign immunity"); *Rodriguez*, 199 F.3d at 281 (stating that *Seminole* made clear Congress may not abrogate state sovereign immunity pursuant to its Article I powers and that it cannot "be sustained as legislation enacted to enforce the guarantees of the Fourteenth Amendment's Due Process Clause").

37 *Allen v. Cooper*, 895 F.3d 337 (4th Cir. 2018).

38 *Cooper*, 224 F. Supp. at 534.

39 *Id.* at 537.

40 *Id.* at 538.

any abrogation of immunity is 'congruent and proportional' to the Fourteenth Amendment injury to be prevented or remedied."[41] The Fourth Circuit decided it was "readily apparent that in enacting the Copyright Remedy Clarification Act,[42] Congress relied on the Copyright Clause in Article I of the Constitution, rather than §5 of the Fourteenth Amendment."[43] It stated: "Neither the text of the statute nor its legislative history indicates any invocation of authority conferred by §5 of the Fourteenth Amendment. And without such an invocation, the Act cannot effect a valid abrogation under §5."[44]

C. JONES ACT

The Jones Act[45] creates a statutory right of recovery for an employer's negligence that results in injury to a seaman in the course of the seaman's employment. Although the Supreme Court early ruled that courts must construe the

---

41 895 F.3d at 349, citing *Florida Prepaid,* 527 U. S. at 639-42. The Fourth Circuit noted the Supreme Court's decision in *Florida Prepaid* wherein it "addressed the constitutionality of the Patent Remedy Act, [35 U.S.C. §§571 et. seq.] which abrogated the States' immunity from suit in federal court for patent infringement." The Fourth Circuit pointed out that the Supreme Court ruled in *Florida Prepaid,* 527 U.S. at 636, "that the Commerce and Patent Clauses could not sustain the Act in light of *Seminole Tribe,*" 517 U.S. at 72-73.

42 17 U.S.C. §§501(a), 511.

43 895 F.3d at 349.

44 *Id.* The Fourth Circuit concluded "that the Copyright Remedy Clarification Act's wholesale abrogation of sovereign immunity for claims of copyright infringement is grossly disproportionate to the relevant injury under the Fourteenth Amendment, and therefore the abrogation cannot be sustained as an enactment that 'appropriately enforces' that Amendment." *Id.* at 353.

45 Section 27 of the Merchant Marine Act of 1920, Pub. L. 66-261, formerly 46 U.S. U.S.C. §688, but codified in 2006 as 46 U.S.C. §30104. The Merchant Marine Act regulates maritime commerce in U.S. waters and between U.S. ports; section 27 of the Act provides rights for seaman. With respect to seaman's rights, the Jones Act states in part: "Any seaman who shall suffer personal injury in the course of his employment may, at his election, maintain an action for damages at law, with the right of trial by jury, and in such action all statutes of the United States modifying or extending the common-law right of remedy in cases of personal injury to railway employees shall apply; and in the case of death of any seaman as a result of any such personal injury, the personal representative of such seaman may maintain an action for damages at law with the right of trial by jury, and in such action all statutes of the United States conferring or regulating the right of action for death in the case of railway employees shall be applicable. Jurisdiction in such actions shall be under the court of the district in which the defendant employer resides or in which his principal office is located.

The saving to suitors clause, 28 U.S.C. §1333, provides state courts with concurrent jurisdiction with Federal courts over claims under the Jones Act.

Act liberally to protect injured workers,[46] there remains the problem that immunity may preclude any redress if the injured seaman's employer is the state or the Federal government.

In *Welch v. Texas Dept. of Highways and Public Transp.*,[47] a state employee who was injured while working on a ferry dock, filed a claim against the state in federal court for damages under the Jones Act. In response to the state's immunity defense, the employee contended that Congress had abrogated the States' Eleventh Amendment immunity from suit.[48] The Supreme Court ruled in a 5-4 decision that because "Congress has not expressed in unmistakable statutory language its intention to allow states to be sued in federal court under the Jones Act,"[49] the Eleventh Amendment bars a state employee from suing the state in Federal court. The Court held that although the Act extended to "any" injured seaman, that general authorization for federal court lawsuits "is not the kind of unequivocal statutory language that is sufficient to abrogate the Eleventh Amendment.[50] The Court did note that the Eleventh Amendment "marks a constitutional distinction between the States and other employers of seaman,"[51] but stated that "the constitutional role of the States sets them apart from other employers and defendants."[52] The dissent in *Welch*[53] disagreed, asserting that the Eleventh Amendment applies "only to diversity suits and not to federal-questions or admiralty suits."[54]

The Supreme Court of Massachusetts later held that defendant states are immune in state courts from suit under the Jones Act unless the state consented

46 *Cosmopolitan Shipping Co., v. McAllister*, 337 U.S. 783, 790, 69 S. Ct. 1317, 93 L. Ed. 1692 (1949).

47 *Welch*, 483 U.S. 468, 469, 107 S. Ct. 2941, 97 L. Ed. 2d 389 (1987).

48 *Id.* at 475.

49 *Id* at 469.

50 *Id.*

51 *Id.*

52 *Id.* at 477.

53 *Id.* at 495 (Brennan, J., with whom Justices Marshall, Blackmun, and Stevens joined).

54 *Id.* at 509. The dissenters were concerned that the Court's expansive scope of the Eleventh Amendment was "protecting the States from the consequences of their illegal conduct" and that the majority decision was "limiting the ability of Congress to take steps it deems necessary and proper to achieve national goals within its constitutional authority." *Id.* at 520-21.

to be sued.[55] In *Morris v. Massachusetts Maritime Academy,* [56] the Massachusetts Supreme Court referred to the Supreme Court's ruling in *Welch* that the Jones Act does not contain sufficiently explicit language to constitute an abrogation of Eleventh Amendment immunity and decided that states may also claim immunity in their own courts.[57] The Massachusetts Supreme Court referred to the state being "hauled into its own courts by the laws of another sovereign" and stated: "We think the Supreme Court's Eleventh Amendment jurisprudence demonstrates a greater respect for the principle of State sovereign immunity."[58] The court then affirmed that because the Jones Act does not abrogate state immunity in federal courts, "it cannot be interpreted as abrogating State court immunity."[59]

The Supreme Court of Alaska also later ruled that the Jones Act did not give a seaman a right to sue the state without the state's consent.[60] The Alaska Court ruled that "under *Alden v. Maine*[61] the only times a private party may sue the state are (1) if the state consented, (2) if Congress had validly abrogated the need for state consent, or (3) under *Ex parte Young*."[62] In referring to the Supreme Court's ruling in *Welch* that "the federal legislation lacked a clear statement of congressional intent to abrogate state sovereign immunity,"[63] the Alaska Court also concluded that the Jones Act did not give a seaman a right to sue the state without the state's consent.[64]

55 *Morris v. Massachusetts Maritime Academy*, 409 Mass. 179, 565 N.E.2d 422 (Mass. 1991). A cadet, who was severely injured by a fire aboard a training vessel used by the Massachusetts Maritime Academy, and the estate of another cadet, who died in the fire, brought action against the Academy seeking damages arising from the injury and death.

56 *Id.* at 426 (citing *Welch v. Texas Dept't of Highways and Pub. Transp.*, 483 U.S. at 474-476.).

57 *Id.*

58 *Id.*

59 *Id.* at 427.

60 *Glover v. State of Alaska*, 175 P.3d 1240 (Alaska 2008).

61 *Alden*, 527 U.S. 706, 19 S. Ct. 2240, 2243,144 L. Ed. 2d 636 (1999).

62 *Glover*, 175 P.3d at 1254 (referring to *Ex parte Young*, 209 U.S. 123, 28 S. Ct. 442, 52 L. Ed. 714 (1908) but also noting that the parties did not attempt to argue the case under *Ex parte Young*).

63 *Glover*, 175 P. 3d at 1254.

64 *Id.* at 1254-55.

Courts have ruled that Congress abrogated Eleventh Amendment immunity with respect to claims under the Civil Rights Act of 1964,[65] referred to as Title VII, and under the Equal Pay Act.[66] However, courts have refused to find abrogation in the Age Discrimination in Employment Act[67] and under Title I of the American with Disabilities Act (ADA).[68] Still, Congress apparently does have authority to abrogate Eleventh Amendment immunity under Title II of the ADA. As a general rule, courts have agreed Congress has the authority to abrogate a state's Eleventh Amendment immunity in civil rights acts but only pursuant to its enforcement powers under Section Five of the Fourteenth Amendment.

1. Title VII, the Civil Rights Act of 1964

The Civil Rights Act of 1964,[69] referred to as Title VII, was enacted to prohibit employment discrimination based on race, color, religion, sex, or national origin.[70] Courts have ruled that Eleventh Amendment immunity does not protect states from Title VII claims.[71] Moreover, following the 1976 Supreme Court opin-

65 42 U.S.C. § 2000e-2000e-17.

66 29 U.S.C. §§201-19.

67 29 U.S.C. §§623 *et seq.*

68 42 U.S.C. §§12101 *et seq.*

69 42 U.S.C. § 2000e-2000e-17.

70 Organizations that are engaged in activities affecting commerce and that have fifteen or more employees on each working day in each of twenty or more calendar weeks in the current or preceding year are subject to the Civil Rights Act of 1964, 42 U.S.C. § 2000e, which is referred to as Title VII. Title VII makes it an unlawful employment practice for any employer to fail or refuse to hire or to discharge any individual, or otherwise to discriminate against any individual with respect to compensation, terms, conditions, or privileges of employment, because of an individual's race, color, religion, sex, or national origin. The Act also prohibits an employer from limiting, segregating, or classifying employees or applicants for employment in any way that would deprive, or tend to deprive, any individual of employment opportunities or would otherwise affect the employee's status as an employee, because of the individual's race, color, religion, sex, or national origin. The Act is enforced by the Equal Employment Opportunity Commission (EEOC). *Id.* at §2000-5.

71 *See, e.g., Fitzpatrick v. Bitzer,* 427 U.S. 445, 453, 96 S. Ct. 2666, 49 L. Ed. 2d 614 (1976) (affirming "there is no dispute that in enacting the 1972 Amendments to Title VII to extend coverage to the States as employers, Congress exercised its power under §5 of the Fourteenth Amendment" and that the Eleventh Amendment "and the principle of state sovereignty which it embodies are necessarily limited by the enforcement provision of the Fourteenth Amendment"); *Ussery v. State of La.,* 150 F.3d 431 (5th Cir. 1998) (Eleventh Amendment bar is not absolute).

ion in *Fitzpatrick v. Bitzer*,[72] courts have repeatedly ruled that Congress validly abrogated states' Eleventh Amendment immunity in its Title VII legislation.[73]

Although courts clearly have ruled that Section Five of the Fourteenth Amendment abrogates state immunity for a state's violation of Title VII,[74] the State of Louisiana argued in *Ussery v. State of Louisiana*[75] that, despite the language in *Fitzpatrick*, none of the cases had addressed whether Title VII contained "the unmistakable congressional waiver of the States' Eleventh Amendment immunity required by the Supreme court in *Atascadero State Hospital v. Scanlon*."[76] The State of Louisiana pointed out that *Atascadero* was decided nine years after *Fitzpatrick*.[77] The Court of Appeals for the Fifth Circuit disagreed with the State of Louisiana, deciding that Congress had "made its intent to abrogate the State's Eleventh Amendment unmistakably clear" when it amended Title VII's definition of "person" to include a "government, governmental agency, and political subdivision" as being an employer that would be subject to Title VII prohibitions "and simultaneously amended the definition of employee to include individuals 'subject to the civil service laws of a State government, government agency, or political subdivision.'"[78]

A discrimination claimant can bring a suit in either federal or state court. However, in considering filing the claim in state court, a claimant is advised that a state may have an immunity statute that a state court interprets as overriding the federal abrogation of state sovereign immunity. For example, consider the

---

72 *Id.*

73 *See, e.g., Whiting v. Jackson State Univ.*, 616 F2d 116, 127 n. 8 (5th Cir. 1980) and *Pegues v. Miss. State Employ. Serv.*, 899 F.2d 1449, 1453 (5th Cir. 1990).

74 *See, e.g., Fitzpatrick*, 427 U.S. at 447, 455 (upholding the constitutionality of the Civil Rights Act to state and local government employees; stating the principle of state sovereignty was necessarily limited by the enforcement provision of the Fourteenth Amendment; and affirming that expansion of congressional power embodied in the Civil Rights Act resulted in "the corresponding diminution of state sovereignty"); *Shawer v. Indiana Univ. of* Penn., 602 F.2d 1161, 1164 (3rd 1979) (stating that it is "clear beyond question that when Congress...extended Title VII to state governments, it did so pursuant to Section 5 of the Fourteenth Amendment and thereby abrogated any existing immunity of the states from liability for discriminatory employment practices"); *United States v. Virginia*, 518 U.S. 515, 534, 116 S. Ct. 2264, 135 L. Ed. 2d 735 (1996) (holding that Virginia was in violation of the Constitution by discriminating against female students at its military institute.)

75 *Ussery*, 150 F.3d 431 (5th Cir. 1998), cert. dismissed, 526 U.S. 1013 (1999).

76 *Atascadero*, 473 U.S. 234, 243, 105 S. Ct. 3142, 3148, 87 L.Ed.2d 171 (1985).

77 *Ussery*, 150 F.3d at 435.

78 *Id.* (quoting the Supreme Court in *Fitzpatrick*, 427 U.S. at 449, n. 2). (Amendment codified at 42 U.S.C. §2000e(f)).

2012 decision of the Texas Supreme Court in *Prairie View A & M University v. Chatha*[79] that has limited victims' Title VII protections against discrimination.

In analyzing the Supreme Court's ruling in *Chatha*, reference must be made to earlier Texas Supreme Court decisions regarding notice requirements of the Texas Commission on Human Rights Act.[80] This Act prohibits an employer from discharging or in any other way discriminating against an employee because of the employee's "race, color, disability, religion, sex, national origin, or age."[81] The Act also prohibits employers from retaliating or discriminating against an employee who engages in certain protected activities under the Act.[82] Because Texas courts have ruled the Texas Legislature intended to correlate state law with federal law with respect to employment discrimination in enacting the Texas Commission on Human Rights Act, the Texas Supreme Court had ruled that courts must look to federal law in interpreting provisions of the Act.[83] Additionally, the Texas Supreme Court earlier ruled that the Texas Act contains an unambiguous waiver of immunity.[84] These cases would lead a litigant

79 381 S.W.3d 500 (Tex. 2012).

80 Tex. Labor Code §§21.001-21.556.

81 *Id.* at §21.051.

82 *Id.* at §21.055. A discrimination claim is filed with the Texas Workforce Commission (TWC) civil rights division. *Id.* at §21.0015. The Texas Workforce Commission replaced the Commission on Human Rights. *Id.* at §21.051. Section 21.051 waives sovereign immunity and provides that an employer may not, on certain specified bases, discriminate, retaliate, or aid and abet in discriminatory behavior against an employee, and that a complainant may bring suit against the employer within sixty days after receiving notice of a right to sue. [Discussion in *Texas Health and Human Services Comm'n v. Olguin,* 532 S.W.3d 403 (Tex. App. Austin 2017).]

A claimant may file a complaint with either the EEOC, the federal agency authorized to investigate charges of discrimination, or the TWC, the Texas equivalent. Tex. Labor Code §21.201; *see* 49 Tex. Admin. Code §819.41(c). When a state has its own employment discrimination statutes, Title VII, 42 U.S.C. §2000e-5(c), requires the EEOC to defer charges of discrimination it receives from employees in those states to state or local fair employment practices agencies for at least sixty days in an attempt to resolve the dispute pursuant to state law. In Texas, a complaint would then be brought initially to the TWC. Complaints filed by Texas employees with the EEOC are filed contemporaneously with the TWC.

83 *See. e.g., M.D. Anderson Hosp. & Tumor Inst. v. Willrich,* 28 S.W.3d 22, 24 (Tex. 2000).

84 *See Mission Consol. Indep. Sch. Dist. v. Garcia,* 253 S.W.3d 653, 660 (Tex. 2008). Later, in *Waffle House, Inc. v. Williams,* 313 S.W.3d 796, 811-13 (Tex. 2010), the Texas Supreme Court ruled that when an employee brings an action against an employer under the Texas Commission on Human Rights Act (TCHRA), the Act preempts any common law claims. In *Waffle House,* the plaintiff sued her employer for sexual harassment under the Act and also for common-law negligence. *Id.* at 800. The jury found for the plaintiff on both claims; she elected to recover on the common law claim, which afforded a far greater monetary recovery. *Id.* However, the Texas Supreme Court ruled the Act is the exclusive remedy for workplace sexual harassment. *Id.* The Supreme Court has also ruled that an employee claiming he or she was terminated in retaliation for complaining of age and race discrimination cannot bring a claim under the Whistleblower Act. *See City of Waco v. Lopez,* 259

to assume that Texas courts would treat a Title VII claim in the same manner as would a federal court and that state sovereign immunity would not be a defense. Nonetheless, in *Prairie View A & M University v. Chatha,*[85] the Texas Supreme Court dismissed a discriminatory action, which was based on salary differentials at a state university, by deciding, contrary to federal law, that a 180-day limitations period on time to file a complaint begins to run "when a discriminatory employment decision is made–not when the effects of that decision become manifest in later events" and that the government has not waived sovereign immunity with respect to notice requirements.[86] The Texas Supreme Court referred in *Chatha* to the Texas Legislature's amendment of Texas Government Code §311.034 and discussed the scope of the amendment in its jurisprudential context.[87] The Texas Court decided the amendment "makes notice requirements, and all other statutory prerequisites to suit, jurisdictional as to governmental entities."[88] This, according to the Texas Supreme Court, preserves "the legisla-

S.W.2d 147, 150 (Tex. 2008) (holding that the plaintiff was obligated to sue under the Commission on Human Rights Act because it provided a "specific and tailored anti-retaliation remedy"). (Discussion of Whistleblower Act in Chapter 4.)

85 *Chatha*, 381 S.W.3d at 503.

86 *Id.* (commenting that its interpretation of Tex. Labor Code §21.202, which obligates a claimant to file a complaint with the TWC or the EEOC not later than the 180th day after the date an allegedly unlawful employment practice occurs "mirrored the United States Supreme Court's interpretation of Title VII until recently"). The Texas Supreme Court noted in *Chatha* that "in 2009, Congress enacted the Lilly Ledbetter Fair Pay Act (Ledbetter Act), Pub. L. No. 111-2, 123 Stat. 5, amending Title VII to provide that a discriminatory pay decision occurs each time a paycheck is received and not just when an initial salary decision is made." *Id* at 510. Thus, as the court stated, "when a claimant files a discriminatory pay claim under federal law, the 180-day limitations period begins each time a claimant receives a paycheck containing a discriminatory amount." However, the Texas Court stated that the law is different in Texas, noting that "the Texas Legislature has not similarly amended the TCHRA." *Id.* The court decided in *Chatha* that it is the Legislature's intent "that all statutory prerequisites are now jurisdictional requirements as to governmental entities." *Id.* at 511. Thus, in Texas, the discriminatory act is deemed to have occurred only when the initial salary decision is made and, if a claimant alleging salary discrimination fails to file a claim with 180 days from that date, the case will be dismissed; failure to file a claim within 180 days of that decision is a jurisdictional bar to suit in Texas.

87 *Id.* The statute was amended in 2005 as a response to the Supreme Court's decision in *Univ. of Tex. Sw. Med. Ctr. at Dallas v. Loutzenhiser*, 140 S.W.3d 351, 359 (Tex. 2004), wherein the Supreme Court had held that because a pre-suit notice requirement in the Texas Tort Claims Act, Tex. Civ. Rem. & Prac. Code §101.106(a) was not a condition of the statute's waiver of immunity, the failure to provide it was not a jurisdictional defect. The court had reasoned that because the provision stated "[a] governmental unit is entitled to receive notice," it was not a mandatory statutory requirement, and because the statute did not specify the consequences of a failure to provide notice, the Texas Court concluded "it was not a condition precedent to suit and the failure to give notice would not deprive the trial court of jurisdiction." *Id.* at 359, 365.

88 *Chatha*, 381 S.W.3d at 503.

ture's interest in managing state fiscal matters through the appropriations process," and ruled that "a statute shall not be construed as a waiver of sovereign immunity unless the waiver is effected by clear and unambiguous language."[89]

The Texas Supreme Court's rigid interpretation of the notice requirements for bringing an EEOC complaint, in conjunction with the Texas Legislature's strict application of the sovereign immunity doctrine, should preclude many discrimination claims brought in courts in Texas.[90] Thus, in some states such as Texas, a better route may be to file in a federal district court.[91]

2. Equal Pay Act

Congress enacted the Equal Pay Act as an amendment to the Fair Labor Standards Act.[92] This Act requires that an employer engaged in commerce or in the production of goods for commerce may not pay different wages to employees of opposite sexes for equal work on jobs the performance of which requires equal skill, effort, and responsibility and that are performed under similar working conditions unless the payment is made pursuant to (1) a seniority system,

---

89 *Id.*

90 The Texas Supreme Court has declared that the "potential absence of equitable defenses against governmental entities that retain their immunity is sovereign immunity's most basic tenet." *Chatha,* 318 S.W.3d at 515. Pursuant to Tex.Gov't Code §311.034, the State of Texas may challenge a court's jurisdiction in a claim against the state by filing a plea to the jurisdiction. This plea will preclude a claimant from proceeding in any manner in a case brought against the government, even obtaining discovery in the case, in the interests, according to the Supreme Court, of the governmental entity effectively avoiding "the time and expense of litigating the merits of a case by first raising the statutory prerequisite issue under section 311.034." *Chatha,* 318 S.W.3d at 515. If a state court denied the plea, the State may challenge the denial in an interlocutory appeal. See Tex. Civ. Prac. & Rem. Code §51.014.

(Chapters 4 and 5 include a discussion of the far-reaching tenets of sovereign immunity in Texas. Refer to discussion in Chapter 4 of Texas Supreme Court decisions that, through a rigid interpretation of the limitations on the waiver provisions in the Texas Tort Claims Act, provide even governmental employees with absolute immunity in most intentional tort claim cases.)

91 Although Title VII requires the filing of a timely charge with the EEOC before filing suit, the U.S. Supreme Court has ruled that exhaustion is not a jurisdictional requirement and may thus be waived or subject to estoppel and equitable tolling. See *Zipes v. Trans World Airlines, Inc.*, 455 U.S. 385, 392-98, 102 S. Ct. 1127, 71 L. Ed. 2d 234 (1982) and *Love v. Pullman,* 404 U.S. 522, 527, 92 S. Ct. 616, 30 L. Ed. 2d 679 (1972) (stating that "technicalities are particularly inappropriate in a statutory scheme in which laymen, unassisted by trained lawyers initiate the process.")

92 29 U.S.C. §§201-19.

(2) a merit system, (3) a system which measures earnings by quantity or quality of production, or (4) a differential based on any factor other than sex.[93]

As originally enacted, the Equal Pay Act was inapplicable to state and local governments. However, coverage was extended to employees of state and local hospitals, institutions, schools, and public transit systems and later was extended to virtually all public employees, except public office holders and their staffs.[94] Courts have ruled that Congress abrogated state's Eleventh Amendment immunity by extending the Act to the states as employers.[95] Moreover, Congress has authority to apply the Act to the states as employers pursuant to Section Five of the Fourteenth Amendment.[96]

---

93 Id at §206(d). The Equal Pay Act is administered by the Equal Employment Opportunity Commission (EEOC). Executive Order 12144, June 12, 1979.

See *Strecker v. Grand Forks County Social Service Board*, 640 F.2d 96, 100 (8th Cir. 1980) (ruling a person alleging unequal pay need not show discriminatory intent; that the Equal Pay Act creates a type of strict liability and no intent to discriminate need be shown.) See also *Brobst v. Columbus Services International*, 761 F.2d 148 (3rd Cir. 1985) (a person establishes a prima facie case by a showing of payment of different wages to employees of opposite sexes for equal work on the job.) In *U.S. EEOC v. Maryland Insurance Admin.*, 879 F.3d 114, 121 (4th Cir. 2018), the court ruled that showing each claimant earned less than at least one male comparator performing substantially equal work under similar working conditions was sufficient to establish a prima facie case of wage discrimination. The court agreed an employer may be entitled to a summary judgment on an Equal Pay Act claim if the employer established an affirmative defense as a matter of law but stated "the burden on the employer necessarily is a heavy one." *Id.* at 120.

Once a prima facie case of unequal pay has been established, the defendant has four affirmative defenses. The defendant must prove that any wage disparity was the result of a seniority system, a merit system, a system which measures earnings by quantity or quality of production, or that the differential was based on any other factor than sex. In *Washington County v. Gunther*, 451 U.S. 161, 178-79, 101 S. Ct. 2242, 68 L. Ed. 2d 751 (1981), the Supreme Court ruled that claims for sex-based wage discrimination can also be brought under Title VII provided the alleged discrimination was not exempt as attributed to seniority, merit, quantity or quality of production or any other factor other than sex.

In *Rizo v. Yovino*, 887 F.3d 453, 456 (9th Cir. 2018), the court ruled that an employer cannot justify a wage differential between male and female employees by relying on a prior salary. In *Rizo*, a female math consultant for a county Office of Education learned her employer was hiring male consultants at higher salary steps. *Id.* at 457-58. The County urged that the fourth statutory exception–any other factor other than sex–applied. *Id.* at 458. The court, however, ruled that "'any other factor other than sex' is limited to legitimate, job-related factors such as a prospective employee's experience, educational background, ability, or prior job performance." *Id.* at 460. It stated, that prior salary "does not fit within the catchall exception because it is not a legitimate measure of work experience, ability, performance, or any other job-related qualify." *Id.* at 467.

94 Discussion in *National League of Cities v. Usery*, 426 U.S. 833, 49 L. Ed. 2d 245, 96 S. Ct. 2465 (1976) (ruling an extension of the Equal Pay Act to states and political subdivisions is a valid exercise of Congress' power under the commerce clause). In *Garcia v. San Antonio Metropolitan Transit Authority*, 469 U.S. 528, 554, 105 S. Ct. 1005, 83 L. Ed.3d 1016 (1985), the Supreme Court overruled *National League* with respect to application of the minimum wage provisions to state governmental entities, stating that there is nothing in the minimum wage provisions "that is destructive of state sovereignty or violative of any constitutional provision."

95 *See., e. g., Ussery v. State of La.*, 150 F.3d 431, 437 (5th Cir. 1998).

96 *Id.* (reasoning that a statute enacted specifically to combat gender discrimination could not fall

In *Varner v. Illinois State University*,[97] the court reasoned that "the wage structure of many segments of American industry has been based on an ancient but outmoded belief that a man, because of his role in society, should be paid more than a woman even though his duties are the same."[98] It stated that "it is precisely these kinds of classifications–those based on outdated and inappropriate assumptions about a woman's place in society–at which the protections of the Fourteenth Amendment are also aimed."[99] One court explained that state discrimination on the basis of race or gender requires high standards of review.[100]

3. Age Discrimination in Employment Act

The Age Discrimination in Employment Act (ADEA),[101] prevents an employer engaged in an industry affecting commerce, with twenty or more employees for each working day in each of twenty or more calendar weeks in the current or preceding calendar year, from failing or refusing to hire or to discharge any individual or otherwise discriminate against any individual because of the individual's age.[102] The purpose of the ADEA was to promote employment of older persons based on their ability rather than on age, to prohibit arbitrary age discrimination in employment, and to help employers and workers find ways of meeting problems arising from the impact of age on employment.

---

outside the authority granted Congress by Section Five"); *Varner v. Illinois State University*, 226 F.3d 927, 936 (7th Cir. 2000) (stating "Congress validly exercised its authority under §5 of the Fourteenth Amendment when it extended the Equal Pay Act to cover wage discrimination on the part of state employers"). *See also Kovacevich v. Kent State Univ.*, 224 F.3d 806 (6th Cir. 2000) (ruling that the Eleventh Amendment defense is in the nature of a jurisdictional bar that "may be raised at any point of the proceedings, including on appeal" but also that the Equal Pay Act "constituted a proper abrogation of Eleventh Amendment immunity") and *Siler-Khodr. v. Univ. of Tex. Health Science Center*, 261 F.3d 542 (5th Cir. 2001) (application of the Equal Pay Act to a state university did not violate the Eleventh Amendment.)

97 *Varner*, 226 F.3d 927 (7th Cir. 2000).

98 *Id.* at 936 (quoting *Corning Glass Works v. Brennan*, 417 U.S. 185, 195, 94 S. Ct. 2223, 41 L.Ed. 2d 1 (1974).

99 *Id.* (concluding that the Equal Pay Act is a "piece of 'remedial or preventive legislation aimed at securing the protections of the Fourteenth Amendment,'"(quoting *Florida Prepaid*, 527 U.S. at 639) and ruling that the university could not assert the Eleventh Amendment as a defense to the plaintiffs' equal pay act claims).

100 *Siler-Khodr*, 261 F.3d at 550.

101 29 U.S.C. §§623 *et seq.*

102 *Id.* at §630(b). The ADEA is limited to persons at least forty years of age. *Id.* at §631.

Title VII standards are applied to charges of age discrimination.[103] The purposes and structure of the acts are similar. However, Title VII standards are not applied automatically in age discrimination cases.[104] An employer can establish a bona fide occupational qualification as a defense to a charge of age discrimination; a business necessity test, not a business convenience test, is used.[105]

The term "employer" in the ADEA includes the federal, state, and local governments.[106] The Court of Appeals for the Ninth Circuit noted that the statute originally applied only to a private-sector employer but was amended in 1974 to extend coverage to the federal, states, and local governments.[107] Still, although the Supreme Court noted that the ADEA contains a clear statement of Congress' intent to abrogate the state's sovereign immunity, it dismissed an age discrimination claim in *Kimel v. Florida Board of Regents*,[108] ruling that the abrogation exceeded Congress' authority under Section Five of the Fourteenth Amendment.[109] The Court decided that "the ADEA prohibits very little conduct likely to be held unconstitutional"[110] and that "Congress never identified any pattern of age discrimination by the States...that rose to the level of constitu-

---

103 *See., e.g., Schwager v. Sun Oil Co. of Penn.*, 591 F.2d 58, 60-61 (10th Cir. 1979).

104 *Tuohy v. Ford Motor Co.*, 675 F.2d 842, 844 (6th Cir. 1982).

105 *Id. See also Gross v. FBL Financial Services, Inc.*, 557 U.S. 167, 129 S. Ct. 2343, 174 L. Ed. 2d 119 (2009).

106 *Guido v. Mount Lemmon Fire Dist.*, 859 F.3d 1168, 1174 (9th Cir. 2017), cert. gr., 138 S.Ct. 1165 (2018), (citing 29 U.S.C. §630(b), which defines the term "employer" to include a State or political subdivision of a State and any agency or instrumentality of a State or a political subdivision of a State"). The court ruled in *Guido* that the twenty employee minimum does not apply to political subdivisions. *Id.* at 1175.

107 *Id.* at 1170 (citing Pub. L. No. 93-259, §28, 88 Stat. 55 (1974)).

108 *Kimel*, 528 U.S. 62, 129 S. Ct. 631, 145 L.Ed.2d 522 (three sets of plaintiffs filed suit under the ADEA, seeking money damages for their state employers' alleged discrimination on the basis of age).

109 *Id.* at 82-83. *See Nanda v. Bd. of Trustees of Univ. of Illinois*, 303 F.3d 817, 825 (7th Cir. 2002) (quoting *Kimel*, 528 U.S. at 91, as observing "that because age discrimination is subject only to rational basis review under the Equal Protection Clause, only irrational age classifications violate the Constitution"). In *Nanda*, the court stated that "Congress' enforcement power must stop short of redefining the States' substantive obligations under the Fourteenth Amendment." *Id.* at 827.

110 *Kimel*, 528 U. S. at 88 (stating that Congress' extension of the ADEA to the States "was an unwarranted response to a perhaps inconsequential problem"). *Id* at 89. In *Kimel*, the Court found that the "substantive requirements the ADEA imposed on state and local governments are disproportionate to any unconstitutional conduct that conceivably could be targeted by the Act" and, in noting that the elderly are not a suspect class, stated that laws discriminating on the basis of age are presumptively valid under rational basis scrutiny. The Court decided that the ADEA prohibits substantially more state employment decisions and practices than would be illegal under the Fourteenth Amendment. *Id.* at 82-86.

tional violation."[111] The Court concluded that the ADEA is not a valid exercise of Congress' power under Section Five of the Fourteenth Amendment in light of the "lack of evidence of widespread and unconstitutional age discrimination by the States and the indiscriminate scope of the Act's substantive requirements."[112]

4. Americans with Disabilities Act

The Americans with Disabilities Act (ADA)[113] represented a "long-delayed but very necessary step to welcome individuals with disabilities fully into the mainstream of American society."[114] Title I of the ADA[115] prohibits a covered entity[116] from discriminating against a "qualified individual with a disability"[117] because of the individual's disability with regard to job application procedures, hiring, advancement, or discharge of employees, employee compensation, job training,

---

111 *Id.*

112 *Id.* at 91.

113 42 U.S.C. §§12101 *et seq.*

114 See Americans with Disabilities Act of 1990, Pub L No. 101-336, 104 Stat 327, 4 US Cong & Admin News 268 (1990). Congress found that some 43,000,000 Americans have one or more physical or mental disabilities and that the number was increasing as the population grew older; that historically, society had tended to isolate and segregate individuals with disabilities; that discrimination against individuals with disabilities persisted in such critical areas as employment, housing, public accommodations, education, transportation, communication, recreation, institutionalization, health services, voting, and access to public services; that individuals who had experienced discrimination on the basis of disability often had no legal recourse to redress such discrimination; and that the continuing existence of discrimination denied persons with disabilities the opportunity to compete on an equal basis and to pursue opportunities. "42 U.S.C. &s;§12101(a).

115 42 U.S.C. §12112.

116 A "covered entity" is an employer engaged in an industry affecting commerce that has fifteen or more employees for each working day of twenty or more calendar weeks in the current or preceding calendar year and any agent of that employer. *Id.* at §12111(5).

117 The term "qualified individual with a disability" means an individual with a disability, who, with or without reasonable accommodation, can perform the essential functions of an employment position the individual holds or desires. *Id.* at §12111(8). A covered entity is deemed to have discriminated against a qualified individual with a disability if the employer does not make reasonable accommodations to the known physical or mental limitations of an otherwise qualified individual with a disability who is an applicant or employee unless the covered entity can demonstrate the accommodation would impose an undue hardship on the entity's business. Further, no qualified individual with a disability can be excluded from participation in or be denied the benefits of services, programs, or activities of a public entity. *Id* at §12112(b)(5).

and other terms, conditions, and privileges of employment.[118] Title II[119] prohibits a public entity[120] from discriminating against "qualified" persons with disabilities in the provisions or operation of public services, programs, or activities.[121]

In *Board of Trustees of the University of Alabama v. Garrett*,[122] the Supreme Court ruled that the Eleventh Amendment bars suits against states by state employees for money damages for failure of a state to comply with Title I of the ADA.[123] However, the Supreme Court ruled shortly thereafter, in *Tennessee v. Lane*,[124] that the Eleventh Amendment does not bar suits against the state under Title II of the ADA.[125] In *Lane*, the Court concluded that Title II is valid Section Five legislation because it applies to the class of cases implicating the

---

118 *Id.* at §12112. The ADA incorporates by reference enforcement provisions of Title VII of the Civil Rights Act of 1964 including injunctive relief and back pay. 42 U.S.C. &s;§12117.

119 *Id* at §12132.

120 The Act defines the term;"public entity;" to include state and local governments, as well as their agencies and instrumentalities. Id. at §12131(1).

121 Title II authorizes suits by private citizens for money damages against public entities that violate §12132. See 42 U.S.C. §12133 (incorporating by reference 29 U.S.C. §794(a)).

122 Garrett, 531 U.S. 356, 148 L. Ed. 2d 866, 121 S. Ct. 955 (2001).

123 *Id.* at 357-58 (ruling the Eleventh Amendment barred state employee suits in federal court to recover money damages under Title I of the ADA; deciding that for Congress to authorize private individuals to recover money damages against a state, there must be a pattern of discrimination by the States that violates the Fourteenth Amendment and "that the remedy imposed by Congress be congruent and proportional to the targeted violation;" and determining that those requirements were not met by Title I of the ADA). *Id.* at 358. The Court ruled that the Fourteenth Amendment does not require states to make special accommodations for the disabled so long as their actions towards these individuals are rational. Although Section Five of the Fourteen Amendment grants Congress the "power to enforce, by appropriate legislation" the Fourteenth Amendment's equal protection guarantee, a majority of the Court decided that the ADA was not an "appropriate" way to enforce this requirement. *Id. at* 357. The majority opined that section Five does not enlarge congressional authority to "rewrite the Fourteenth Amendment law." *Id. at* 358.

124 *Lane*, 541 U. S. 509, 124 S. Ct. 1978, 158 L. Ed. 2d 820 (2004).

125 *Id.* at 533-34 (acknowledging: "Title II, as it applies to the class of cases implicating the fundamental right of access to the courts, constitutes a valid exercise of Congress' §5 authority to enforce the guarantees of the Fourteenth Amendment").

accessibility of judicial services.[126] The Court further ruled in *United States v. Georgia*,[127] that "insofar as Title II creates a private cause of action for damages against the States for conduct that actually violates the Fourteenth Amendment, Title II validly abrogates state sovereign immunity."[128]

Even prior to the Supreme Court's ruling in *Lane*, the Court of Appeals for the Ninth Circuit had affirmed that the Eleventh Amendment does not bar claims against a state brought under Title II of the ADA,[129] but in *Wessel v. Glendening*,[130] the Court of Appeals for the Fourth Circuit had ruled that the Eleventh Amendment does bar claims against a state under Title II.[131] A district court later declared that *Lane* did not overturn *Wessel* and that the Fourth Circuit's ruling in *Wessel* continues to control within the Fourth Circuit.[132] More recently, the Seventh Circuit Court of Appeals disagreed that Congress' abrogation of Eleventh Amendment immunity in Title II ADA claims applied to a suit brought by a deaf plaintiff against a state court, alleging the court's refusal to provide him with an interpreter during mediation violated Title II of the ADA. In *King v. Marion Circuit Court*,[133] the Seventh Circuit ruled that the state court had sovereign immunity from the plaintiff's suit. The court decided the plaintiff had not made a showing that "limits on the subsidy of court-annexed mediation services can deny him, or anyone else, access to judicial services," and determined the plaintiff had not brought forward a "right of access to the courts"

---

126 *Id.* at 531-533 (stating Title II's requirement of program accessibility "is congruent and proportional to its object of enforcing the right of access to the courts"). *Id.* at 531. The Court stated: "This duty to accommodate is perfectly consistent with the well-established due process principle that, 'within the limits of practicability, a State must afford to all individuals a meaningful opportunity to be heard' in its courts.'" *Id.* at 532 (citing *Boddie v. Connecticut*, 401 U.S. 371, 379, 91 S. Ct. 780, 28 L. Ed. 2d 113 (1971) and stating that "Title II's affirmative obligation to accommodate persons with disabilities in the administration of justice cannot be said to be 'so out of proportion to a supposed remedial or preventive object that it cannot be understood as responsive to, or designed to prevent, unconstitutional behavior'" (quoting *Boerne*, 521 U.S. at 532, and *Kimel*, 528 U. S. at 86)).

127 *Georgia*, 546 U.S. 151, 126 S. Ct. 877, 163 L. Ed. 2d 650 (2006).

128 *Id.* at 159.

129 *Lovell v. Chandler*, 303 F.3d 1039 (9th Cir. 2002).

130 *Wessel*, 306 F.3d 203 (4th Cir. 2002).

131 *Id.* (stating that Congress' power under Section Five of the Fourteenth Amendment is not unlimited and that Congress did not validly abrogate Eleventh Amendment immunity of states when it enacted Title II of the ADA).

132 *Costello v. University of North Carolina*, 394 F. Supp. 2d 752 (D.C.N.C. 2005) (ruling that the defendants retained their Eleventh Amendment immunity).

133 *Marion Circuit Court*, 868 F.3d 589 (7th Cir. 2017), Cert. Denied, 138 S.Ct. 1582 (2018).

issue.[134] The Seventh Circuit concluded the plaintiff's claim "has no constitutional dimension at all."[135]

In *Savage v. Glendale Union High School, Dist. No. 205, Maricopa County,*[136] in an ADA claim brought against a school district, the Court of Appeals for the Ninth Circuit determined that the school district was not an agent of the State of Arizona and thus was not entitled to sovereign immunity under the Eleventh Amendment. The court referred to five factors it earlier set out in *Mitchell v. Los Angeles Community College Dist,*[137] that a court must examine to determine whether a governmental entity is an arm of the state for Eleventh Amendment purposes. These are: (1) whether a money judgment would be satisfied out of state funds; (2) whether the entity performs central governmental functions; (3) whether the entity may sue or be sued; (4) whether the entity has the power to take property in its own name or only in the name of the state; and (5) the corporate status of the entity.[138] In considering these factors, the court concluded the school district was not an arm of the state. The court also noted Arizona law defines school districts as political subdivisions and stated that political subdivisions are not included in the law's definition of "state."

In summary, courts agree that Title VII abrogated the state's Eleventh Amendment immunity. Further, a state cannot assert Eleventh Amendment immunity as a defense in an action under the Equal Pay Act. Nonetheless, the

134 *Id.* at 592.

135 *Id.* at 593.

136 *Savage,* 343 F.3d 1036 (9th Cir. 2003), cert. denied, 124 S. Ct. 2067 (2004).

137 *Mitchell,* 861 F. 2d 198 (9th Cir. 1988).

138 *Savage,* 343 F.3d at 1040-41 (noting that it had found California school districts were state agencies entitled to Eleventh Amendment immunity in *Belanger v. Madera Unified School Dist.*, 963 F2d 248 (9th Cir. 1992) but that Nevada school districts were not arms of the state entitled to sovereign immunity, citing *Eason v. Clark County School Dist.*, 303 F3d 1137 (9th Cir. 2002), cert. denied, 537 US 1190 (2003)). The Ninth Circuit decided in *Savage* that Arizona school districts were more akin to Nevada's than to California's and therefore were subject to suit in federal court. *Id.* at 1041. The court concluded that the Arizona State treasury would not be vulnerable to a money judgment against the school district because it decided the state guarantees only a minimum amount of per pupil spending and school districts may generate funds in addition to those provided by the state. The Ninth Circuit further concluded that the Arizona law grants local school districts enormous autonomy in the management of public education and noted that Arizona school districts are empowered by statute to hold and convey property for the use and benefit of the district. Finally, it noted that Arizona law defines school districts as political subdivisions and stated political subdivisions are not included in the law's definition of "state" The court commented that most communities value local control of their schools, stating that when a state chooses to vest the control of school districts in local school boards, a school district cannot invoke the protection of the Eleventh Amendment to immunize themselves from appropriate lawsuits in federal court. *Id.* at 1044.

Supreme Court has ruled that Congress exceeded its authority in abrogating Eleventh Amendment immunity in the Age Discrimination in Employment Act. Further, the Court held that Congress did not validly abrogate sovereign immunity under Title I of the ADA, which prohibits employers from discriminating against an individual because of the individual's disabilities with respect to hiring, advancement, and firing. Even so, the Supreme Court has ruled that Congress did validly abrogate sovereign immunity under Title II of the ADA, which prohibits public entities from discriminating against persons with disabilities in the provisions or operations of public services, programs, or activities. Nonetheless, some federal courts of appeal have found reasons to grant states Eleventh Amendment immunity likewise in claims brought under Title II of the Act.

E. BANKRUPTCY PROCEEDINGS

The United States Constitution[139] provides Congress with power to establish "uniform Laws on the subject of Bankruptcies throughout the United States."[140] In *Tennessee Student Assistance Corp. v. Hood*,[141] the Supreme Court upheld the application of the Bankruptcy Code[142] to proceedings initiated by a debtor against a state agency to determine the dischargeability of a student loan debt, but did not determine whether the Bankruptcy Clause in the Constitution gives Congress the authority to abrogate States' immunity from private suits.[143] Two years after its decision in *Hood*, the Supreme Court ruled, in *Central Virginia.*

139 United States Constitution, Article 1, §8.

140 Discussion in *Central Va. Community College v. Katz*, 546 U.S. 356, 126 S. Ct. 990, 163 L. Ed. 2d 945 (2006).

141 *Hood*, 541 U.S. 440, 443, 124 S.Ct. 1905, 58 L.Ed. 2d 764 (2004).

142 11 U.S.C. §§101 *et seq.*

143 Section 106(a) of the Bankruptcy Code attempts to abrogate the sovereign immunity of all government units with respect to disputes under the Code. Section 106(b) provides for a deemed waiver of immunity when a governmental agency engages in certain conduct, such as filing a proof of claim for a claim that arises out of the same transaction or occurrence as claims held by a bankruptcy estate against the government entity (i. e., compulsory counterclaims). Section 106(c) provides that if an estate holds a claim against the entity that did not arise out of the same transaction or occurrence as a claim held by the entity (i. e., permissive counterclaims), the entity's immunity is deemed waived to the extent that the estate's claim can be offset against the entity's claim.

Community College v. Katz,[144] that Congress did validly abrogate the State's sovereign immunity in bankruptcy proceedings. The Court stated in *Katz*: "The Bankruptcy Clause's history, the reasons it was adopted, and the legislation proposed and enacted under it immediately following ratification demonstrate that it was intended not just as a grant of legislative authority to Congress, but also to authorize limited subordination of state sovereign immunity in the bankruptcy arena."[145] The Court reasoned that the "relevant question is not abrogation, but whether Congress' determination that States should be amenable to preferential transfer proceedings is within the scope of its power to enact 'Laws on the subject of Bankruptcies'" and stated "[b]eyond peradventure, it is."[146]

In *Katz*, the Court listed "[c]ritical features of every bankruptcy proceeding" as being "the exercise of exclusive jurisdiction over all of the debtor's property, the equitable distribution of that property among the debtor's creditors, and the ultimate discharge that gives the debtor a 'fresh start' by releasing him, her, or it from further liability for old debts" and stated: "Under our longstanding precedent, States, whether or not they choose to participate in the proceeding, are bound by a bankruptcy court's discharge order no less than other creditors."[147] The Court noted that bankruptcy jurisdiction "is principally *in rem* jurisdiction" and that because "the court's jurisdiction is premised on the debtor and his estate, and not on the creditors," the exercise of a court's jurisdiction "does not, in the usual case, interfere with state sovereignty even when states' interests are affected."[148] The Court decided that when the states ratified the Bankruptcy Clause, "the states acquiesced in a subordination of whatever sovereign immunity they might otherwise have asserted in proceedings necessary to effectuate the *in rem* jurisdiction of the bankruptcy courts."[149]

144 *Katz*. 546 U.S. at 379.

145 *Id.* at 361. The Court ruled that an adversary proceeding brought by a Chapter 11 trustee to set aside alleged preferential transfers that the debtor had made to state agencies was not barred by the agencies' sovereign immunity.

146 *Id.* at 357-58.

147 *Id.* at 363-64.

148 *Id.* at 369.

149 *Id.* at 378. In *In re Soileau*, 488 F.3d 302 (5th Cir. 2007), the Court of Appeals for the Fifth Circuit applied *Hood* and *Katz* to a case involving a bail bondsman's petition for Chapter 7 relief to obtain discharge of debts to the State of Texas. The State of Texas, as the creditor holding judgment debts, moved to dismiss the petition based on the state's Eleventh Amendment immunity. The Firth Circuit noted that the petitioner was "neither seeking the return of any funds already in the State's possession nor bringing an adversarial proceeding against the State" and stated: "She asks nothing more

In ruling the State could not claim sovereign immunity in a bankruptcy proceeding, the Court of Appeals for the Fifth Circuit[150] has stated that the *Katz* decision provides lower courts with "three crucial facets of the exercise of *in rem* jurisdiction" that reject a state's sovereign immunity defense--(1) exercise of jurisdiction over the estate of the debtor, (2) equitable distribution of the estate's property among creditors, and (3) discharge."[151]

With respect to a bankruptcy trustee's ability to recover federal tax payments, the Court of Appeals for the Seventh Circuit[152] considered the issue of whether a debtor, acting with state-law avoidance powers of unsecured creditors, had a viable cause of action against the United States to avoid the tax payments. A Chapter 11 debtor, organized as a subchapter S corporation, had brought adversary proceedings to avoid, as fraudulent transfers, payments it had made to cover individual pass-through federal tax liability of three shareholders. The courts below, relying on §106(a)(1) of the Bankruptcy Code, had concluded that a debtor in possession could use §544(b)(1) of the Bankruptcy Code to bring a state fraudulent-transfer action against the IRS. However, the Seventh Circuit ruled §106(a)(1) did not displace the actual-creditor requirement in §544(b)(1).[153] The Seventh Circuit noted that outside of bankruptcy, sovereign immunity would bar a regular creditor from bringing a state-law fraudulent-transfer suit against the federal government and ruled that §106(a)(1) did not confer such a right.[154] The Seventh Circuit affirmed that it construes "any ambiguities in the scope of a waiver in favor of the sovereign."[155]

---

than that the bankruptcy court exercise its *in rem* jurisdiction over her bankruptcy estate by adjudicating the rights of the State as a creditor." *Id.* at 308. The court concluded that because the case was "an exercise of *in rem* jurisdiction...indisputably contemplated by *Katz,* the State's sovereign immunity claim must fail." *Id.* The court also rejected the argument advanced by the State of Texas "that finding bail bond forfeiture debts dischargeable would undermine the effective administration of its criminal justice system." *Id.* at 309.

150 *In re Soileau,* 488 F.3d at 307-08.

151 In *In re Cox,* 433 B.R. 911 (N.D. Ga., 2010), the United States Bankruptcy Court applied these principles to decide that a state's Eleventh Amendment immunity did not bar a proceeding to determine whether a bankruptcy estate had an interest in prize money the debtor had designated as a charitable contribution to the state's Department of Education.

152 *In re Equipment Acquistion Resources, Inc.*, 742 F.3d 743 (7th Cir. 2014).

153 *Id.* at 745. The Seventh Circuit stated: "Ordinarily a creditor cannot bring an Illinois fraudulent-transfer claim against the IRS; therefore, under §544(b)(1), neither can the debtor in possession."

154 *Id.* at 746.

155 *Id.* at 750. The Seventh Circuit explained that to determine the IRS's liability, it had to "undertake two analytically distinct inquiries...[t]he first inquiry is whether there has been a waiver of sov-

The Court of Appeals for the Ninth Circuit disagrees with the Seventh Circuit.[156] That court has ruled that a trustee's adversary proceeding to recover, on a fraudulent transfer theory, a debtor's prepetition tax payments to the federal government is not barred by the government's sovereign immunity.[157] The Ninth Circuit recognized that outside of bankruptcy, there would be no actual unsecured creditor who could pursue a claim against the IRS because sovereign immunity would preclude the claim; however, the court decided §106(a)(1) "unambiguously abrogates the federal government's sovereign immunity with respect to section 544."[158] The Ninth Circuit reasoned that "[i]n allowing for the avoidability of transfers made to the IRS, Congress ensured that the IRS is on equal footing with all other creditors[159] and referred to the explanation of the Court of Appeals for the Tenth Circuit[160] that the waiver of sovereign immunity contained in the Bankruptcy Code 'is based on equity...'" The Tenth Circuit has decided that "it would be unfair for a governmental unit to participate in the distributions of a bankruptcy case while at the same time shielding itself from liability."[161] The Ninth Circuit agreed and opined that Congress "provided for a waiver of sovereign immunity...because it aligns with the primary goal of federal bankruptcy law—collecting and preserving a debtor's assets for equitable distribution among all creditors."[162]

---

ereign immunity...the second inquiry...is whether the source of substantive law upon which the claimant relies provides an avenue of relief." *Id.* at 747. The court agreed there was a waiver of sovereign immunity but noted that the Illinois Uniform Fraudulent Transfer Act did not provide an avenue for relief, stating that any unsecured creditor who brought such a claim against the IRS in Illinois would be barred by the government's sovereign immunity.

156 See *In re DBSI, Inc. v. United States*, 869 F.2d 1004 (9th Cir. 2017).

157 The district court had entered judgment directing the IRS to return approximately $13.4 million of a total of $17 million in fraudulent tax transfers. The Ninth Circuit declined the government's request to reverse that judgment and rule that sovereign immunity precluded the return of the $13.4 million. *Id.* at 1009.

158 *Id.* at 1010. The Ninth Circuit stated its "interpretation of the interplay between Section 106(a)(1) and section 544(b)(1) is bolstered by the fact that Section 106(a)(1) was enacted after Section 544(b)(1)." *Id* at 1011.

159 *Id.* at 1016.

160 *In re Franklin Savings Corp.*, 385 F.3d 1279, 1290 (10th Cir. 2004).

161 *Id.*

162 *In re DBSI*, 869 F.3d at 1016.

CHAPTER 4.
EXCEPTIONS TO SOVEREIGN OR GOVERNMENTAL IMMUNITY

Congress can abrogate Eleventh Amendment immunity for states under circumstances noted in Chapter 3. In addition, sovereign immunity does not apply in certain cases. As examples, federal courts have denied states immunity from payment of federal taxes[1] and have ruled that states cannot erode federal authority in areas traditionally subject to federal statutory regulations.[2] Further, to counter a strict and inflexible application of the sovereign and governmental immunity doctrine that runs counter to "notions of reason and justice," courts early distinguished between "governmental" and "proprietary" functions--sometimes characterized as "discretionary" versus "ministerial" duties–and have decided governments and their officials should not have immunity for their "proprietary" or "ministerial" functions.[3] Additionally, Congress and state legislatures

1 *See State of New York v. United States,* 326 U.S.572, 574, 66 S. Ct. 310, 9; L. Ed. 326 (1946) (states were denied immunity from federal taxes on liquor businesses when states sought to control the liquor traffic by going into the liquor business). The Court rejected "reciprocal intergovernmental immunity." *Id.* at 577.

In *Travis v. Reno,* 163 F.3d 1000, 1003 (7th Cir. 1998), the court upheld a federal statute that levied fines upon states for failure to comply with federal regulations and in *Ohio v. United States,* 849 F.3d 313, 320 (6th Cir. 2017), the court ruled that one of the tax provisions in the Patient Protection and Affordable Care Act (ACA) "applies to state government employers with the same force that it applies to private employers," deciding that the ACA's application did "not run afoul of the important principles of federalism or the Tenth Amendment to the United States Constitution." *Id.* at 325.

2 *United Transp. Union v. Long Island R. Co.,* 455 U.S. 678, 687, 102 S. Ct. 1349, 71 L. Ed. 2d 547 (1982) (holding that states are not immune from minimum wage and overtime requirements of the Fair Labor Standards Act (FLSA), 29 U.S.C. §201 *et. seq.; Garcia v. San Antonio Metropolitan Transit Authority,* 469 U.S. 528, 105 S. Ct. 1005 (1985) ("There is nothing in the overtime and minimum-wage requirements of the FLSA...that is destructive of state sovereignty or violative of any constitutional provisions.").

3 *State of South Carolina v. United States,* 199 U.S. 437, 26 S. Ct. 110, 50 L. Ed 261 (1905); *State of Ohio v. Helvering,* 292 U.S. 360, 369, 54 S. Ct. 725, 78 L. Ed. 1307 (1934). Justice Frankfurter expressed concern that governmental immunity runs counter to "prevailing notions of reason and justice," in a dissent-

can waive sovereign immunity.[4] The discussion in this chapter focuses on Texas law and court decisions to point out the limitations some states, such as Texas, have placed on waivers of sovereign immunity to preserve, as the Texas Supreme Court has articulated, a continuation of strict application of the immunity doctrine to ensure its "roots remain secure within the sovereign,"[5] and to demonstrate that a rigid application of that doctrine precludes protection for victims of governmental wrongdoing.

A. TAKINGS CLAUSES AND INVERSE CONDEMNATION SUITS

The Fifth Amendment states: "[N]or shall private property be taken for public use, without just compensation." Claims for just compensation are grounded in the Constitution itself.[6] Because the constitutional mandate is self-executing, sovereign immunity cannot defeat the requirement of the Fifth Amendment for "just compensation" when a taking of property occurred for a public use.[7] In *Arnberg v. United States*,[8] the Court of Appeals for the Ninth Circuit stated that the principle--the United States cannot be sued without its consent--does not apply to suits directly authorized by the Constitution.[9] This exception to

---

ing opinion in *Larson v. Domestic & Foreign Commerce Corp.*, 337 U.S. 682, 709, 69 S. Ct. 1457, 93 L. Ed. 1628 (1949).

4 Discussion *infra*. The waiver principles under federal law and state law are essentially the same although some state courts have construed waiver language more strictly in favor of retaining sovereign immunity.

5 *See, Wasson Interests, Ltd. v. City of Jacksonville*, 489 S.W.3d 427, 432 (Tex. 2016).

6 *First Evangelical Lutheran Church of Glendale v. County of Los Angeles*, 482 U.S.304, 315, 107 S. Ct. 2378, 96 L.Ed.26 250 (1987).

7 *See e. g., U.S. v. Clark*, 445 U.S. 253, 257, 100 S.Ct. 1127, 63 L.Ed.2d 373 (1980) (emphasizing that, because the Constitution requires a landowner to be compensated justly for a governmental taking of land, the landowner is entitled to bring suit against the governmental entity to ensure compensation).

8 *Arnberg*, 757 F.2d 971, 980 n. 7 (9th Cir. 1984).

9 The Fifth Amendment to the U.S. Constitution provides for "just compensation" for a taking of property for a public purpose.

In *Rohland v. United States*, 136 Fed. Cl. 55 (2018), the Court of Federal Claims referred to the Tucker Act, 28 U.S. C. §1491(a)(1), which is the principal statute governing the jurisdiction of that court, and noted that it "waives sovereign immunity for claims against the United States, not sounding in tort, that are founded upon the Constitution, a federal statute or regulation, or an express or implied contract with the United States" (quoting *United States v. White Mountain Apache Tribe*, 537 U.S. 465, 472, 123 S.Ct. 1126, 155 L.Ed.2d 40 (2003)). 136 Fed. Cl. at 64. Still, as the Court of Federal Claims noted, the statute "does not create any

immunity governs suits to recover money damages for private property taken by the United States.[10] Moreover, because the Fifth Amendment explicitly grants a right to sue the government for redress, a litigant bringing a takings claim is not required to establish a specific waiver of immunity.[11] The Supreme Court has explained: "The Fifth Amendment's guarantee that private property cannot be taken for a public use without just compensation was designed to bar Government from forcing some people alone to bear public burdens which, in all fairness and justice, should be borne by the public as a whole."[12] A claim for compensation under the Fifth Amendment initially is brought to the Court of Federal Claims pursuant to the Tucker Act.[13]

States generally have takings clauses in their state constitutions. For example, the Utah Constitution prohibits private property from being "taken or damaged for public use without just compensation."[14] The takings clause in the Texas Constitution[15] states: "No person's property shall be taken, damaged or destroyed for or applied to public use without adequate compensation being

---

substantive right that is enforceable against the United States for money damages" (citing *United States v. Testan*, 424 U.S. 392, 398, 9 6 S.Ct. 948, 47 L.Ed. 2d 114 (1976) and stating that the substantive right must appear in another source of law, such as a 'money-mandating constitutional provision, statute or regulation… or an express or implied contract with the United States" (citing *Loveladies Harbor, Inc. v. United States*, 27 F.3d 1545, 1554 (Fed. Cir. 1994). 136 Fed Cl. at 64.

10 As discussed *infra*, the Tucker Act waives sovereign immunity for claims against the United States. However, a claim must be against the United States, not against individual federal officials. See *Brown v. United States*, 105 F.3d 621, 624 (Fed. Cir. 1997) and *Cleavinger v. Saxner*, 474 U.S. 193, 199, 106 S. Ct. 496, 88 L. Ed. 2d 507 (1985).

11 *T.O.F.C.,Inc. v. United States*, 683 F.2d 389, 393 (Ct. Cl. 1982).

See 28 U.S.C. § 1491(a)(1), which states that the Court of Federal Claims has jurisdiction to render judgment upon any claim against the United States founded on the Constitution. In *United States v. Causby*, 328 U.S. 256, 267, 66 S.Ct.1062, 90 L.Ed.2d 1206 (1946), the Supreme Court recognized that the Court of Claims [now titled Court of Federal Claims] had jurisdiction over takings claims.

12 *Armstrong v. United States*, 364 U.S. 40, 80 S. Ct. 1563, 4 L.Ed.2d 1554 (1960).

13 28 U.S.C. §1491(a)(1), (discussed *infra* under "Breach of Contract Claims). Discussion in *James v. United States*, 130 Fed. Cl. 707, 719 (2017) (citing *Eastern. Enterprises. v. Apfel*, 524 U.S. 498, 520, 118 S. Ct. 2131, 141 L.Ed.2d 451 (1998)). As the court ruled in *Moden v. United States*, 404 F.3d 1335, 1341 (Fed. Cir. 2005), to the extent a claimant has "a nonfrivolous takings claim founded upon the Fifth Amendment, jurisdiction under the Tucker Act is proper."

"Absent an express statutory grant of jurisdiction to the contrary, the Tucker Act provides the Court of Federal Claims exclusive jurisdiction over takings claims for amounts greater than $10,000." *Preseault v. Interstate Commerce* Comm'n, 494 U.S. 1, 12, 110 S.Ct. 914, 108 L.Ed. 2d 1 (1990) (quoting *United States v. Causby*, 328 U.S. 256, 267, 66 S. Ct. 1062, 90 L. Ed. 1206 (1946)).

14 Utah Constitution, Article I, §22.

15 Texas Constitution, Article I, §17.

made, unless by the consent of such person."[16] Sovereign immunity does not provide a shield from claims under a constitutional takings provision.[17] The state constitution itself is a waiver of governmental immunity for the taking, damaging, or destruction of property for public use.[18]

Neither should the sovereign immunity doctrine apply to an inverse condemnation lawsuit.[19] Inverse condemnation occurs when the State or its agency physically takes or invades property or unreasonably interferes with a property owner's right to use and enjoy it.[20] The Supreme Court has defined inverse condemnation as a "shorthand description of the manner in which a landowner recovers just compensation for a taking of his property when condemnation proceedings have not been instituted."[21] To defeat a government's summary judgment motion or plea to the jurisdiction in an inverse condemnation suit, the property owner must plead sufficient facts to show the elements of an inverse condemnation cause of action.[22]

---

16 *Id.*

17 See *Steele v. City of Houston*, 603 S.W.3d 786, 791 (Tex.1980).

18 *Id.*

19 *See Moden v. United States*, 404 F.3d at 1343 (ruling the Court of Federal Claims had subject matter jurisdiction over a nonfrivolous inverse condemnation claim but deciding the plaintiffs did not prove a valid protectable property interest they alleged the government had taken).

20 *Texas Parks & Wildlife Dep't v. Callaway*, 971 S.W.2d 145, 148 (Tex. App.–Austin 1998, no pet.) An inverse condemnation proceeding is an avenue of relief available when the state takes (or damages) property for a public use without compensation or pursuant to a proper condemnation proceeding, and the owner wants to recover compensation for his loss. To have standing to sue for inverse condemnation, a party must have a vested property interest at the time of the taking. *City of Keller v. Wilson*, 168 S.W.3d 802, 808 (Tex. 2005).

To recover damages for inverse condemnation, the property owner must prove that a governmental entity intentionally took the owner's property for public use without paying adequate compensation or was substantially certain such a taking would be the result of its intentional acts. *City of Dallas v. Jennings*, 142 S.W.3d 310, 313-14 (Tex. 2004).

21 *United States v. Clarke*, 445 U.S. 253, 257, 100 S.Ct. 1127, 63 L. Ed.2 d 373 (1980) (stating it is a cause of action against the government to recover the value of property taken by the government without formal exercise of the power of eminent domain.)

22 *See., e. g., Kerr v. Dep't of Trans.*, 45 S.W.3d 248, 251 (Tex. App.–Houston [lst Dist.] 2001) and *Moden*, 404 F.3d at 1343.

B. IMMOVABLE PROPERTY

There is "no immunity from jurisdiction with respect to actions relating to immoveable property."[23] Courts have referred to the "immovable-property" exception to sovereign immunity as being "well established."[24] This exception to immunity "is a corollary of the ancient principle of *lex rei sitae*," the principle providing that "land is governed by the law of the place where it is situated."[25]

The Supreme Court very early ruled that property ownership is not an inherently sovereign function.[26] Consequently, sovereign immunity is not applicable to land owned by a state; a state can be made a party to an action to obtain possession of, or establish a property interest in, immovable property located in that state or in another state.[27]

The Georgia Supreme Court stated in *State of Ga. v. City of Chattanooga*:[28] "Having acquired land in another state for the purpose of using it in a private capacity, Georgia can claim no sovereign immunity or privilege in respect of its expropriation." The Supreme Court ruled that when Georgia obtained land in Tennessee, it occupied the same position in Tennessee as did a private corporation and that it could not claim sovereign privilege or immunity. It held that Georgia's acquisition and use of land in Tennessee subjected Georgia to condemnation proceedings in Tennessee.[29]

C. GOVERNMENTAL/PROPRIETARY AND DISCRETIONARY/ MINISTERIAL DICHOTOMIES

The Supreme Court has recognized an important limitation on the principle of sovereign immunity as it applies to local governments and political subdivisions of a state, explaining the principle "bars suits against States but not lesser

23 *See Upper Skagit Indian Tribe v. Lundgren*, 138 S. Ct. 1649, 200 L. Ed. 2d 931 (2018).

24 *Id.*

25 *Id.* quoting F. Wharton, Conflict of Laws §273, p. 607 (G. Parmele ed., 3d ed. 1905).

26 *See Schooner Exchange v. McFaddon*, 7 Cranch 116, 145, 13 L. Ed. 287 (1812).

27 *State of Ga. v. City of Chattanooga*, 264 U.S. 472, 44 S. Ct. 369, 68 L. Ed. 796 (1924).

28 *Id.* at 479-80.

29 *Id.* at 480-81.

entities."[30] Additionally, the Court early decided "there is a Constitutional line between the State as government and the State as trader" and that the exercise of the right to go into business "is not the performance of a governmental function."[31]

Political subdivisions of the state–such as counties, municipalities, and school districts–do share in a state's immunity.[32] Immunity is referred to as "governmental immunity" for these lesser state entities. Still, in applying a "governmental immunity" concept to local governments, courts have distinguished "between those acts performed as a branch of the state," for which there is immunity, and "those acts performed in a proprietary, non-governmental capacity,"[33] for which there is no immunity.[34] Courts have also referred to discretionary

---

30 *Alden v. Maine*, 527 U. S. 706, 756, 119 S. Ct. 2240, 144 L. Ed. 2d 636 (1999) (noting that immunity does not extend to suits prosecuted against a municipal corporation or other governmental entity that is not an arm of the state, citing *Mt. Healthy City Bd. of Ed. v. Doyle*, 429 U. S. 274, 280, 97 S. Ct. 568, 50 L. Ed. 2d 471 (1977)).

31 Early decisions in *State of South Carolina v. U. S.*, 199 U.S. 437, 26 S. Ct. 110, 50 L. Ed. 261 (1905) and *State of Ohio v. Helvering*, 292 U.S. 360, 54 S. Ct. 725, 78 L. Ed. 1307 (1934). In a 1946 decision, *State of New York*, 326 U.S. at 580, the Supreme Court noted New York's urging that it should not be taxed because its sale of mineral waters was connected with the State's conservation policy. The Court agreed that "liquor control by a State certainly concerns the most important of a State's natural resources–the health and well-being of its people," citing *Mugler v. State of Kansas*, 123 U.S. 623, 661, 8 S. Ct. 273, 297, 31 L.Ed. 205 (1887), but decided a state could be taxed as others engaged in the liquor business even though its sale of its mineral waters had a relation to its conservation policy. *Id.* at 313-14. The Court referred to its earlier holding *United States v. State of California*, 297 U. S. 175, 185, 56 S. Ct. 421, 80 L. Ed. 567 (1936), wherein it had ruled that by engaging in the railroad business a State could not withdraw the railroad from the power of the federal government to regulate commerce.

32 *See discussion in Reata Constr. Corp. v. City of Dallas*, 197 S.W.3d 371, 374 (Tex. 2006) (stating though that these political subdivisions "represent no sovereignty distinct from the state and possess only such powers and privileges as have been expressly or impliedly conferred upon them," citing *Payne v. Massey*, 196 S.W.2d 493, 495 (Tex. 1946)).

33 *Jean Moreau & Associates, Inc. v. Health Center Comm'n*, 720 S.E.2d 105, 110 (Va. 2012) (citing *Carter v. Chesterfield County Health Comm'n*, 527 S.E.2d 783,785 (S. Car. 2000) and *Wasson Interests, Ltd. v. City of Jacksonville*, 489 S.W.3d 427, 430 (Tex. 2016) (citing *Dilley v. City of Houston*, 222 S.W.2d 992, 993 (Tex.1949) and *City of Galveston v. Posnainsky*, 62 Tex. 118, 127 (Tex. 1884)). In *Jean Moreau*, 720 S.E.2d at 110, the Virginia Supreme Court stated: "Municipal corporations are immune from liability 'when performing governmental functions, but are not when exercising proprietary functions,'"(citing Carter, id. at 785).

The Texas Supreme Court provided its rationale for denying a city governmental immunity for its proprietary acts in *Wasson Interests*, 489 S.W.3d at 434, stating that "acts performed as part of a city's proprietary function do not implicate the state's immunity for the simple reason that they are not performed under the authority, or for the benefit, of the sovereign" (citing *Fort Worth Indep. Sch. Dist. v. City of Fort Worth*, 22 S.W.3d 831, 840 n. 12 (Tex. 2000)).

34 In *City of Va. v. Carmichael Development Co.*, 527 S.E.2d 778, 782 (Va. 2000), the Virginia Supreme Court stated: "It is a frequently recited proposition that a municipality is authorized to perform both

duties of governmental employees that provide for immunity, versus ministerial duties that do not.[35]

In differentiating "proprietary" activities of local governments from their "governmental" functions, the Supreme Court has acknowledged it had been unable to provide a basis for the governmental/proprietary distinction in many instances.[36] Further, the Supreme Court early concluded that efforts to define "traditional" or "integral" state government functions had failed.[37] The Court decided there is no "unchanging line of demarcation between essential and non-essential governmental functions" and a rule "that looks to the 'traditional,' integral,' or 'necessary' nature of governmental functions" invites a judiciary "to make decisions about which state policies it favors and which ones it dislikes."[38] In *Garcia*,[39] the Court rejected "as unsound in principle and unworkable in practice, a rule of state immunity" that is a judicial appraisal as to "whether a particular governmental function is 'integral' or 'traditional,'"[40] and restored the Court's earlier rulings that Congress can regulate state entities "so long as it is not destructive of state sovereignty or violative of any constitutional power."[41]

---

governmental and proprietary functions. Governmental functions, as the term implies, are powers and duties to be performed exclusively for the public welfare. When a municipality exercises, or fails to exercise, a governmental function, it is shielded from liability by sovereign immunity on the theory that the municipality is performing as an agency of the state. In contrast, proprietary functions are privileges and powers performed primarily for the benefit of the municipality and, thus, do not enjoy the shield of sovereign immunity."

35 Discussed *infra.*

36 See *Garcia v. San Antonio Metropolitan Transit Authority,* 469 U.S.528, 540, 105 S. Ct. 1005, 83 L. Ed. 2d 1016 (1985) (disavowing "a static historical view of state functions generally immune from federal regulation," citing *United Transp. Union v. Longland R. Co.,* 455 U.S. 678, 686, 102 S. Ct. 1349, 71 L. Ed. 2d 547 (1982)). The Court referred in *Garcia* to its ruling in *United Transp., id* at 686-87, that "the inquiry into a particular function's 'traditional' nature was merely a means of determining whether the federal statute at issue unduly handicaps 'basic state prerogatives,'" *id.* at 540, and overruled, id. at 531, its earlier decision in *National League of Cities v. Usery,* 426 U.S. 833, 842, 96 S. Ct. 2465, 49 L. Ed. 2d 245 (1976) wherein the Court had decided the Tenth Amendment provided credence to contentions that the Constitution provided limits upon Congress's power to waive state sovereign immunity. In *Garcia,* the Court revisited cases that had raised the issue in *Usery* that the Commerce clause does not empower Congress to enforce provisions of the Federal Labor Standards Act (FLSA) against the states in the area of traditional governmental functions and decided that the FLSA was not destructive of state sovereignty or violative of any constitutional provision. *Id.*

37 *Garcia, cited in note 36,* 469 U. S. at 554.

38 *Id.* at 546.

39 *Id.* at 546-47.

40 *Id.*

41 *Id.* at 554. *See, e. g.,* its earlier decisions in *Brown v. Walker,* 161 U.S. 591, 16 S. Ct. 644, 40 L. Ed. 819

The Texas Supreme Court[42] has referred to the distinction between governmental and proprietary functions as being "premised on the derivative nature of governmental immunity," stating that a "state's immunity is inherent in its sovereignty," whereas cities "derive their immunity from the state."[43] Noting this distinction, the Texas Court recognized a city's immunity as extending "as far as the state's immunity but no further" and explained that "a city is cloaked in the state's immunity when it acts as a branch of the state but *only* when it acts as a branch of the state."[44]

State courts have experienced difficulties in applying both the governmental/proprietary distinctions and the discretionary/ministerial dichotomy to the many, varying activities of the government, especially local governments. The Supreme Court of Virginia[45] has stated: "A function is governmental in nature if it is directly related to the general health, safety, and welfare of the citizen," and that, "[i]n contrast, a function is proprietary in nature if it involves a privilege and power performed primarily for the benefit of the [municipal corporation]."[46] The Virginia Supreme Court has ruled that providing specialized health services should be designated as "an essential governmental function."[47] The Texas Supreme Court has designated a municipality's operation of a public utility as a proprietary function, [48] but has ruled garbage and solid waste removal, collection and disposal is governmental.[49] A court in Ohio decided the negligent posting of an incorrect clearance sign on a county-owned bridge, as part of the county operating its roads and bridges, was not protected by sovereign immunity.[50] In

---

(1896), *Reina v. U. S.*, 364 U.S. 507, 81 S. Ct. 260, 5 L. Ed. 2d 249 (1960), and *Fry v. U. S.*, 421 U.S. 542, 95 S. Ct. 1792, 44 L. Ed. 2d 363 (1975).

42 *Wasson Interests*, 289 S.W.3d at 437.

43 *Id.*

44 *Id.* (citing *Tooke v. City of Mexia*, 197 S.W.3d 325, 343 (Texas. 2006)).

45 *Jean Moreau & Assoc., Inc. v. Health Center Com'n*, 720 S.E.2d 105, 113 (Va. 2012) (citing *Gambrell v. City of Norfolk*, 593 S.E.2d 246, 249 (Va. 2004)).

46 *Id.*

47 *Pike v. Hagaman*, 787 S.E.2d 89, 93 (Va. 2016).

48 Discussion in *Wheelabrator Air Pollution Control, Inc. v. City of San Antonio*, 489 S.W.3d 448, 452 (Tex. 2016) (citing *San Antonio Indep. Sch. Dist. v. City of San Antonio*, 550 S.W.2d 262, 264 (Tex. 1976)).

49 *Wheelabrator*, 489 S.W.3d at 452.

50 *Covent Insurance Co., ltd. v. Carroll County Commissioners*, 2 Ohio App. 3d 410, 442 N.E.2d 486 (Oh. App.1981) (still sovereign immunity of the county for the operation of roads and bridges had been abrogated by a state statute, R.C. 305.12).

noting a different focus in deciding whether governmental units had immunity for their actions, the Texas Supreme Court[51] recently referred to amendments to the Texas Tort Claims Act,[52] which reclassified as governmental functions public transportation systems that previously were proprietary functions.[53]

The distinction between "discretionary" and "ministerial" functions is a more comprehensive criterion for determining when a governmental unit is entitled to immunity. The Virginia Supreme Court has stated: "The presence of discretion supports a finding of immunity."[54] A ministerial function, in contrast, does not. The Michigan Supreme Court[55] has explained the distinction between discretionary and ministerial functions as discretionary acts being "those which require personal deliberation, decision and judgment" while ministerial acts "constitute merely an obedience to orders or the performance of a duty in which the individual has little or no choice."[56] However, another Michigan court observed that distinction provided it "no 'bright line' standard by which to determine whether an employee was performing a discretionary or ministerial act."[57]

---

51 *Fort Worth Transp. Authority v. Rodriguez,* 547 S.W.3d 830 (Tex. 2018).

52 Tex. Civ. Prac. & Rem. Code §101.001-.009. Discussion of the Texas Tort Claims Act *infra.*

53 *City of Fort Worth,* 22 S.W.3d at 840 (citing the limited waiver provisions of the Texas Tort Claims Act (TTCA) [Tex. Prac. & Rem. Code §101.021(1)(1)] and the damages cap in TTCA, §101.023 and noting the reclassification placed the transportation systems "within the bounds of governmental immunity," although subject to a limited waiver of immunity.)

54 *Pike,* 787 S.E.2d at 93 (citing *Lohr v. Larsen,* 431 S.E.2d 642, 645 (Va. 1993) and further stating that "regardless of the existence of discretion in the overall job, there is no sovereign immunity for the negligent performance of ministerial acts" (citing *First Va. Bank-Colonial v. Baker,* 301 S.E.2d 8,11 (1983)). The Virginia Supreme Court admonished that the sovereign immunity defense "applies only to acts of judgment and discretion which are necessary to the performance of the governmental function itself." 787 S.E.2d at 93.

55 *Ross v. Consumers Power Company,* 420 Mich. 567, 634-35, 363 N.W.2d 641, 668 (Mich.1985), superseded by statute as stated in I*n re Bradley Estate,* 494 Mich. 367, 835 N.W.2d 545 (Mich. 2013) (stating the court could not exercise its contempt power to punish a sheriff's department for allegedly contemptuous conduct by awarding indemnification damages. The court noted that the Michigan tort claims act, M.C.L. §691.1407(1), immunizes governmental agencies from tort liability. 494 Mich. at 398.) (Discussion of Michigan's governmental tort liability act in Chapter 6.)

56 *Ross,* 363 N.W. 2d at 668 (citing Prosser, [Torts (4th ed)] §132, p. 988). The Michigan court decided "the distinction between 'discretionary' and 'ministerial' acts is that the former involves significant decision-making, while the latter involves the execution of a decision and might entail some minor decision-making." 429 Mich. at 635.

In *Joplin v. Univ. of Mich.* Bd. of Regents, 173 Mich. App. 149, 433 N.W.2d 830, 833 (Mich. App. 1988), the court ruled surgeons employed by a state university hospital were entitled to immunity for allegedly improperly performing an abortion, deciding the performance of dilatation and evacuation procedure was discretionary, not ministerial in nature.

57 *Sayles v. Baughman,* 163 Mich. App. 58, 62, 413 N.W.2d 730 (Mich. App. 1987) (citing *Davis v. Lhim,*

In considering the discretionary/ministerial dichotomy regarding actions of local governmental officials, a Georgia court ruled that while removal of garbage and trash and other health and sanitation measures protecting the health and welfare of the public would be considered *governmental* functions,[58] such activities could become a "source of revenue" for a local government, instead of a "purely incidental profit." The activity would become a quasi-public business, a *ministerial* function, for which there would be no immunity.[59] The Mississippi Supreme Court has held the duty of the state's department of transportation to maintain and repair state highways to be ministerial.[60] The Iowa Supreme Court[61] has ruled that a school district's "hiring, retention, and supervision of a middle-school teacher was not an exercise of judgment of the kind that would be subject to the discretionary function exception;"[62] thus, the school's actions were not shielded by governmental immunity.

Some courts have referred to a two-prong test for determining whether a discretionary function immunity applies in a particular case against the government.[63] The first inquiry should be whether challenged conduct was a matter of choice for an acting employee.[64] Then, if there is an element of judgment

---

147 Mich. App. 8, 11, 382 N.W.2d 195 (Mich. App. 1985) and ruling an assistant resident doctor at a hospital wholly owned and operated by a city, was not entitled to immunity from liability).

58 *City of Atlanta v. Whatley,* 161 Ga. App. 705, 289 S.E.2d 541, 543 (Ga. App. 1982).

59 *Id.,* 289 S.E.2d at 543. The court characterized cleaning up a street and a cleanup campaign, which would include keeping the streets safe for travel, as a ministerial function even though the activity would include health and sanitation measures.

60 *Mississippi Transp. Com'n v. Adams,* 197 So.3d 406, 414 (Miss. 2016) (concluding the defendants did not enjoy discretionary-function immunity). In *Brantley v. City of Horn Lake,* 152 So.3d 1106, 1110-18 (Miss. 2014), the Mississippi Supreme Court created a new test for determining the discretionary-function immunity that a justice in *Crider v. Desoto County Convention and Visitors Bureau,* 201 So. 3d 1063 (Miss. 2016) called an abandonment of a "long-standing precedent" (J. Maxwell, concurring in part only, stating that the test in *Brantley* omitted "to consider whether the alleged activity involved a policy decision" and that the omission "undermines the very purpose of discretionary-function immunity–'to prevent judicial second -guessing' of legislative and administrative decisions *grounded in social, economic, and political policy* through the medium of an action in tort.") *Id.* at 1067. [In Crider, the Mississippi Supreme Court ruled a county visitors' bureau was entitled to discretionary function immunity under the Mississippi tort claims act, Miss. Code 11-46-9(1).]

The Mississippi Tort Claims Act is discussed in Chapter 6.

61 *Doe v. Cedar Rapids Community Sch. Dist.,* 652 N.W.2d 439 (Iowa 2002).

62 *Id.* at 442.

63 *Berkovitz v. United States,* 486 U.S. 531, 536, 108 S. Ct. 1954, 100 L. Ed. 2d 531 (1988).

64 *Discussion in Crete v. City of Lowell,* 418 F.3d 54, 61 (1st Cir. 2005) (stating most states consider claims of negligent hiring to be barred by the discretionary function exception).

involved in the challenged conduct, a court should determine whether the judgment was of the kind the discretionary function exception was designed to shield.[65] If the answer to either of the inquiries was negative, the discretionary function exemption would not apply.[66]

In *United States v. Gaubert*,[67] the Supreme Court explained that a governmental employee is not protected if the employee violates a mandatory regulation "because there is no room for choice and the action will be contrary to policy" but, on the other hand, when established governmental policies, "as expressed or implied by statute, regulation, or agency guidelines," permit a governmental employee to "exercise discretion, there is a strong presumption that the agent's acts are grounded in policy when exercising that discretion."[68] The Court stated: "The focus of the inquiry is not on the agent's subjective intent in exercising the discretion conferred by statute or regulation, but on the nature of the actions taken and on whether they are susceptible to policy analysis."[69] Still, Congress later enacted the Federal Employees Liability Reform and Tort Compensation Act[70] to eliminate a requirement that a federal employee had to show he or she was performing a "discretionary" function to have immunity. The Act provided

---

65 *Discussion in Goodman v. City of LeClaire*, 587 N. W. 2d 232, 237-38 (Iowa 1998).

66 *See discussion in City of Cedar Falls v. Cedar Falls Cmty. Sch. Dist.*, 617 N.W.2d 11, 19 (Iowa 2000) (stating the second prong of the test protected governmental actions and decisions based on considerations of public policy grounded on social, economic, and political reasons.)

67 *Gaubert*, 499 U.S. 315, 322, 111 S. Ct. 1267, 1271, 113 L. Ed. 2d 335 (1991).

68 *Id.* at 322. In *Gaubert*, the Supreme Court rejected the planning/operational level dichotomy prevalent in several state tort claims acts. The Court stated, 111 St. Ct. at 1274-75: "In addition to planning-level decisions, which are clearly protected by the discretionary function exception, also protected may be decisions at the operational level involving the necessary element of choice and grounded in social, economic, or political goals," emphasizing that "it is the nature of the conduct, rather than the status of the actor' that governs whether the exception applies" (quoting *U. S. v. Variq Airlines*, 467 U.S. 797, 813, 104 S. Ct. 2755, 81 L.Ed.2d 660 (1984)).

69 *Id.* at 325. In *Searles v. Agency of Transp.*, 762 A.2d 812, 813 (Vt. 2000), the Vermont Supreme Court referred to the decision of the U.S. Supreme Court in *Gaubert* and noted that the Vermont Torts Claims Act, 12 Vt. Stat. §§5601-06, is "nearly identical" to the Federal Tort Claims Act. 762 A.2d at 816, n. 1. The Vermont Supreme Court stated in *Estate of Gage v. State*, 882 A.2d 1157, 1160, n. 6: "Because the discretionary function exception to the Vermont Tort Claims Act is nearly identical to that of the Federal Tort Claims Act, '[t]his Court therefore looks to case law interpreting the federal provision to guide us in analyzing 12 V.S.A. §5601(e)'" (quoting *Lane v. State*, 811 A.2d 190, 192, n. 2 (Vt. 2002)).

Vermont's Tort Claims Act is briefly reviewed in Chapter 6.

70 Pub. L. No, 100-694, 102 Stat. 4563, codified as amended at 28 U.S.C. §2679(b)(1).

governmental employees with absolute immunity so long as they act within the scope of their employment.[71]

The Texas Supreme Court has explained that the common law defense of official immunity protected governmental employees from personal liability in performing in good faith "discretionary" duties within the scope of their authority.[72] However, Texas courts have denied immunity to governmental officials for failure to perform a "purely ministerial act" based on another criterion—whether a governmental official's act is *ultra vires.*[73] The Texas Supreme Court has referred to *ultra vires* acts of local governments as being outside the protection of governmental immunity, justifying an *ultra vires* exception to immunity by characterizing such acts as being "without authority" and explaining that such acts "should not be considered acts of the state at all."[74] The Texas Supreme Court has stated that "a government officer with some discretion to interpret and apply a law may nonetheless act 'without legal authority,' and thus *ultra vires*, if he exceeds the bound of his granted authority or if his acts conflict with the law itself."[75] The Texas Court compared such acts with "ministerial acts," which it described as those "where the law prescribes and defines the duties to be performed with such precision and certainty as to leave nothing to the exercise of discretion or judgment."[76] The Texas Supreme Court defined "an *ultra vires* claim based on actions taken 'without legal authority'" as having "two fundamental components: (1) authority giving the official some (but not absolute) discretion to act and (2) conduct outside of that authority."[77]

---

71 Discussion *infra* under "Tort Claims Acts."

72 *Brown & Gay engineering, Inc. v. Olivares*, 461 S.W.3d 117, 128 (Tex. 2015) (citing *Kassen v. Hatley,* 887 S.W.2d 4, 8 (Tex. 1994) and *Ballantyne v. Champion Builders, Inc.*, 144 S.W.3d 417, 414 (Tex. 2004). The Texas Court noted that "unlike sovereign immunity from suit...official immunity is an affirmative defense that must be pled and proved by a party asserting it" (citing *City of Lancaster v. Chambers,* 883 S.W. 2d 650, 653 (Tex. 1998)).

73 *See, e.g., City of El Paso v. Heinrich*, 284 S.W.3d 366, 372 (Tex. 2009) and *Hall v. McRaven*, 508 S.W. 3d 232, 238 (Tex. 2017) (citing *Houston Belt & Terminal Ry. Co. v. City of Houston*, 487 S.W.3d 154, 158 (Tex. 2016), wherein the Texas Supreme Court "clarified what it means for an official to act 'without legal authority'").

74 *McRaven*, 508 S.W.3d 238. (citing *Cobb v. Harrington,* 190 S.W.3d 709 (Tex. 1945)).

75 *Id.* (citing *Houston Belt*, 487 S.W.3d at 158).

76 *Id.* (citing *Bell Tel. L.P. v. Emmett,* 459 S.W.3d 578, 587 (Tex. 2015)).

77 *Id.* at 239, 241 (citing *Houston Belt,* 487 S.W.3d at 158) and stating "higher authority has created a ministerial (nondiscretionary) duty for the subordinate official to engage in conduct the plaintiff claims is wrongful," clarifying there are two general means of proving an *ultra vires* claim: (1) an action "without legal authority" or (2) failure to "perform a purely ministerial act."

D. WAIVER OF SOVEREIGN IMMUNITY

The Supreme Court has ruled consistently that only Congress can waive the United States' right to assert the doctrine of sovereign immunity and that a statute's text must contain an "unequivocally clear statement of a wavier of sovereign immunity."[78] Courts are to construe strictly any waiver of governmental sovereign immunity;[79] therefore, the Supreme Court has required courts to "construe ambiguities in favor of immunity."[80] Still, in referring to actions Congress and state legislatures have taken to ameliorate the hardship of the immunity doctrine, one Supreme Court justice avowed that the Court's "stubborn insistence on 'clear statements' burdens the Congress with unnecessary reenactment of provisions that were already plain enough when read literally."[81]

In *Federal Aviation Administration v. Cooper*,[82] the Supreme Court ruled that a provision in the Privacy Act[83] that expressly authorized recovery from the government for "actual damages" did not authorize an award of damages for mental or emotional distress.[84] In deciding the question at issue concerned the *scope* of the waiver in the Privacy Act, the Court stated: "For the same reason that we refuse to enforce a waiver that is not unambiguously expressed in the

78 See., e.g., *Lane v. Pena*, 518 U.S. 187, 192, 116 S.Ct. 2092, 135 L. Ed.2d 486 (1996) (citing *United States v. Nordic Village, Inc.*, 503 U.S. 30, 34 (1992)) (discussing the right of Congress to waive the United States' sovereign immunity through a clear statement of waiver).

79 *Id.* (citing *United States v. Williams*, 514 U.S. 537, 531 (1995)).

80 *Williams*, 514 U.S. at 531. *See also Federal Aviation Admin.. v. Cooper*, 566 U.S. 284, 290-91, 132 S. Ct. 1441, 182 L. Ed.2d 497 (2012) ("Ambiguity exists if there is a plausible interpretation of the statute that would not allow money damages against the Government," citing *Nordic Village*, 503 U.S. at 37).

81 *Nordic Village*, 503 U.S. at 45 (Stevens, J., dissenting).

82 *Cooper*, 566 U.S. at 291, 304.

83 5 U.S.C. §552a.

84 *Cooper*, 566 U.S. at 304 (concluding that because Congress did not "speak unequivocally" [in the Privacy Act], it adopted "an interpretation of 'actual damages' limited to proven pecuniary or economic harm" and explaining: "To do otherwise would expand the scope of Congress' sovereign immunity waiver beyond what the statutory text clearly requires." Three dissenting justices expressed concern that in the Court ruling "actual damages" is limited to pecuniary loss, "individuals can no longer recover what our precedents and common sense understand to be the primary, and often only, damages sustained as a result of an invasion of privacy, namely mental or emotional distress." The dissenting justices stated: "That result is at odds with the text, structure, and drafting history of the Act. And it cripples the Act's core purpose of redressing deterring violations or privacy interests." *Id.*

statute, we also construe any ambiguities in the scope of a waiver in favor of the sovereign."[85]

In *College Savings Bank v. Florida Prepaid Postsecondary Education Expense Board*,[86] the Supreme Court explained that "a state does not consent to suit in federal court merely by consenting to suit in the courts of its own creation."[87] According to a plurality of the Court, Congress must refer specifically to state sovereign immunity and the Eleventh Amendment to make its intention clear.[88] One Supreme Court Justice criticized this position of the Court, opining that when "judge-made rules require Congress to use its valuable time enacting and reenacting provisions whose original intent was clear to all but the most skeptical and hostile reader, those rules should be discarded."[89]

The Texas Supreme Court also has ruled that to waive sovereign immunity effectively "a statute or resolution must contain a clear and unambiguous expression" of the State's waiver,[90] but has stated it should "have little difficulty

---

85 *Id.* at 291 (quoting *Lane,* 518 U.S. at 192)).

86 *College Savings*, 527 U.S. 666, 676, 119 S. Ct. 2219, 144 L. Ed. 2d 605 (1999).

87 *Id.*, (citing *Smith v. Reeves*, 178 U.S. 436, 441-45,20 S. Ct. 919, 44 L. Ed. 1140 (1900)). This position was reaffirmed, based on the doctrine of *stare decisis.* The Court clarified that a state does not "consent to suit in federal court merely by stating its intention to 'sue and be sued.'" *Id.*

88 *See Dellmuth v. Muth*, 491 U.S. 223, 231, 109 S. Ct. 2397, 105 L. Ed. 2d 181 (1989) (holding that reference to the Eleventh Amendment or the states' sovereign immunity is necessary to convey an intent to abrogate the sovereign authority of the states), *superseded by statute*, Individuals with Disabilities Education Improvement Act of 2004, Pub. L. No. 108-446, §101, §604, 118 Stat. 2464, 2659.

89 *Lane*, 518 U.S. at 212 (Stevens, J., dissenting).

90 *Wichita Falls State Hospital v. Taylor,* 106 S.W.3d 692, 696 (Tex. 2003) (noting that the Texas Legislature ratified this waiver approach by adding §311.034 to the Texas Government Code, which states: "In order to preserve the legislature's interest in managing state fiscal matters through the appropriate process, a statute shall not be construed as a waiver of sovereign immunity unless the waiver is effected by clear and unambiguous language." See also *Tex. Dep't of Trans. v. City of Sunset Valley,* 146 S.W.3d 637, 641 (Tex. 2004) (reiterating that sovereign immunity cannot be waived without the Texas legislature providing an apparent and express intent to do so).

A plaintiff must affirmatively demonstrate the court's subject-matter jurisdiction "by alleging a valid waiver of immunity." *Dallas Area Rapid Transit v. Whitley*, 104 S.W.3d 540, 542 (Tex. 2003) (noting that a plaintiff must plead a waiver of immunity because governmental immunity is superior to the court's subject-matter jurisdiction).

In statutes with language stating that immunity from suit is waived to the extent of liability, the court has ruled that "immunity from suit and liability are co-extensive."*State v. Lueck*, 290 S.W.3d 876, 880 (Tex. 2009); *see also Tex. Dept't of Parks & Wildlife v. Miranda*, 133 S.W.3d 217, 224 (Tex. 2004) (stating that "the Tort Claims Act creates a unique statutory scheme in which the two immunities are co-extensive"). In such cases, the court must consider the "facts alleged by the plaintiff and, to the extent it is relevant to the jurisdictional issue, the evidence submitted by the parties." *Dallas Area Rapid Transit*, 104 S.W.3d at 542. The court has held that, if pleadings affirmatively negate the existence of jurisdiction, it will grant a plea to the jurisdiction without permitting a plaintiff the opportunity to amend. *City of Cameron v. Brown*, 80

recognizing the Legislature's intent to waive immunity from suit when a statute provides that a state entity may be sued or that "sovereign immunity to suit is waived."[91] Yet, in *Harris County Hospital District v. Tomball Regional Hospital*, in applying the court's reasoning that in "a world with increasingly complex webs of governmental units, the Legislature is better suited to make the distinctions, exceptions, and limitations that different situations require,"[92] the Texas Supreme Court referred to a heavy presumption in favor of sovereign immunity derived "from principles related to separation of powers"and from practical concerns.[93]

The Texas Supreme Court's opinion in *Harris County Hospital* appears devoid of any deference to legislative distinctions and exceptions. For example, the court decided that language in the Texas Health and Safety Code, which provides that boards of hospital districts "may sue and be sued,"[94] does not waive the district's immunity from suits.[95] The court reasoned that when an entity's organic statute

---

S. W.3d 549, 555 (Tex. 2002).

Discussion of the state's assertion of sovereign immunity through a plea to the jurisdiction and further discussion of waiver of immunity in Texas in Chapter 6.

91 *Wichita Falls State Hospital*, 106 S.W.3d at 696-97.

92 *Harris Cnty. Hosp.*, 283 S.W.3d 838, 848 (Tex. 2009) (quoting *City of Galveston v. State*, 217 S.W.3d 466, 469 (Tex. 2007)) and (analyzing language cited in the Texas Constitution and various statutes to conclude that none of them, when read individually or together, clearly and unambiguously waived the hospital district's governmental immunity from suit). The court ruled the defendant in the suit, a hospital district, was immune from a suit brought by a hospital authority that sought to recover the cost of medical care its hospital rendered to indigent patients. 283 S.W.3d at 841. The court determined that none of the constitutional and statutory provisions asserted by the plaintiff showed an intent to waive the hospital district's immunity from suit. *Id.*

See Leach v. Texas Tech University, 335 S.W.3d 386, 393 (Tex. App.–Amarillo 2011), discussed in more detail *infra*, wherein the Seventh Court of Appeals referred to "observations" and "hypotheticals" of the Texas Supreme Court set out in *Federal Sign v. Texas S. Univ.* 951 S.W. 2d 401 (Tex. 1997), discussed *infra*, as "hardly" comporting "with the idea that only the legislature can decide when, where, and how to waive sovereign immunity."

93 *Harris Cnty. Hosp.* 283 S.W.3d at 842-43 (citing Tex. Gov't Code §311.034); *Tooke v. City of Mexia*, 197 S.W.3d 325, 328-29 (Tex. 2006), (quoting from *Nueces County v. San Patricio County*, 246 S.W.3d 651, 653 (Tex. 2008)).

94 Tex. Health & Safety Code §281.056(a).

95 *Harris Cnty. Hosp*, 283 S.W.3d at 843. The court stated that it construes a statute "to determine and give effect to the Legislature's intent,"looking at not only the statute as a whole, rather than as isolated parts, but also "the 'plain and common meaning of the statute's words.'" *Id.* at 842 (quoting *State v. Gonzalez*, 82 S.W.3d 322, 327 (Tex. 2002)). However, the court failed to mention that it also generally seeks to "give effect to legislative intent...expressed by the plain meaning of words used in the statute unless the context necessarily requires a different construction, a different construction is expressly provided by statute, or such an interpretation would lead to absurd or nonsensical results." *City of Waco v. Kelley*, 309 S.W.3d 536, 542 (Tex. 2010) (Emphasis added). The court concluded it "must examine the Legislature's words or parts of the statute as a whole and not consider words

states the entity may "sue and be sued," the phrase in and of itself does not mean that immunity to suit is waived.[96] The Texas Supreme Court also ruled that a section of the Texas Constitution, which requires a hospital district to assume full responsibility for providing medical and hospital care to needy inhabitants of the county and prohibits county and cities from levying any other tax for hospital purposes,[97] does not waive immunity because the constitutional language as adopted did not address waiver of a hospital district's immunity.[98] Indeed, among the guiding principles the court developed to help analyze statutes for legislative consent to suit, the court enumerated that ambiguity as to waiver favors retaining immunity.[99]

The inherent problem appears to be that the Texas Supreme Court applies judge made immunity rules to determine the manner in which the Legislature can adequately waive immunity,[100] but, the court's "judge-made" immunity rules can leave the court in a quandary. In *Engelman Irrigation Dist. v. Shields Brothers, Inc.*, [101] a governmental entity sought a court declaration court that a "decades-old" judgment against it was void. The Supreme Court again affirmed that the decision to waive sovereign immunity is largely left to the Legislature and ruled anew that "it remains the judiciary's responsibility to define the boundaries of the doctrine;" it then abandoned its strict application of the sovereign immunity doctrine to rule against the governmental entity.[102]

---

or parts of a statute in isolation." *Id.*

96 *Harris Cnty. Hosp.*, 283 S.W.3d at 843.

97 Texas Constitution, Article IX, §4.

98 *Harris Cnty. Hosp,* 283 S.W.3d at 843-44. A question the court did not address is whether the Texas Constitution abrogated immunity so that waiver should not have been an issue.

99 283 S.W.3d at 844. In the end, the court declined to remand the hospital district case to permit the hospital authority to replead and seek equitable relief. *Id.* at 849 (dismissing the case because the suit remained one for money damages and the plaintiff did not request an opportunity to replead and seek injunctive relief).

100 *See. e.g., Lane v. Pena,* 518 U.S. at 200-12 (Stevens, J., dissenting and criticizing the majority's use of strict judge-made rules for determining statutory waiver of sovereign immunity that defeat the clear intent of Congress).

101 *Engelman Irrigation Dist. v. Shields Brothers, Inc.*, 514 S.W.3d 746, 751 (Tex. 2017). The court declined to equate immunity to a lack of subject-matter jurisdiction, deciding that the Legislature can waive immunity from suit but cannot waive subject-matter jurisdiction (referring to Hecht, J. concurring and noting: "The Court does not equate immunity to a lack of subject-matter jurisdiction...").

102 *Id.* at 753 (ruling the judgment against the governmental entity was not void but rather that *res judicata* barred the government's effort to attack the judgment collaterally). The court referred to its decision that "to waive sovereign immunity is largely left to the Legislature" but declared that

1. Breach of Contract Claims

For a time governmental immunity fell into disfavor in the United States.[103] A "chilling feeling against sovereign immunity" was reflected in federal legislation as early as 1797, when Congress determined that once the United States sues an individual, the individual could offset any amount due from the federal government.[104] However, this early trend to waive immunity of the federal government did not appear again until 1855 when Congress enacted legislation to establish the Court of Claims, permitting citizens to sue the United States for debts of the federal government.[105] While there was no general provision governing claims against the United States for more than sixty years after adoption of the Constitution, the 1855 Act reflected a congressional decision that individuals and entities should be able to bring claims against the government based on acts of Congress, executive regulations, and express or implied contracts with the government.[106] Congress established the Court of Claims in 1855 to permit a defined class of claims brought against the government.[107]

Approximately thirty years later, in 1887, Congress enacted the Tucker Act,[108] which not only waived immunity for suits arising out of express or implied contracts to which the federal government was a party but also extended the jurisdiction of the Court of Claims to constitutional claims and claims for damages "in cases not sounding in tort," to include a governmental taking of the property for which the Fifth Amendment provides compensation, and claims founded on

---

it has "also recognized that sovereign immunity is a common-law creation," and stated "it remains the judiciary's responsibility to define the boundaries of the doctrine." *Id.* Interestingly, the Texas Supreme Court ruled against the government's contention in *Engelman* that "the law has changed regarding the entity's sovereign immunity." The court stated: "Later developments in the common law on sovereign immunity do not undermine the finality of the *Engelman* judgment." *Id.* at 755.

103 *Nat'l City Bank v. Republic of China*, 348 U.S. 356, 359 (1955).

104 *Id.*

105 Act of Feb. 24, 1855, ch 122, 10 Stat. 612 (stating the Court of Claims "shall hear and determine all claims founded upon any law of Congress,...any regulation of an executive department, or...any contract, express or implied, with the government of the United States"). See now 28 U.S.C. §1491.

106 *Id; see also Nat'l City Bank*, 348 U.S. at 359-60 (discussing how the creation of the Court of Claims made it possible for the United States to be held accountable for its actions).

107 *Nat'l City Bank,* 348 U.S. at 359-60.

108 *See* Tucker Act, ch. 359, 24 Stat. 505 (1887) (providing the Court of Claims jurisdiction over "all claims founded upon the Constitution, except for pensions, or upon any regulation of an Executive Department, or upon any contract, express or implied, with the Government of the United States....")

acts of Congress or regulations of executive departments. Today, similar provisions remain in force for the United States Court of Federal Claims.[109] Some courts have noted that there is no reason why the government should be treated differently from its citizens, particularly in its status as a creditor.[110] For a time, the course of court decisions reflected the conflicting considerations that apply to the sovereign immunity doctrine, for in "varying degrees, at different times, the momentum of the historic doctrine" was arrested or deflected "by an unexpressed feeling that governmental immunity runs counter to prevailing notions of reason and justice."[111]

Many states do not have legislation similar to the Tucker Act that permits its citizens to sue the state on its contracts.[112] For example, in contrast to federal immunity law, the Texas Supreme Court ruled in *Federal Sign v. Texas Southern University*[113] that the State of Texas maintains sovereign immunity even with

---

109 *See, e.g.*, 28 U.S.C. §1491(a)(1) (" The United States Court of Federal Claims shall have jurisdiction to render judgment upon any claim against the United States founded either upon the Constitution, or any Act of Congress or any regulation of an executive department, or upon any express or implied contract with the United Sates, or for liquidated or unliquidated damages not sounding in tort."). If a plaintiff seeks damages of $10,000 or less, any federal district court has jurisdiction along with the United States Court of Federal Claims. If damages sought exceed that amount, the Court of Federal Claims has exclusive jurisdiction. *Id.* at §1346(a). (The Court of Federal Claims is an Article I court. Article I courts are agencies of the legislative or executive branch. Because the jurisdiction of the Court of Federal Claims is permissive only, Congress can prescribe rules and procedures to be followed in pursuing claims against the government. The judicial functions exercised by Article III courts, on the other hand, cannot be performed by Congress nor delegated to agencies under its supervision and control.)

In *Franklin-Mason v. Mabus*, 742 F.3d 1051, 1055 (D.C.Cir. 2014), the court noted that, while courts have construed the Tucker Act as granting exclusive jurisdiction to the Court of Federal Claims for contract disputes seeking more than $10,000 in damages, the Tucker Act does not grant the Court of Federal Claims exclusive jurisdiction for all contract claims over $10,000 (citing *Tritz v. U.S. Postal Serv.*, 721 F.3d 1133, 1137 (9th Cir. 2013)).

110 *See United States v. Whiting Pools, Inc.*, 462 U.S. 198, 209, 103 S. Ct. 2309, 76 L. Ed. 2d 515 (1983) (discussing how there is no reason to treat a government entity differently than a normal citizen concerning debt collection); *see also United States v. Nordic Village, Inc.*, 503 U.S. 30, 43-4 (1991) (citing with approval the analysis in *Whiting Pools*).

111 Frankfurter, J. dissenting in *Larson v. Domestic & Foreign Commerce Corp.*, 337 U.S. 682, 709, 69 S.Ct. 1457, 93 L.Ed. 1628 (1949).

112 In 1999, Texas did enact a statute that provides for dispute resolution and negotiation of some claims against the State for breach of contract. Tex. Gov't Code §2260.001-.108. This provision applies to contracts with independent contractors but does not apply to contracts between the State and its employees. *Id.* at §2260.051.

113 *Federal Sign*, 951 S.W.2d. 401, 412 (Tex. 1997) (holding that sovereign immunity applies to contracts between the state and individuals absent legislative consent to sue), but *superseded by statute*, Act of May 30, 1999, 76th Leg. R.S., ch. 1352, §9, 1999 Tex. Gen. Laws 4578, 4583-87, Tex. Gov't Code §§2260.001-.108, as to contracts with independent contractors, and *as recognized in Gen. Servs.*

respect to contract claims. Additionally, in a "matter of first impression," the Virginia Supreme Court ruled that municipal corporations performing governmental functions have immunity from a breach of contract claim.[114]

The Texas Supreme Court held in *Federal Sign* that, while the state may be liable on its contracts as if it were a private person, it only waives immunity from liability and not immunity from suit.[115] A private citizen must have legislative consent to sue the state on a breach of contract claim.[116]

Comm'n v. Little-Tex Insulation Co., 39 S.W.3d 591 (Tex. 2001).

The administrative scheme in Tex. Gov't Code §§2260.001 et seq. "applies to all written contracts for the sale of goods, services, or construction" and is intended "to promote mediation and settlement." *Gen. Servs.,* 39 S.W.3d at 596, and Tex. Govt' Code §2260.001(1). The Texas Supreme Court set out the administrative procedures required in *Gen Servs.* and ruled that "there is but one route to the courthouse for breach-of-contract claims against the State, and that route is through the Legislature." *Gen Servs.,* 39 S.W.3d at 597. The Supreme Court stated: "Chapter 2260's express language states that the administrative proceedings are a precursor to legislative consent to sue under Chapter 107," citing Tex. Gov't Code §2260.005. It ruled that "[c]ompliance with Chapter 2260...is a necessary step before a party can petition to sue the State." *Id.* The court referred to Chapter 107 as being "the typical means for seeking redress in breach-of-contract cases against the State..." The Supreme Court further concluded "that the State does not waive its immunity from a breach-of-contract action by accepting the benefits of a contract." *Id.* at 598.

114 *Jean Moreau & Associates, Inc. v. Health Center Com'n,* 720 S.E.2d 105, 111 (Va. 2012). The Virginia Supreme Court thought there was no reason to differentiate a municipal's immunity for tort claims from "quasi-contractual claims." *Id.* It stated: "If municipal corporations act as arms or agencies of the State when they exercise governmental functions, then they should be protected–like the Commonwealth–from both tort and quasi-contractual claims." *Id.* It ruled that recovery from municipal corporations on a quantum meruit basis is limited to proprietary functions. *Id.*

115 *Federal Sign,* 952 S.W.3d at 412. The Texas Supreme Court in *Federal Sign* expressly overruled any cases that held to the contrary. Four Justices wrote a separate opinion because they thought the parties and the public were owed an explanation. *Id.* at 412 (Hecht, J., concurring). Three justices dissented because they thought the opinion called "into question the enforceability of State contracts and [was] counter to the national trend recognizing that a State waives sovereign immunity when it enters contracts." *Id.* at 416 (Enoch, J., dissenting). These justices thought that just as the state university in the case expected parties with which it contracted to honor their obligations (and could and would seek redress when they failed to do so), it also should honor its obligations. *Id.* at 418. The dissent opined that the majority opinion held that the "State can be liable for its breach of contract but it cannot be *held* liable." *Id.* at 420.

116 *Id.* at 408 (majority opinion). A party who contracts with the State and contends the State has breached the contract can seek redress by requesting the Legislature to waive immunity from suit presumably to permit the Legislature to resolve matters of public concern. However, an earlier report showed that only six percent of the requests to sue were granted in a period of eight years. *Id.* at 413 (Hecht, J., concurring) (citing Tex. H. Comm. On Civ. Prac., Interim Report 75th Leg. at 9 (1996).

In *Gen. Servs. Com'n v. Little-Tex Insulation Co., Inc.,* 39 S.W.3d at 596, the Supreme Court referred to Chapter 107 of the Texas Civil Practices and Remedies Code as generally providing the permission and procedure to sue the state. The court referred to Chapter 2260 of the Texas Government Code, specifically §2260.005, as requiring that its procedures be followed as "a prerequisite to suit under Chapter 1-7" for a breach-of-contract claim.

Although the Texas Supreme Court established in *Federal Sign* that the act of contracting does not waive the state's immunity from suit, the court left open the possibility that the State may waive its immunity by conduct other than simply executing a contract so that it is not always immune from suit when it contracts.[117] Nonetheless, in *General Servs. Comm'n v. Little-Tex Insulation Co.,*[118] the Texas Supreme Court expanded its ruling in *Federal Sign* that the state maintains sovereign immunity with respect to contract claims, holding "that the State does not waive its immunity from a breach-of-contract action by accepting the benefits of a contract." Still, in 2002, after its 1997 ruling in *Federal Sign* and its 2001 ruling in *General Servs. Comm'n,* the Texas Supreme Court did adopt, in *Texas A & M University-Kingsville v. Lawson,*[119] a waiver exception for immunity in a breach of contract case involving the enforcement of a settlement agreement.[120] Lawson had settled a suit against a public university under the Texas Whistleblowers' Act[121] but later sued the university for allegedly violating the terms of the agreement.[122] In a 5-4 decision, the court reasoned that a suit for a breach of a settlement agreement is separate and apart from suit on the settled claim, thus, it held, but only in a 5-4 decision, that enforcement of a settlement from which immunity was waived should not be barred by immunity.[123]

117 *Federal Sign*, 951 S.W.2d at 408 n. 1. In a concurring opinion, Justice Hecht stated that the court ruled "only that the mere execution of a contract for goods and services, without more, does not waive immunity from suit." *Id.* at 413 (Hecht, J., concurring). He commented that the university defendant terminated its agreement with Federal Sign before Federal Sign had delivered anything to the university. Justice Hecht noted the court did not address whether the State would be immune from suit on debt obligations, such as bonds. He also questioned whether the State would be immune if Federal Sign had complied fully with the contract and the university then refused to pay the agreed price. *Id.* at 412. He commented that the court's decision in *Federal Sign* did not hold that "the State is always immune from suit for breach of contract absent legislative consent." *Id.* at 413. However, later, in *Gen. Servs. Comm'n v. Little-Tex Insulation Co.*, 39 S.W.3d at 598, the Supreme Court concluded "that the State does not waive its immunity from a breach-of-contract action by accepting the benefits of a contract."

118 *Gen. Servs. Comm'n,* 39 S.W.3d at 598.

119 *Lawson*, 87 S.W.3d 518 (Tex. 2002).

120 *Id.* at 512 (discussing that, if the state waives immunity in a previous suit, it cannot assert immunity in a suit to enforce the settlement from the prior suit).

121 Discussed *infra.*

122 *Id.* at 519.

123 *Id.* at 521. The Texas Supreme Court did reject the court of appeals' adoption of a broad waiver by conduct exception to sovereign immunity as well as the dissent's rigid view of immunity from suit for breach of contract. *Id.* at 522-3; *see also Catalina Development Inc. v. County of El Paso*, 121 S.W.3d 704 (Tex. 2003), (establishing that the court evaluates the facts of each case to determine if waiver-by-conduct exception to sovereign immunity exists).

In *Wasson Interests, Ltd. v. City of Jacksonville*, the Texas Supreme Court ruled the governmental proprietary dichotomy applies in the contract-claims context.[124] The court stated:[125] "Yet, although the rationale for governmental immunity remains firmly established in our jurisprudence, we have never decided whether the distinction between governmental and proprietary acts–sometimes referred to as the proprietary governmental dichotomy–applies to breach-of-contract claims against municipalities."[126] The court further commented that "[L]ike *ultra vires* acts, for which government officers do not enjoy immunity, a city's proprietary functions are not performed under the authority or for the benefit of the state, and thus such functions do not share a common root with the state's sovereign immunity."[127] The court reiterated that *ultra vires* acts are distinct from a city acting in its proprietary function, but concluded "the rationale for not extending immunity is similar because a city's proprietary functions are not done pursuant to the will of the people, protecting them via the state's immunity is not an efficient way to ensure efficient allocation of state resources."[128]

The Texas Supreme Court neither answered whether the state's refusal to honor its contractual obligations is an "efficient way to ensure efficient allocation of state resources" nor whether that refusal is "done at the will of the people." It would seem that even advocates of a state's sovereign immunity would agree that a breach-of-contract claim against the government does not have "a common root with a state's sovereign immunity." Additionally, "reason and justice" would dictate that the government, like private citizens, must honor

124 *Wasson Interests, Ltd. v. City of Jacksonville*, 489 S.W.3d 427, 434-35, 439 (Tex., 2016) (stating that in *Tooke v City of Mexia*, 197 S.W 3d 325, 343 (Tex. 2006), it "simply declined to address whether the dichotomy applied because to do so was unnecessary in that case."). [Discussion of the governmental/proprietary and discretionary/ministerial dichotomies *supra*.]

125 *Id.* at 432.

126 *Id.*, (citing *Tooke v. City of Mexia*, 197 S.W.3d at 343 (Tex. 2006)).

127 *Id.* at 436-37 (citing *Houston Belt*, 487 S.W.3d at 157 and noting "that 'extending immunity to officials using state resources in violation of the law would not be an efficient way of ensuring those resources are spent as intended,'" citing *City of El Paso v. Heinrich*, 284 S.W.3d 366, 372 (Tex. 2009)).

128 *Id.* The court had to address an attempt by the governmental entity "to declare void a decades-old final money judgment on grounds that the law has changed regarding the entity's sovereign immunity." Although the court generally has imposed immunity on virtually all suits against the state or its agencies, in *Engleman Irrigation Dist. v. Shields Brothers, Inc.*, 514 S.W.3d 746 (Tex. 2017), the Texas Supreme Court refused to rule that a final money judgment could be set aside as being void based on a theory that the earlier court had lacked subject-matter jurisdiction to render judgment against the state agency.

its contracts and that the doctrine of sovereign immunity cannot justify a refusal to do so.

In 1999, following the Supreme Court's decision in *Federal Sign*, the Texas Legislature enacted a mediation and settlement statute for breach-of-contract claims involving state contracts with independent contractors;[129] however, the statute did not provide for mediation of claims from individuals, including state employees.

Texas courts have had difficulty in barring breach-of-contract claims brought by individuals against the state based on sovereign or governmental immunity defenses. Despite the rulings of the Texas Supreme Court in *Federal Sign* and *General. Serv. Comm'n,* in 2007, the Texas First Court of Appeals[130] recognized and identified a "waiver-by-conduct" exception to sovereign immunity.[131] This court ruled that "legislative control over waiving immunity from suit does not mean the State can breach contracts with private parties freely or that the State can use sovereign immunity as a shield to avoid paying for benefits the State accepts under a contract."[132] Therefore, as the First Court of Appeals held, sovereign immunity would not defeat the trial court's subject-matter jurisdiction over a claim of breach of contract when the state entity accepted substantial benefits under a contract.[133]

Still, later, in 2011, in a case involving a former coach suing a state university for breach of contract when the university refused to pay amounts due him under his contract with the university,[134] the Texas Seventh Court of Appeals refused to

---

129 Tex. Gov't Code §§ 2260.001-.108.

130 *Texas Southern University v. State Street Bank and Trust Company,* 212 S.W.3d 893 (Tex. App. Houston [lst Dist] 2007, pet. denied).

131 *Id.* at 908 (discussing how Texas Southern University's conduct created a waiver-by-conduct exception by entering into a $13 million contract for equipment and services, allowing delivery, and then refusing to pay and claiming sovereign immunity). The court noted an additional fact in the case that governmental officials had lured the party to the contract "with false promises that the contract would be valid and enforceable, then disclaimed any obligation on the contract by taking the position the contract was not valid after all." *Id.*

[Tex. Gov. Code §2260, discussed *supra,* applies to state contracts with independent contractors and is not applicable to state contracts with employees of the state. *See* §2260.001(2)(B).]

132 *Texas Southern University,* 212 S.W.3d at 901. (The contract was entered into prior to the effective date of the statute providing for dispute resolution and negotiation of claims relating to controversies with the state regarding performance on its contracts, Tex. Gov' Code §2260 *et. seq.,* n. 302.)

133 See *id.* at 908 (holding that the facts were enough to constitute a waiver of sovereign immunity, giving the trial court subject-matter jurisdiction).

134 *Leach v. Texas Tech Univ,* 335 S.W. 3d 386 (Tex. App.–Amarillo 2011), pet. denied.

find the university waived immunity by conduct related to the coach's breach of contract claim and dismissed the claim.[135] The Seventh Court of Appeals deferred to the ruling of the Texas Supreme Court in *General Servs. Comm'n* that "there is but one route to the courthouse for breach-of-contract claims against the State and that route is through the Legislature."[136]

It is interesting that in 2016, in *Wheelabrator Air Pollution Control, Inc. v. City of San Antonio,*[137] the Texas Supreme Court ruled that a city-owned electric and gas utility did not have immunity for its breach of contract.[138] Further, in 2017, in *Engelman Irrigation Dist. v. Shields Brothers, Inc.,*[139] the Supreme Court was faced with a dilemma regarding its statements that sovereign immunity is a jurisdictional bar in all suits against the government. In *Engelman,* a governmental entity sought a declaration that a judgment against it was void based on what the governmental entity suggested was "changed precedent involving government immunity."[140] The Supreme Court did refuse to declare the judgment to be void.

In sum, a citizen can sue the federal government for debts of the federal government. However, in some states, a citizen cannot sue the state for its debts. In Texas, the State Legislature has enacted a statute that the state must enter into dispute resolution and negotiation for breach of contract claims brought

---

135 *Id.* at 401. After the Texas Supreme Court denied a petition for review in *Leach,* the decision of the Seventh Court of Appeals became a final decision that rendered unenforceable an $800,000 contract the coach had entered into with Texas Tech University. Later, and *during* the appeal of a case wherein the Seventh Court also rendered a favorable decision for Texas Tech University, the university employed all of the then justices of that court to serve as adjunct professors in the university's law school. The chief justice of the Seventh Court self-reported his university employment to the Texas State Commission on Judicial Conduct.

136 *General Servs. Comm'n.,* 39 S.W.3d at 597. The Seventh Court did not note in *Leach* that in *Gen. Servs. Comm'n,* the Supreme Court did not defer to the Legislature but rather concluded "that the State does not waive its immunity from a breach-of-contract action by accepting the benefits of a contract." *Id.* at 598.

137 *Wheelabrator,* 489 SW.3d 448 (Tex. 2016).

138 *Id.* (relating to a claim for breach of a contract to install pollution control equipment at a power plant and ruling the action was proprietary and therefore the city was not immune from suit based on government immunity).

139 *Engleman,* 514 S.W.3d 746 (Tex. 2017).

140 Id. The court had to address an attempt by the governmental entity "to declare void a decades-old final money judgment on grounds that the law has changed regarding the entity's sovereign immunity." Although the court generally has imposed immunity on virtually all suits against the state or its agencies, in *Engleman,* the Texas Supreme Court refused to rule that a final money judgment could be set aside as being void based on a theory that the earlier court had lacked subject-matter jurisdiction to render judgment against the state agency.

by independent contractors, but it is apparent that before most Texas courts will recognize a breach-of-contract claim from an individual claimant, the Texas Legislature must extend the mediation process to all state contracts. The State of Texas, as well as some other states that adhere to absolute state sovereign immunity, continues to have immunity with respect to contracts between the State and individuals, including its employees.

2. Tort Claims Act

In 1945, the immunity of the United States government as a territorial sovereign came under attack again when the sovereign immunity doctrine was increasingly "found to be in conflict with the growing subjection of governmental action to the moral judgment."[141] At that time, the Supreme Court observed that "prerogatives of the government must yield to the needs of the citizen" if governments seek "to ameliorate inequalities as necessities permit."[142] Following a few limited statutes waiving immunity, the Federal Tort Claims Act[143] was enacted in 1946. This Act waived the federal government's immunity from suits due to damage to or loss of property, or on account of personal injury or death, caused by the negligent or wrongful act of any governmental employee while acting within the scope of the employee's office or employment. The Act applied under circumstances where the United States would be liable to the claimant if it were a private person.[144] The Act did not, however, provide a waiver of immunity for intentional torts, to include, among others, "assault, battery, false imprisonment, false arrest, malicious prosecution, abuse of process, libel, slander, misrepresentation, deceit, or interference with contract rights," and claims arising

---

141 *See National City Bank of New York v. Republic of China,* 348 U.S. 356, 359 (1955) (discussing how the doctrine of sovereign immunity has received increased scrutiny due to the moral implications of being immune from suit or liability or alleged wrongdoing).

142 *United States v. Shaw,* 309 U.S. 495, 501, 60 S.Ct. 659, 84 L.Ed. 888 (1940).

143 Pub. L. No. 79-601, Ch. U53, tit. IV, 60 Stat. 842 (codified as amended in scattered sections of 28 U.S.C., including §§1291, 1346(b), 1402(b), 1504, 2110, 2401(b), 2402, 2411-2, 2671-2680).

144 28 U.S.C. §§1346(b) and 2674.

Discussion in *United States v. Yellow Cab Co. v. United States,* 340 U.S. 543, 549, 71 S.Ct. 399, 95 L.Ed. 523 (1951) and *F.D.I.C v. Meyer,* 510 U.S. 471, 114 S. Ct. 996, 127 L.Ed. 2d 308 (1994). In *Yellow Cab. Co,* 340 U.S. at 549, the Court recognized that the government's obligation to pay claims for negligent or wrongful actions by its employees was not new and could be seen in the many relief acts passed. In *F.D.I.C.,* the Court decided a constitutional tort claim was not cognizable under the Act, 28 U.S.C. § 1346(b), because the section did not provide a cause of action for such a claim. *Id.* at 477. The Court also discussed how "sue and be sued" language can constitute a waiver of sovereign immunity. *Id.* at 483.

out of combatant activities of the military.[145] The Act also did not apply to claims "based upon the exercise or performance or the failure to exercise or perform a discretionary function or duty on the part of a federal agency or an employee of the Government...."[146] The Supreme Court has stated "the exception covers only acts that are discretionary in nature, acts that 'involv[e] an element of judgment or choice'"[147] and "it is the nature of the conduct rather than the status of the actor that governs whether the exception applies."[148]

As discussed *supra*, there had been complexity in applying the discretionary function exception to immunity. However, the problem was eliminated in determining whether a federal employee has immunity from liability based on a common law tort claim when the Federal Employees Liability Reform and Tort Compensation Act[149] was enacted in 1988 to provide absolute immunity to governmental employees when they act within the scope of employment.[150] This Act

---

145 28 U.S.C. §2680(h). Other torts for which there is no waiver are listed in 28 U.S.C. §2680. The exceptions to waiver, among others, do not apply to acts or omissions of federal investigation or law enforcement officers with respect to "assault, battery, false imprisonment, false arrest, abuse of process, or malicious prosecution." *Id.*

146 *Id.* at §2680(a). This exception is frequently litigated; if the exception applies, the claim will be dismissed.

147 *U.S. v. Gaubert*, 499 U.S. 315, 322, 111 S. Ct. 1267, 1271 113 L. Ed. 2d 335 (1991) (quoting *Berkovitz v. United States*, 486 U.S. 531, 536, 108 S. Ct. 1954, 100 L. Ed. 2d 531 (1988) and *Dalehite v. United States*, 346 U.S. 15, 34, 73 S. Ct. 956, 967, 94 L. Ed 1427 (1953) and stating: "The discretionary function exception covers acts involving an element of judgment or choice if they are based on considerations of public policy.")

148 *Gaubert*, 499 U.S. at 322 (adding the exception protects actions of government employees involving the necessary element of choice, the purpose of the exception being to 'prevent judicial 'second-guessing' of legislative and administrative decisions grounded in the social, economic, or political policy through the medium of an action in tort,'" quoting *United States v. Varig Airlines*, 467 U.S. 797, 814, 104 S. Ct. 2755, 81 L. Ed. 2d 6609 (1984)).

149 Pub. L. No. 100-694, 102 Stat. 4563, codified as amended in relevant part at 28 U.S.C. §2679(b)(1). The Act reads: "The remedy against the United States provided by [the Federal Tort Claims Act] for injury or loss of property, or personal injury or death arising or resulting from the negligent or wrongful act or omission of any employee of the Government while acting within the scope of his office or employment is exclusive of any other civil action or proceeding for money damages by reason of the same subject matter against the employee whose act or omission gave rise to the claim or against the estate of such employee. Any other civil action or proceeding for money damages arising out of or relating to the same subject matter against the employee or the employee's estate is precluded without regard to when the act of omission occurred."

150 The Act was a response to a Supreme Court decision in 1988 in *Westfall v. Erwin*, 484 U.S. 292, 108 S. Ct. 580, 98 L. Ed. 2d 619 (1988), wherein the Supreme Court added an additional requirement for immunity when a federal governmental employee was sued in the employee's personal capacity. The Court ruled in *Westfall* that for a federal employee to have immunity from suit on a common law tort, the employee had to show that the employee was acting within the scope of employment and was performing a discretionary function. *Id.* at 296-97. In enacting the Federal Employees Liability

substitutes the federal government for the employee in a suit against a federal employee for tortious misconduct if the employee was acting within the scope of employment when performing the tortious act;[151] the Act confers immunity upon government employees by making a Federal Tort Claims Act (FTCA) claim "against the Government the exclusive remedy for torts committed by government employees in the scope of their employment."[152] Moreover, the Act authorizes the Attorney General to issue a certification that a defendant employee was acting within the scope of the employee's office or employment at the time of the incident out of which a claim against the employee arose.[153]

In determining whether an employee acted within the scope of employment, courts "consider the substantive law of the jurisdiction where the employment relationship exists."[154] Generally, however, the Attorney General's certification "begins and ends the scope-of-employment analysis."[155] When the Attorney

---

Reform and Tort Compensation Act, often referred to as the "Westfall Act," Congress removed the second requirement, viewing it as exposing employees to unwarranted liability.

In *United States v. Smith*, 499 U.S. 160, 111 S. Ct. 1180, 113 L. Ed2d 134 (1991), the Court referred to the Act as the Liability Reform Act. The court recognized that the Act establishes absolute immunity for government employees by making a Federal Tort Claims action against the government the exclusive remedy for torts committed by government employees in the scope of their employment.

151 28 U.S.C. §2679(d)(1).

152 *United States v. Smith*, 499 U.S. at 162.

153 *Id.* If the Attorney General certifies an federal employee was acting within the scope of employment when a tortious act occurred, any action brought against the employee is an action against the United States; the United States is substituted as a party defendant. Accordingly, any action brought in a state court is removed to a federal district court and deemed to be an action or proceeding against the United States. The case then proceeds as an action filed against the United States pursuant to 28 U.S.C. §1346(b) of the Federal Tort Claims Act and is subject to the limitations and exceptions applicable to actions against the United States. 28 U.S.C. §2679(d)(4). If the Attorney General refuses certification, the federal employee may petition the court to find and certify that the employee was acting within the scope of employment. *Id* at (d)(3). Should the court disagree with the Attorney General's determination, the tort suit can proceed against the defendant government employee in the employee's personal or individual capacity. *Gutierrez de Martinez v. Lamagno*, 515 U.S. 417, 423-24, 434, 115 S. Ct. 2227, 132 L. Ed.3d 375 (1995).

154 *See Jacobs v. Brobel,* 724 F.3d 217, 221 (D.C. Cir. 2013) (ruling courts in the District of Columbia analyze the issue "via a test established by the Second Restatement of Agency, which states: "(1) Conduct of a servant is within the scope of employment if, but only if: (a) it is of the kind he is employed to perform; (b) it occurs substantially within the authorized time and space limits; [and] (c) it is actuated, at least in part by a purpose to serve the master. (2) Conduct of a servant is not within the scope of employment if it is different in kind from that authorized, far beyond the authorized time or space limits, or too little actuated by a purpose to serve the master." Restatement (Second) of Agency 228 (1958).

155 In *Harbury v. Hayden*, 522 F.3d 413, 417 (D.C. Cir.2008). In *Wilson v. Libby,* 535 F.3d 697, 711 (D.C. Cir. 2008) the court stated: "The certification carries a rebuttable presumption that the employee has

General certifies a federal employee acted within the scope-of-employment in a tort claims action, the Federal government becomes the sole party defendant and the suit proceeds under the FTCA.[156] The problem is that "the FTCA is only a *limited* waiver of sovereign immunity."[157] There generally is no waiver of the government's immunity; thus, when Congress has not waived the government's sovereign immunity under the FTCA, the Attorney General's scope-of-employment certification has the effect of converting a tort claim into "an FTCA case over which the federal courts lack subject-matter jurisdiction."[158] Additionally, courts have given very expansive interpretations of scope-of-employment coverage; some courts having ruled that sexual harassment, a shooting, armed assault, and rape fell within the scope of a defendant's employment.[159] As the court explained in *Harbury v. Hayden*, "the combination of the scope-of-employment determination and the FTCA's exceptions may absolutely bar a plaintiff's case."[160]

---

absolute immunity from the lawsuit and that the United States is to be substituted as the defendant." In *Jacobs v. Vrobel*, 724 F.3d 217, 221 (D.C. Cir. 2013), the court stated: To rebut the certification, the plaintiff must allege, either in the complaint or a subsequent filing, specific facts 'that taken, as true, would establish that the defendant['s] actions exceed the scope of ... employment,'" citing *Stokes v. Cross*, 327 F.3d 1210, 1215 (D.C. Cir. 2003). If the plaintiff satisfies the burden, the court stated the plaintiff could "if necessary, attain 'limited discovery' to resolve any factual disputes over jurisdiction,'" citing *Wuterich v. Murtha*, 562 F.3d 375, 381 (D.C. Cir. 2009) and quoting *Stokes*, 327 F.3d at 1214, 1216).

156 *Id.*

157 *Id.*

158 *Id.* The political question doctrine bars state law tort claims against federal employees in their personal capacities. In *Baker v. Carr*, 369 U.S. 186, 217, 82 S. Ct. 91, 7 L. Ed.2d 663 (1962), the Supreme Court held that the political question doctrine bars judicial resolution of certain issues textually and exclusively committed by the Constitution to one or both of the other branches of the Federal Government. The Court recognized that judicial restraint is often appropriate in the area of foreign affairs because these cases "frequently turn on standards that defy judicial application, or involve the exercise of a discretion demonstrably committed to the executive or legislature." *Id.* at 211. *See also Nixon v. United States*, 506 U. S. 224, 113 S. Ct. 732, 122 L.Ed. 2d 1 (1993) and *Goldwater v. Carter*, 444 U.S. 996, 1002, 100 S. Ct. 533, 62 L. Ed.2d 428 (1979).

There also is an exception, among others, to the FTCA's waiver of sovereign immunity for suits based on injuries suffered in a foreign country. See 28 U.S.C. §2680. In *Sosa v. Alvarez-Machain*, 542 U.S. 692, 712, 124 S. Ct. 2739, 159 L. Ed. 2d 718 (2004), the Supreme Court ruled that the foreign country exception to the FTCA "bars all claims based on any injury suffered in a foreign country."

159 Discussed in *Harbury*, 522 F.3d at 422 (citing *Howard Univ. v. Best*, 484 A.2d 958, 987 (D.C. 1984) (sexual harassment); *Johnson v. Weinberg*, 434 A.2d 404, 409 (D.C. 1981) (a shooting); *Lyon v. Carey*, 533 F.2d 649, 652 (D.C. Cir. 1976) (a rape).

160 *Harbury*, 522 F.3d at 417 (citing *United States v. Smith*, 499 U.S. at 166). A victim then of a Federal governmental employee's tortious actions often has no remedy.

In *Lewis v. Clarke*,[161] in an individual-capacity action brought against a tribal governmental employee to impose individual liability upon the employee, the Supreme Court pointed out that a governmental employee "may be able to assert personal immunity defenses but not sovereign immunity."[162] The Court also ruled that an indemnification statute for governmental employees "does not extend sovereign immunity to individual employees who would otherwise not fall under its protective cloak."[163] The Court stated: "Personal-capacity suits... seek to impose *individual* liability upon a government officer for actions taken under color of state law"[164] and further commented that "officers sued in their personal capacity come to court as individuals."[165] Even though the defendant was a tribal employee, the decision demonstrates that a victim of a governmental employee's misconduct should file suit against the employee in the employee's individual, rather than official, capacity.

Additionally, there are two exceptions to the Federal Employees Liability Reform and Tort Compensation Act's provision, discussed *supra*, that federal employees have absolute immunity if they act within the scope of their employment. The Act specifically exempts any civil action brought against a federal employee for a violation of the Constitution[166]–the *Bivens* action discussed in Chapter 2 (although courts have substantially limited its application as noted in Chapter 2) –and an action under a statute that specifically authorizes recovery against an individual employee.[167]

With respect to state immunity for governmental tortious acts, most states have enacted tort claims acts. These acts, which are set out in Chapter 6, have differing impact on victims' abilities to sue the government successfully for

161 *Lewis v. Clarke*, 137 S. Ct. 1285, 197 L.Ed. 2d 631 (2017).

162 *Lewis v. Clarke*, 137 S. Ct. at 1287 (quoting *Hafer v. Melo*, 502 U.S. 21, 30-31, 112 C. Tt. 358, 116 L. Ed. 2d 301 (1991)). The Court referred to its cases establishing that "in the context of lawsuits against state and federal employees or entities, courts should look to whether the sovereign is the real party in interest to determine whether sovereign immunity bars the suit" *id.* at 1290 (quoting *Hafer*, 502 U.S. at 25).

163 *Id.* The Court stated that it had "never held that a civil rights suit under 42 U.S.C. §1983 against a state officer in his individual capacity implicates the Eleventh Amendment and a State's sovereign immunity from suit."

164 *Id.* at 1291 (quoting *Hafer*, 502 U.S. at 25).

165 *Id.* (quoting *Hafer*, 502 U.S. at 27).

166 28 U.S.C. §2679(b)(2)(1)(A).

167 *Id.* at (b)(2)(1)(B). Discussion in *United States v. Smith*, 499 U.S. at 173.

its tortious conduct and/or that of its employees. As an example, the Texas Legislature enacted the Texas Tort Claims Act[168] to waive sovereign immunity for some tortious governmental conduct but only "to the extent of liability" created by that Act.[169] A person having a claim under the Act may sue a governmental unit for damages permitted by the Act[170] only for: (1) wrongful acts or omissions or negligence of an employee acting within the scope of employment when operating a motor-driven vehicle or motor-driven equipment if the employee would be personally liable to the claimant[171] and (2) personal injury and death caused by a condition or use of tangible personal or real property if the governmental unit would be liable to the claimant if it were a private person.[172] Additionally, although the governmental units covered by the Texas Tort Claims Act include school districts, which are political subdivisions of the state,

---

168 Texas Tort Claims Act, 69th Leg., R.S., ch. 959 §1, §§101.101-.109, 1985 Tex. Gen. Laws. 3301 (codified as amended at Tex. Civ. Prac. & Rem. Code, §§101.001-.109).

169 Tex. Civ. Prac. & Rem. Code, §101.025.

170 Section 101.025 states: "(a) Sovereign immunity to suit is waived and abolished to the extent of liability created by this chapter. (b) A person having a claim under this chapter may sue a governmental unit for damages allowed by this chapter."

171 Tex. Civ. Prac. & Rem. Code §101.021(1)(A). However, liability from this waiver of immunity is limited to a maximum amount of $100,000 money damages for each person. Id. 101.023(b). Because "a regional transportation authority might delegate some or all of the operation of its public transportation system to one or more independent contractors," the Texas Supreme Court pointed out in *Fort Worth Transportation Authority v. Rodriguez*, 547 S.W.3d 830 (Tex. 2018) that "the Legislature contemplated liability for such a situation" and provided that an independent contractor of the authority that performs a function of the authority is subject to the same liability cap. Tex. Transp. Code §452.056(d). In *Rodriguez,* a plaintiff sued three such independent contractors, seeking the statutory maximum of $100,000 from each entity. The court, however, ruled that "the liability of any number of independent contractors performing essential governmental functions for an authority under chapter 452 is limited to a single damages cap..." It held that the three entities were "cumulatively liable up to a single $100,000 damages cap."

Interestingly, the court in *Rodriguez* also ruled that the bus driver was protected by governmental immunity, ruling the election-of-remedies provision, discussed *infra,* which provides absolute immunity to governmental employees who act within the scope of employment when they perform tortious acts, applied to the bus driver as well even though she was working for a private entity, the independent contractor, rather than for the state. The court held that an employee of an independent contractor that performs an essential governmental function under the Transportation Code chapter 452, who is acting within the scope of employment, is afforded protection under the Tort Claims election-of-remedies provision as if she were an employee of the government.

172 Tex. Civ. Prac. & Rem. Code §101.021. These exceptions have been referred to as three areas: use of publicly owned automobiles, premises defects, and injuries arising out of conditions or use of property. See *Tex. Dep't of Trans. v. Able*, 35 S.W.3d 608, 611 (Tex. 2000). Section 101.058 of the Tort Claims Act further modifies a governmental unit's waiver of immunity from suit by imposing limitations of liability articulated in the recreational use statute.

school districts have special treatment under the Act in that a school district is liable only for tort claims involving the use or operation of motor vehicles.[173]

Moreover, the Texas Supreme Court had also adopted a rigid application of the Texas Tort Claims Act that substantially precludes a victim from any redress from the government for its tortious actions. As an example, the Act requires that a party who asserts a tort claim against a governmental unit must give the governmental unit formal notice of the claim within six months after the incident that gave rise to the claim.[174] However, the notice-of-claim requirements do "not apply if the governmental unit has actual notice" of the injury or that the claimant's property was damaged.[175] Still, in *City of San Antonio v. Tenorio*,[176] the Texas Supreme Court "tilted the scales" in favor of the government in dismissing a case brought by a motorcyclist against a city arising from a collision caused by city officers pursuing a suspect in an armed robbery. The Texas Court ruled that the city did not have "actual" notice that it was at fault in causing the collision, which the court stated was required for waiver of governmental immunity. In response to the plaintiffs' contention that the city was aware of its role in contributing to the injuries, the Texas Supreme Court interpreted the "actual notice" requirement to mean that "a governmental unit must have the same knowledge it is entitled to receive under the written notice provisions" of the Texas Tort Claims Act.[177] Four justices dissented, one stating: "At minimum, the jurisdictional evidence raises a fact issue regarding the City's actual knowledge of potential fault"[178] and the majority's "ever narrower construction of the Tort Claims Act's actual-notice exception is discordant with legislative intent plainly expressed in the statute and our precedent construing the statute."[179] The three other dissenting justices contended the courts should "avoid rewriting statutes;" that "our very freedom depends on it."[180]

173 *Id.* at §101.051 ("Except as to motor vehicles, this chapter does not apply to a school district'). *See Mission Consol. Indep. Sch. Dist. v. Garcia*, 253 S.W.3d 653, 676 (Tex. 2008).

174 *Id.* at §101.101(a).

175 *Id.* at §101.101(c).

176 *City of San Antonio v. Tenorio*, 543 S.W.3d 772, 774 (Tex. 2018).

177 *Id.* at 775.

178 *Id.* at 783.

179 *Id* at 785.

180 *Id.* at 787. These dissenting justices stated: "The Texas Constitution's separation-of-powers provision 'reflects a belief on the part of those who drafted and adopted our state constitution that one of

In *Texas Department of Parks & Wildlife v. Miranda*,[181] the Texas Supreme Court ruled that the Texas Tort Claims Act provides "a limited waiver of sovereign immunity"[182] and referred to two distinct principles of sovereign immunity: "immunity from suit and immunity from liability."[183] The court decided that the "Tort Claims Act creates a unique statutory scheme in which the immunities are co-extensive."[184]

When the Texas Torts Claims Act was first enacted in 1969, "the Act did little to limit claims against public employees, providing only that such claims were barred by a judgment in an action or settlement of a claim against the governmental employer."[185] While the Act "effectively conferred immunity on employees who otherwise had only qualified immunity," plaintiffs often sought to avoid strictures in the Act by suing governmental employees in their individual capacities--there was no immunity bar against these claims and the State would indemnify governmental employees for damages if they were found liable for committing toritous acts within the scope of their employment.[186] The Texas Supreme Court pointed out that "to prevent such circumvention, and to

---

the greatest threats to liberty is the accumulation of excessive power in a single branch of government,'" quoting *Armadillo Bail Bonds v. State*, 802 S.W.2d 237, 239 (Tex. Crim. App. 1990)). *Id.* The justices further commented: "It is not hyperbole to say that a court's well-intended effort to 'help' the Legislature or 'do justice' by rewriting a statute in a given case threatens the very foundation on which our liberty rests. A little tweak here or a little addition there may seem harmless enough at the time, but each little chip in the wall that separates the branches weakens the fortress safeguarding our freedom." *Id.*

181 *Tex. Dep't of Parks & Wildlife*, 133 S.W.3d 217 (Tex. 2004).

182 *Id.* at 224.

183 *Id.*

184 *Id.* It referred to the provision in Tex. Civ. Prac. & Rem. Code §101.025(a) which states: "Sovereign immunity to suit is waived and abolished to the extent of liability created by this chapter."

As noted *infra*, this language is present in the Texas Whistleblowers Act. Tex. Gov't Code, §554.0035 states: Sovereign immunity is waived and abolished to the extent of liability for the relief allowed under the chapter for a violation of this chapter. However, while the Texas Supreme Court has recognized this sentence waives sovereign immunity from suit, it ruled in *Texas Department of Transportation v. Lueck*, 290 S.W.3d 876, 882 (Tex. 2009) that the second sentence of §554.0035, which is the waiver of immunity from liability, simply limits judgments against the State to "the extent of liability for the relief allowed under this chapter for a violation of this chapter." The court concluded the "second sentence not only waives immunity from liability, but confines the scope of the State's consent to suit that was established in the first sentence." *Id.* It then reasoned, in most confusing language, that "like the Texas Tort Claims Act, the Whistleblower Act imposes a limited waiver of immunity that allows consideration of the section 554.002(a) elements, to the extent necessary in determining whether the claim falls within the jurisdictional confines of section 554.0035." *Id.*

185 Discussion in *University of Texas Health Science Center at Houston v. Rios*, 542 S.W.3d 530 (Tex. 2017).

186 *Id.* See Tex. Civ. Prac. & Rem. Code §§104.001-.002.

protect governmental employees," the Texas Legislature enacted a "comprehensive election-of-remedies provision in 2003."[187]

In *Mission Consolidated Indep. Sch. Dist. v. Garcia,*[188] the Texas Supreme Court stated that the purpose of the election-of-remedies provisions, Texas Practice and Remedies Code §101.106, "was to force a plaintiff to decide at the outset whether an employee acted independently and is thus solely liable, or acted within the general scope of his or her employment such that the governmental unit is vicariously liable."[189] As the Court of Appeals for the Fifth Circuit declared in *Wilkerson v. University of North Texas,*[190] the election-of-remedies provision, §101.106 "mandates plaintiffs to pursue lawsuits against governmental units rather than their employees"[191] and "entitles" a governmental "employee 'to dismissal' of the relevant tort claim."[192] The Fifth Circuit cited the Texas Supreme Court in *Goodyear Tire & Rubber Co. v. Mayes,*[193] in ruling that "even if the employee performs negligently or is motivated by ulterior motives or personal animus," there may be "a connection between the employee's job duties and the alleged tortious conduct."[194]

The problem for victims of government misconduct is that the Texas Supreme Court's interpretation of §101.106 prevents any claims based on the intentional torts of governmental employees. The State is substituted as the defendant in a tort claims suit against a governmental employee, and the State has absolute immunity for intentional torts.

The Texas Tort Claims Act does not waive immunity for any actions against the government except, as noted above, for the use of publicly owned

---

187 *Id.*

188 *Garcia,* 253 S.W.3d 653 (Tex. 2008).

189 *Id.* at 657.

190 *Wilkerson,* 878 F.3d 147, 159 (5th Cir. 2017).

191 *Id.* citing *Tex. Adjutant Gen.'s Office v. Ngakoue,* 408 S. W.3d 350, 352 (Tex. 2013).

192 *Id.* citing *Laverie v. Wetherbe,* 517 S.W.3d 748, 752 (Tex. 2017).

See, however, *Lewis v. Clarke,* 137 S. Ct. at 1287-89, wherein the U.S. Supreme Court ruled a governmental employee sued in the employee's individual capacity is not entitled to sovereign immunity and reversed a decision of the Connecticut Supreme Court that had granted the employee immunity. Additionally, the Supreme Court ruled in *Lewis v. Clarke,* 137 S. Ct. at 1292, that an indemnification statute for governmental employees does not make the government the real party in interest to support state sovereign immunity.

193 *Mayes,* 236 S.W.3d 754, 757 (Tex. 2007).

194 *Wilkerson,* 878 F.3d at 160 (citing Mayes, 236 S.W.3d at 757.) See also *Laverie v. Wetherbe,* 517 S.W.3d at 753).

automobiles, premises defects, and injuries arising out of conditions or use of property. Further, with the election-of-remedies provision, Texas Civil Practice and Remedies Code §101.106, effectively negating any tort claims against governmental employees, victims are effectively barred from suing the State. Section 101.106(a) states that, if a claimant files a tort claim against a governmental unit, the claimant cannot also sue the governmental employee regarding the *same* subject matter.[195] While a public employee can be liable individually for the employee's tortious conduct outside the general scope of employment, §101.106(b) of the Act requires a plaintiff to make an irrevocable election at the time suit is filed between suing the governmental unit under the Act or proceeding against the employee alone.[196] If a plaintiff sues *both* the government unit and any of its employees, §101.106(e) requires the suit against the employee to be dismissed on the governmental unit's motion. Further, §101.106(f) provides that, if a suit is filed against a governmental employee based on conduct within the general scope of that person's employment and the suit could have been brought against the governmental unit, the suit is considered to be against the employee in the employee's official capacity only.[197] If the employee files a motion to dismiss the suit, the plaintiff must amend the pleading to instead name the governmental unit as the defendant.[198] However, as noted previously, the Texas Tort Claims Act retains absolute immunity for the governmental unit for intentional tort claims.

---

195 Tex. Civ. Prac. & Rem. Code §101.106(a). Thus, as to *same subject matter* suits, a plaintiff must elect to file suit against the employee individually or against the governmental unit. Section 101.106(b) states: "The filing of a suit against any employee of a governmental unit constitutes an *irrevocable election* by the plaintiff and immediately and *forever bars any suit or recovery by the plaintiff against the governmental unit regarding the same subject matter* unless the governmental unit consents." (Emphasis added.) If a suit is filed against both the governmental unit and any of its employees, the governmental unit can file a motion to dismiss the suit against the individual employees. *Id.* at §101.106(e).

196 *University of Texas Health Science Center v. Rios*, 542 S.W.3d 530 (Tex. 2017) (noting that if a "plaintiff nevertheless sues both employer and employee, section 101.106(e) requires that the employee 'immediately be dismissed'" and ruling that the government's "statutory right to dismissal accrues when the motion is filed and is not impaired by later amendments to the pleadings or motions").

197 Section 101.106(f), Tex. Civ. Prac. & Rem. Code, states: "If a suit is filed against an employee of a governmental unit *based on conduct within the general scope of that employee's employment and if it could have been brought under this chapter against the governmental unit,* the suit is considered to be against the employee in the employee's official capacity only." (Emphasis added.)

198 *Id.*

In *Franka v. Velasquez*,[199] the Texas Supreme Court ruled the phrase in §101.106(f) that if a suit "could have been brought under this chapter," i. e., the Tort Claims Act, to mean that *any* "tort claim against the government is brought 'under' the Act for purpose of section 101.106, even if the Act does not waive immunity."[200] In response to the contention that "brought under this chapter" should encompass only tort claims for which the Tort Claims Act waives immunity, the Court ruled that "all common-law tort theories alleged against a government unit are assumed to be under the Act for purposes of section 101.106."[201] The Texas Supreme Court pointed to the Federal Employees Liability Reform and Tort Compensation Act (Westfall Act)[202] and stated that §101.106 "achieves the same end under Texas law as the Westfall Act does under federal law."[203] In *Franka,* the Supreme Court reasoned that "restrictions on government employee liability have always been part of the tradeoff" for the Texas Tort Claim Act's waiver of immunity, "expanding the government's own liability for its employees' conduct, and thus, 'a reasonable exercise of the police power in the interest of the general welfare.'"[204]

There is a question of what "tradeoff" exists when (1) the Texas Supreme Court's restrictions placed on governmental employee liability have eliminated any redress through suit against an employee for the employee's misconduct because a claim must be brought against the state rather than the employee and (2) there is no "expansion" of the government's liability because the Texas Tort Claims Act bars all intentional tort claims against the government.[205]

---

199 *Franka*, 332 S.W.3d 367 (Tex. 2011).

200 *Id.* at 375, 385. The Texas Supreme Court observed in *Franka, id.* at 372, n. 9, that while §101.106(f) does not use the term 'bars any action,' "four other subsections speak of a bar from suit or recovery and we think the character of the statute as one conferring immunity remains unchanged" (referring to an earlier Supreme Court decision, *Newman v. Obersteller*, 960 S.W.2d 621, 623 (Tex. 1997) that construed a prior version of §101.106 as "an immunity statute").

201 *Id.* at 367.

202 28 U.S.C. §2679 (discussed *supra*).

203 *Franka*, 332 S.W.3d at 385.

204 *Id.*, quoting *Tex. Workers' Comp. Comm'n v. Garcia*, 893 S.W.2d 504, 520 (Tex. 1995).

205 Recall that in *Laverie v. Wetherbe*, 517 S.W. 3d at 752, the Texas Supreme Court ruled §101.106(f) requires plaintiffs to pursue lawsuits against governmental units rather than their employees. That section then permits dismissal of tort claims against governmental employees because the Texas Tort Claims Act bars intentional tort actions against the State. See also *Tex. Adjutant Gen.'s Office v. Ngakoue*, 408 S.W.3d 350, 352 (Tex. 2013).

The Texas Supreme Court has ruled that "Texas is inviolably sovereign," that "sovereignty is inherent in its statehood," that "sovereignty is vested in 'the people' of the state," and that "it is firmly established" that a purpose of immunity is "to shield the public from the costs and consequences of improvident acts of their government."[206] In *Laverie,*[207] the Texas Supreme Court explained that the election-of-remedies provision in the Texas Tort Claims Act "favors "an expedient dismissal of governmental employees" to reduce resources the government and its employees must use in defending "redundant litigation"[208] The Supreme Court has not considered that victims of improvident governmental actions view immunity much differently. Victims, who would not characterize their claims against the government for its tortious acts as "redundant litigation," view the Texas Supreme Court's strict interpretation of the Act as having a purpose to "shield" the government, not the public, from "improvident acts of their government."

Although a governmental employee can be held liable for tortious wrongdoing if the employee is sued in his or her individual capacity and the wrongdoing occurred outside the scope of employment, Texas courts have interpreted government employee's actions that occur "within the scope of employment" very expansively to protect further governmental employees at the expense of their victims. In *University of Texas Health Science Center v. Rios,* [209] the Texas Supreme Court ruled that government employees are not required to prove their subjective intent to be dismissed from a suit pursuant to the election-of-remedies provision. The court stated there may be a connection between an employee's job duties and an alleged tortious conduct "even if the employee performs negligently or is motivated by ulterior motives or personal animus so long as the conduct itself was pursuant to her job responsibilities."[210]

206 See, e. g. *Wasson Interests, ltd. v. City of Jacksonville,* 489 S.W.3d 427 (Tex. 2016); *Tex. Nat Res. Conservation Comm'n v. IT-Davy,* 74 S.W.3d 849, 853 (Tex. 2002); and *Tooke v. City of Mexia,* 197 S.W.3d 325, 332 (Tex. 2006).

207 517 S.W.3d at 755.

208 *Id.*, citing *Mission Consol. Indep. Sch. Dist. v. Garcia,* 253 S. W. 3d 653, 657 (Tex. 2008). In *Laverie,* 527 S.W.3d at 755, the court stated the "function of the election-of-remedies provision...is..to quickly dismiss government employees when the suit should be brought against their employer" quoting *Tex. Adjutant Gen.'s Office v. Ngakoue,* 408 S.W.3d at 355.

209 *Rios,* 542 S.W.3d 530, 535 (Tex. 2017).

210 *Id.* (quoting *Laverie v. Wetherbee,* 517 S.W.3d at 753).

In *Jackson v. Texas Southern University,*[211] a federal district court included a male professor's assaulting a female professor while the two professors were proctoring examinations as occurring within the scope of the male professor's employment. The court ruled that even if the male professor "was motivated in part by personal animosity" toward the female professor, he acted within the scope of his employment in proctoring an exam that the university "lawfully assigned" to him "substantially within the authorized time and space limits of the university's scheduling."[212] The court dismissed the female professor's assault claim without considering any facts relating to the assault.[213]

While the Texas Supreme Court continues to assume a "general need for the doctrine of sovereign immunity, depicting it "as a doctrine of constitutional dimension and one based on the need to allow governments to perform their necessary functions,"[214] in some recent cases it has become somewhat "guarded" in its "description of the interplay of jurisdiction and sovereign immunity."[215] In *Fort Worth Transportation Authority v. Rodriguez,*[216] the Supreme Court did finally express some concern about the potential and considerable unfairness of the doctrine--stating that while immunity protects the public as a whole, the protection "comes at a cost;" the court acknowledged that "in protecting the public by shielding government funds from the costs of litigation, immunity 'places the burden of shouldering those costs and consequences on injured individuals.'" Further, in *Mariono v. Lenoir,*[217] the court declined to apply §101.106(f) to a malpractice claim against a resident physician. The court ruled that a resident physician who allegedly caused the death of a pregnant patient and her two unborn children was not protected by governmental immunity because the court found she was an employee of a university's foundation, rather than the

211 *Texas Southern University,* 31 F. Supp. 3d 884 (S.D. Tex. 2014).

212 *Id.* at 888.

213 *Id.* at 889.

214 *Engelman Irrigation District v. Shields Brothers, Inc.*, 514 S.W.3d 746, 752 (Tex. 2017).

215 *Id.* (pointing to three of its decisions–*Houston Belt & Terminal Railway Co. v. City of Houston,* 487 S.W.3d 154 (Tex. 2016); *Manbeck v. Austin Independent School District,* 383 S.W.3d 528 (Tex. 2012); and *Rusk State Hospital v. Black,* 392 S.W.3d 88 (Tex. 2012). The court stated in these cases "quite deliberately," that "sovereign immunity 'implicates' the trial court's subject-matter jurisdiction" but does not equate "to a lack of subject-matter jurisdiction for all purposes."

216 *Rodriguez,* 547 S.W.3d 830 (Tex. 2018), quoting *IT-Davy,* 74 S. W. 3d at 853-54.

217 *Lenoir,* 526 S.W.3d 403 (Tex. 2017).

university, and thus was not an employee of a governmental unit.[218] In *Engelman Irrigation District v. Shields Brothers, Inc.*,[219] the court determined that sovereign immunity does not so implicate "subject-matter jurisdiction that it allows collateral attack on a final judgment" and denied the state a declaration that a "decades-old final money judgment" against the state was void. A review of Texas cases importantly illustrates the extent to which courts will protect the government from its misconduct; such a review also points to the need for victims of governmental misconduct to obtain documents and other evidence prior to filing a claim against the government or its employees to avoid an immediate dismissal of the claim.[220]

In summary, the Federal government has absolute immunity from liability for intentional torts of its employees. Further, its employees have absolute immunity for their tortious acts if they were acting within the scope of employment when the acts occurred. Federal employees are no longer required to have been performing a "discretionary" function to have immunity. However, the Supreme

218 *Id.* at 404-405. The court found that powers of the University of Texas System Medical Foundation, a non-profit organization, included the employment of qualified persons to serve as residents or interns on the staff of any hospital owned or operated by the University of Texas System and that the resident physician had been appointed to the university's residency program under a contractual notice of appointment with the Medical Foundation. The court found she was paid by the foundation and that the university did not have the "legal right to control" her under the evidence presented.

Previously, however, in *Klein v, Hernandez*, 315 S.W.3d 1, 7-8 (Tex. 2010), the Texas Supreme Court did treat, as a state employee for the purpose of sovereign immunity, a resident physician of a private medical school, Baylor College of Medicine. The physician worked at a public hospital under an agreement with his private medical school. Underlying litigation in the case arose from the physician's work at the public hospital. The court reasoned in *Klein* "that the Legislature sought to encourage private medical schools to cooperate with public hospitals through clinical education programs for their residents." In giving "effect to this intent," the court concluded "the Legislature intended to treat these private medical schools like other governmental entities at public hospitals, extending the same protection and benefits to Baylor and its residents who work at these hospitals." *Id.* at 8.

219 514 S.W. 3d at 746, 752.

220 The Texas Supreme Court stated in *Texas Dept. of Parks and Wildlife v. Miranda*, 133 S.W.3d 217, 225-26 (Tex.2004): "The trial court must determine at its earliest opportunity whether it has the constitutional or statutory authority to decide the case before allowing the litigation to proceed," citing *Austin & N.W.R. Co. v. Cluck*, 77 S.W.403, 405 (Tex. 1903). The court further stated that "sovereign immunity defeats a trial court's subject matter jurisdiction and thus is properly asserted in a plea to the jurisdiction," quoting Tex. *Dep't of Transp. v. Jones*, 8 S.W.3d 636, 637 (Tex. 1999). If the evidence creates a fact question regarding the jurisdictional issue, then the trial court cannot grant the plea to the jurisdiction, and the fact issue will be resolved by the fact finder. However, if the relevant evidence is undisputed or fails to raise a fact question on the jurisdictional issue, the trial court rules on the plea to the jurisdiction as a matter of law." 133. S.W. 3d at 227-28.

Court has pointed out[221] that in a suit brought against a tribal governmental employee in an individual-capacity action that imposes individual liability upon a government employee, the employee cannot assert sovereign immunity and has ruled that an indemnification statute for governmental employees does not extend sovereign immunity to individual governmental employees. The Court has stated that state employees sued in their personal capacity "come to court as individuals."[222] The case involved a tribal employee but nonetheless a victim of a governmental employee's misconduct should file suit against the employee in the employee's individual, rather than official, capacity. Additionally, Federal employees can possibly be liable for a violation of the Constitution–the *Bivens* action–despite the fact that the Supreme Court disfavors expanding the *Bivens* remedy as discussed in Chapter 2, and for an action under a statute that authorizes recovery against an individual employee as discussed in Chapter 3.

The State of Texas has absolute immunity for tort claims except in three areas: use of publicly owned vehicles or motor-driven equipment, premises defects, and injuries arising out of conditions or use of property. Additionally, Texas governmental employees have absolute immunity if they were acting within the scope of employment when they engage in tortious acts--with the Texas Supreme Court having expanded "scope of employment" to include almost all acts performed pursuant to job responsibilities, even those "that are motivated by ulterior motives or personal animus."[223] A review of sovereign immunity law in Texas becomes relevant as the reader encounters the means by which a state can deprive its citizens of access to the courts through a state's strict application of the sovereign immunity doctrine.

3. Whistleblowers' Acts

In 1989, Congress enacted the federal Whistleblower Protection Act[224] to help eliminate wrongdoing within the federal government. Among other provisions, the Act mandates that federal employees not suffer adverse consequences as a

221 *Lewis v. Clarke*, discussed *supra*, 137 S. Ct. at 1287, and *Hafer v. Melo*, 502 U.S. at 30-31.

222 *Id.* quoting *Hafer*, 502 U.S. at 27.

223 See *Univ. of Texas Health Science Center v. Rios*, 542 S.W.3d at 535, and discussed *supra*.

224 Whistleblower Protection Act of 1989, Pub. L. No. 101-12, §2(b), 103 Stat. 16, 16, codified at 5 U.S.C. §§1201 et seq. ("the purpose of this Act is to strengthen and improve protection for the rights of Federal employees, to prevent reprisals, and to help eliminate wrongdoing within the Government..."

result of disclosing evidences of a violation "of any law, rule or regulation," or "gross mismanagement, a gross waste of funds, [or] an abuse of authority."[225] Later, in 2012, the Whistleblower Protection Enhancement Act[226] was enacted as a comprehensive amendment to several provisions of the Whistleblower Act to clarify "the breadth of disclosures that are afforded protection," to expand "the right to bring reprisal claims for certain protected activities," and to enhance "the remedies available to federal whistleblowers."[227] The Act also expanded judicial review to extend beyond being limited to the Federal Circuit. Claims can now be brought to any court of appeals.[228]

A federal whistleblower complaint is filed with the Office of Special Counsel (OSC), which is the "federal office charged with investigating allegations that an agency has violated the Whistleblower Protection Act by retaliating against its employee for disclosing a 'violation of law, rule, or regulation.'"[229] If the OSC declines to investigate, appeal is to the Merit Systems Protection Board.[230] The Board evaluates a case to determine if the employee established a prima facie case by demonstrating four facts: "(1) the acting official has the authority to take, recommend, or approve any personnel action; (2) the aggrieved employee made a protected disclosure; (3) the acting official used his authority to take, or refuse to take, a personnel action against the aggrieved employee; and (4) the protected disclosure was a contributing factor in the agency's personnel action."[231] The employee bears the burden of proof by a preponderance of the evidence.[232] If the employee establishes a prima facie case, the burden shifts to the agency to show

225 5 U.S.C. §2302(b)(8).

226 Whistleblower Protection Enhancement Act, Pub. L. 112-199, 126 Stat. 1465 (2012) (amending several provisions of the Whistleblower Act).

227 *See Delgado v. Merit Systems Protection Board*, 880 F.3d 913. 927 n. 1 (7th Cir. 2018) (referring to statements from U.S. Gov't Accountability Office (GAO)).

228 5 U.S.C. 7703(b)(1)(B).

229 5 U.S.C. §§1214(a)(1)(A) and 2302(b)(8). An agency cannot terminate an employee for making a protected disclosure. 5 U.S.C. §2302(a).

230 *See* 5 U.S.C. §1214(a)(3). The Board has issued regulations setting out what must be include in an appeal. See 5 C.F.R. §§1209.6(a)(1), 1201.14(a)(1)-(9).

231 *Flynn v. U. S. Securities & Exchange Comm.*, 877 F.3d 200, 204 (4th Cir. 2017) (citing *Chambers v. Dep't of Interior*, 602 F.3d 1370, 1376 (Fed. Cir. 2010) and 5 U.S.C. §2302(b)(8)).

232 *Id.* citing 5 C.F.R. §1209.7(a).

"by clear and convincing evidence" that it would have taken the same personnel action in the absence of the disclosure.[233]

The Court of Appeals for the Fourth Circuit stated:[234] "At its core, whistleblowing involves 'the making of a protected disclosure.'" The court commented that the "law prohibits certain agency actions in response to receiving such disclosures from whistleblowers."[235] Although the Court of Appeals for the Fifth Circuit[236] early recognized that "[t]here is perhaps no subset of 'matters of public concern' more important than bringing official misconduct to light," whistleblower victims nonetheless have had difficulty in finding protection in the Federal Act.[237]

Additionally, some state courts have more strictly applied exceptions to state whistleblower acts than those imposed by federal courts to limit even more the protection of whistleblowers. For example, the Texas Supreme Court has enforced what it has termed the Texas Legislature's "narrower view" regarding internal reporting of violations of law, to preclude any protection for whistleblowers in Texas courts.[238] Decisions of that court, discussed *infra*, point to the Texas Supreme Court, rather than the Texas Legislature, as having both instituted and enforced the "narrower" view of the state's whistleblower law, one

233 *Id.* citing *Chambers*, 601 F.3d at 1376 and 5 C.F.R. §1209.7(b).

234 *Flynn*, 877 F.3d at 203, citing 5 C.F.R. §1209.4(b).

235 *Id.* The Federal law prohibits taking a "personnel action" against an employee because the employee disclosed information that the employee thought evidenced a violation of any law, rule, or regulation or gross mismanagement, a gross waste of funds, an abuse of authority, or a substantial and specific danger to public health or safety."

236 *Davis v. Ector County, Texas*, 40 F.3d 777, 782 (5th Cir. 1995) (citing *Thompson v. City of Starkville*, 902 F.2d 456, 463 (5th Cir. 1990)).

237 In *Delgado*, 880 F.3d at 927 n. 1, the Court of Appeals for the Seventh Circuit pointed out that the Government Accounting Office had found that, despite "enhanced protections implemented by the Whistleblower Protection Enhancement Act of 2012, the Merit Systems Protection Board adjudicated on the merits only fifteen percent of whistleblower appeals during the three years after passage" of the expansion amendment. *Id.* As that court noted, the GAO report did show that "roughly one third of appeals were either withdrawn or settled," but also that data showed "that the Board consistently dismissed more than half of all contested appeals without a hearing." *Id.* In expressing concern about some of claimant's problems, the Seventh Circuit criticized "the Board's stringent application of the Whistleblower Protection Act's exhaustion requirement" stating that its requirement "can effectively prevent all but the savviest federal whistleblowers from receiving a hearing on the merits." *Delgado*, 880 F.3d at 924-25. The Seventh Circuit ruled that "a claimant is not required to submit evidence or to include every detail that might be necessary to prove at trial."

238 *See Univ. of Texas Southwestern Mecical Center v. Gentilello*, 398 S.W.3d 680 (Tex. 2013), but also a somewhat less narrow focus in *McMillen v. Tex. Health & Human Services Comm'n*, 485 S.W.3d 427 (Tex. 2016), both decisions discussed *infra*.

that runs counter to the Texas Legislature's purpose in seeking to protect those who "bring official misconduct to light."[239]

Rulings of the Texas Supreme Court that demonstrate that court's "narrower" view of the state's whistleblower act are reviewed in this discussion to emphasize again the harsh and unfair impact a strict application of sovereign immunity principles inflicts on victims of improvident governmental conduct when a court will not protect those who bring governmental misconduct to light. Unfortunately, the Texas Supreme Court has refused to protect governmental employees who report governmental wrongdoing through a curiously unshakable goal to ensure the state's absolute sovereign immunity.

In 1993, the Texas legislature enacted the Texas Whistleblowers Act,[240] which prohibits a governmental entity from retaliating against "a public employee who in good faith reports a violation of law by the employing governmental entity or another public employee to an appropriate law enforcement authority."[241] In *Texas Department of Assistive and Rehabilitative Services v. Howard,*[242] the Third Court of Appeals stated the Texas Whistleblowers' Act "is designed to enhance openness in government and compel the State's compliance with law by protecting those who inform authorities of wrongdoing."[243] The court viewed "whistleblowing by a public employee as a courageous act of loyalty to a larger community"[244] and further stressed that, because "the Act is remedial in nature," the Act "should be liberally construed to effect its purpose."[245] Nevertheless, the Texas Supreme Court has reversed judgments of several Texas courts of appeal wherein the courts of appeal, in liberally construing the Act, had denied the state's plea to the jurisdiction.[246] Overall, the Texas Supreme Court has appeared

---

239 *Davis,* 40 F.3d at 782.

240 Act of May 4, 1993, 73d Leg., R.S., ch. 268, §1, 1993 Tex. Gen. Laws 583, 609-11, codified as amended at Tex. Gov't Code §§554.002-.010.

241 Tex. Gov't Code §554.002(a). See *Serna v. City of San Antonio,* 244 F.3d 479, 482 (5th Cir. 2001).

242 *Howard,* 182 S. W.3d 393 (Tex. App.–Austin 2005, pet. denied),

243 *Id.* at 399 (citing *City of New Braunfels v. Allen,* 132 S.W.3d 157, 161 (Tex. App.–Austin 2004, no pet.)

244 *Id.* at 396. The Third Court of Appeals also commented that "[t]he State of Texas elevates public employees who report legal wrongdoing to a protected status as a matter of fundamental policy." *Id.*

245 *Id.* at 399, citing *Hill v. Burnet County Sheriff's Dep't,* 96 S.W.3d 436, 440 (Tex. App.– Austin 2002, pet. denied) and *Allen,* 132 S.W.3d at 161.

246 See, e. g., *Univ. of Tex. Sw. Med. Ctr. at Dallas v. Gentilello,* 260 S.W.3d 221, 224 (Tex. App.–Dallas 2008) (recounting how the plaintiff, a tenured professor of medicine, was stripped of faculty chair positions after internally reporting what he believed were violations of federal regulations), *rev'd,*

unconcerned that whistleblowers not only risk the loss of their jobs and reputations when they come forward with reports of governmental wrongdoing but also has ignored the fact that whistleblowers' reports often provide the only means to bring official misconduct to light.[247] Another problem for whistleblower litigants is the burden of paying for their attorneys while the State enjoys a substantial advantage of being represented without charge by the Texas Office of the Attorney General.[248]

In *State v. Lueck*,[249] the Texas Supreme Court imposed a "jurisdictional hurdle" that despite language in the Whistleblowers Act has erected a significant immunity bar in a whistleblower case.[250] In *Lueck*, the Texas Supreme Court reversed

---

300 S.W.3d 753 (Tex. 2009); *see also Tex. Dep't of Human Servs. v. Okoli*, 263 S.W.3d 275, 277 (Tex. App.–Houston [lst Dist.] 2007) (describing how the plaintiff, a former state employee, had his employment terminated after reporting alleged illegal activity to two supervisors and a manager), *rev'd sub. nom. Tex. Dep't of Health & Human Servs. v. Okoli*, 295 S.W. 3d 667 (Tex. 2009).

247 *Id.*

248 See Tex. Civ. Prac. & Rem. Code §§104.001-.002, .004 (requiring the attorney general to defend state officials for damages resulting from acts or omissions made within the course and scope of employment). Although the public funds the Office of the Attorney General, its services are provided to governmental officials without charge. See *id.*§104.007 ("Only funds appropriated from the General Revenue Fund to the attorney general may be used to conduct the defense...."). Further, through the use of dilatory tactics and interlocutory appeals available to the government, but not private litigants, the State can delay proceedings against it for years. See *id.* §51.014(a)(5) (providing for an interlocutory appeal of a denial of a summary judgment motion "based on an assertion of immunity by an individual who is an officer or employee of the state or a political subdivision of the state"); *id.* §51.014(a)(8) (providing for an interlocutory appeal of a grant or denial of "a plea to the jurisdiction by a governmental unit"). As a result, private litigants must incur substantial costs, including necessary attorney fees, in their attempts to challenge governmental misconduct while the State of Texas pays all costs for the governmental tortfeasor.

Even if victims of governmental misconduct can afford legal representation, they may be faced with a court granting governmental attorneys immunity even for egregious procedural misconduct. In *OAG v. Weatherspoon*, 435 S.W.3d 844 (Tex. App. –Dallas 2014) and 472 S.W.3d 280 (Tex. 2015), discussed *infra*, the facts show that the Texas Office of Attorney General terminated an assistant attorney when she refused to sign a false affidavit to report false interactions about a judge with whom that office did not agree. The Texas Supreme Court dismissed the whistleblower case she filed after that office terminated her in retaliation for refusing to sign the affidavit she stated "constituted subornation of perjury." 435 S.W.3d at 847.

249 *Lueck*, 290 S.W.3d 876 (Tex. 2009).

250 *Id.* at 884. In confusing language in *Lueck*, the Texas Supreme Court interpreted the first sentence of the whistleblower act to mean that the Act waives sovereign immunity from suit, but decided the second sentence of Tex. Gov't Code §554.0035 "simply limits judgments against the State to "the extent of liability for the relief allowed under [the Act] for a violation of [the Act]" and that the "second sentence not only waives immunity from liability, but confines the scope of the State's consent to suit that was established in the first sentence." 290 S.W.3d at 882. The court concluded that, "like the Texas Tort Claims Act, the Whistleblower Act imposes a limited waiver of immunity that allows consideration of the section 554.002(a) elements, to the extent necessary in determining whether the claim falls within the jurisdictional confines of section 554.0035." *Id.* The court held that the Whistleblower Act, like the Texas Tort Claims Act, creates a statutory scheme in which the dual

the Third Court of Appeals, which had affirmed a district court's dismissal of the State's plea to the jurisdiction in a suit against the State under the Texas Whistleblowers' Act.[251] The Texas Supreme Court ruled as a matter of law that Lueck, a public employee, did not allege a violation of the Texas Whistleblowers' Act and dismissed his case for lack of subject-matter jurisdiction.[252] Although Lueck had attached to his petition a copy of an e-mail report he sent to his supervisor warning of regulatory non-compliance by a state agency, the court reasoned that the e-mail did not report "a violation of law...within the meaning of the Whitleblower Act."[253] In addition, the court determined that an agency supervisor "is not an appropriate law enforcement authority to whom a report should be made."[254] For these two reasons, the court held that "Lueck's allegation affirmatively negate[d] the court's subject-matter jurisdiction over the cause."[255]

In *Lueck*, the court referred to the general principle that "clear and unambiguous language" is necessary to waive sovereign immunity[256] and ruled[257] that, for a waiver of immunity from suit, the language in Texas Government Code §554.0035--the Texas Whistleblowers Act--requires a plaintiff not only to allege a violation of the Act but also to provide a trial court with facts supporting the elements of §554.002(a) immediately upon filing a complaint.[258] Lueck contended that "section 554.002(a) contains non-jurisdictional elements that speak to the underlying merits of the claim and, therefore, [could not] be considered

immunity system in Texas is co-extensive. Thus, the Texas Supreme court concluded in *Lueck* that "it necessarily follows" from language of §554.0035 that a plaintiff "must actually allege a violation of the Act for there to be a waiver from suit." It ruled that the elements of §554.002(a) "can be considered as jurisdictional facts when it is necessary to resolve whether a plaintiff has alleged a violation under the Act." *Id.* at 881.

251 290 S.W.3d at 878-80.

252 *Id.* at 886.

253 *Id.* at 885.

254 *Id.*

255 *Id.* at 878.

256 *Lueck*, 290 S.W.3d at 880 (quoting Tex. Gov't Code §311.034) (noting that state agencies "are immune from suit and liability in Texas unless the Legislature expressly waives sovereign immunity").

257 *Id.* at 881.

258 Section 554.002(a) provides that a "governmental entity may not... take [any] adverse personnel action against a public employee who in good faith reports a violation of law by the employing governmental unit or another public employee to an appropriate law enforcement authority."

when determining jurisdiction."[259] However, the Supreme Court reasoned that, because §554.0035 directs the immunity inquiry to §554.002(a),[260] holding those elements as jurisdictional facts was consistent with the principle that mere reference to the Act "does not establish the state's consent to be sued and thus is not enough to confer jurisdiction on the trial court."[261] In sum, the court announced that a public employee must be able initially to show that the employee reported a violation of law to an "appropriate law enforcement authority" to even file a whistleblower suit against the State and, if the plaintiff's pleadings "affirmatively negate the existence of those jurisdictional facts, the court must dismiss without an opportunity for a plaintiff to amend.[262]

In *Lueck*, the Texas Supreme Court referred to the Texas Tort Claims Act,[263] which the Court contends created a "unique statutory scheme" in which "two immunities are co-extensive."[264] As noted *supra*, when addressing the question of sovereign immunity in Texas, courts look at "not only whether the State has consented to suit, but whether the State has accepted liability."[265] To file

259 *Id.*

260 *Id.* at 882.

261 *Id.* at 881-82 (quoting *Tex. Dep't of Criminal Justice v. Miller*, 51 S.W.3d 583, 587 (Tex. 2001).

262 *Lueck*, 290 S.W.3d at 884-86 (dismissing the case for lack of subject-matter jurisdiction because "Luecks's pleadings affirmatively demonstrate[d] that he did not allege a violation under the Whistleblower Act"); see also *Tex. Dep't of Parks & Wildlife v. Miranda*, 133 S.W.3d at 227 ("If the pleadings affirmatively negate the existence of jurisdiction, then a plea to the jurisdiction may be granted without allowing the plaintiff an opportunity to amend.").

263 Tex. Civ. Prac. & Rem. Code, Ch.101. See discussion of Texas Tort Claims Act *supra.*

264 *Lueck*, 290 S.W. 3d at 881. See Tex. Civ. Prac. & Rem. Code § 101.025.

Under a "two immunity scheme," immunity from suit is a jurisdictional question of whether the State has expressly consented to suit while immunity from liability determines whether the State has accepted liability even after it has consented to suit. The Texas Supreme Court considered the "two immunity scheme" in a suit against the State pursuant to the Texas Whistleblowers' Act. *Lueck*, 290 S.W.3d at 880-2. See *Wichita Falls State Hosp. v. Taylor*, 106 S.W.3d at 696-7 and *Tex. Dep't of Parks & Wildlife v. Miranda*, 133 S.W.3d at 224. The court ruled that Lueck did not allege a violation of the Whistleblower Act because his supervisor was not "an appropriate law enforcement authority." *Id.* at 885-86.

265 *Wichita Falls Sate Hosp. v. Taylor*, 106 S.W.3d 692, 696 (Tex. 2003). Under this two-immunity scheme, immunity from suit is a jurisdictional question of whether the State has expressly consented to suit, while immunity from liability asks whether the State has accepted liability even after it has consented to suit. *Id.* In *Lueck*, the state agency argued that the substantively identical language in the Texas Tort Claims Act was dispositive of the jurisdictional requirements for waiving immunity under the Texas Whistleblower Act. 290 S.W.3d at 882; *see also Miranda*, 133 S.W.3d at 224 (opining that the Texas Tort Claims Act "creates a unique statutory scheme in which the two immunities are co-extensive'). Although the Texas Supreme Court declined to permit the Texas Tort Claims Act to control the analysis, noting that it considers immunity statutes standing alone, it nevertheless implicitly determined that a co-extensive immunity scheme applies to a suit against the State under

a sustainable action under the Texas Whistleblowers' Act, the Texas Supreme Court requires that a claimant not only allege status as a public employee and a violation of the Act, but also demonstrate a good-faith report of a violation of law to an appropriate law enforcement authority and facts to verify that report.[266] Thus, alleging facts to support these prerequisites is necessary to show the trial court the Legislature has in fact consented to the plaintiff's particular cause of action before the plaintiff can produce through discovery evidence to prove retaliation.[267] If any of these required allegations are insufficient to demonstrate jurisdiction affirmatively, the Supreme Court takes the position that the plaintiff's pleadings fail to show the Legislature has waived immunity from suit.[268] The Texas Supreme Court dismissed the plaintiff's case in *Lueck*, because, according to the court, the plaintiff did not allege the required jurisdictional facts, i.e., reporting "a violation of the law" to "an appropriate law enforcement authority."[269] Still, the Supreme Court stated that its ruling in *Lueck* was limited--that it did not mean a whistleblower plaintiff "must prove his claim in order to satisfy the jurisdictional hurdle."[270] Lueck, as well as others who read that court's decision setting out its requirements to file a sustainable whistleblowers complaint, might disagree.

---

the Texas Whistleblower Act. See *Lueck*, 290 S.W.3d at 882-83 (holding "that the elements of section 554.002(a) can be considered to determine both jurisdiction and liability").

266 *Lueck*, 290 S.W.3d at 882.

267 *Id.* See also *Miranda*, 133 S.W.3d at 227. Further, the Texas Supreme Court will dismiss the plaintiff's cause of action without permitting the plaintiff an opportunity to amend. *Lueck*, 290 S.W.3d at 882-3.

268 The Court in *Lueck* reversed the court of appeals' judgment and dismissed the plaintiff's cause for lack of subject-matter jurisdiction because the Court decided the plaintiff's allegation that the Department failed to remedy non-compliance with federal and state reporting requirements did not "equate to a violation of law." 290 S.W.3d at 882, 885-6. It further decided that as a matter of law the email report to his supervisor, which the plaintiff attached to his pleadings, was not a report to an appropriate law enforcement authority. (Both the trial court and the court of appeals had dismissed TxDOT's plea to the jurisdiction reasoning that the plaintiff's pleadings "affirmatively demonstrate the district court's jurisdiction to hear the case." *Id.* at 880.)

269 *Lueck*, 290 S.W. 3d. at 881, 886.

270 *Id.* at 884. The Court in *Lueck* quoted *Miranda*, 133 S.W.3d at 227, regarding a requirement that a trial court consider evidence prior to ruling on the state's plea to the jurisdiction: "When the consideration of a trial court's subject matter jurisdiction requires the examination of evidence, the trial court exercises its discretion in deciding whether the jurisdictional determination should be made at a preliminary hearing or await a fuller development of the case." Accordingly, the court's ruling in *Lueck* should caution a litigant bringing suit under the Texas Whistleblower Act to draft a petition carefully, making certain it meets the jurisdictional challenge, and to request the trial court to defer ruling on the State's plea to the jurisdiction until the Plaintiff can develop the case more fully.

The jurisdictional hurdle pronounced in *Lueck* presents concerns that the Texas Supreme Court has circumvented the Texas Legislature's clear intent to protect a whistleblower from retaliatory actions of governmental officials in instances when a whistleblower reports illegal governmental actions. Moreover, the Texas Supreme Court's strict adherence to the sovereign immunity doctrine poses a question whether that court has effectively abandoned its reasoning in *Nueces County v. San Patricio County*,[271] wherein it emphasized "the Legislature is better suited to make the distinctions, exceptions, and limitations that different situations require."[272]

In *Texas Department of Transportation v. Garcia*,[273] the public-employee plaintiff contended a co-worker directed him to use property belonging to the Texas Department Public Safety (TxDOT) "to 'do private work' during state work hours."[274] The plaintiff claimed that he "refused to perform the requested acts and reported the co-worker's actions to 'enforcement authorities within the Texas Department of Transportation, but no action was taken.'"[275] The plaintiff also "alleged that on another occasion he saw a TxDOT employee 'drinking on the job and driving a company vehicle.'"[276] He also reported that incident; "again no action was taken."[277] The plaintiff finally resigned "out of despair," and thereafter sued TxDOT under the Texas Whistleblowers Act.[278] The Thirteenth Court of

271 *Nueces*, 246 S.W.3d 651(Tex. 2008).

272 *Id.* at 653 (quoting *City of Galveston v. State*, 217 S.W.3d 466, 469 (Tex. 2007). Moreover, it seems questionable whether the *Lueck* holding is consistent with *Hernandez v. Ehrom*, 289 S.W.3d 316, 318 (Tex. 2009), in which the Texas Supreme Court acknowledged that it does not give effect to words in a statute if the "context necessarily requires a different construction." An additional query is how the Texas Supreme Court will apply the Lueck approach in conjunction with the principle that pleadings must be construed liberally in favor of the plaintiff. *See Miranda*, 133 S.W.3d at 226-7 (citing *Tex. Ass'n of Bus. v. Tex. Air Control Bd.*, 852 S.W.2d 440, 446 (Tex. 1993) (stating that courts, in plea to the jurisdiction challenges, "construe the pleadings liberally in favor of the plaintiff and looks to the pleader's intent.")

273 *Garcia*, 243 S.W.3d 759 (Tex. Civ. App.–Corpus Christi, 2007), *rev'd*, 293 S.W.3d 195 (Tex. 2009).

274 *Id.* at 760.

275 *Id.*

276 *Id.* at 760-61.

277 *Id.* at 761.

278 *Id.* at 761. The State's attorneys filed a plea to the jurisdiction, contending the plaintiff "failed to invoke the [Whistleblower] Act because the record [did] not reflect evidence" that the employee had alleged a violation of the law. *Id.* at 761-2. The state's attorneys also asserted the plaintiff failed to plead and "show as a matter of law" that he reported to "an appropriate law enforcement authority," *id.* at 761-62, citing Tex. Gov't Code §554.002(a). The State's attorneys contended a public employee

Appeals looked to the Act as the source of jurisdictional requirements for the case.[279] The court determined the Act makes the only jurisdictional prerequisites to maintaining a suit the plaintiff's status as a public employee "and the sufficiency of the whistleblower's allegations;" it ruled those prerequisites were met.[280] However, the Texas Supreme Court reversed the Thirteenth Court of Appeals, applying the holding in *Lueck* that "the elements of section 554.002(a) can be considered to determine both jurisdiction and liability."[281] Upon remand, the court of appeals held that, under the reasoning in *Lueck*, the plaintiff's reports to TxDOT were not a report of violations of law to enforcement authorities.[282]

"must allege specific facts relating to the merits of the claim." *Id.* The court of appeals disagreed with the state's attorneys and affirmed the district court's denial of the state's plea to the jurisdiction. *Id.* at 760. The court of appeals adopted the reasoning in *Texas Bd. of Pardons & Paroles v. Feinblatt*, 82 S.W.3d 513 (Tex. App.–Austin 2001) that "an element of a plaintiff's cause of action does not affect the trial court's subject matter jurisdiction; rather, it affects the merits of the cause of action." *Garcia*, 243 S.W. 3d at 762-63, *rev'd* 293 S.W.3d 195 (Tex. 2009).

279 *Garcia*, 243 S.W.3d at 763.

280 *Id.* Under the Whistleblower Act, § 554.002(a), a state or local governmental entity may not suspend or terminate employment of, or take other adverse personnel action against, a public employee who in good faith reports a violation of law by the employing governmental entity or another public employee to an appropriate law enforcement authority." The Act further provides, §554.002(b), that "a report is made to an appropriate law enforcement authority if the authority is a part of a state or local governmental entity or of the federal government that the employee in good faith believes is authorized to: (1) regulate under or enforce the law alleged to be violated in the report, or (2) investigate or prosecute a violation of criminal law."

281 *Garcia*, 293 S.W.3d at 196 (quoting *State v. Lueck*, 290 S.W. 3d 876, 883 (Tex. 2009)). Similarly, in *University of Houston v. Barth*, 313 S.W.3d 817 (Tex. 2010), the Supreme Court reversed and remanded a decision of the First Court of Appeals, ruling that the question--whether a professor's reports to state university officials of his dean's contracting and accounting irregularities were "good-faith reports of a violation of law to an appropriate law-enforcement authority"–was jurisdictional and could be raised for the first time on appeal. At trial, the jury found that the university did retaliate against the tenured professor plaintiff for reporting the dean's alleged financial malfeasance and awarded the professor damages. *Id.* On appeal, the university argued that "the verdict was not supported by legally sufficient evidence that Barth made a good-faith reports to an appropriate law-enforcement authority." *Id.* The court of appeals held that the university "had waived its legal sufficiency challenge" to some of the elements of the professor's whistleblower claims. *Id.* In reversing the court of appeals, the Texas Supreme Court ruled that the question of whether the professor had made "good-faith reports of a violation of law to an appropriate law-enforcement authority is a jurisdictional question...and may not be waived by the parties." *Barth*, 313 S.W.3d at 818. The court then remanded the case to the court of appeals "to determine, under the analysis set forth in *Lueck*, Barth's claims [met] the Whistleblower Act's jurisdictional requirements for suit against a governmental entity and, thus, whether the trial court had jurisdiction over Barth's suit." *Id.*

282 *Tex. Dep't of Trans. v. Garcia*, 2010 WL 2543899 (Tex. Civ. App.–Corpus Christi 2010). The Thirteen Court of Appeals decided TxDOT was not an "appropriate law enforcement authority" for purposes of reporting a "violation of the law." *Id.* The court referred to *Tex. Dep't of Trans. v. Needham*, 82 S.W.2d 3d 314, 317 (Tex. 2002) wherein the Supreme Court held an employer's power to conduct internal investigations or disciplinary practices would not satisfy the 'appropriate law enforcement

In *University of Texas Southwestern Medical Center at Dallas v. Gentilello*,[283] a professor sued the University of Texas Southwestern Medical Center under the Texas Whistleblower Act, alleging he was demoted and stripped of two faculty chair positions for reporting violations of Medicare and Medicaid regulations to his supervisor. The Medical Center filed a plea to the jurisdiction asserting his claims were barred by governmental immunity because he failed to allege a violation under the Whistleblower Act.[284] The trial court denied the plea to the jurisdiction and the appellate court affirmed.[285] The Supreme Court reversed and remanded, directing the lower court "to determine whether under the analysis set forth in *Lueck*" the plaintiff had alleged a violation under the Act.[286] The Supreme Court ruled that "whether the reporting of violations of Medicare and Medicaid regulations to a supervisor is a good faith report of a violation of law to an appropriate law-enforcement authority is a jurisdictional question."[287]

However, on remand, the Fifth Court of Appeals decided that a fact-finder could determine the plaintiff "had a good faith belief that he reported to an appropriate law enforcement authority."[288] The Fifth Court of Appeals determined that a fact issue existed on whether the plaintiff had a good faith belief that he reported to an "appropriate law enforcement authority" when the plaintiff reported violations of Medicare and Medicaid rules and regulations to the person at the Medical Center who set policies regarding the presence of attending physicians and who had the power to investigate internal Medicare and Medicaid violations.[289] In contrast, the Medical Center took the position the plaintiff must plead specifically that the physician to whom he reported "had been delegated 'federal enforcement authority' by the Medicare and Medicaid statutes and regulations" or that the physician "had some sort of criminal

authority' standards under the Act. The Thirteenth Court noted that in *Needham*, the Texas Supreme Court ruled "TxDOT is not considered an 'appropriate law enforcement authority.'" *Id.* (citing *Needham*, 82 S.W.3d at 320).

283 *Gentilello*, 300 S.W.3d 753, 754 (Tex. 2009).

284 *Id.*

285 *Id.*

286 *Id.*

287 *Id.*

288 *Univ. of Texas Southwestern Medical Center at Dallas v. Gentilello*, 317 S. W.3d 865, 867 (Tex. Civ. App.–Dallas 2010).

289 *Id.* at 867-71. After the plaintiff reported the violations, "he alleged he was demoted because of his good faith report." *Id.* at 868.

jurisdiction."[290] According to the Medical Center, "unless the employing agency is itself a law enforcement agency, a supervisor can never be an appropriate law enforcement authority as a matter of law."[291] The Fifth Court disagreed and ruled that "a plaintiff can reasonably believe a report to an appropriate law enforcement authority may be made internally."[292]

The Texas Supreme Court again granted the Medical Center's petition for review in *Gentilello* II and reversed the Fifth Court, ruling that the surgery professor's report to his supervisor was not protected by the Texas Whistleblowers Act.[293] The Supreme Court stated: "Federal and other state whistleblower laws explicitly protect purely internal reports to supervisors; Texas law does not."[294] The court ruled that, "by its text and structure," the Texas act "restricts the term 'law enforcement authority.'"[295]

In denying whistleblower victims' relief, the Texas Supreme Court has placed its strict interpretations of the Texas Whistleblower Act on the Texas Legislature, stating: "This is a legislatively-mandated legal classification, one tightly drawn, and we cannot judicially loosen it."[296] Unfortunately, rather than "loosening" the legislature's classification, the Supreme Court has "tightened" it. Dissenting justices actually characterized the majority court's strict interpretation of the Act's requirements that a victim make a "good faith" report to an "appropriate law-enforcement authority" as having eliminated any "good faith standards."[297]

The Supreme Court commented that it has had "three occasions to...protect internal reports to workplace supervisors" but "all three times has declined to do so."[298] The first of these "three occasions" was the court's interpretation of good

290 *Id.* at 867.

291 *Id.*

292 *Id.* at 869.

293 *Gentilello II,* 398 S.W.3d 680, 687 (Tex. 2013).

294 *Id.* at 689.

295 *Id.*

296 *Id.*

297 *Tex. Dep't Health & Human Services v. Okoli,* 440 .W.3d 611, 618 (Devine, J., joined by Willett, J. and Lehrmann, J.).

298 *Id.* at 683. The three decisions were rendered in 2002, 2009, and 2010 in *Texas Department of Transportation v. Needham,* 82 S.W.3d 214 (Tex. 2002); *State v. Lueck,* 290 S.W.3d 876 (Tex. 2009); and *City of Elsa v. Gonzales,* 325 S.W.3d 622 (Tex. 2010).

faith in 2002 in *Texas Dept. of Transportation v. Needham.*[299] In *Needham*, the Texas Supreme Court defined "good faith" to mean "(l) the employee believed the governmental entity was authorized to (a) regulate under or enforce the law alleged to be violated in the report, or (b) investigate or prosecute a violation of criminal law; and (2) the employee's belief was reasonable in light of the employee's training and experience."[300] In *State v. Lueck*,[301] the Texas Supreme Court took the position that "when the facts underlying the merits and subject-matter jurisdiction are intertwined, the State may assert sovereign immunity from suit by a plea to the jurisdiction, even when the trial court must consider evidence 'necessary to resolve the jurisdiction issues raised.'"[302] *In City of Elsa v. Gonzalez*,[303] the Texas Supreme Court stated that whether a court has subject matter jurisdiction under the Whistleblower Act is a question of law that a court reviews *de novo*.[304] The court again held that if the relevant evidence is undis-

299 *Needham*, 82 S.W.3d at 321.

300 *Id.* at 321. In *Texas Department of Assistive and Rehabilitative Services v. Howard*, 182 S.W.3d 393, 401 (Tex.App.–Austin 2005), the Third Court of Appeals discussed the "first prong" of the good faith test as a consideration of an "employee's subjective belief: whether the employee honestly believed the conduct reported was a violation of law." In contrast, the court noted, that "[t]he second prong is objective because it measures the employee's belief against that of a reasonably prudent employee in similar circumstances." *Id.* The court further clarified that "[a] report of an alleged violation of law may be in good faith even though incorrect." *Id.* The Third Court of Appeals appeared to follow Texas Supreme Court precedent. *See Wichita County, Tex. v. Hart*, 917 S.W.3d 779, 784-5 (Tex. 1996) (adopting the two-prong definition of "good faith" to include objective and subjective elements).

301 *State v. Lueck*, 290 S.W.3d at 880 (quoting *Bland Indep. Sch. Dist. v. Blue*, 34 S.W.3d 47, 555 (Tex. 2000).

302 *Id.* at 884 (requiring the plaintiff's pleadings to prove affirmatively the jurisdictional facts of Tex. Gov't Code §554.002(2) when the opposing party challenges the jurisdiction of the plea). In fact, a court may deny a plaintiff the chance to amend the pleading if the original plea effectively negates jurisdiction even with supporting evidence. See *id.* at 880 (dismissing the case for lack of subject-matter jurisdiction because the original plea affirmatively negated jurisdiction by stating specific assertions contrary to the required elements under the Texas Whistleblower Act).

Because the State can immediately file a plea to the jurisdiction and, if denied, subsequently file an interlocutory appeal before the plaintiff may have sufficient evidence, the result may often preclude any fair consideration whatsoever of the plaintiff's claim, much less his or her good faith. Consequently, under the analysis in *Lueck*, whistleblower plaintiffs potentially face a major problem with satisfying the elements of § 554.002(a) of the Whistleblowers' Act based solely on their pleadings. Indeed, given the Texas Supreme Court's view of a limited waiver of immunity in the Texas Whistleblowers Act, if a plaintiff cannot persuade a trial court to delay ruling on the plea to the jurisdiction until the plaintiff has had the opportunity to discover the necessary evidence to prove the plaintiff's claim, the plaintiff may be required "to prove up his case before the court assume[s] jurisdiction." Lueck, 290 S.W.3d at 881, 884 (implying that a whistleblower plaintiff must present sufficient evidence, in addition to the allegations in the pleadings, to establish the court's subject-matter jurisdiction under the Texas Whistleblower Act).

303 *City of Elsa*, 325 S.W. 3d at 625.

304 *Id.* (citing *Tex. Dep't. of Parks & Wildlife v. Miranda*, 133 S.W.3d 217, 226 (Tex. 2004).

puted or fails to raise a fact question on the jurisdictional issue, a trial court must rule on the plea to the jurisdiction as a matter of law.[305]

In *Galveston Independent School District v. Jaco*,[306] the Supreme Court again reversed lower court decisions that had provided redress for a whistleblower plaintiff, remanding the case with directions for the court of appeals to follow the approach in *Lueck* that §554.002(a) of the Texas Whistleblowers' Act is jurisdictional.[307] The Texas Supreme Court held that, in deciding whether a school district's immunity under the Texas Whistleblower Act is waived, the trial court was required to determine whether an athletic director's reporting of a high school football player's violations of league rules and regulations to an interscholastic league was "a good-faith report of a violation of law to an appropriate law-enforcement authority."[308]

In *Tex. Dep't. Health & Human Services v. Okoli*,[309] the First Court of Appeals determined the Whistleblower Act "makes the only jurisdictional prerequisites to maintaining a whistleblower suit, the plaintiff's status as a public employee and the sufficiency of his whistleblower allegations."[310] The court decided the question of whether the plaintiff "actually reported to an appropriate law enforcement authority, or whether he had a good-faith belief" that the entity to which he reported was such an authority, were each an element of his whistleblower claim and could not be a jurisdictional prerequisite to suit.[311] The Supreme Court reversed, explaining that, under the reasoning in *Lueck*, the element of whether the plaintiff in that case made "a good faith report of a violation of law to an appropriate law enforcement authority is a jurisdictional question."[312]

The plaintiff in *Okoli* had reported internal falsification of dates and documents to supervisors and a manager in the Texas Department of Human Services

---

305 *Id.* at 626 (citing *Miranda*, 133 S.W.3d at 228.)

306 *Jaco*, 303 S.W.3d 699 (Tex 2010).

307 *Id.* at 699-700. Prior to the reversal, the court of appeals had held that elements of §554.002 of the Texas Whistleblowers Act are not jurisdictional. *Galveston Indep. Sch. Dist. v. Jaco*, 278 S.W.3d 477, 482-83 (Tex. App.–Houston [14th Dist.] 2009, *rev'd* 303 S.W.3d 699 (Tex. 2010).

308 *Id.* at 699-700. The Supreme Court remanded the case for a determination of whether the plaintiff alleged a violation of the Whistleblower Act. *Id.* at 700.

309 *Okoli*, 263 S.W.3d 275 (Tex. App.–Houston [1st Dist.] 2007), *rev'd*, 295 S.W.3d 667 (Tex. 2009).

310 *Id.* at 282, citing *State v. Lueck*, 212 S.W.3d at 636.

311 *Id.*, citing *Lueck*, 212 S.W.3d at 637-38.

312 *Tex. Dep't of Health & Human Servs. v. Okoli*, 295 S.W.3d 667, 668 (Tex. 2009).

(TDHS).[313] On remand, the First Court of Appeals held that the plaintiff had made a report to "an appropriate law enforcement within TDHS."[314] The plaintiff argued that his report to TDHS was to an appropriate law enforcement authority because the Department of Human Services was the governmental entity authorized to regulate under and enforce the subject law.[315] The plaintiff further asserted that he, in good faith, believed that his supervisors "were authorized to regulate and enforce" the subject law "because his work rules required employees to make reports of fraudulent conduct to their supervisors."[316] In addition, he contended "that TDHS was authorized to "refer and fund district attorney's special welfare fraud units for prosecution."[317] The First Court of Appeals noted that the Whistleblower Act was "designed to enhance openness in government and to compel the government's compliance with law by protecting those who inform authorities of wrongdoing"and that because the Act is remedial in nature, the court would "construe its provisions liberally."[318] Referring to the fact that the plaintiff "was instructed by TDHS to report the criminal conduct at issue in this case 'up his chain of command,'" the court reasoned the governmental entity and supervisors were appropriate law enforcement authorities authorized to investigate the alleged criminal conduct.[319] As an alternative basis for the plaintiff to move forward with the suit, the court also held that he "had a good faith belief" he was "reporting the alleged criminal conduct to appropriate law enforcement authorities."[320] Thus the court decided that "under the plain language of the Whistleblower Act," the plaintiff was "entitled to the Act's

313 *Okoli*, 263 S.W.3d at 277.

314 *Okoki*, 317 S.W.3d 800, 809-10 (Tex. Civ. App.–Houston [1st Dist.] 2010).

315 *Id.*

316 *Id.* at 804.

317 *Id.*

318 *Id.* at 805 n.10 (citing *City of Houston v. Levingston*, 221 S.W.3d 204, 219 (Tex. App.–Houston [1st Dist.] 2006, no pet.); *Tex. Dep't of Criminal Justice v. McElyea*, 239 S.W.3d 842, 849 (Tex. App.–Austin 2007), pet. denied)).

319 *Okoli*, 317 S.W.3d at 808-09. The Uniform Law Commission states, within the Uniform Electronic Recordation of Custodial Interrogations Act, that: "'Law enforcement agency' means a governmental entity or *person authorized by a governmental entity* or by state law to enforce criminal laws or investigate suspected criminal activity. The term includes a *nongovernmental entity* that has been delegated the authority to enforce criminal laws or investigate suspected criminal activity." Unif. Elec. Recordation of Custodial Interrogations Act §2(3) (2010) (Emphasis added.)

320 *Okoli*, 317 S.W. 3d at 809-10.

protection for whistleblowing about the alleged unlawful conduct to those in his chain of command."[321]

However, in its 2014 opinion in *Tex. Dep't of Health & Human Servs. v. Okoli*,[322] and its second review of the First Court of Appeals, the Texas Supreme Court dismissed the court of appeals' determination to provide the plaintiff with the protection set out in the Texas Whistleblower Act.[323] In *Okoli* II, the Supreme Court refused anew "to remove the objective element and protect internal reports to workplace supervisors,"[324] requiring again that to be protected by the Texas Whistleblower Act, "a plaintiff's belief that he or she reported a violation of the law to an appropriate law enforcement agency, no matter how sincere, must not only be made in good faith, but must be 'objectively reasonable' as well."[325] The dissent disagreed, stating that the court's opinion "parses the whistleblower statute so finely as to eliminate any good-faith standards," and concluded that "statutory good faith has no meaning under the Court's writing."[326] The dissent stated: "In *Gentilello*, we left open the door that good faith might bridge the gap between internal agency reports and reports to an appropriate law enforcement authority in limited circumstances. Today, the Court closes that door and with it any meaning the Legislature might have intended for 'good faith.'"[327]

In *University of Houston v. Barth*,[328] the Texas Supreme Court ruled that a "professor's reports to a university chief financial officer, general counsel, and internal auditor of alleged statutory violations" that included violations of state civil and criminal law by a college dean "were not reports made to appropriate law enforcement authority." The court noted that the professor's report of the violation to the university's police department occurred after the alleged

---

321 *Id.* at 810.

322 *Okoli*, 440 S.W.3d 611 (Tex. 2014).

323 *Id.* (ruling that the plaintiff's "up-the-chain-of-command reports" to his superiors did not satisfy the requirement to report wrongdoing to "an appropriate law-enforcement agency).

324 *Id.* at 614.

325 *See Connally v. Dallas Indep. Sch. Dist.*, 506 S.W.3d 767, 777 (Tex. App.–El Paso 2016) (quoting *Gentilello*, 398 S.W.3d at 687.)

326 *Okoli*, 440 S.W.3d at 618 (Devine, J., joined by Willett, J. and Lehrmann, J., dissenting).

327 *Id.*

328 *Barth*, 403 S.W.3d 852, 853 (Tex. 2013).

retaliatory acts had occurred, stating that such a report "may well have been sufficient, but only if it preceded the retaliatory action."[329]

In *Texas Comm'n on Environmental Quality v. Resendez*,[330] the Texas Supreme Court held that a report to a state senator's office about alleged fraud in distribution of assets of a governmental agency "was not a report to 'appropriate law enforcement authority'" despite the plaintiff's contention that "it is objectively reasonable for a layperson like herself to believe that a state senator has authority to investigate violations of law, especially fraud on the government."

One must question the reasoning of the Texas Supreme Court that, in its need to protect the public fisc through its absolute state immunity posture, a most strict interpretation of the Texas Legislature's waiver provision in the Texas Whistleblowers' Act provides that purpose. The Supreme Court's adherence to absolute sovereign immunity, despite the waiver provision in the whistleblower act, effectively prevents whistleblower claims, most of which involve reports of waste, misuse and illegal use of governmental property. The Texas Supreme Court has effectively limited the ability of the Texas Legislature to take the steps it deemed necessary and proper to achieve state goals in encouraging state employees to report governmental waste, improvident conduct, and illegal activities by protecting those persons who risk their reputations and employment when they report such activity. The importance and requirements the Texas Supreme Court has placed on requiring a claimant to report properly an ill-defined "good faith" report to a most ill-defined "appropriate law enforcement authority" is most difficult to comprehend. One must consider that the Supreme Court's required technicalities are "particularly inappropriate in a statutory scheme in which laymen, unassisted by trained lawyers, initiate the process."[331]

In *Office of the Attorney General v. Weatherspoon*,[332] the Texas Supreme Court held that an assistant attorney general's report to a division within the Office of the Attorney General (OAG) was not a report to "an appropriate law enforcement authority" within the meaning of the Whistleblower Act. Weatherspoon, an assistant attorney general, alleged "that two senior attorneys tried to coerce her to sign a false affidavit regarding her interactions with a

329 *Id.* at 857.

330 *Resendez*, 450 S.W.3d 520 (Tex. 2014).

331 *Love v. Pullman Company*, 404 U.S. 522, 527, 92 S. Ct. 616, 30 L. Ed. 2d 679 (1972).

332 *Weatherspoon*, 472 S.W.3d 280 (Tex. 2015).

judge."[333] Weatherspoon stated the two senior regional OAG attorneys ordered her to report interactions she had with a district judge and sent her an e-mail with an attached affidavit for her to sign concerning her conversation with the judge.[334] A managing attorney with the OAG informed Weatherspoon that they "intended to use the affidavit as evidence to have the judge recused from hearing cases involving the OAG" and that the "affidavit was also going to be used to support a judicial misconduct complaint against the judge."[335] Weatherspoon refused "to sign the affidavit stating that she believed it misrepresented various facts regarding her conversation with the judge and mischaracterized the tone and nature of the conversation."[336] Weatherspoon testified that an OAG attorney then sent her "an e-mail ordering her to sign the affidavit." She responded that the affidavit was false as written and asked if she could revise it, but the OAG attorney "rejected her request."[337] Weatherspoon alleged she was "ordered into a separate room and was told she could not leave until she had prepared a written statement against the judge."[338] Weatherspoon reported the OAG attorney's attempts to force her to sign the allegedly false affidavit to another division within the OAG. She claimed the attorneys' conduct in insisting that she sign a false affidavit "constituted subornation of perjury in violation of federal law."[339] Weatherspoon contended that, after she reported the alleged violations to a division within the OAG, "she was retaliated against and eventually terminated from her position."[340] The court of appeals ruled that the assistant attorney general's report to a division head in the OAG was made to an appropriate law enforcement under the Texas Whistleblowers Act.[341] The Supreme Court reversed and dismissed the case, ruling that "the authority of some OAG

333 *Id.* at 281.

334 *OAG v. Weatherspoon*, 435 S.W.3d 844, 846 (Tex. App.–Dallas 2014).

335 *Id.*

336 *Id.*

337 *Id.*

338 *Id.*

339 *Id.* at 847.

340 *Id.*

341 *Id* at 845.

divisions to investigate or prosecute crime does not transform the entire OAG into an appropriate law-enforcement authority."[342]

The following year, in *McMillen v. Texas Health & Human Servs. Comm'n*,[343] the Texas Supreme Court deflected and ruled that the plaintiff, an attorney who had served as Deputy Counsel for the Commission's Office of the Inspector General (OIG), made a report to an "appropriate law-enforcement authority" even though the plaintiff reported a violation of the law to the OIG.[344] The court ruled that the reported-to authority must have "outward-looking powers;" it must have authority to enforce, investigate, or prosecute violations of law against third parties outside of the entity, or it must have authority to promulgate regulations governing the conduct of third parties. The court decided the OIG is an appropriate law-enforcement authority because it "is responsible for the investigation of fraud and abuse in the provision of health and human services and the enforcement of state law relating to the provision of those services."[345] Thus, in *McMillen*, the court held that "an appropriate authority can 'include someone within an OIG or even an OIG within the same agency as the whistleblower, because the OIG has outward-looking-law-enforcement authority.'"[346] However, in *Weatherspoon*, the court refused to consider the OAG as an "outward-looking-law-enforcement authority" when an OAG attorney filed a report with the OAG despite the fact that the OAG is the chief law enforcement agency in Texas.

In summary, whistleblowers have some limited protection under both the Federal Whistleblower Act and state whistleblower acts. However, while the Federal Whistleblower Act and whistleblower statutes in most other states protect internal reports to supervisors, Texas does not. Whistleblower claims in Texas are dismissed if the whistleblower does not report a good faith violation of law to "an appropriate law enforcement authority" that has "outward looking powers." The question of what can be included in a "law enforcement authority that has outward looking powers" is unanswered although the Texas Supreme Court has ruled that the OIG can be included but the OAG cannot. The Texas

342 OAG v. Witherspoon, 472 S.W.3d 280, 283 (Tex. 2015).

343 *McMillen*, 485 S.W.3d 427, 429 (Tex. 2016)

344 *Id.* (stating "the authority's power to 'regulate under' or 'enforce' must pertain to 'the law alleged to be violated in the report,'" citing Tex. Gov't Code §554.002(b)(1).

345 *Id.* at 300. The court distinguished *Gentilello*, stating that the department chair in *Gentilello* 'had power only to ensure internal compliance with certain Medicare and Medicaid requirements" where the OIG has "outward-looking powers."

346 *Id.* (quoting *Tex. Dep't of Human Servs. v. Okoli*, 440 S.W.3d 611, 617 (Tex. 2014)).

Supreme Court's harsh decisions in its whistleblower cases are examples of the problems victims of governmental misconduct encounter in finding redress for their injuries or damages when a state mandates absolute sovereign immunity.

E. OPEN COURT RESTRICTIONS

Most states have some variation of an Open Courts Clause that provide an individual cannot "be arbitrarily deprived of effective remedies designed to protect basic individual rights."[347] A state legislature does not have "unbridled power" to create and define the law;[348] thus, as the Supreme Court of Utah stated the Open Courts Clause in its Constitution "acts as a substantive check on legislative power."[349]

The Texas Supreme Court has indicated that an open courts challenge to a state's sovereign immunity would fail.[350] The Texas Court has ruled that "proof of an open courts violation requires two elements: (1) a cognizable, common-law claim that is statutorily restricted, and (2) the restriction is unreasonable or arbitrary when balanced against the statute's purpose and basis."[351] The Texas Supreme Court has further ruled that the test for violation of the open courts provision applies only to common law causes of action and there is "no common law right to sue the government."[352]

The Texas Supreme Court is incorrect in concluding that the election of remedies provision[353] and a court's reading of that provision do not violate the State

347 *Waite v. Utah Labor Commission*, 416 P.3d 635, 654 (Utah 2017). The Utah Constitution's Open Courts Clause, Utah Constitution, Article 3, §11, states: "All courts shall be open, and every person, for an injury done to him in his person, property or reputation, shall have remedy by due course of law, which shall be administered without denial or unnecessary delay; and no person shall be barred from prosecuting or defending before any tribunal in this State, by himself or counsel, any civil cause to which he is party."

348 Discussion in *Waite v. Utah Labor Commission*, 416 P.3d at 642.

349 *Id.* at 642.

350 See., e.g., *Franka v. Velasquez*, 322 S.W.3d 367, 385 (T ex. 2011).

351 *Yancy v. United Surgical Partners Intern'l, Inc.*, 236 S.W.3d 778 (Tex. 2007). The open courts provision of the Texas Constitution, Article 1, §13, provides: "All courts shall be open and every person for an injury done him, in his lands, goods, person or reputation, shall have remedy by due course of law." See discussion of provision in *Tenet Hospital Limited v. Rivera*, 445 S.W.3d 698 (Tex. 2014).

352 *Union Carbide Corp. v. Synatzske*, 438 SW.3d 39, 55 (Tex. 2014).

353 Tex. Civ. Prac. & Rem. Code §101.106(f).

Constitution's Open Courts provision. The Texas Supreme Court earlier stated: "Although a plaintiff who pursues the statutory remedy against the government may lose his or her common law remedy against the employee, the plaintiff is not required to follow this course. He or she may still opt to pursue the full common law remedy against the responsible employee, foregoing or postponing any attempt to recover from the government."[354] Unfortunately, however, the Texas Supreme Court's reading of the election of remedies provisions in the Texas Torts Claims Act no longer permits a plaintiff to pursue a common law remedy against a governmental employee. Importantly, common law causes of action for intentional torts of governmental officials have been completely precluded through the interpretation the Texas Supreme Court places upon the election of remedies provision of the Texas Tort Claims Act,[355] discussed *supra.* As noted *supra*, when a suit is brought against a governmental employee for conduct occurring within the general scope of employment so that suit could have been brought under the Texas Tort Claims Act against the government, the election of remedies provision[356] provides that "the suit is considered to be against the employee in the employee's official capacity only."[357] Additionally, the Texas Supreme Court has interpreted "scope of employment" most broadly to include almost any act that occurred when a governmental employee was "discharging the duties generally assigned to him."[358] Moreover, the Texas Supreme Court's current interpretations of the Texas Whistleblower Act also has precluded any protection for those who bring to light state official and employee violations of the law.

In considering that the Texas Tort Claims Act retains absolute immunity for the governmental unit for intentional tort claims and that the Texas Supreme Court has effectively precluded whistleblowers from filing claims against the

354 *Thomas v. Oldham*, 895 S.W.2d 352, 357-58 (Tex. 1995).

355 Tex. Civ. Prac. & Rem. Code §101.106(a)-(f).

356 *Id.* at §106(f).

357 *McFadden v. Olesky*, 517 S.W.3d 287, 296 (Tex. 2017) (quoting *Alexander v. Walker*, 435 S.W.3d 789, 791 (Tex. 2014).

358 As noted previously, in *University of Texas Health Science Center v. Rios*, 542 S.W.3d at 535, the Texas Supreme Court ruled that government employees are not required to prove their subjective intent to be dismissed from a suit pursuant to the election-of-remedies provision. The court stated there may be a connection between an employee's job duties and an alleged tortious conduct "even if the employee performs negligently or is motivated by ulterior motives or personal animus so long as the conduct itself was pursuant to her job responsibilities." *Id.* (quoting *Laverie v. Wetherbee*, 517 S.W.3d at 753).

State, victims of intentional torts committed by governmental employees within a broadly expansive "scope of employment" have no recourse in Texas courts. There is then a question whether the Texas Supreme Court's current reading and application of those provisions violates the Texas Constitution's Open Courts provision as well as the Due Process Clause of the Fourteenth Amendment to the United States Constitution. As the Utah Supreme Court concluded with respect to a state legislature--that it does not have "unbridled power" to create and define the law--,[359] a state supreme court also does not have that power.

Concerns that victims of the harsh application of sovereign immunity principles are precluded access to the courts should be at issue in all states that retain absolute sovereign immunity. Additionally, amendments to the Federal Tort Claims Act, discussed *supra*, now effectively preclude federal tort claims against it and its employees. A denial of a recourse for citizens who are injured or damaged by their government must be addressed, not only to provide redress for victims of improvident governmental action, but also to ensure a democratic state based on transparency and accountability of its governmental entities and their employees. Victims of governmental wrongdoing who are denied access to the courts based on a jurisdictional sovereign immunity bar should bring forward allegations of open court violations as well as violations of the Due Process Clause of the Fourteenth Amendment to the United States Constitution.

359 *Waite v. Utah Labor Commission*, 416 P. Ed at 642.

CHAPTER 5.
TRIBAL NATIONS AND FOREIGN STATES SOVEREIGN IMMUNITY

Tribal nations are domestic "nations" and, as such, have absolute sovereign immunity. With respect to foreign States, immunity is statutory pursuant to the Foreign Sovereign Immunities Act.[1] Still, that Act excepts immunity for enumerated transactions, the principal ones being a foreign State's commercial activities in the United States and its taking of property in violation of international law.[2] Foreign States can be sued in courts in the United States in limited circumstances.

A. TRIBAL NATION IMMUNITY

Tribal nations are "'domestic dependent nations' that exercise 'inherent sovereign authority.'"[3] The Supreme Court has acknowledged that tribal nations "are subject to plenary control by Congress" but that "'they remain 'separate sovereigns pre-existing the Constitution'" so that "'unless' and 'until' Congress acts, the tribes retain' their historic sovereign authority.'"[4] The Court affirmed: "Among the core aspects of sovereignty that tribes possess–subject to congres-

1 28 U.S.C. §§1602-11, discussed *infra.*

2 *Id.* at §1605(a)(2) and (3). Provisions of the Act as well as its exceptions for foreign State immunity discussed *infra.*

3 *Michigan v. Bay Mills Indian Community,* 134 S.Ct. 2024, 2027, 188 L. Ed. 2d 1071 (2014) (quoting *Oklahoma Tax Comm'n v. Citizen Band Potawatomi Tribe of Okla.,* 498 U.S. 505, 509, 111 S. Ct. 905, 112 L. Ed. 2d 1112 (1991) and *Cherokee Nation v. Georgia,* 5 Pet. 1, 17, 81 L. Ed. 25 (1831)).

4 *Id.* at 2017 (quoting *United States v. Lara,* 541 U.S. 193, 200, 124 S. Ct. 1628, 158 L. Ed. 2d 420 (2004), *Santa Clara Pueblo v. Martinez,* 436 U.S. 49, 56, 98 S. Ct. 1670, 56 L. Ed. 2d 106 (1978), and *United States v. Wheeler,* 435 U.S. 313, 313, 98 S.Ct. 1079, 55 L.Ed. 2d 303 (1978).

sional action–is the 'common-law immunity from suit traditionally enjoyed by sovereign powers.'"[5] The Court has explained that immunity is "a necessary corollary to Indian sovereignty and self-governance."[6] In addressing a question of whether tribal sovereign immunity barred a state's suit against a tribe for opening a casino outside Indian lands, the Supreme Court ruled in *Michigan v. Bay Mills Indian Community*,[7] that immunity protected the tribe from the legal action. The Court referred to its earlier decision in *Kiowa Tribe of Okla. v. Manufacturing Technologies, Inc.*[8] wherein it had declined to make any exception for tribal immunity "for suits arising from a tribe's commercial activities, even when they take place off Indian lands."[9] While Congress can abrogate tribal immunity, it "must 'unequivocally' express that purpose."[10] Any ambiguity is resolved in favor of sovereign immunity,[11] and abrogation of tribal sovereign immunity may not be implied.[12]

Tribal employees do not have tribal sovereign immunity if they are sued in their individual capacities and a tribe's indemnification statute for its employees "cannot, as a matter of law, extend sovereign immunity to individual employees;" an indemnification statute does not make the tribe the real party in interest to support tribal sovereign immunity.[13]

---

5 *Id.* (citing *Santa Clara Pueblo*, 436 U.S. at 59, in acknowledging that "immunity applies whether a suit is brought by a State...or arises from a tribe's commercial activities off Indian lands" (citing *Puyallup Tribe, Inc. v. Department of Game of Wash.*, 433 U.S. 165, 97 S. Ct. 2616, 53 L. Ed.2d 667 (1977) and *Kiowa Tribe of Okla. v. Manufacturing Technologies, Inc.*, 523 U.S. 751, 118 S. Ct. 1700, 140 L.Ed. 2d 981 (1998)).

6 *Three Affiliated Tribes of Fort Berthhold Reservation v. Wold Engineering, P.C.*, 476 U.S. 877, 890, 106 S. Ct. 2305, 90 L. Ed.2d 881 (1986). The Court stated that tribal immunity "is a matter of federal law and is not subject to diminution by the States." *Id.* at 891.

7 *Bay Mills Indian Community*, 134 S. Ct. at 2038.

8 *Kiowa Tribe*, 523 U.S. at 758.

9 *Bay Mills Indian Community*, 134 S. Ct. at 2031.

10 *Id.* (quoting *C & L Enterprises, Inc. v. Citizen Ban Potawatomi Tribe of Okla*, 532 U.S. 411, 418, 121 S. Ct. 1589, 149 L. Ed. 2d 623 (2001) and stating that "courts will not lightly assume that Congress in fact intends to undermine Indian self-government." 134 S. Ct.. at 2032.

11 *White Mountain Apache Tribe v. Bracker*, 448 U.S. 136, 143-44, 100 S. Ct. 2578, 65 L. Ed. 2d 665 (1980).

12 *Santa Clara Pueblo v. Martinez*, 436 U. S. at 58.

13 *Lewis v. Clarke*, 137 S. Ct. 1285, 1286-87, 197 L. Ed.2d 631 (2017). In reversing the Supreme Court of Connecticut that ruled tribal sovereign immunity barred a suit against a tribal employee, the U.S. Supreme Court held that "in a suit brought against a tribal employee in his individual capacity, the employee, not the tribe, is the real party in interest and the tribe's sovereign immunity is not implicated." *Id.* at 1288. The U.S. Supreme Court stated: "Officers sued in their personal capacity come to

Although the Supreme Court has also recognized that there may be an exception to immunity for immovable property, which a tribe purchased in the same manner as a private individual,[14] it decided to forego consideration of the immovable-property rule in a recent decision in *Upper Skagit Indian Tribe v. Lundgren.*[15] In a concurring opinion, two Supreme Court justices stated that a tribe should not be able to "wield sovereign immunity as a sword and seize property with impunity,"[16] noting that "property ownership is not an inherently sovereign function."[17] Two dissenting justices recognized the immovable-property exception to sovereign immunity as being "well established" and stated that "it plainly extends to tribal immunity, as it does to every other form of sovereign immunity."[18]

B. SOVEREIGN IMMUNITY AS A DOCTRINE OF INTERNATIONAL LAW

The Supreme Court has pointed out that "international law is distinct from domestic law in its domain as well as its objectives."[19] Additionally, "international law has shaped the development of the common law of foreign sovereign immunity."[20] Some of the principal concerns regarding the immunity of

court as individuals," citing *Hafer v. Melo*, 502 U.S. 21, 27, 112 S. Ct. 358, 116 L. Ed. 2d 301 (1991).

14 See *Upper Skagit Indian Tribe v. Lundgren*, 138 S.Ct. 1649, 200 L. Ed. 2d 931 (2018). The Court granted certiorari in *Upper Skagit Indian Tribe* because of lower courts disagreements about the significance of its decision in *County of Yakima v. Confederated Tribes and Bands of Yakima Nation*, 502 U.S. 251, 112 S. Ct. 683, 116 L. Ed. 2d 687 (1992). Still, the Court noted that *Yakima* did not address the scope of tribal sovereign immunity. Additionally, the Court's opinion in *Upper Skagit Indian Tribe* also left questions about the extent of tribal sovereignty.

15 *Upper Skagit*, 138 S. Ct. at 1654-55.

16 *Id.* at 1655, Justices Roberts and Kennedy, concurring.

17 *Id.*, quoting *Permanent Mission of India to United Nations v. City of New York*, 551 U.S. 193, 199, 127 S. Ct. 2352, 168 L. Ed. 2d 85 (2007) and explaining that "since the 18th century, it has been a settled principle of international law that a foreign state holding real property outside its territory is treated just like a private individual," citing *Schooner Exchange v. McFaddon*, 7 Cranch 116, 145, 3 L. Ed. 287 (1812)).

18 *Upper Skagit Indian Tribe*, Justices Thomas and Alito, dissenting.

19 *Jesner v. Arab Bank, PLC*, 138 S. Ct. 1386, 1401, 200 L.Ed. 612 (2018).

20 Discussion in *Yousuf v. Samatar*, 699 F.3d 763, 774 (4th Cir. 2012) (citing *Schooner Exchange v. M'Faddon*, 11 U.S. (7 Cranch 116), 136 (1812) ("noting 'a principle of public law' derived from 'common usage' and 'common opinion' that 'national ships of war, entering the port of a friendly power

foreign States for violation of international law relate to international human-rights norms that "prohibit acts repugnant to all civilized peoples–crimes like genocide, torture, and slavery that make their perpetrators 'enemies of all mankind.'"[21] In recognizing that "respect for fundamental human rights" is in "the individual and collective interest" of the international community, international law imposes duties on nation-states and their officials to protect individuals from inhuman treatment and from the taking of their property in violation of international law.[22] While courts in the United States have addressed suits filed against foreign States and foreign officials by claimants seeking redress for violations of international human-rights protections,[23] a major problem for these victims is that the courts generally grant foreign States immunity for their tortious acts, and often their officials as well, and dismiss the victims' claims.

The Alien Tort Claims Act[24] was enacted in 1789 to recognize a limited category of "torts in violation of the law of nations"[25] and to ensure "the availability of a federal forum."[26] However, while some suits against foreign States and foreign officials have been brought under this Act, victims filing claims against foreign nations as well as against foreign officials are limited because the Act does not have a sovereign immunity waiver.[27] An important purpose of the Foreign

open for their reception, are to be considered as exempted by the consent of that power from its jurisdiction'").

21 *Jesner*, 136 S. Ct. at 1401-02 (quoting *Sosa v. Alvarez-Machain*, 542 U.S. 692, 732, 124 S. Ct. 2739, 159 L. Ed. 2d 718 (2004)).

22 *Id.* at 1400 (quoting *Filartiga v. Pena-Irala*, 630 F.2d 876, 890 (2nd Cir.1980); *Kiobel v. Royal Dutch Petroleum Co.*, 569 U.S. 108, 118, 133 S. Ct. 1659, 185 L. Ed. 2d 671 (2013)).

23 *Id.* at 1398.

24 18 U.S.C. §1350.

25 *Sosa*, 542 U.S. at 714.

26 *Id.* at 755-19.

27 Further, the Act was later amended to limits its liability to individuals. The Torture Victim Protection Act of 1991, Pub. L. No. 102-256, 106 Stat. 73, amended the Alien Tort Claims Act to create an express cause of action for victims of torture and extrajudicial killing in violation of international law, but the Act limited liability to individuals. Additionally, based on this limitation, the Supreme Court has ruled that the Act also does not provide a private right of action against foreign corporations. *Jesner*, 138 S. Ct. at 1408.

The Foreign Sovereign Immunities Act (FSIA), 28 U.S.C. §§1602-11,which was enacted in 1976, defines the jurisdiction of United States courts in suits against foreign states. This act provides the sole basis for jurisdiction over a foreign State. Although the Act provides foreign nations with immunity from suit in United States, some exceptions enumerated in the Act, and discussed *infra*, do waive sovereign immunity for foreign states.

Sovereign Immunities Act was to codify the theory of sovereign immunity. The Act adopted a "restrictive theory" of immunity which Congress recognized as consistent with extant international law."[28] The restrictive theory deviates from absolute immunity--the Act sets outs some specific acts of a foreign State that are exceptions to immunity.[29] One of the exceptions is the taking of property in "violation of international law."[30] Even though this "expropriation" exception relates to the taking of "property," because "violation of international law" has been interpreted to encompass genocide,[31] the Foreign Sovereign Immunity Act has become the basic statute practitioners must address not only in filing property claims against foreign States, but also for claims of genocide.

Sovereign immunity as a doctrine of international law differs from diplomatic immunity and was first recognized in a United States court in 1812 in *Schooner Exchange v. M'Faddon*,[32] wherein Chief Justice Marshall upheld a plea of immunity that was "supported by an executive branch suggestion, by noting that a recognition of immunity was supported by the law and practice of nations."[33] The Supreme Court later began to place "less emphasis on whether immunity was supported by the law and practice of nations, and relied instead on the practices and policies of the State Department."[34]

There have been "two conflicting concepts of sovereign immunity, each widely held and firmly established."[35] The "classical or absolute theory of sovereign immunity" prescribes that without consent, a sovereign cannot "be made a

28 *Id.* Under the FSIA, courts, rather than the State Department, decide claims of foreign immunity based on principles set out in the statute.

29 *Id.* at §1605, discussed *infra.*

30 *Id.* at §1605(a)(3).

31 *Simon v. Republic of Hungary*, 812 F.3d 127, 142-43, 146 (D.C. Cir. 2016).

32 *Schooner Exchange*, 7 Cranch 116, 136 (1812) (ruling that while foreign sovereigns had no right to immunity in United States courts, "as a matter of comity, members of the international community had implicitly agreed to waive the exercise of jurisdiction over other sovereigns in certain classes of cases.") Justice Marshall concluded that the "implied waiver theory" exempted a French national armed vessel from jurisdiction in United States courts. The Supreme Court commented in *Republic of Austria v. Altmann,* 541 U.S. 677, 688, 124 S.Ct. 2240, 159 L. Ed. 2d 1 (2004), that Chief Justice Marshall's opinion in *Schooner Exchange* "is generally viewed as the source of our foreign sovereign immunity jurisprudence."

33 *Schooner Exchange*, 7 Cranch at 134.

34 H.R. Rep. 94-1487, at 8, 94th Cong., 2nd Sess. 1976, 1976, U.S.C.C.A.N. 6604, 6606 (referring to *Ex Parte Peru*, 318 U. S. 578, 63 S. Ct. 793, 87 L. Ed. 1014 (1943) and *Republic of Mexico v. Hoffman*, 324 U.S. 30, 65 S. Ct. 530, 89 L. Ed. 729 (1945)).

35 Discussion in *Republic of Austria v. Altmann*, 541 U.S. at 690.

respondent in the courts of another sovereign."[36] A later theory of "restrictive" sovereign immunity recognized the immunity of the sovereign "with regard to sovereign or public acts" but "not with respect to private acts." Countries in Western Europe "followed the restrictive principle of sovereign immunity" and denied pleas of immunity in tort and contract cases.[37]

The Supreme Court noted in *Verlinden B.V. v. Central Bank of Nigeria*,[38] that it had consistently "deferred to the decisions of the political branches,"in particular, those of the Executive Branch, on whether to take jurisdiction over actions against foreign governments. "The Executive Branch originally followed a policy of requesting immunity in all actions against friendly sovereigns."[39] A two-step procedure was followed "for resolving a foreign state's claim of sovereign immunity, typically asserted on behalf of seized vessels."[40] "Under that procedure, "the diplomatic representative of the sovereign could request a 'suggestion of immunity' from the State Department."[41] If the State Department granted a sovereign's diplomatic request for a "suggestion of immunity," the district court surrendered jurisdiction, but if the State Department refused, the court would decide the immunity issue.[42] "Although cases involving individual foreign officials as defendants were rare, the same two-step procedure was typically followed when a foreign official asserted immunity."[43]

After World War II, the United States became increasingly involved in litigation in foreign courts in activities such as "the purchase of goods and services by our embassies, employment of local personnel by our military bases, the construction or lease of buildings for our foreign missions, and traffic accidents involving U.S. Government-owned vehicles."[44] "When the United States

---

36 *Id.*

37 *Id.*

38 *Verlinden*, 461 U.S. 480, 486, 103 S. Ct. 1962, 76 L. Ed. 2d 81 (1983) (citing *Ex Parte Peru*, 318 U.S. at 586-90, and *Republic of Mexico*, 324 U.S. at 33-36)).

39 *Republic of Austria*, 541 U.S. at 689-90 (citing *Verlinden*, 461 U.S. at 486).

40 Discussion in *Samantar v. Yousuf*, 560 U.S. 305, 308, 130 S. Ct. 2278, 176 L.Ed.2d 1047 (2010) (citing *Ex Parte Peru*, 318 U.S. at 587-89, and *Republic of Mexico*, 324 U.S. at 34-36.)

41 *Samantar*, 460 U.S. at 308 (citing *Ex parte Peru*, 318 U.S. at 581).

42 *Ex Parte Peru*, 318 U. S. at 581.

43 *Samantar*, 460 U.S. at 312 (citing *Heaney v. Government of Spain*, 445 F.2d 501, 504-505) (2nd Cir. 1971)).

44 H.R. Rep. 94-1487, 94th Cong., 2nd Sess., 1976, at 9, 1976 U.S.C.C.A.N., 6604, 6607.

became involved in foreign suits on a large scale, foreign counsel retained by the Department of Justice were instructed to plead sovereign immunity in almost every instance."[45]

In 1952, and pursuant to a letter from Jack B. Tate, the Acting Legal Adviser in the Department of State, referred to as the "Tate Letter,"[46] the State Department announced its adoption of the "restrictive" theory of sovereign immunity and began to "recognize immunity in cases based on a foreign state's public acts, but not in cases based on commercial or private acts."[47] Additionally, beginning in the 1970's, the Department of Justice adopted a practice of not pleading sovereign immunity abroad where, under the Tate letter standards, the Department would not recognize a foreign state's immunity in this country.[48]

In referring to the 1952 "Tate Letter" in *Republic of Austria v. Altmann*,[49] the Supreme Court explained that while the State Department would thereafter apply the 'restrictive theory' of sovereign immunity," the "Tate Letter" had "little, if any impact on federal courts' approach to immunity analyses," stating that courts continued to abide by the State Department's "suggestions of immunity."[50]

Congress sought to remedy problems relating to the inconsistent application of sovereign immunity by enacting the Foreign Sovereign Immunities Act in 1976.[51] The Act was to insure that the "restrictive principle of immunity" was applied in litigation in U.S. courts.[52] Additionally, the Act provided a statutory procedure for making service upon, and obtaining in personam jurisdiction over, a foreign state.[53] Moreover, it provided a judgment creditor some remedy if

---

45 *Id.*

46 26 Department of State Bulletin 984.

47 H. R Rep. 94-1487, at 9, 1976 U.S.C.C.A.N. at 6607-08.

48 *Id.*

49 *Republic of Austria*, 541 U.S. at 689-90.

50 *Id.* at 692.

51 *Id.* See also *Semantar,* 560 U.S. at 313.

52 *Id.* The Committee on the Judiciary pointed out that courts did not always apply the restrictive principle. H. R. Rep. 94-1487, at 7, 1976 U.S.C.C.A.N. at 6605-06. It stated: "Today, when a foreign state wishes to assert immunity, it will often request the Department of State to make a formal suggestion of immunity to the court. Although the State Department espouses the restrictive principle of immunity, the foreign state may attempt to bring diplomatic influences to bear upon the State Department's determination." *Id.*

53 H. R. Rep. 94-1487, at 8, 1976 U.S.C.C.A.N. at 6606. As the Committee stated: "This would render un-

a foreign State failed to satisfy a final judgment.[54] As the Supreme Court stated in *Samantar v. Yousuf*, [55] the Act's two primary purposes were: "(1) to endorse and codify the restrictive theory of sovereign immunity, and (2) to transfer primary responsibility for deciding 'claims of foreign states to immunity' from the States Department to the courts."

C. ALIEN TORT CLAIMS ACT

The Alien Tort Claims Act,[56] sometimes referred to as the Alien Tort Statute (ATS), provides a court with jurisdiction over claims for violations of a treaty of the United States and for violations of the law of nations.[57] The Supreme Court[58] has stated that Congress enacted the Act as part of the Judiciary Act of 1789 to provide then new federal district courts with "cognizance, concurrent with the courts of the several States, or the circuit courts" in cases where an alien sued for a tort but only in violation of the law of nations or under a treaty of the United States.[59] Much later, in 1991, Congress enacted the Torture Victim Protection Act,[60] as an amendment to the ATS, to create "an express cause of action for

necessary the practice of seizing and attaching the property of a foreign government for the purpose of obtaining jurisdiction."

54 *Id.* This remedied the then "predicament of a plaintiff who has obtained a judgment against a foreign state" for under the then existing law, a foreign state enjoyed absolute immunity from execution in U.S. courts, "even in ordinary commercial litigation where commercial assets [were] available for the satisfaction of a judgment." The Act conformed "the execution immunity rules more closely to the jurisdiction immunity rules." *Id.*

55 *Samantar*, 560 U.S. at 313.

56 18 U.S.C. §1350.

57 *Id.* The Act states: "The district courts shall have original jurisdiction of any civil action by an alien for a tort only, committed in violation of the law of nations or a treaty of the United States."

58 *Sosa v. Alvarez-Machain*, 542 U.S. 692, 124 S. Ct. 2739, 159 L. Ed. 2d 718 (2004).

59 *Id.* at 712-13 (citing the Judiciary Act of 1789, ch. 20, §9, 1 Stat. 77). The Court stated: "When the United States declared their independence, they were bound to receive the law of nations, in its modern state of purity and refinement" (citing *Ware v. Hylton*, 3 Dall. 199, 182, l L. Ed. 58 (1796)). *Id.* at 714. The Court acknowledged that "this law of nations comprised two principal elements." The first covered the "general norms governing the behavior of national states with each other." The second was a more pedestrian element that implicated mercantile questions, such as bills of exchange and the like, all marine causes, and disputes. *Id.* at 715-17.

60 Pub. L. No. 102-256, 106 Stat. 73 (1991), which amended the Alien Tort Claims Act. The Court stated in *Jesner* that this act did not permit suits against corporate entities. The court referred to its "key feature" being that "it limits liability to individuals." 138 S. Ct. at 1404.

victims of torture and extrajudicial killing in violation of international law." The Torture Victim Protection Act stated explicitly, what was "perhaps implicit in the Act of 1789–that the law of nations is incorporated into the law of the United States and that a violation of the international law of human rights is (at least with regard to torture) *ipso facto* a violation of U.S. domestic law."[61] In enacting this amendment to the ATS, "Congress essentially created an express private right of action for individuals victimized by torture and extrajudicial killings that constitute violations of *jus cogens* norms,"[62] i.e, the commission of international crimes.

One court drew inferences from history of the Torture Victim Protection Act to decide that Congress intended the ATS to furnish jurisdiction for a "relatively modest set of actions alleging violations of the law of nations."[63] Apparently only a few torts in violation of the law of nations were understood to be within the common law.[64]

Victims suing under the ATS are limited for several reasons. First, the ATS itself does not include a waiver of sovereign immunity. Thus, victims are precluded from seeking redress under the ATS against foreign States as well as the Federal government.[65] Additionally, the Supreme Court has severely restricted

---

61 *Wiwa v. Royal Dutch Petroleum Co.*, 226 F.3d 88, 105 (2nd Cir. 2000).

62 *Samantar*, 699 F.3d 763, 777 (4th Cir. 2012).

63 *Sosa v. Alvarez-Machain*, 542 U.S. at 720. These included offenses against ambassadors, violations of safe conduct, and individual actions arising out of prize captures and piracy.

64 *Id. Jus cogens* includes human rights violations such as genocide.

65 The Foreign Sovereign Immunities Act provides sovereign immunity for foreign States but does provide exceptions for certain specified activities that are set out in the Act and discussed *infra*. Thus, this Act authorizes some lawsuits to be brought against foreign States.

The only remedy against the Federal government for its tortious actions is that provided in the Federal Torts Claims Act, which is discussed in Chapter 4. As noted in Chapter 4, the Federal Torts Claims Act protects the sovereign immunity of the United States government with respect to intentional torts. Additionally, the Federal Employees Liability Reform and Tort Compensation Act, Pub. L. No. 100-694, 102 Stat. 4563, codified as amended in relevant part at 28 U.S.C. §2679(b)(1) and referred to as the Westfall Act or the Liability Reform Act, was enacted in 1988 to provide absolute immunity for governmental employees when they act within the scope of employment. As discussed in Chapter 4, this Act was a response to a Supreme Court decision in 1988 in *Westfall v. Erwin*, 484 U.S. 292, 108 S. Ct. 580, 98 L. Ed. 2d 619 (1988), wherein the Supreme Court added an additional requirement for immunity when a federal governmental employee was sued in the employee's personal capacity. The Court ruled in *Westfall* that for a federal employee to have immunity from suit on a common law tort, the employee had to show that the employee was acting within the scope of employment *and* was performing a discretionary function. *Id.* at 296-97. In enacting the Federal Employees Liability Reform and Tort Compensation Act, often referred to as the "Westfall Act," Congress removed the second requirement, viewing it as exposing employees to unwarranted liability. In *United States v. Smith*, 499 U.S. 160, 111 S. Ct. 1180, 113 L. Ed2d 134 (1991), the Court, in referring to the Westfall Act as the Liability Reform Act, recognized that the Act established absolute immunity for

claims under the ATS allegedly based on a reluctance to extend judicially created private rights of action.[66] The Court has ruled that providing a private right of action under the ATS for violating international law has "implications for the foreign relations of the United States" and would impinge "on the discretion of the Legislative and Executive Branches in managing foreign affairs."[67] In *Sosa v. Alvarez-Machain*,[68] the Supreme Court held that the ATS is "strictly jurisdictional" and does not provide for a private cause of action for international law violations" that occurred in a foreign country even though "arguably caused both by action in the foreign country and planning in the United States."[69] An additional problem in filing a claim under the ATS is that the ATS does not provide a definition of a cause of action for "international-law violations."[70]

In *Kiobel v. Royal Dutch Petroleum Co.*,[71] the Supreme Court dismissed a claim brought under the ATS against holding companies incorporated in the Netherlands and the United Kingdom for aiding and abetting the Nigerian Government in human rights abuses. The Court ruled that dismissal was required based on the presumption against extraterritorial application of statutes.[72] In addressing the extraterritorial application of the ATS, the Court expressed concern that "other nations, also applying the law of nations, could hale our citizens

---

government employees.

66 *Sosa*, 542 U.S. at 692. The Court further ruled in *Sosa* that the Federal Tort Claims Act's exception to waiver of sovereign immunity for claims arising in a foreign country, 28 U.S.C. §2680(k), bars claims based on any injury suffered in a foreign country regardless of where the tortious act or omission occurred.

67 *Sosa*, 542 U.S. at 727.

68 *Id.* at 692. In *Sosa*, a Mexican acquitted of murder after being abducted and transported to the United States to face prosecution brought action under the ATS against the United States and its agents alleging that his abduction violated his civil rights. The Court ruled "a single illegal detention of less than a day, followed by the transfer of custody to lawful authorities and a prompt arraignment, did not violate any "norm of customary international so well defined as to support the creation of a federal remedy." *Id* at 738.

69 *Id.* at 693, 713-14. The injuries in *Sosa* rested on events that occurred in Mexico.

70 *Id.* The Court announced a two-part test that federal courts must apply before recognizing an ATS common-law action. The threshold question is whether a plaintiff can demonstrate that the alleged violation is "of a norm that is specific, universal, and obligatory." *Id.* at 732. If such a norm can control, a court must determine whether permitting the case to proceed under the ATS is a proper exercise of judicial discretion or whether caution requires the political branches to grant specific authority before imposing corporate liability. *Id.*

71 *Kiobel*, 569 U.S. 108, 123, 133 S. Ct. 1659, 185 L. Ed. 2d 671 (2013).

72 *Id.* at 124. All the relevant conduct took place outside the United States.

into their courts for alleged violations of the law of nations occurring in the United States, or anywhere else in the world."[73]

In *Jesner v. Arab Bank*,[74] the Supreme Court pointed out the ATS was invoked only a few times over its first 190 years, but with "the evolving recognition–e.g., in the Nuremberg trials–that certain crimes against humanity violate basic precepts of international law, courts began to give some redress to violations of clear and unambiguous international human-rights protections..." Congress followed this trend by enacting the Torture Victim Protection Act[75] to create "an express cause of action for victims of torture and extrajudicial killing in violation of international law,"[76] However, while more ATS suits were filed, the Supreme Court referred to an earlier decision in *Sosa v. Alvarez-Machain*[77] that "ATS litigation implicates serious separation-of-powers and foreign-relations concerns."[78] In *Jesner*, "foreign nationals were seeking millions of dollars in damages from a major Jordanian financial institute for injuries suffered in attacks by foreign terrorists in the Middle East."[79] The Court pointed out that the only alleged connections to the United States were "CHIPS transactions[80] in Arab Bank's New York branch and a brief allegation about a charity in Texas"[81] and that at "a minimum, the relatively minor connection between the terrorist attacks and the alleged conduct in the United States illustrate[d] the perils of extending the scope of ATS liability to foreign multinational corporations like Arab Bank."[82]

---

73 *Id.*

74 *Jesner*, 138 S. Ct. 1386, 200 L. Ed. 2d 612 (2018).

75 Pub. L. No. 102-256, 106 Stat. 73 (1991), which amended the Alien Tort Claims Act. As noted *supra*, the Court stated in *Jesner* that this act did not permit suits against corporate entities; the Court referred to the Act's "key feature" being that "it limits liability to individuals." 138 S. Ct. at 1404.

76 *Jeswner*. 138 S.Ct. at 1389, 1398.

77 *Sosa*, 542 U.S. 692, 124 S. Ct. 2739, 159 L. Ed. 2d 718 (2004).

78 *Jesner*, 138 S. Ct. at 1389 (citing *Sosa*, 542 U.S. at 732).

79 *Id.* at 1390.

80 An elaborate system to clear dollar-dominated transactions through the Clearing House Interbank Payments System is referred to as CHIPS. *Id.* at 1395.

81 The charity was the Texas-based Holy Land Foundation for Relief and Development that the plaintiffs alleged was affiliated with Hamas. *Id.* According to the plaintiffs, Arab Bank used its New York branch to facilitate the transfer of funds from the Holy Land Foundation to the bank accounts of terrorist-affiliated charities in the Middle East.

82 Accordingly, the Court ruled that foreign corporations could not be defendants in suits brought

In 2017, in *Al-Tamimi v. Adelson*,[83] Palestinians and Palestinian-American from East Jerusalem, the West Bank, and the Gaza Strip, and five Palestinian village councils brought action against forty-nine defendants alleging a civil conspiracy to expel all non-Jews from East Jerusalem, the West Bank, and the Gaza Strip.[84] The court ruled that the plaintiffs' request for the court to adjudicate and resolve the lawfulness of the development of the Israeli settlements in Gaza, the West Bank, and East Jerusalem stretches "over thirty years into the past" and that issue, "both close to the heart of the ongoing Israeli-Palestinian conflict and central to the United States' foreign policy decision-making in the region," was inappropriate for the court to resolve.[85] The court ruled "these issues must be decided by the political branches" and granted defendants' motions to dismiss.[86]

In *Comparelli v. Republica Bolivariana De Venezuela*,[87] the Court of Appeals for the Eleventh Circuit ruled that a reference to the ATS did not preclude the court from recognizing that the plaintiffs had invoked jurisdiction, alleging a taking of their property by a Venezuelan company in violation of international law, under an expropriation exception to immunity in the Foreign Sovereign Immunities Act,[88] discussed *infra*. The Eleventh Circuit reversed the district court's dismissal of the foreign plaintiffs' actions.[89]

---

under the ATS. *Id.* The Court stated: "For 13 years, this litigation has caused considerable diplomatic tensions with Jordan, a critical ally that considers the litigation an affront to its sovereignty."

The Court considered the history of the ATS to debate the extent of causes of action under the ATS and stated: "The First Congress enacted the ATS to help the United States avoid diplomatic friction. Putting that objective together with the rules governing federal common law generally, the following principle emerges: Federal courts should decline to create federal common law causes of action whenever doing so would not materially advance the ATS's objective of avoiding diplomatic strife. Applying that principle here, it is clear that courts should not create causes of action under the ATS against foreign corporate defendants. Customary international law does not generally require corporate liability, so declining to create it under the ATS cannot give other nations just cause for complaint against the United States. To the contrary, creating causes of action against foreign corporations under the ATS may instead provoke exactly the sort of diplomatic strife inimical to the statute's fundamental purpose. *Id.* at 1392.

83 *Adelson*, 264 F. Supp. 3d 69 (D.C. D.C. 2017).

84 They also alleged genocide, crimes against humanity, and violation of the Alien Tort Claims Act and the Torture Victim Protection Act.

85 264 F. Supp. 3d at 87.

86 *Id.*

87 *Camparelli*, 891 F.3d 1311 (11th Cir. 2018).

88 28 U.S.C. §1605(a)(3).

89 891 F.3d at 1318, 1326.

The Foreign Sovereign Immunities Act (FSIA)[90] is "'the sole basis for obtaining jurisdiction over a foreign state'" in United States courts.[91] Under the FSIA, '"a foreign state is immune from the jurisdiction of the United States unless an FSIA statutory exemption is applicable.'"[92] The Supreme Court has stated that sovereign immunity reflects "comity or mutual respect" that "is essential in dealings between sovereign nations.[93] The ATS reflects this principle as it does not waive immunity for foreign States. In contrast, although the FSIA specifically provides for immunity for foreign States from suits in U.S. courts,[94] exceptions to immunity in specific cases set out in FSIA permit some claims against foreign States to be brought in courts in the United States.[95] Nonetheless, if no exception applies, a trial court lacks subject-matter jurisdiction."[96]

The FSIA clarified the confusion that developed after the executive branch shifted from a long-standing policy of asserting sovereign immunity on behalf of friendly sovereigns under almost all circumstances to a more restrictive approach to immunity that would permit U.S. courts to exercise jurisdiction over claims against foreign sovereigns generally based on their commercial activities[97] but also under FSIA's expropriations exception. The FSIA "starts from a

90 28 U.S.C. §§1602-11.

91 *Comparelli*, 891 F.3d at 1318-19 (quoting *Argentine Republic v. Amerada Hess Shipping Corp.*, 488 U.S. 428, 434, 109 S. Ct. 683, 102 L. Ed 2d 818 (1989)).

92 *Id.* at 1319 (citing *Calzadilla v. Banco Latino International*, 413 F.3d 1285, 1296 (11th Cir. 2005).

93 *Republic of Philippines v. Pimental*, 553 U.S. 851, 865, 128 S. Ct. 2180, 171 L. Ed. 2d 131 (2008) (class action by and for human rights victims (Pimental class) of Ferdinand Marcos while he was President of the Republic of the Philippines).

94 28 U.S.C. at §1604.

95 As the Supreme Court stated in *Bolivarian Republic of Venezuela v. Helmerick & Payne*, 137 S. Ct. 1312, 197 L. Ed. 2d 663 (2017), the FSIA shields foreign states from suits in United States courts with some exceptions. The FSIA defines "the jurisdiction of United States courts in suits against foreign states, the circumstances in which foreign states are immune from suit and in which execution may not be levied on their property." The purpose of the Act "is to provide when and how parties can maintain a lawsuit against a foreign state or its entities in the courts of the United States and to provide when a foreign state is entitled to sovereign immunity." *See* H.R. Rep. 94-1487, at 1, 94th Cong., 2nd Sess. 1976, 1976 U.S.C.C.A.N. 6604.

96 *Comparelli*, 891 F.3d at 1319.

97 *See, e.g.*, discussion in *Republic of Austria v. Altmann*, 541 U.S. at 690-91, and *Verlinden*, 461 U.S. at 487-88.

premise of immunity and then creates exceptions to the general principle."[98] Thus, while a foreign sovereign and its instrumentalities are immune from suit in U.S. courts,[99] the following specific statutory exception apply:[100] (1) the foreign state has waived immunity either explicitly or by implication;[101] (2) the action is based upon a commercial activity carried on in the United States by the foreign state;[102] (3) in cases in which rights in property taken in violation of international law are in issue and property, or property for which it was exchanged, is in the United States (an expropriation exception);[103] (4) in cases in which rights in property in the United States acquired by gift or succession or rights in immovable property situated in the United States are in issue; and (5) where money damages are sought against a foreign state for personal injury or death or damage or loss of property caused by the tortious act or omission of that foreign state or one of its employees while acting within the scope of office or employment.[104]

---

98 *Verlinden,* 461 U.S. at 493 (citing H.R. Rep. No. 94-1487, at 17.) The Supreme Court ruled *in Bolivarian Repub. of Venezuela v. Hermerich & Payne,* 137 S. Ct. 1312, 1318, 197 L. Ed. 2d 663 (2017), that FSIA's statutory language makes foreign sovereign immunity jurisdictional.

99 28 U.S.C. at §1604.

100 *Id.* at §1605(a).

101 Still courts have construed very narrowly this waiver exception set out in §1605(a)(1). Courts have seldom found that a nation has waived its sovereign immunity. *See e.g., Frolova v. Union of Soviet Socialist Republics,* 761 F.2d 370, 377 (7th Cir. 1985); *Argentine Republic v. Amerada Hess Shipping Corp,* 488 U.S. 428, 442-43, 109 S. Ct. 683, 102 L. Ed. 2d 818 (1989); and *Sampson v. Federal Republic of Germany,* 250 F.3d 1145, 1150 (7th Cir. 2001).

102 Under the commercial activity exception, "'a foreign state may be liable for its commercial activities outside the territory of the United States having a 'direct effect' inside the United States." *Camparelli, id.* at 1325 (citing *Amerada Hess,* 488 U.S. at 441)).

103 The expropriation exception requires a claimant to show "(1) that rights in property are at issue; (2) that property was taken; (3) that the taking was in violation of international law; and (4) that at least one of ... two statutory nexus requirements are satisfied." *Camparelli,* id. at 1319. The court stated: "The nexus requirement is satisfied if the property in question or any property exchanged for such property is either (a) 'present in the United States in connection with a commercial activity carried on in the United States by the foreign state;'or (b) 'is owned or operated by an agency or instrumentality of the foreign state and that agency or instrumentality is engaged in a commercial activity in the United States.'" *Id.* at 1325. The court reasoned that the nexus requirement of §1605(a)(3) is the connection to the United States. Id at 1326.

104 The exceptions for the most part involve commerce or immovable property located in the United States although violations of international law have become important considerations in determining sovereignty in suits against foreign governments.

The immovable-property exception in FSIA is based on the ancient principle of *lex rei sitae*[105] and "reflects the fact that a sovereign 'cannot suffer its own laws...to be changed' by another sovereign."[106] In recognizing that "property ownership is not an inherently sovereign function," the Supreme Court has stated that the FSIA was "meant to codify the real property exception recognized by international practice at the time of its enactment."[107] Additionally, the Court has ruled that the FSIA does not immunize a foreign sovereign from a lawsuit to declare the validity of tax liens on property held by a sovereign.[108] Although the Court recognized that the exception in FSIA as to immovable property[109] "focuses more broadly on 'rights in' property," it decided that a suit to establish the validity of a tax lien placed "rights in immovable property" in issue and, thus, a foreign government was not immune from a lawsuit to declare the validity of tax liens on a sovereign's property located in the United States.[110]

Decisions in the following cases illustrate that courts in the United States have granted, and generally continue to grant, foreign States immunity from suit even for claims involving violations of international law, but the cases also exemplify the difficulties courts have had in resolving immunity issues, particularly when claimants are victims of foreign States' violations of international law. The landmark case of *Republic of Austria v. Altmann*,[111] represented the Supreme Court's affirmation in 2004 that the immunity exceptions in FSIA, although not enacted until 1976, apply retroactively to permit victims to bring claims in United States courts against foreign States relating to genocide and the taking of victims' property in violation of international law, including violations that occurred before and during World War II. Victims of crimes involving violations of international law have filed numerous claims in United States courts subsequent to *Altmann*; however, in addressing these claims, the courts have

105 Discussion in *Upper Skagit Tribe v. Lundgren*, 1375 S. Ct. 1649, 200 L Ed. 231 (2018), Thomas, J, dissenting, joined by Alito, J., stating: "the principle provides that 'land is governed by the law of the place where it is situated,'" quoting, F. Wharton, Conflict of Laws §273, p. 607 (G. Parmele ed. 3d ed 1905)).

106 *Id.*, citing H. Wheaton, Elements of International Law §81, p. 114 (1866).

107 *Permanent Mission of India to the United Nations v. City of New York*, 551 U.S. 193, 194, 127 S. Ct. 2352, 168 L,Ed. 2d 85 (2007).

108 *Id.* at 195.

109 28 U.S.C. §1605(a)(4).

110 *Permanent Mission of India*, 554 U.S. at 202.

111 *Republic of Austria v. Altmann*, 541 U.S. 677, 124 S. Ct. 2240, 159 L. Ed. 2d 1 (2004).

rendered conflicting decisions relating to the immunity of foreign States, as well as their officials, for their tortious acts.

In 2004, in *Republic of Austria v. Altmann*, the Supreme Court affirmed a decision of the Court of Appeals for the Ninth Circuit that courts in the United States had jurisdiction to hear a claim of a Holocaust victim as against the Republic of Austria. Maria Altmann brought a claim against the Republic of Austria for the recovery of six Gustav Klimt paintings the Nazis took from her deceased Jewish uncle, Ferdinand Bloch.[112] The Republic of Austria contended it was immune from the jurisdiction of courts in the United States under the FSIA. However, the Ninth Circuit affirmed the decision of the district court that a foreign state is not immune from the jurisdiction of courts in the United States when the issue is whether rights in property were taken in violation of international law. The Ninth Circuit decided that Austria could not expect immunity in light of its complicity in, and perpetuation of, the discriminatory expropriation of the Klimt paintings. It noted that the seizures violated both Austria's and Germany's obligations under the 1907 Hague Convention on the Laws and Customs of War on Land and that Austria's Second Republic officially repudiated all Nazi transactions in 1946. Although the Supreme Court did not endorse the reasoning of the Ninth Circuit,[113] it affirmed that court's ruling determining that the FSIA also applies to appropriation takings that occurred prior to the Act's enactment in 1976.[114]

In 2006, in *Intel Corp. v. Commonwealth Scientific and Indus. Research*,[115] the court ruled patent licensing negotiations engaged in by Australia's national science agency in the United States qualified as "commercial activity" within the meaning of the exception to immunity under the FSIA and thus the science agency was not entitled to immunity. The court referred to the statutory definition of commercial activity in FSIA and decided it means "either a regular course of commercial conduct or a particular commercial transaction or act."[116] The court decided that because Congress did not set forth an exhaustive list of

---

112 See *Altmann v. Republic of Austria*, 317 F.3d 954 (9th Cir. 2002) and 327 F.3d 1246 (9th Cir. 2003).

113 541 U.S. at 700.

114 *Id.* at 697. The Court decided that Congress intended the FSIA to apply to preenactment conduct.

115 *Intel*, 455 F.3d 1364 (Fed. Cir. 2006).

116 *Id.* at 1369-70 (citing 28 U.S.C. §1603(d)).

activities that would constitute "commercial activity," it left the courts with "a great deal of latitude" in deciding what is a "commercial activity."[117]

In 2010, in *Samantar v. Yousuf,*[118] natives of Somalia brought action against a former high-ranking government official for alleged acts of torture and human rights violations committed against them by government agents.[119] The Supreme Court ruled that an individual foreign official sued for conduct undertaken in the individual's official capacity is not a "foreign state" entitled to immunity from suit under FSIA. The Court noted that FSIA specifies that a foreign state includes a political subdivision or any agency or instrumentality of a state, which are all entities, and that the list in the FSIA does not suggest that officials are included.[120] As further discussed *infra*, a question remains with the courts whether foreign officials have common law immunity.

In *Rosenberg v. Lashkar-E-Taiba,*[121] American and Israeli citizens who were injured or had relatives killed during a terrorist attack in India filed claims against an alleged terrorist organization designated by the United States government as a Foreign Terrorist Organization, one that based its operations in Pakistan. The plaintiffs also alleged that Pakistani members of the organization planned, trained, and prepared for the Mumbai terror attacks in Pakistan. All ten of the terrorists who committed the Mumbai terror attacks were Pakistani nationals. The court referred to the Supreme Court's opinion in *Samantar v. Yousuf* that while the FSIA does not provide immunity for officials, the officials "might" have immunity under the common law.[122]

In 2010, in *Cassirer v. Kingdom of Spain,*[123] an American citizen, Claude Cassirer, whose grandmother's Pissarro painting allegedly was confiscated in 1939 by an agent of the Nazi government in Germany because she was Jewish, filed suit to recover the painting from the Kingdom of Spain and the Thyssen-

117 *Id.* at 1370.

118 *Samantar*, 560 U.S. 305, 130 S. Ct. 2278, 176 L. Ed. 2d 1047 (2010).

119 The former high-ranking government official, Mohamed Ali Samantar, originally was the First Vice President and Minister of Defense of Somalia but later served as its Prime Minister. Respondents, who were natives of Somalia, alleged that they, or members of their families, were the victims of torture and extrajudicial killings while Samantar served in his official capacities. *Id.* at 308.

120 *Samantar*, 560 U.S. at 306 (citing 28 U.S. §1603(a)).

121 *Rosenberg*, 980 F. Supp. 2d 336 (E.D.N.Y. 2013), *aff'd Rosenberg v. Pasha*, 577 Fed. Appx. 22 (2nd Cir. 2014).

122 980 F. Supp. 2d at 344-45.

123 *Cassirer*, 616 F.3d 1019 (9th Cir. 2010), cert. den., 131 S. Ct. 3057 (2011).

Bornemisza Collection Foundation, an instrumentality of Spain that had possession of the painting and claimed ownership of it.[124] The Court of Appeals for the Ninth Circuit ruled the expropriation exception to FSIA was applicable even though neither the Kingdom of Spain nor the Foundation took the painting from its owner.[125] The Ninth Circuit further ruled that Cassirer was not required to exhaust judicial remedies available in Germany or Spain before suing in the United States under the expropriation exception.[126] The court decided that because Congress had not mandated exhaustion, sound judicial discretion governed. The Ninth Court also found that the Foundation had engaged in sufficient commercial activity in the United States to support jurisdiction pursuant to FSIA.[127]

---

124 Spain and the Foundation moved to dismiss, asserting that sovereign immunity pursuant to the FSIA made them immune from suit in the United States courts. Cassirer relied on the "international takings" or "expropriation" exception in FSIA that confers subject matter jurisdiction over a foreign state when rights in property taken in violation of international law are at issue and when the instrumentality is engaged in a commercial activity in the United States. Spain and the Foundation maintained the exception was not applicable because the painting was taken in violation of international law by Germany, and not by either of them, and because the Foundation was not engaged in commercial activity in the United States sufficient to trigger the exception. In 1939, Lilly Cassirer, Claude Cassirer's grandmother, decided she had to leave Germany. German Jews had been deprived of their civil rights, their property was being "Aryanized," and the Kristallnacht pogroms had taken place throughout the country. Although Lilly wished to take the painting with her, an official appraiser appointed by the Nazi government refused to permit her to take the painting out of Germany and demanded she give it to him for approximately $360. Fearing she would not otherwise be permitted to go and knowing she would not obtain the money as the funds would be paid into a blocked account, Lilly complied. *Id.* at 1023-25. The appraiser traded the painting to another art dealer who also was persecuted and fled Germany for Holland. After Germany invaded Holland, the Gestapo confiscated the painting and returned it to Germany where it was sold at auction to an anonymous purchaser in 1943. It appeared in a New York gallery in 1952 and was sold to a St. Louis collector. It was sold again in 1976 to a New York art dealer who, in turn, sold it to Baron Hans-Heinrich Thyssen-Bornemisza. Bornemisza lived in Switzerland. In 1988, Spain paid the Baron $50 million to lease his collection for ten years. Five years later Spain paid the Foundation $327 million to purchase the entire collection, including the Pissarro painting. As part of the agreement, Spain provided without charge the Villahermosa Palace in Madrid to the Foundation for use as the Thyssen-Bornemisza Museum. Claude Cassirer discovered the painting was on display at the museum in Madrid in 2000. He requested Spain's Minister for Education, Culture and Sports, who was chair of the Foundation's board, to return the painting. The request was refused. In 2003, five members of Congress wrote the Minister requesting return of the painting; this request also was refused. *Id.* at 1023-24.

125 *Id.* at 1028-31.

126 *Id.* at 1034.

127 The Foundation had borrowed art works from American museums, had encouraged United States citizens to visit the museum and had accepted entrance fees from them, had sold various items to United States citizens including images of the painting, and had maintained a web site where United States citizens could buy admission tickets using United States credit cards to view paintings on display. *Id.* at 1032.

In 2011, in *Orkin v. Swiss Confederation*,[128] the court ruled that the "takings" exception of the FSIA does not apply when the property at issue passed in the first instance to a private individual and then, from the private individual, to a foreign government.[129] According to the court, the FSIA will apply only if property initially was taken or expropriated by other sovereigns. When an acquisition is by a private individual, the court ruled there is no subject matter jurisdiction under the FSIA's "taking" clause.[130]

In 2011, in *Rubin v. Islamic Republic of Iran*,[131] judgment creditors sought to enforce a judgment they had obtained against the Islamic Republic of Iran for injuries sustained in a suicide bombing in Israel carried out by a terrorist organization with the assistance of Iranian material support and training. They attempted to collect their judgment by executing or attaching various collections of Persian artifacts in the possession of a museum and a university.[132] Iran claimed FSIA immunity from attachment of the collections.[133] The Court of Appeals for the Seventh Circuit referenced the commercial-activity exception in the FSIA[134] but stated the exception permits execution against property of a foreign state in the United States only if that property has been used for commercial activity. The court ruled that the property of a foreign state in the United States is presumed immune from attachment, that immunity inheres in the property, and that it does not depend on an appearance or special pleading by the foreign State.[135] Further, it ruled a court must satisfy itself that an

---

128 *Orkin*, 770 F. Supp. 2d 612 (S.D.N.Y. 2011).

129 The property at issue, a Van Gogh pen and ink drawing, was sold by a German of Jewish descent to a Swiss art collector to help fund her family's escape from the Nazis. The drawing passed to the Swiss Confederation as a bequest from the art collector. *Id* at 613-14.

130 *Id.* at 617.

131 *Rubin*, 637 F.3d 783 (7th Cir. 2011).

132 Two of the collections of Persian antiquities were owned by Iran but were on long-term academic loan to the University of Chicago's Oriental Institute. One collection was owned by Chicago's Field Museum of Natural History; however, plaintiffs contested the Field Museum's title. The judgment creditors claimed Iran owned the collection because Ernst Herzfeld, from whom the Field Museum purchased the collection, allegedly stole the artifacts and smuggled them out of Iran in the 1920s and 1930s. Iran did not claim ownership of the collection. *Id.* at 787.

133 28 U.S.C. §1609.

134 *Id.* at §1610(b).

135 637 F.3d at 800-01.

exception to the FSIA[136] applies before it can order attachment or other execution on foreign-state property in the United States.[137]

In 2013, in *Rubin v. Islamic Republic of Iran*,[138] the Court of Appeals for the First Circuit ruled that antiquities allegedly belonging to Iran but in possession of museums in the United States were not "blocked assets" that were subject to attachment under the Terrorism Risk Insurance Act (TRIA).[139] Judgment creditors in the case sought to attach by trustee process various antiquities allegedly belonging to Iran following the creditors obtaining a $109 million default judgment against the Islamic Republic of Iran.[140] The museum contended that Iran did not own the antiquities and that, even if it did, the antiquities would be immune under the FSIA.[141] Although under certain circumstances TRIA permits the attachment of property that might otherwise be immune under the FSIA, the museums contended the TRIA does not displace the traditional rule that a judgment creditor may execute only against assets that a judgment creditor owns and that the district court was correct in concluding that Iranian law did not vest title to the antiquities in Iran.[142] The First Circuit determined that the antiquities were not "contested" assets and, thus, they could not qualify as "blocked assets" under TRIA.[143] The First Circuit ruled that because Iran had never made a claim to, or directed transfer of, any of the antiquities at issue in the case, the antiquities were not "contested;" thus, even if the antiquities qualified as "assets of Iran" under the TRIA, they would be "uncontested" assets. The First Circuit ruled that the judgment creditors had failed to demonstrate that any of the antiquities in the museums' possession fell within the narrow exception in

136 *Id.* at §1610(a).

137 637 F.3d at 801.

138 *Rubin*, 709 F.3d 49 (1st Cir. 2013).

139 28 U.S.C. §1610(g). The TRIA was enacted in 2002 to permit attachment in aid of execution of a FSIA judgment. The act permits claimants to impose liens on property of State sponsors of terrorism.

140 709 F.3d at 50. The creditors obtained the judgment after a suicide bombing was carried out by an Iran-sponsored terrorist group. The creditors were United States citizens who were injured in a 1997 terrorist attack that Hamas orchestrated in Jerusalem. They sued the Islamic Republic of Iran alleging that Iran had provided material support to Hamas and was therefore liable for the attack. They sought to collect their default judgment by attaching certain antiquities they claimed were the property of Iran but that were in the possession of two U.S. museums. *Id.*

141 *Id.* at 52.

142 *Id.* at 51.

143 TRIA defines a "blocked asset" as any asset seized or frozen by the United States under the International Emergency Economic Powers Act. 50 U.S.C. §§1701-1702.

TRIA that excluded foreign sovereign property from immunity from attachment and execution.[144]

In 2016, in *Bennett v. Islamic Republic of Iran*,[145] the Court of Appeals for the Ninth Circuit ruled that four groups of American victims of Iranian terrorist acts, who had obtained judgments against the Islamic Republic of Iran, had priority with respect to certain blocked assets the companies owed to the national bank of Iran. The court held the bank's assets were subject to attachment under the FSIA and the Terrorism Risk Insurance Act (TRIA).[146] The court noted TRIA permits judgment creditors to attach assets held by the instrumentalities of state sponsors of terrorism and that FSIA permits attachment of an execution against property held by a foreign terrorist state's instrumentality that is a separate juridical entity.[147]

In 2018, in *Rubin v. Islamic Republic of Iran and Field Museum of Natural History*,[148] the Supreme Court affirmed the ruling of the Seventh Circuit,[149] that families who had obtained judgment against the Islamic Republic of Iran under the FSIA for injuries sustained in terrorist groups' suicide bombing, could not execute the judgment against Iranian antiquities currently on loan to a university and museum. The Court ruled the university's alleged commercial use of artifacts did not trigger the FSIA exception to executive immunity for property of a foreign state "used for a commercial activity" in the United States and held that the FSIA provision,[150] permitting attachment of and execution against property held by a foreign terrorist state's instrumentality "that is a separate juridical entity" was not a freestanding "terrorism" exception to execution immunity. The Seventh Circuit had agreed with the district court,[151] that a United States

144 *Id.* at 58. The court ruled that the TRIA did not nullify the antiquities immunity from execution as provided in the FSIA. See 28 U.S. C. §1609. The general rule is that foreign sovereign property in the United States is immune from attachment and execution. However, while the FSIA makes property of a foreign State that is located in the United States immune from attachment and execution, there are exceptions, one of which permits attachment of foreign State property if it is used for commercial activities in the United States.

145 *Islamic Republic of Iran*, 825 F.3d 949 (9th Cir. 2016)

146 Pub. L. No 107-297, 1216 Stat. 2322.

147 825 F. 3d at 957-58.

148 *Rubin v. Islamic Republic of Iran*, 138 S. Ct. 816 (2018).

149 *Rubin*, 830 F.3d 470 (7th Cir 2016).

150 28 U.S. C. §1610(g).

151 33 F. Supp. 3d 1003 (N.D. Ill. 2014).

museum was not an agent of the Republic of Iran for purposes of the commercial activity exception to FSIA. Some artifacts in the museum belonged to the National Museum of Iran and were on long-term loan to the University of Chicago's Oriental Institute for scholarly study. The museum purchased other artifacts, but the museum lacked provenance of the items. The Supreme Court ruled that while the FSIA provision stating that certain property will be subject to attachment in aid of execution upon judgment under FSIA's terrorism exception, the provision does not provide a freestanding basis for parties holding such a judgment to attach and execute against property of a foreign state.[152]

Holocaust survivors and heirs of other Holocaust victims have sued several Hungarian banks and the Hungarian national railway asserting that the banks and the national railway participated in expropriating property from Hungarian Jewish victims of the Holocaust. The victims alleged takings in violation of international law and the aiding and abetting of genocide as violations of international law. The banks and the railway moved to dismiss for lack of subject-matter jurisdiction based on a defense of sovereign immunity under the FSIA.[153] In one of these cases, *Victims of Hungarian Holocaust v. Hungarian State Railways*,[154] the federal district court ruled that the takings exception in the FSIA[155] was sufficiently alleged and the victims were not required to exhaust remedies in Hungarian courts. Similarly, in the second of these two cases, *Holocaust Victims of Bank Theft. v. Magyar Nemzeti Bank*,[156] the federal district court found that the plaintiffs had alleged sufficient facts to show that the expropriation exception to the FSIA applied to their claims. However, in *Abelesz v. Magyar Nemseti Bank*,[157] in the appeal of both these cases, the Court of Appeals for the Seventh Circuit ruled that the plaintiffs were required either to exhaust any available Hungarian remedies or to present to the district court a legally compelling reason for failure to do so.[158] The Seventh Circuit explained that "the requirement that domestic

---

152 *Rubin v. Islamic Republic of Iran*, 138 S. Ct. at 825-27.

153 28 U.S.C. §1604.

154 *Victims of Hungarian Holocaust*, 798 F. Supp. 2d 934 (N.D. Ill. 2011).

155 28 U.S.C. §1605(a)(3).

156 *Holocaust Victim of Bank Theft*, 807 F. Supp. 2d 689, 697 (N.D. Ill. 2011).

157 *Abelesz*, 692 F.3d 661 (7th Cir. 2012).

158 *Id.* at 666-696. See also *Fischer v. Magyar Allamvasutak Zrt*, 777 F.3d 847 (7th Cir. 2015). In *Fischer*, the Seventh Circuit summarized the exhaustion inquiry to be a requirement for a court answer two questions: (1) whether plaintiffs have alleged a taking in violation of international law where "in-

remedies for expropriation be exhausted before international proceedings may be instituted "to be a well-established rule of customary international law."[159] In *Fischer v. Magyar Allamvasutak Zrt*,[160] the court recognized that FSIA does not require an exhaustion prerequisite but nonetheless stated that the exhaustion requirement was "made clear" from the statute's "reliance on international law norms," that includes exhaustion.[161] That court explained that "exhaustion of domestic remedies is preferred in international law as a matter of comity" and that plaintiffs must either show they have exhausted a foreign sovereign's own domestic remedies or that to do so would be futile.[162]

In d*eCsepel v. Republic of Hungary*,[163] the Court of Appeals for the District of Columbia affirmed a district court's ruling that victims' claims against the Republic of Hungary and a number of its museums for their refusal to return pieces of art confiscated from the victims' ancestor, the Baron Mor Lipot Herzog, and their alleged breach of bailment agreements entered into in World War II, fell within the FSIA's commercial activity exception.[164] Additionally, the court

ternational law favors giving a state accused of taking property in violation of international law an opportunity to 'redress it by its own means, within the framework of its own legal system before the same alleged taking may be aired in foreign courts,'" citing *Abelesz*, 692 F.3d at 680, and (2) whether plaintiffs have exhausted domestic remedies in the country where the taking occurred or, if not whether plaintiffs can "show convincingly that such remedies are clearly a sham or inadequate or that their application is unreasonably prolonged," again citing *Abelesz*, 692 F.2d at 681. In *Fischer*, the Seventh Circuit states that "principles of international comity make clear" that a plaintiff "must attempt to exhaust domestic remedies" except where the remedies are "futile or imaginary." 777 F. 3d at 852, 858.

159 692 F.3d at 679.

160 *Fischer*, 777 F.3d at 854-55.

161 *Id.*

162 *Id.* at 859.

163 *deCsepel*, 714 F.3d 591 (D.C.C. 2013)

164 *Id.* at 600-01. The court ruled that there was a jury question whether the claims were time-barred and reversed the district court's finding of comity regarding a Hungarian judgment which dismissed claims to eleven pieces of artwork. The appellate court ruled that there was a jury question as to whether a Hungarian judgment was entitled to comity. The victims alleged that at least forty works of art were known to be in the possession of Hungarian museums and that several were openly exhibited as "From the Herzog Collection." The court pointed out that the relevant statute of limitations is the District of Columbia's three-year limitations period for claims relating to the recovery of personal property or damages for its retention. Pursuant to the statute, a bailment claim accrues when a victim demands the return of the property and the current possessor refuses, or the possessor takes some action that a reasonable person would understand to be either an act of conversion or inconsistent with a bailment. The appellate court reversed the district court's granting comity to a Hungarian judgment that dismissed the Herzog family's claim to eleven pieces of artworks. The appellate court ruled that granting comity would be inappropriate if the Hungarian

ruled the expropriation exception to FSIA also applied to their claims. The court decided the inherited paintings constituted genocidal takings in violation of international law and that the Treaty of Peace with Hungary did not provide the exclusive means of recovery for Hungarian Holocaust victims. The court further determined the plaintiffs' actual cause of action was not based upon Hungary's solicitation of United States tourists or other limited activities in the United States but rather on the postwar bailments and actions that took place in Hungary.[165] The court found there was evidence of express and implied bailments, some of which involved Holocaust victims residing in the United States. Additionally, the court decided the complaint alleged a cause of action falling squarely within the expropriation exception to FSIA.[166]

In 2016, in *Simon v. Republic of Hungary*,[167] the Court of Appeals for the District of Columbia Circuit ruled the 1947 Treaty of Peace with Hungary did not provide the exclusive means of recovery for Hungarian Holocaust victims and that United States federal courts have jurisdiction over claims for personal injury or death against a foreign sovereign. The court agreed that the plaintiffs' alleged confiscation of survivors' personal property constituted genocide.[168] The court held that the plaintiffs had established jurisdiction under the expropriation exception to the FSIA because expropriations undertaken to bring about a protected group's physical destruction qualify as genocide. Further, in contrast to the ruling of the Court of Appeals for the Seventh Circuit in *Abelesz*, discussed *supra*, that the victim of the Hungarian holocaust were required to exhaust

proceedings failed to provide an opportunity for a full and fair trial under "a system of jurisprudence likely to secure an impartial administration of justice." *Id.* at 606-07.

165 The court stated the relevant question was whether Hungary and the plaintiffs formed any bailment agreements that necessarily contemplated the United States as the place of performance. *Id.* at 599-601.

166 On remand, 169 F. Supp. 3d 143, 148-49 (D.C.D.C 2016), the court found that forty-two of the forty-four artworks named in the complaint were taken in violation of international law, noting that the Court of Appeals for the District of Columbia, in *Simon v. Republic of Hungary*, 812 F.3d 127, 142-43 (D.C. Cir. 2016), ruled that takings of Jewish property by the Republic of Hungary during World War II were expropriations that were "themselves genocide."

167 *Republic of Hungary*, 812 F.3d 127 (D.C. Cir. 2016).

168 *Id.* at 142. The court stated: "Such takings did more than effectuate genocide or serve as a means of carrying out genocide. Rather, we see the expropriations themselves as genocide." The court stated that genocide perpetuated by a state against its own nationals is a violation of international law. The court ruled that while an "intrastate taking–a foreign sovereign's taking of its own citizens' property–does not violate the international law of takings," *id.* at 144, "an intrastate taking can nonetheless subject a foreign sovereign and its instrumentalities to jurisdiction in the United States where the taking amounted to the commission of genocide." *Id.* at 142.

remedies in Hungarian courts, the court did not rule that customary international law obligates a plaintiff to exhaust domestic remedies before attempting to bring suit against a foreign sovereign in a United States court. The District of Columbia Circuit found jurisdiction over the victim's property-based claims under the FSIA's expropriation exception but remanded the case to the district court for it to decide whether exhaustion of remedies was required before the plaintiffs' claims could proceed in United States courts.[169]

On remand,[170] however, the district court dismissed the case, ruling that the plaintiffs had not shown that pursuing their claims in Hungary would be futile or that Hungary is an inadequate alternative forum.[171] Despite the plaintiffs arguments "that they would face 'manifest religious and ethnic prejudice' in the Hungarian courts" and irrespective of the court's statement that the "rise of anti-Semitism in Hungary and elsewhere, even close to home, is enormously disturbing," the district court decided "such concern [was] insufficient to conclude that bringing the plaintiffs' claims before Hungary's judicial system would be futile."[172]

In 2017, in de *Csepel v. Republic of Hungary*,[173] the Court of Appeals for the District of Columbia Circuit agreed the plaintiffs' claims for at least some of the artworks confiscated by the Republic of Hungary during World War II satisfied the expropriation exception. However, the appellate court ordered the district court to dismiss the Republic of Hungary as a defendant. The appellate court did permit the plaintiffs to amend their complaint against the other defendants, including Hungarian museums, in light of the Holocaust Expropriated Art Recovery Act,[174] which was enacted in 2016 to provide for a federal six-year statute of limitations that will not begin to run until a claimant's actual discovery

169 *Id.* at 133.

170 *Simon v. Republic of Hungary*, 277 F. Supp. 3d 42 (D.C.D.C. 2017, app. filed).

171 *Id.* at 51-52 (citing the decisions of the Court of Appeals for the Seventh Circuit in *Abelesz* and *Fischer* discussed *supra*). The district court thought the same considerations the Seventh Circuit decided warranted dismissal of the claims in *Abelesz* and *Fischer* for failure to exhaust Hungarian remedies applied in the case before it.

172 *Id.* at 61.

173 *Republic of Hungary*, 859 F.3d 1094 (D.C. Cir. 2017), pet. for cert. filed.

174 22 U.S. C. §1621.

of artwork or other property lost during the period of 1933 to 1945 because of Nazi persecution.[175]

In 2017, in *Philipp v. Federal Republic of Germany*,[176] legal successors of estates of consortium members of three art dealer firms in Germany brought action against the Federal Republic of Germany and an instrumentality of Germany alleging that the German instrumentality was in wrongful possession of a collection of medieval relics because sale of the collection to the former State of Prussia, a political subdivision of the Third Reich, was coerced as part of Nazi persecution of Jewish sellers.[177] The court ruled that application of the expropriation exception to sovereign immunity was appropriate under the FSIA and that the successors' claims were not preempted on the basis the claims were already adjudicated through a German advisory commission created to hear the claims.[178] The court also ruled international comity did not require the court to defer to the advisory commission's non-binding decisions that there was not a compulsory sale of the collection.[179] On appeal, the Court of Appeals for the District of Columbia Circuit[180] explained that it was "asked for the first time whether seizures of art may constitute 'takings of property that are themselves genocide'"[181] and stated that its answer "is yes."[182] Additionally, the court ruled the claimants were not required to exhaust remedies in German courts, as a matter of international comity, before bringing an action against Germany.[183]

175 *Id.* Actual discovery of the identify and location of artwork or other property is deemed to occur on the date on which there are facts sufficient to form a substantial basis to believe the artwork or other property is lost property. The act preempts any provision of federal or state law or any defense at law relating to the passage of time. *Id.*

176 *Federal Republic of Germany*, 248 F. Supp. 3d 59 and 253 F. Supp. 3d 84 (DC DC 2017), aff'd, *Phillipp v. Federal Republic of Germany*, 849 F.3d 406 (D.C Cir. 2018).

177 248 F. Supp. at 68.

178 *Id.* at 75-76.

179 *Id.* The court did dismiss five of the claims. *Id.* at 87.

180 *Phillipp v. Federal Republic of Germany*, 894 F.3d 406 (D.C. Cir. 2018).

181 *Id.* at 411, citing *Simon*, 812 F.3d at 144.

182 *Id.*

183 *Id.* at 416. The court stated that the FSIA, "which 'is, and always has been, a 'matter of grace and comity,'" (quoting *Verlinden*, 461 U. S. at 486) "leaves no room for a common-law exhaustion doctrine based on the very same considerations of comity."

In 2017, in *Bolivarian Republic of Venezuela v. Helmerich & Payne Intern'l Drilling Co.*,[184] the Supreme Court addressed the issue of whether a sovereign's taking of its own nationals' property can amount to an expropriation that violates international law. An American parent company and its Venezuelan subsidiary brought action against the Venezuelan government and two government-owned entities under the expropriation exception of the FSIA. The subsidiary of an American company had supplied oil rigs to oil development entities that were part of the Venezuelan government. The Venezuelan government had failed to pay more than $10 million that it owed the subsidiary, and at that point, sent troops to the equipment yard where the rigs were stored, prevented the subsidiary from removing the rigs, and issued a Decree of Expropriation, nationalizing the rigs. The plaintiffs alleged that Venezuela had unlawfully expropriated the subsidiary's rights by nationalizing them while the Venezuelan Government's argued that international law does not cover expropriations of property belonging to a country's own nationals.[185] The Supreme Court ruled that a case falls within the scope of the expropriation exception only if the property in which the party claims to hold rights was property taken in violation of international law and remanded the case for a consideration of the parent corporation's rights in property in the subsidiary. Additionally, the Court ruled that a court should decide the foreign sovereign's immunity defense at "the threshold of the action."[186]

In 2018, in *Devengoechea v. Bolivarian Republic of Venezuela*,[187] the Court of Appeals for the Eleventh Circuit considered another claim brought against Venezuela, in this case by the owner of a collection of historical artifacts, called the Bolivar Collection.[188] After the owner had taken the collection to Venezuela

184 *Bolivarian Republic of Venezuela*, 137 S. Ct. 1312, 197 L. Ed.2d 663 (2017).

185 *Id.* at 1314-15.

186 *Id.* at 1318-24 (citing V*erlinden*, 461 U. S. at 493).

187 *Bolivarian Republic of Venezuela*, 889 F.3d 1213 (11th Cir. 2018).

188 The plaintiff's great, great grandfather, who was a friend of Simon Bolivar, obtained a treasure trove of Bolivar's possessions (the "Bolivar Collection"). Because Bolivar, who was born in 1783, was a contemporary of George Washington and a founding father in South America not long after Washington played that role in North America, the collection had great significance. When Venezuela learned of the collection, it sent officials to the United States to meet with the plaintiff and negotiate. The parties reached an agreement that the plaintiff would take the Bolivar Collection to Venezuela for further inspection and Venezuela would either purchase it or return to the plaintiff. Five years after the plaintiff took the collection to Venezuela and despite repeated inquiries about obtaining payment or return, Venezuela had not returned nor paid for the collection.

for inspection in connection with that nation's prospective purchase of the collection, Venezuela refused to pay for the artifacts or to return them. The court ruled that the district court had jurisdiction under FSIA's commercial-activity exception.[189]

In summary, while the Alien Torts Statute (ATS) has provided limited access to the courts for victims of violations of international law, principally because the ATS does not waive immunity for foreign States, the FSIA, in contrast, sets out exceptions to immunity that permit courts in the United States to exercise jurisdiction over claims against foreign sovereigns in specific cases. The exceptions generally involve foreign States' commercial activities in the United States or those that occur under an expropriation exception applicable to violations of international law. Courts seemingly have latitude in deciding what constitutes "commercial activity." With respect to "violations of international law," courts are divided as to whether victims must exhaust remedies in the foreign State prior to filing a claim in a court in the United States.

E. WAIVER OF IMMUNITY FOR FOREIGN OFFICIALS

In *Samantar v. Yousuf*,[190] natives of Somalia brought an action under the Torture Victim Protection Act and the Alien Tort Statute seeking to impose liability and recover damages from a foreign high-ranking government official for alleged acts of torture and human rights violations committed against them by government agents. The official claimed statutory immunity under the FSIA. The Supreme Court clarified that the FSIA does not govern determinations of sovereign immunity for foreign officials.[191] As noted previously, the Supreme Court ruled that an individual foreign official sued for conduct undertaken in his official capacity is not a "foreign State" entitled to immunity from suit under FSIA. The Court noted that FSIA specifies that a foreign State includes a political subdivision or any agency or instrumentality of a State, and that these are all entities. Additionally, the list of exceptions to immunity in the FSIA, even if illustrative rather than exclusive, does not suggest that officials are included as being

189 The plaintiff also filed his claim against Venezuela under the commercial-activity exception to FSIA, 28 U.S. C. §1605(a)(2).

190 *Samantar*, 560 U.S. at 324-27.

191 *Id.*

entitled to immunity.[192] The Court commented that the sovereign immunity doctrine "developed as a matter of common law long before FSIA was enacted in 1976"[193] and that FSIA's history and purposes did "not show that when Congress codified state immunity, it intended to codify *sub silentio* official immunity."[194] Nonetheless, the Court decided action against a foreign official could still be barred under the common law[195] and remanded the case to determine whether the official would be entitled to immunity under the common law.

On remand,[196] the Court of Appeals for the Fourth Circuit decided that, "[b]efore proceeding further," it had to decide "the appropriate level of deference courts should give to the Executive Branch's views on case-specific questions of individual foreign sovereign immunity."[197] It noted that the United States "takes the position that federal courts owe absolute deference to the State Department's view of whether a foreign official is entitled to sovereign immunity" and that "the State Department's opinion of any foreign immunity issue is binding on the courts."[198] The Fourth Circuit stated: "The State Department's position allows for the federal courts to function as independent decision makers on foreign sovereign immunity questions in only one instance: when the State Department remains silent on a particular case."[199] Further, it noted that the United States had contended that "the State Department resolved the issues once it presented the district court with its view that [the foreign official] Samantar was not entitled to immunity."[200] The court referred to the Constitution[201] that assigns the power to "receive Ambassadors and other public Ministers" to the Executive Branch and decided that this ability "includes by implication, the power to accredit diplomats and recognize foreign heads of state."[202] It noted that courts had gener-

192 *Id.* at 306 (citing 28 U.S. §1603(a)).

193 *Id.* at 311.

194 *Id.* at 306.

195 *Id.* at 324.

196 *Yousuf v. Samantar*, 699 F.3d 763 (4th Cir. 2012).

197 *Id.* at 768.

198 *Id.* at 769.

199 *Id.*

200 *Id.* at 769-70.

201 United States Constitution, Article II, §3.

202 *Yousuf*, 699 F. 3d at 772.

ally treated executive "suggestions of immunity" for heads of state as a function of the Executive's constitutional power and, therefore, as controlling on the judiciary;[203] consequently, if the Executive Branch determined that a foreign head of state was immune from suit, that determination was conclusive and a court must accept the determination.[204] The Fourth Circuit ruled that when the Executive Branch "'has filed a Suggestion of Immunity as to a recognized head of a foreign state, the jurisdiction of the Judicial Branch immediately ceases.'"[205] Accordingly, the court concluded "that the State Department's pronouncement as to head-of-state immunity [was] entitled to absolute deference."[206] However, the Fourth Circuit also ruled that with respect to conduct-based immunity, while the State Department's determination "carries substantial weight in our analysis of the issue," it is not controlling.[207] The court referred to "customary international law" that had "long distinguished between status-based immunity afforded to sitting heads-of-state and conduct-based immunity available to other foreign officials, including former heads-of-state." The court opined that conduct-based immunity for a foreign official derives from the immunity of the State and "the international law principle that sovereign immunity, which belongs to a foreign *state*, extends to an individual *official* acting on behalf of that foreign state."[208] Thus, the immunity of a foreign State extended to any official with respect to acts performed in that individual's official capacity if the effect of exercising jurisdiction would be to enforce a rule of law against the State.

The Fourth Circuit additionally ruled that immunity was extended to a foreign official only when that official was acting *on behalf* of the State,[209] referring to decisions of the Court of Appeals for the Ninth Circuit to support its determination.[210] The Fourth Circuit "sketched" out the general contours of official-

203 *Id.* (quoting *Ye v. Zemin,* 383 F.3d 610, 626 (7th Cir. 2004)).

204 *Id.* (citing *Doe v. State of Israel,* 400 F. Supp. 2d 86, 111 (D.C.D.C. 2005)).

205 *Id.* (quoting *United States v. Noriega,* 117 F.3d 1206, 1212 (11th Cir. 1997)).

206 *Id.* at 773.

207 *Id.*

208 *Id.* at 774 (quoting the Supreme Court in *Underhill v. Hernandez,* 168 U.S. 250, 252, 18 S. Ct. 83, 42 L. Ed. 456 (1897)).

209 *Id.* at 774-75.

210 *Id.* referring to *Chuidian v. Philippine Nat'l Bank,* 912 F.3d 1095, 1106 (9th Cir. 1990) (recognizing that an individual is not "entitled to sovereign immunity for acts not committed in his official capacity") and *Hilao v. Estate of Marcos,* 25 F.3d 1467, 1472 (9th Cir. 1994) (stating that immunity "is extended to an individual only when acting on behalf of the state because actions against those individuals

act immunity as being that "a foreign official may assert immunity for official acts performed within the scope of his duty, but not for private acts where 'the officer purports to act as an individual and not as an official, [such that] a suit directed against that action is not a suit against the sovereign.'"[211] The court pointed to an increasing trend in international law to abrogate foreign official immunity for individuals who commit acts, otherwise attributable to the State, that violate *jus cogens* norms.[212] "A *jus cogens* norm, also known as a 'peremptory norm of general international law,' can be defined as 'a norm accepted and recognized by the international community of States as a whole as a norm from which no derogation is permitted and which can be modified only by a subsequent norm of general international law having the same character."[213] The court recognized that "*jus cogens* violations may well be committed under color of law and, in that sense, constitute acts performed in the course of the foreign official's employment by the Sovereign,"[214] but stated that "as a matter of international and domestic law, *jus cogens* violations are, by definition, acts that are not officially authorized by the Sovereign.[215] The court referred to a number of decisions from foreign national courts that "have reflected a willingness to deny official-act immunity in the criminal context for alleged *jus cogens* violations."[216] In also denying the official immunity, the Fourth Circuit observed that courts in the United States "have generally followed that trend, concluding that *jus cogens* violations are not legitimate official acts and therefore do not merit foreign official immunity."[217]

---

are the practical equivalent of a suit against the sovereign directly and a lawsuit against a foreign official acting outside the scope of his authority does not implicate any of the foreign diplomatic concerns involved in bringing suit against another government in United States courts").

211 *Yousuf*, 699 F.3d at 774 (quoting *Chuidian*, 912 F.2d at 1106).

212 *Id.* at 776.

213 *Id.* at 775, citing *Vienna Convention on the Law of Treaties*, Article 53, May 23, 1969, 1155 U.N.T.S. 331.

214 *Id.* at 775-76.

215 *Id.* at 776. Still, the court did state that "head-of-state immunity, based on status, is of an absolute nature and that it can apply even against *jus cogens* claims."

216 *Id.* referring "most notably the British House of Lords' *Pinochet* decision denying official-acts immunity to a former Chilean head of state accused of directing widespread torture," i. e., *Regina v. Bartle, ex parte Pinochet*, 38 I.L.M. 581, 593-95 (H.L.1999) (concluding that official-acts immunity is unavailable to shield foreign officials from prosecution for international crimes because acts of torture do not constitute officially-approved acts).

217 *Id.* at 778. Even the State Department had denied immunity for Samantar. The State Department had submitted a suggestion of non-immunity for Samantar, the individual in question, because

In 2013, in *Rosenberg v. Lashkar-e-Taiba*,[218] the court rejected the analysis of the Fourth Circuit in *Yousuf v. Samantar* and dismissed an action against a foreign official because that court decided that the official in question had immunity under the common law. On appeal, the Court of Appeals for the Second Circuit[219] affirmed, referring to its decision in *Matar v. Dichter*,[220] wherein it had pointed out that, although the FSIA is silent with regard to the immunity of former foreign governmental officials, there is no provision in FSIA that "bespeaks intent to abrogate [the] common-law scheme with respect to former officials."[221] The Second Circuit decided that because there is no general *jus cogens* exception to FSIA immunity, foreign officials are immune under common-law principles that "pre-date, and survive," the enactment of FSIA. The Second Circuit thought that, in the common-law context, a court must defer to the Executive Branch's determination of the scope of immunity.[222] Consequently, the Second Circuit ruled in *Rosenberg* that a claim of *jus cogens* does not withstand foreign service immunity.[223]

In 2018, in *Ben-Haim v. Edri*,[224] the court addressed the issue of whether a state court had jurisdiction to hear civil claims against foreign officials when

---

Samantar, as a former official of a state, did not have a currently recognized government that would request immunity on his behalf or that could take a position as to whether the acts in question were taken in an official capacity and additionally because Samantar's status was that of a permanent legal resident. The State Department decided that U.S. residents who enjoy the protections of U.S. law ordinarily should be subject to the jurisdiction of U.S. courts, particularly when sued by U.S. residents or naturalized citizens, such as the two of the plaintiffs. *Id.* at 777. The Fourth Circuit agreed with the State Department's determination, reasoning that "both factors the State Department considered added substantial weight to its decision to deny immunity." The court opined that because the State Department had not recognized officially a Somali government, the court did "not face the usual risk of offending a foreign nation by exercising jurisdiction over the plaintiffs' claims" and, "as a permanent legal resident, Samantar has a binding tie to the United States and its court system." *Id.* at 777-78.

218 *Rosenberg*, 980 F. Supp. 2d 336, 344 (E.D.N.Y. 2013).

219 *Rosenberg v. Pasha*, 577 Fed. Appx. 22 (2nd Cir. 2014).

220 *Matar*, 563 F.3d 9, 15 (2nd Cir. 2009).

221 *Id.* at 14-15.

222 *Id.*

223 577 Fed. Appx. at 23-24, citing *Matar*, 563 F.3d at 15. The Second Circuit referred in *Matar* to the ruling of the Seventh Circuit in *Ye v. Zemin*, 383 F.3d 620, 627 (7th Cir. 2004) that a claim premised on the violation of *jus cogens* does not withstand foreign service immunity. The Seventh Circuit considered and rejected the argument that "a foreign state should be deemed to have forfeited its sovereign immunity when it engages in conduct that violate fundamental humanitarian standards."

224 453 N.J. Super 526 (N. J. App. Ct. 2018).

the United States, through the State Department, had issued a suggestion of immunity (SOI) determining that the officials were entitled to immunity. Following divorce and child custody proceedings in Israel, a husband filed a civil complaint against Rabbinical Courts of Israel, six Israeli rabbinical judges, and an official of the Rabbinical Courts of Israel for aiding and abetting in the kidnapping of his daughter and for defamation. The court referred to the Supreme Court's statement in *Samantar v. Yousuf*[225] that claims against foreign officials may be governed by the common law. Accordingly, the court ruled that if the State Department determines a foreign official is entitled to immunity that decision is binding on the courts so that, once a court receives an SOI from the State Department, the court loses jurisdiction.[226] The court ruled that the SOI was binding; it was based on a finding by the State Department that foreign officials were acting within the scope of their authority for a foreign sovereign nation.

In *Mamani v. Berzain*,[227] the court considered claims brought under the Torture Victim Protection Act by nine Bolivian residents and citizens, who were relatives of eight Bolivian civilians that the Bolivian military allegedly killed deliberately. The plaintiffs claimed that two former high-ranking Bolivian government officials masterminded a violent military campaign that led to the deaths of their relatives, all in an effort to quell public opposition to their unpopular political agenda. In *Mamani*, the court did not refer to immunity issues with regard to the Bolivian officials but, in denying the defendants' summary judgment motion, the court ruled that the plaintiffs had exhausted their remedies under Bolivian law.

In sum, while the Supreme Court has clarified that the FSIA does not grant foreign State officials immunity, the Supreme Court has not addressed directly the issue of whether former foreign State officials have immunity under the common law. The Court of Appeals for the Fourth Circuit has ruled that *jus cogens* violations are not legitimate official State acts and therefore former officials who committed these violations do not merit foreign official immunity. In contrast, the Court of Appeals for the Second Circuit would defer to the Executive Branch's determination of the scope of immunity, ruling that *jus cogens* violations do not withstand foreign service immunity.

---

225 *Samantar*, 560 U.S. at 311.

226 *Id.*

227 309 F. Supp. 3d 1274 (D.C. S.D. Fla. 2018).

CHAPTER 6.
STATE SOVEREIGN IMMUNITY PROVISIONS

This chapter includes summaries of the sovereign and governmental immunity doctrine as it is applied in all the states, including the District of Columbia. The reader is cautioned that the discussion of each state's treatment of its sovereign immunity laws is a summary and some specialized provisions relating to a state's sovereign immunity laws are reviewed only briefly, or, for some states, are not discussed. As examples, each state has specific statutes of limitation for claims; requirements for notice differs in the states; and some states permit claims against an agency if liability insurance is available even if immunity is not waived. These very specialized provisions, are generally summarized tersely if they are covered. Although the state summaries in this chapter either do not cover specialized provisions or reviews them only cursorily with respect to some states, the summaries do provide a valuable starting point in determining a specific state's sovereign immunity law.

It should be noted that Alabama, Arkansas, Texas, and West Virginia are four states with an established and forceful protection of state sovereign immunity. Alabama's Constitution specifically provides for an inherent sovereign immunity law; its Constitution states that the state cannot be sued.[1] Because the source of immunity in Alabama is constitutionally based, Alabama courts have ruled that neither courts nor the Alabama legislature have power to waive a state's immunity.[2] The Arkansas Constitution states: "The State of Arkansas shall never be made defendant in any of her courts."[3] West Virginia's Constitution also provides for absolute state immunity. It states[4] that "West Virginia shall never be

1 Alabama Constitution, Article I, §14. See discussion *infra.*

2 *See, e. g., Ex parte Cranman,* 792 So. 2d 392, 399 (Ala. 2000).

3 Arkansas Constitution, Article 5, §20.

4 West Virginia Constitution, Article 6, §35. See discussion *infra.*

made defendant in any court of law or equity...." Texas courts have recognized judge-made sovereign immunity law as "a common-law doctrine that initially developed without any legislative or constitutional enactment,"[5] but nonetheless the Texas Supreme Court has ruled that "Texas is inviolably sovereign," that "sovereignty is inherent in its statehood," and that "sovereignty is firmly established."[6]

The strict sovereign immunity jurisprudence in Alabama, Arkansas, Texas, and West Virginia contrasts sharply with Washington statutory law that has abolished sovereign immunity for a state's tortious conduct, recognizing the sovereign immunity doctrine "springs from [an] archaic concept."[7] Additionally, several states have enacted torts claims acts that limit substantially those states' immunity from liability. In abrogating the state's immunity, the North Dakota Supreme Court[8] decided that "whatever justifications initially existed for sovereign immunity, they are no longer valid in today's society" and noted that few principles of modern law have been so uniformly and soundly criticized.

The opinion of the North Dakota Supreme Court must be compared with the earlier reasoning of the Virginia Supreme Court[9] that the doctrine "serves a multitude of purposes, including but not limited to protecting the public purse, providing for smooth operation of government, eliminating public inconvenience and danger that might spring from officials being fearful to act, assuring that citizens will be willing to take public jobs, and preventing citizens from improperly influencing the conduct of governmental affairs through the threat or use of vexatious litigation." The Virginia Court referred to the doctrine "as a rule of social policy, which protects the state from burdensome interference with the performance of its governmental functions and preserves its control over state funds, property and instrumentalities." It stated: "Given the several purposes of the doctrine, it follows that in order to fulfill those purposes, the protection

5 *Reata Const. Corp. v. City of Dallas*, 197 S.W.3d 371, 374 (Tex. 2006), citing *Cohens v. Virginia*, 6 Wheat 264, 19 U.S. 264, 293, 5 L. Ed. 257 (1821) and *Hosner v. De Young*, 1 Tex. 764, 769 (1847) (recognizing the doctrine was without statutory or constitutional authority).

6 See, e. g. *Wasson Interests, ltd. v. City of Jacksonville*, 489 S.W.3d 427 (Tex. 2016); T*ex. Nat Res. Conservation Comm'n v. IT-Davy*, 74 S.W.3d 849, 853 (Tex. 2002); and *Tooke v. City of Mexia*, 197 S.W.3d 325, 332 (Tex. 2006). See discussion *infra* and detailed discussion of Texas cases interpreting Texas sovereign immunity law in Chapter 4.

7 *Kelso v. City of Tacomo*, 390 P.2d 1, 4 (1964); Rev. Code of Wash. 4.92.090.

8 *Bulman v. Hulstrand Constr. Co., Inc.*, 521 N.W. 2d 632, 638 (N.D. 1994).

9 *Messina v. Burden*, 321 S.E.2d 657 (Va. 1984)

afforded by the doctrine cannot be limited solely to the sovereign." The court decided: "Unless the protection of the doctrine extends to some of the people who help run the government, the majority of the purposes for the doctrine will remain unaddressed."[10]

The reader must decide which position, that of the Supreme Court of North Dakota or that of the Virginia Supreme Court, is most accurate and preferable or whether, in the alternative, there should be an intermediate and limited application of the doctrine, which is present in many of the states and should be noted from the summaries *infra* of all of the states' sovereign immunity laws.

There is differing treatment in the states regarding specialized provisions. For example, notice requirements differ in the states as well as the applicable office--supervisor of an agency, a claims commission, or the attorney general of the state--that must receive a required notice. Additionally, a state generally will have differing requirements depending on whether the claim is a tort, contract or property claim. If a state has waived immunity for some claims, most states will not permit punitive damages, attorney's fees, costs, and/or interest; many may have caps on damages and, if so, the amount of the damage limitations will differ. Schools and municipalities are treated differently in the states with respect to immunity. In some states, police agencies and some firefighting agencies have separate statutory requirements regarding waiver of governmental immunity. Discretionary or governmental functions versus proprietary or ministerial acts have different treatment in some of the states.

With the exception of Alabama and Arkansas, the states have enacted some form of a torts claims act that waives sovereign and governmental immunity for specified tort claims. Most retain immunity for discretionary acts and for legislative, judicial, and administrative acts, and many states provide a waiver for the negligent use of motor vehicles but retain a state's immunity for damages or injury caused by intentional torts. In defining the "discretionary function or duty" exception, several states adopted the "public policy function test" enunciated by the U.S. Supreme Court in *United States v. Gaubert*[11] and discussed in Chapter 4.

The law in Texas on sovereign immunity is discussed in more detail and is highlighted in this chapter to emphasize that state's strict endorsement of the doctrine of sovereign immunity. Additionally, because Texas statutes and cases

10 *Id.* at 660-61.

11 *Gaubert*, 499 US.315, 322, 111 S. Ct. 1267, 113 L. Ed.2d 335 (1991).

set out the major principles relating to sovereign immunity, a reading of these statutes and cases provide a means to address other states' harsh application of the doctrine. In considering the Texas Supreme Court's strict application of the sovereign immunity doctrine, which precludes almost all actions against the state, as well as court decisions and damages cap in other states that have substantially limited claims against the states, the reader must consider whether the law in these states has set the functional equivalent of an absolute bar to access to the courts that should be a violation of the open courts provision in a state's Constitution and the Due Process Clause of the Fourteenth Amendment to the United States Constitution.

A. ALABAMA

Alabama is a solid protector of sovereign immunity. Its Constitution[12] states: "The State of Alabama shall never be made a defendant in any court of law or equity." Alabama courts have referred to this constitutional provision as rendering state immunity impregnable, one court stating the "wall of 'governmental immunity' is almost invincible."[13] In *Hutchinson v. Board of Trustees of Univ. of Alabama,*[14] the Alabama Supreme Court maintained that the state's strict application of the sovereign immunity doctrine was "made so by the people through their Constitution as interpreted by this Court"[15] and has even ruled that sovereign immunity cannot be waived.[16] Still, the Alabama Supreme Court has found the constitutional provision to be limited in that it "extends only to 'the protection of *immediate and strict* governmental agencies of the State'" and "does not apply to country and city boards of education."[17]

12 Alabama Constitution, Article I, §14.

13 *Hutchinson v. Board of Trustees of Univ. of Alabama,* 256 So. 2d 281, 284 (Ala. 1971).

14 *Id.*

15 *Id.* In *Hutchinson,* an expectant patient sued the University of Alabama hospital seeking relief when she was told that the hospital had given her the wrong baby. The court ruled that even though the hospital accepted paying patients, its operation was a governmental function; therefore, the hospital had state agency immunity and could not be sued. Id at 283.

16 *Alabama State University v. Danley,* 282 So.3d 112, 122 (Ala. 2016); Ex *parte Cranman,* 792 So. 2d 392, 399 (Ala. 2000); *Larkins v. Department of Mental Health & Mental Retardation,* 806 So. 2d 358, 363 (Ala. 2001); and *Patterson v. Gladwin Corp.,* 835 So. 2d 137, 142 (Ala. 2002).

17 *Ex parte Cranman,* 792 So.2d at 408, (quoting *City of Foley v. Terry,* 175 So. 2d 461, 465 (Ala 1965)

In *Armory Commission of Alabama v. Staudt*,[18] the Alabama Supreme Court discussed the proper test to determine whether an agency is an arm of the State of Alabama and therefore immune from suit, stating: "Whether a lawsuit against a body created by legislative enactment is a suit against the state depends on the (1) character of power delegated to the body, (2) the relation of the body to the state, and (3) the nature of the function performed by the body. All factors in the relationship must be examined to determine whether the suit is against an arm of the state or merely against a franchisee licensed for some beneficial purpose."[19] Although counties and municipalities are not specifically afforded the state constitutional immunity protection, common law does afford governmental immunity to Alabama counties and municipalities.[20] Additionally, a party may not indirectly sue the state by suing its officers or agents when a result favorable to plaintiff would directly affect the financial status of the state treasury.[21]

While the Alabama Constitution[22] prevents a suit against the state as well as suits against its agencies, there was a question whether a breach-of-contract claim against the State or its officials is also barred by the Constitution. In *State of Alabama Highway Dep't v. Milton Construction Co.*,[23] the Alabama Supreme Court reasoned that when a state agency "has legally contracted under state law for goods or services and accepts such goods or services," the state agency would become "legally obligated to pay for the goods or services accepted in accordance with the terms of the contract;" it ruled a contractual claim in *Milton*

and *Ex parte Board of School Comm'rs of Mobile County*, 161 So. 108, 109 (1935)). In *Cranman*, the court stated that just empowering a physician does not necessarily give the physician State-agent immunity for his discretionary acts, or those involving skill or judgment.

18 *Staudt*, 388 So. 2d 991 (Ala. 1980).

19 In *Health Care Auth. For Baptist Health v. Davis*, 158 So. 3d 397 (Ala. 2013), in applying these factors, the Alabama Supreme Court held that a health-care authority organized under a state act is not an immediate and strictly governmental agency of the state, and therefore, is not entitled to State immunity under §14 of the Alabama Constitution.

20 Still, the Alabama Supreme Court refused to extend this protection to health care authorities organized under Alabama law. *Id.* at 418. The Supreme Court further found that the determination of which kinds of entities or persons fall within the constitutional immunity is a judicial function for the courts, not the legislature. *Id.*

21 *State Docks Comm'n v. Barnes*, 143 So. 581, 582 (1932).

22 Article I, §14.

23 *Milton*, 586 So. 2d 872, 875 (Ala 1991).

was not barred.[24] However, in *Alabama State Univ. v. Danley,*[25] the court clarified *Milton* to rule that the state was obligated to pay for services only after it had contracted for the services and had accepted the services.[26] In expressing concern with the majority opinion, a dissenting justice commented:[27] "Moreover, if we hold that breach-of-contract claims against the State generally are barred ..., then what reason would people have to contract with the State?"

Immunity in Alabama is available to the State of Alabama in an action against the State of Alabama called "State Immunity"[28] as opposed to "State-agent immunity,"[29] which may be available to individual defendants who are sued on behalf of the State of Alabama.[30] The Alabama Supreme Court recognizes immunity for state officers and employees, both in their official and individual capacities, "when the action is, in effect, one against the State."[31] The court "considers the nature of the suit or the relief demanded, not the character of the office of the person against whom the suit is brought."[32]

24 *Id.*

25 *Danley*, 212 So. 3d at 128.

26 Discussion at 212 So. 3d at 147. In *Danley*, 212 So. 3d at 126, the Alabama Supreme Court provided immunity protection for its institutions of higher learning in preventing an athletic director from recovery in a breach of contract claim for backpay the director filed after being terminated. The case illustrates that the Alabama Supreme Court extends the prohibition in its Constitution, §14, which states that "the State of Alabama shall never be made a defendant in court of law or equity" to a contract with the State of Alabama. The Alabama Court noted in *Danley, id.* at 125, that its decision in *Sims v. Etowah Country Bd. of Educ.*, 338 So.2d 1310 (Ala. 1976)--that country boards of education have the rights to sue and to contract and that those rights carry the implied right to be sued on contracts–was overruled in *Ex parte Hale County Bd. of Educ.*, 14 So.3d 844, 848 (Ala. 2009) (declaring that country boards of education are local agencies of the State and, thus, are "clothed in constitutional immunity from suit.")

27 *Id.* at 147-48, Moore, Chief Justice (concurring in part and dissenting in part).

28 Alabama Constitution, Article I, §14.

29 See *DeStafney v. University of Alabama*, 413 So.2d 391, 393 (Ala. 1981).

30 In *Ex parte Cranman*, 792 So. 2d at 400, the Alabama Supreme Court referred to its much earlier decision in *Elmore v. Fields*, 45 So. 661 (Ala. 1907), where it "recognized the right of a citizen to sue a State employee for a tort committed in the line of duty." It noted in *Cranman*, 792 So. 2d at 400, that "*Elmore* was the first Alabama case ever to deal with the issue of immunity for State agents sued in their individual capacity for the commission of a tort" and that the Alabama Supreme Court at that time "recognized no immunity," citing *State v. Hill,* 54 Ala 67 (1875).

31 *Phillips v. Thomas*, 555 So. 2d 81, 83 (Ala. 1989).

32 *Ex parte Carter*, 395 So. 2d 65, 67-68 (Ala. 1980) (stating an action is one against the state "when a result favorable to the plaintiff would directly affect a contract or property right of the State." *Id.* at 68. See also *Alabama State University v. Danley*, 212 So.3d at 124 (stating "this Court considers 'whether a result favorable to the plaintiff would directly affect a contract or property right of the

The Alabama Supreme Court has referred to six general categories of actions not barred by the general rule of immunity.[33] These are: "(1) actions brought to compel State officials to perform their legal duties; (2) actions brought to enjoin State officials from enforcing an unconstitutional law; (3) actions to compel State officials to perform ministerial acts; (4) actions brought against State officials under the Declaratory Judgments Act...,[34] seeking construction of a statute and its application in a given situation; (5) valid inverse condemnation actions brought against State officials in their representative capacity; and (6) actions for injunction or damages brought against State officials in their representative capacity and individually where it was alleged that they had acted fraudulently, in bad faith, beyond their authority, or in a mistaken interpretation of law."[35] These "'exceptions' to sovereign immunity apply only to actions brought against State officials; they do not apply to actions against the State or against State agencies."[36]

Because immunity afforded state employees even when sued in their official capacities "is not unlimited" in Alabama,[37] in *Ex Parte Cranman*,[38] the Alabama Supreme Court stated: "The Legislature, should it see fit to do so, can create a mechanism for providing State employees with liability insurance or it can propose a constitutional amendment that would authorize statutory procedures to make the State amenable to lawsuits for the torts of its agents while protecting State employees from lawsuits."[39] In *Cranman*, the Supreme Court restated the rule governing State-agent immunity as follows:

> A State agent *shall* be immune from civil liability in his or her personal capacity when the conduct made the basis of the claim against the agent is based upon the agent's ....
>
> (1) formulating plans, policies, or designs; or

State,'" quoting *Mitchell v. Davis*, 598 So. 2d 801, 806 (Ala. 1992).

33 *Danley*, 212 So. 3d at 123. See also *Ingle v. Adkins*, 2017 WL 5185288 (Ala. 2017).

34 Ala. Code §§6-6-220 *et seq.*

35 *Id.*

36 *Id.*, citing *Alabama Dep't of Transp.*, 990 So. 2d 831, 840-41 (Ala. 2008).

37 *See e. g. Unzicker v. State*, 346 So.2d 931 (Ala. 1977).

38 *Cranman*, 792 So. 2d at 405.

39 *Id.* at 405-406.

(2) exercising his or her judgment in the administration of a department or agency of government, including, but not limited to, examples such as:

(a) making administrative adjudications;

(b) allocating resources

(c) negotiating contracts;

(d) hiring, firing, transferring, assigning, or supervising personnel;

or (3) discharging duties imposed on a department or agency by statute, rule, or regulation, insofar as the statute, rule, or regulation prescribes the manner for performing the duties and the State agent performs the duties in that manner; or

(4) exercising judgment in the enforcement of the criminal laws of the State, including, but not limited to, law-enforcement officers' arresting or attempting to arrest persons; or

(5) exercising judgment in the discharge of duties imposed by statute, rule, or regulation in releasing prisoners, counseling or releasing persons of unsound mind, or educating students.

Still, the Court negated immunity for a state agent in the agent's personal capacity (1) when the Constitution or laws of the United States, or the Constitution of the state, or laws, rules, or regulations of the state enacted or promulgated for the purpose of regulating the activities of a governmental agency require otherwise; or (2) when the state agent acts willfully, maliciously, fraudulently, in bad faith, beyond his or her authority, or under a mistaken interpretation of the law.

There is no tort claims act in Alabama. The Legislature provides some relief to compensate persons injured in specified situations by appropriating money to the State Board of Adjustment for payment of claims for injuries by the State of Alabama.[40] This legislation sets out the procedure for an injured person to

40 Code of Alabama §41-9-62. In *Cranman*, 792 So.2d at 399, n. 9, the court referred to an "only statutory basis presently existing for making compensation available to citizens of the State who have suffered injuries caused by the State or its agencies." That statute, Ala Code §§41-9-60 to -74, established "the Board of Adjustment, which functions outside the judicial system." The Alabama Supreme Court stated in *Cranman* that the Legislature recognized in those Code sections "a moral obligation where there is no legal obligation," citing *Hawkins v. State Bd.of Adjustment*, 7 So. 2d 775 (Ala. 1942). The court noted that these Code sections extend "a measure of compensation or relief when the rule of sovereign immunity exempts the State and its respective agencies from suit," citing *State, McQueen v. Brandon*, 12 So. 2d 319 (Ala. 1943).

receive compensation if the person suffers injury because of actions of the state, its agents or its employees.[41]

B. ALASKA

Alaska has "abolished the common law doctrine of sovereign immunity by statute."[42] "The Constitution of the State of Alaska granted the legislature sole and exclusive power to enact laws establishing the terms and conditions upon which the state may be sued...."[43] The Alaskan Legislature enacted the Alaska Tort Claims Act to permit contract, quasi-contract, or tort claims, even discretionary acts, against the state by a person or corporation.[44] The Alaska Supreme Court has stated that, with respect to claims against the State of Alaska, "liability is the rule, immunity is the exception, placing the burden of showing a presumption of immunity on a state instrumentality wishing to invoke it."[45]

Still, the Alaska Legislature provided an exception to the waiver of the State's immunity; it retained "the State's sovereign immunity in tort cases where the actions are based upon the exercise or performance or the failure to exercise or perform a discretionary function or duty on the part of a state agency or an employee of the state."[46] The Alaska Supreme Court has stated: "Discretionary function immunity seeks to ensure that private citizens do not

41 Code of Alabama §§41-9-60 *et seq.*

In *Alabama State Univ. v. Danley*, 121 So. 3d at 148, the dissenting chief justice was concerned about the state claiming immunity from liability on a contract and referred to the a victim having a remedy with the Board of Adjustment, but stated: "If the State can breach its contracts before it has fully accepted the services rendered by the non-breaching parties and claim immunity under §14 [of the Alabama Constitution], then, although an aggrieved party may have a remedy with the Board of Adjustment, he or she will find no justice in a court of law."

42 *Steward v. State of Alaska*, 322 P.3d 860, 863 (Ala. 2014).

43 *Alaska v. O/S Lynn Kendall*, 310 F.Supp. 433 (D.Alaska 1970).

The Alaska Constitution, Article II, §21, requires the legislature to "establish procedures for suits against the State."

44 Alaska Code §§09.50.250-.300. Still, an action may not be brought against the state if the claim is against an employee exercising due care in the execution of a statute or regulation, negligent medical treatment during a quarantine or isolation, intentional tort, use of ignition interlock, or an action under the Jones Act. *Id.* (The Jones Act is discussed in Chapter 3.)

45 *Douglas Indian Ass'n v. Cent. Council of Tlingit & Haida Indian Tribes of Alaska*, 403 P.3d 1172, 1178 (Alaska 2017).

46 Discussion in *Steward v. State of Alaska*, 322 P.3d at 863.

interfere with or inhibit the governing process by challenging through private tort actions basic governmental policy decisions."[47] The Supreme Court has ruled that, when determining whether discretionary immunity applies to a specific act of a government employee, planning functions of employees enjoy immunity, but operational functions do not.[48] Planning decisions are decisions that involve policy formation, whereas operational decisions involve policy execution or implementation.[49]

Courts have given federally recognized tribes in Alaska federal tribal sovereign immunity in Alaska state courts to ensure tribal assets are used as a tribe chooses, without threat of litigation.[50]

C. ARIZONA

The Arizona Constitution states: "The Legislature shall direct by law in what manner and in what courts suits may be brought against the State,"[51] thus, as the Arizona Supreme Court has stated:[52] "The legislature is constitutionally empowered to 'direct by law the manner in which suits may be brought against the state.'" The Legislature has granted a public entity in Arizona with absolute immunity and has provided that the State cannot be liable if employees are exercising a judicial, legislative, or administrative function.[53] Public employees of

---

47 *Id.*

48 *Id.*

49 *State, Dep't of Transportation & Pub. Facilities v. Sanders,* 944 P. 2d. 453 (Alaska 1997). Because operating decisions are "normal day-by-day operations" of the government and are not planning decisions, these functions are not entitled to immunity under the discretionary function exception. *Steward v. State of Alaska,* 322 P.3d at 863.

The Alaska Supreme Court earlier decided the University of Alaska was entitled to immunity because the "University is an integral part of the state government and an instrumentality of the state in performing its educational function." *University of Alaska v. National Aircraft Leasing,* 536 P.2d. 121 (Ala. 1975).

50 Discussion in *Douglas Indian Ass'n,* 403 P.3d at 1176-79.

51 Arizona Constitution, Article 4, Pt. 2, §18.

52 *Kohl v. City of Phoenix,* 160 P.3d 170 (Ariz. 2007) (citing *Clouse ex rel. Clouse v. State,* 16 P. 3d 757, 764 (Ariz. 2001)).

53 A.R.S. §2-820.01. The Supreme Court stated in *Kohl:* "In promulgating A.R.S. §12-820.01, the legislature exercised its authority and specifically declared that certain spheres of governmental conduct shall be absolutely immune from liability. The legislature declared that "[a] public entity *shall* not be liable for acts and omissions of its employees constituting...[t]he exercise of an administrative function involving the determination of fundamental governmental policy,'" citing A.R.S. §12-820.01.A.

Arizona have qualified immunity when acting within the scope of employment unless they are involved in an intentional or grossly negligent act.[54]

"Examples of policy decisions entitled to immunity may include such matters as whether government or its agencies should pursue one general course of action over another, whether an agency of government should construct a particular building or where the building should be located, or a decision as to the direction and focus of an entire regulatory scheme,...or decisions on whether to provide resources for the purchase of equipment, the construction or maintenance of facilities, the hiring of personnel, the provision of governmental services, and the licensing and regulation of professions and occupations."[55]

D. ARKANSAS

The Arkansas Constitution states that "[t]he State of Arkansas shall never be made defendant in any of her courts,"[56] The Arkansas Supreme Court[57] has ruled that "[s]overeign immunity is jurisdictional immunity from suit,"[58] and has stated: "In determining whether the doctrine of sovereign immunity applies, the court should determine if a judgment for the plaintiff will operate to control the action of the State or subject it to liability. If so, the suit is one against the State and is barred by the doctrine of sovereign immunity."[59]

As the court pointed out in *Kohl,* "[t]he legislature then identified certain determinations that, as a matter of law, constitute 'fundamental governmental policy,'" identifying those set out in §12-820.01.B, which includes acts involving the exercise of discretion.

54 A.R.S. §12-820.02.

55 *Fidelity Sec. Life Ins. Co. v. Department of Ins.*, 954 P.2d 580, 583-584 (Ariz. 1998).

56 Arkansas Constitution, Article 5, §20.

57 *Clowers v. Lassiter,* 213 S.W.3d 6 (Ark. 2005).

58 *Id.* at 9, citing *Ark. Tech Univ. v. Link*, 17 S.W.3d 809 (Ark. 2000). The Supreme Court further stated that jurisdiction must be determined entirely from the pleadings.

59 *Id.* The court did acknowledge that enforcing a ministerial action required by statute is not barred by the doctrine of sovereign immunity.

The Arkansas Supreme Court early ruled that a suit against a state employee is not a suit against the state. *McConnell v. Ark. Brick & Mg. Co.* 69 S.W. 559 (Ark. 1902). The Supreme Court recently noted that "a suit against a public official in his or her official capacity is essentially a suit against that official's agency." *Ark. State Medical Bd. v. Byers,* 521 S.W.3d 459, 460 (Ark. 2017) (citing *Ark. Dep't of Human Servs. v. Ft. Smith Sch. Dist,* 455 S.W.3d 294 (Ark. 2015)).

Although the Supreme Court "has held that the doctrine of sovereign immunity is rigid," it has also held "that it may be waived in limited circumstances."[60] The Supreme Court "has recognized that a claim of sovereign immunity may be surmounted in the following three instances: (1) when the State is the moving party seeking specific relief; (2) when an act of the legislature has created a specific waiver of sovereign immunity and (3) when the state agency is acting illegally or if a state agency officer refuses to do a purely ministerial action required by statute."[61] Additionally, a state agency or officer may be enjoined from an action that is *ultra vires.*[62]

The Supreme Court of Arkansas recently confirmed that the "avenue for financial redress is through the Claims Commission...."[63] The Arkansas Legislature has given the Arkansas State Claims Commission jurisdiction to determine payment of claims filed with Commission.[64] Upon recommendation of the Attorney General of Arkansas, the State of Arkansas will pay actual damages for claims against an officer or employee of the State of Arkansas if the officer or employee was acting without malice and in good faith within the scope of employment.[65]

E. CALIFORNIA

The California Constitution states: "Suits may be brought against the state in such manner and in such courts as shall be directed by law ;"[66] thus, California statutes determine if a city, county, or state entity is liable. The California leg-

---

60 *Bd. of Trustees of the Univ. of Ark. v. Andrews*, 535 S.W.3d 616 (Ark. 2018) (citing *Office of Child Support Enf't v. Mitchell*, 954 S.W.2d 907 (Ark. 1997)).

61 *Id.* at 619-20. See also *LandsnPulaski, LLC. v. Ark. Dep't. of Correction*, 269 S.W.3d 793 (Ark. 2007) (stating: An action against a state agency or officer is not prohibited "[i]f the state agency is acting illegally or if a state agency officer refused to do a purely ministerial action required by statute" (citing *Parker v. Moore*, 262 S.W.2d 891 (Ark. 1953)). The court ruled that the Arkansas Constitution, Article 5, §20, "does not prohibit the State from waiving immunity or voluntarily entering its appearance" in a case. *Id.* at 796.

62 *Id.* A state agency or officer may be enjoined from acting arbitrarily, capriciously, in bad faith, or in a wantonly injurious manner. *Ark. State Medical Bd.*, 521 S.W.3d at 463 (citing *Ark. Dep't of Envt. Qual. v. Oil Producers of Ark.*, 318 S.W.3d 570 (Ark. 2009)).

63 *Ark. Veterans Affairs v. Mallett*, 2018 Ark. 217, 2018 WL 3061691 (Ark. 2018).

64 Ark. Stat. Ann. §§21-9-201 *et seq.*

65 *Id.* at §21-9-203.

66 California Constitution, Article III, §5.

islature enacted the California Tort Claims Act to determine governmental liability,[67] but in governmental tort cases, "the rule is liability and immunity is the exception."[68]

The tort liability of a public entity in California is wholly statutory as provided under the California Tort Claims Act.[69] "There is no common law governmental tort liability in California and a public entity is not liable for any act or omission of itself, a public employee, or any other person unless otherwise provided by statute."[70] City council persons, mayor, board members or public entities are not vicariously liable for the acts or omissions of public entities or advisory bodies.[71]

"A public entity is not liable for an injury, whether such injury arises out of an act or omission of the public entity or public employee, except as provided by statute."[72] The public entity or public employee is entitled to any immunity provided by statute and any defense provided a private person.[73] "A public entity is liable for injuries proximately caused by an act or omission of an employee of the public entity acting within the scope of his employment if the act or omission would have given rise to a cause of action against that employee or personal

67 Cal. Govt. Code §§810-996.6. "The Act governs all public entities and their employees (§§811.2, 811.4) and all noncontractual bases of compensable damage or injury that might be actionable between private persons (§§810.8, 814). It establishes the basic rules that public entities are immune from liability except as provided by statute (§815, subd. (a)), that public employees are liable for their torts except as otherwise provided by statute (§810, subd. (a)), that public entities are vicariously liable for the torts of their employees (§815.2, subd. (a)), and that public entities are immune where their employees are immune, except as otherwise provided by statute (§815.1, subd. (b))." *Caldwell v. Montoya*, 897 P.2d 1320, 1325 (Cal. 1995).

68 *Ramos v. County of Madera*, 484 P.2d. 93 (Cal. 1971).

69 *Tolan v. State of California ex rel. Dept. of Transportation*, 100 Cal. App. 3d 980 (Cal. App. 4th Dist. 1979).

70 *Cowing v. City of Torrance*, 60 Cal. App. 3d 757 (Cal. App. 2d Dist. 1976). In *Hoff v. Vacavill Unified School Dist.*, 968 P. 2d 522 (Cal. 1998), the California Supreme Court found that a school district, even though vicariously liable for its school personnel, had no duty under respondent superior to supervise a student as he exited an overflow parking lot and struck the plaintiff.

71 Cal. Govt. Code §820.9.

72 *Id.* at §815(a). "Public entity" includes "the state, the Regents of the University of California, the Trustees of the California State University and the California State University, a county, city, district, public authority, public agency, and any other political subdivision or public corporation in the State of California." *Id.* at §811.2. "Public employee" means an employee of a public entity. *Id.* at §811.4.

73 *Id.* at §815(b).

representative,"[74] but "[a] public entity is not liable for an injury resulting from an act or omission of an employee of the public entity where the employee is immune from liability, except as provided by statute."[75] The California Supreme Court has stated: "The rule has become established that government officials are not personally liable for their discretionary acts within the scope of their authority even though it is alleged that their conduct was malicious."[76]

A basic policy decision in the province of a coordinate branch of government may be discretionary, and, as such, the governmental entity will be entitled to governmental immunity "if the governmental unit shows that [the action] was taken with a conscious balancing of risks and advantages; nevertheless, subsequent ministerial actions in the implementation of that basic decision must still face case-by-case adjudication on the question of negligence."[77] A public entity may be liable for the intentional torts of elected officials, if co-defendants and the elected official's intentional tort arose from and was directly related to the performance of the elected official's duties.[78] "A public entity is liable for death or injury to person or property proximately caused by a negligent or wrongful act or omission in the operation of any motor vehicle by an employee of the public entity acting within the scope of his employment."[79] "A public employee is liable for injury caused by his act or omission to the same extent as a private person, except as provided by statute."[80] A public employee is entitled to any defenses available to a private person.[81]

74 *Id.* at §815.2(a). In *Lugtu v. California Highway Patrol,* 28 P.3d 249 (Cal. 2001), the Supreme Court ruled a California Highway Patrol, acting within the scope of his employment, would be liable for injuries to the occupants of a vehicle he stopped in the center median for a traffic violation if the officer failed to exercise reasonable care for the safety of the occupants of the stopped vehicle.

75 Cal. Govt. Code §815.2(b).

76 *Lipman v. Bribane Elementary Sch. Dist.*, 359 P.2d. 465 (Cal. 1961).

77 *Johnson v. State,* 447 P.2d. 352 (Cal. 1968) (discussing Govt. Code §815.2 (b)).

78 *Id.* at §815.2.

79 Cal. Veh. Code §17001. The Supreme Court ruled in *Thomas v. City of Richmond,* 892 P.2d. 1185 (Cal. 1995), that Cal. Govt. Code §845.8 does not provide immunity to public entities for liability based upon Cal. Veh. Code §17001, when a suspect was injured because of the city's police officers negligent or intentional use of excessive force. If the prisoner injures herself during an attempted escape, immunity exists because this is not an action against the operation of a motor vehicle. *Ladd v. County of San Mateo*, 911 P.2d 496 (Cal. 1996).

80 Cal. Govt. Code §820(a).

81 *Id.* at 820(b).

A public employee is not liable for an injury, except as provided by statute, for discretionary acts or omissions even if abused.[82] Statutorily, neither the public entity nor the public employee are liable for injuries caused by negligent misrepresentation or intentional misrepresentation,[83] issuance or denial of license or other authorization,[84] adoption or failure to adopt or enact or enforce laws,[85] to inspect property,[86] or to give advice to small claims litigants.[87]

The California Legislature has set the procedures and deadlines to make a claim against a public employee or public entity. A claim relating to a cause of action for death or for injury to a person or to personal property must be presented not later than six months after the accrual of the cause of action.[88] All other claims must be brought not later than one year after the accrual of the cause of action.[89] The Board of Control must act on the claim within forty-five days after the claim is presented or the claim is deemed rejected.[90]

An action brought "against a public entity for claims of discharge from or termination of employment grounded on a whistleblower claim are not barred by governmental immunity."[91] Although Indian tribes have immunity under federal law, the California Supreme Court has ruled that, to maintain the integrity

---

82 *Id.* at §820.2. The California Supreme Court has ruled that breaches by public employees of actionable duty are immune from liability if the public employee's actions are discretionary. *Caldwell v. Montoya,* 42 Cal. Rptr. 2d 842, 897 P.2d 1320 (Cal. 1995) The court has defined immune discretionary acts as those that draw "the line between 'planning' and 'operational' functions of government" and has determined "there is no basis for immunizing lower-level, or 'ministerial,' decisions that merely implement a basic policy already formulated." 897 P.2d at 1325, 26. "[V]otes by members of a school district's governing board whether to renew the superintendent's employment contract qualify as discretionary acts...." 42 Cal. Rptr. 2d at 982.

83 Cal. Govt. Code Sec. 818.8; 822.2 ...unless the public employee is guilty of actual fraud, corruption or actual malice.

84 *Id.* at §§818.4; 821.2.

85 *Id.* at §§818.2; 821.

86 *Id.* at §§818.6; 821.

87 *Id.* at §818.9.

88 *Id.* at §911.2.

89 *Id.*

90 *Id.* at §912.4.

91 *Whitehall v. Cnty. of San Bernardino,* 17 Cal. App. 5th 352, 365, 225 Cal. Rptr. 3d 321 (2017) (citing *Southern Cal. Rapid Transit Dist. v. Superior Court,* 30 Cal. App. 4th 713, 715, 36 Cal Rptr. 2d 665 (1994)).

of the election process, tribes allowed to participate in the state electoral process are not immune from reporting requirements under California state law.[92]

F. COLORADO

The Colorado Governmental Immunity Act (CGIA)[93] established sovereign immunity for public entities from all suits.[94] The Act created for the state "a right to be free from all suits and not merely immune from liability;" it gives a public entity the right to waive immunity by resolution.[95] Failure to comply with the Colorado Governmental Immunity Act requires that an action be dismissed.[96]

The Colorado Supreme Court has stated:[97] "Because governmental immunity established by the CGIA derogates Colorado's common law, we strictly construe the Act's immunity provisions, and as a logical corollary, we broadly construe its waiver provisions." The Supreme Court has commented that while the CGIA "recognizes that governmental immunity is sometimes inequitable," the Act "also recognizes that governmental entities provide many essential services that unlimited liability could disrupt or make prohibitively expensive."[98]

"Under the CGIA, there are several different circumstances that—upon sufficient proof of particular jurisdictional facts–automatically waive a public entity's immunity."[99] The Supreme Court has explained that "[i]mmunity is

92 *Agua Caliente Band of Cahuilla Indians v. Superior Court*, 148 P.3d 1126 (Cal. 2006).

93 Colo. Rev. Stat. §§24-10-101 *et seq.*

94 *Aspen Orthopaedics & Sports Medicine v. Aspen Valley*, 353 F3d 832, 846 (10th Cir. 2003).

95 Colo. Rev. Stat. §24-10-104.

96 *Denver v. Desert Truck Sales, Inc.*, 837 P.2d 759 (Colo. 1992).

97 *Young v. Brighton School Dist.*, 325 P.3d 571 (Colo. 2014) (citing *Springer v. City and Cnty. Of Denver*, 13 P.3d 794, 798 (Colo. 2000)).

98 *Burnett v. State Dep't of Natural Resources*, 346 P.3d 1005 (Colo. 2015). The Supreme Court noted that, in 1971, in *Evans v. Bd. of Cnty. Comm'rs*, 482 P.2d 968, 972 (Colo. 1971), it "held that judicially imposed sovereign immunity was inappropriate and abolished such immunity at every level of government, but that in "[t]he next year, the General Assembly enacted the CGIA to reestablish governmental immunity, excepting a finite number of specific circumstances in which public entities waive immunity." *Id.* at 1009.

99 *Young*, 325 P.3d. at 576-77, citing §24-10-106(l)(a)-(h), which provides a list of immunity waivers. The court noted that "the CGIA does not provide specific guidance as to how the immunity waivers interact with one another, nor does it specify what should be done when more than one waiver provision could be triggered in a particular factual scenario." *Id.* at 577. The court ruled that "the CGIA's waiver provisions are not mutually exclusive." It stated: "Rather, each provision provides an

a threshold issue, as it is designed to protect a public entity from liability in the most preliminary stages of a lawsuit" and that "courts regularly test multiple waiver provisions at the same time in determining whether a plaintiff has alleged sufficient facts to waive immunity."[100]

Sovereign immunity is waived by a public entity for the operation of a motor vehicle, public hospital, and correctional facility, for dangerous condition of a public building or public highway, or if a public employee would be personally liable.[101] The Supreme Court had decided that "sovereign immunity does not apply with respect to man-made objects and does apply to natural objects."[102]

G. CONNECTICUT

The Connecticut Constitution requires claims against the State of Connecticut to be "resolved as provided by law."[103] The Connecticut Supreme Court has ruled that "when the state waives sovereign immunity by statute a party attempting to sue under the legislative exception must come clearly within its provisions, because statutes in derogation of sovereignty should be strictly construed in favor of the state, so that its sovereignty may be upheld and not narrowed or destroyed...."[104] The Supreme Court stated: "Where there is any doubt about the meaning or intent of a statute in derogation of sovereign immunity, it is given the effect which makes the least rather than the most change in sovereign immunity."[105] It affirmed that "[t]he state's sovereign right not to be sued may be

---

alternative avenue for stripping a public entity of its immunity, which may (or may not) be triggered by a particular factual scenario." *Id.*

100 *Id.*

101 Colo. Rev. Stat. §24-10-106.

102 *Burnett,* 346 P.3d at 1010. It determined that a "natural condition of any unimproved property' includes native trees originating on unimproved property" and ruled that the state is immune from liability for an injury caused by a limb from such a tree. *Id.*

103 Connecticut Constitution, Article XI, §4.

104 *Babes v. Bennett,* 247 Conn. 256, 721 A.2d 511, 514 (Conn. 1998) (citing *Berger, Lehman Associates, Inc. v. State,* 178 Conn. 352, 356, 411 A.2d 168 (Conn. 1979)).

105 *Babes,* 721 A.2d at 515 (citing *Federal Deposit ins. Corp. v. Peabody,* 239 Conn. 93, 101-102, 680 A.2d 1321 (Conn. 1996)).

waived by the legislature, provided clear intention of that effect is disclosed by the use of express terms or by force of a necessary implication."[106]

The Connecticut Legislature has enacted the Claims Against the State[107] that provides immunity for state officers and employees.[108] Additionally, "a suit against a state officer concerning a matter in which the officer represents the state is, in effect, against the state" because as the Connecticut Supreme Court has ruled: "a state can act only through its officers and agents."[109] The Supreme Court has determined that "[c]laims involving the doctrines of common-law sovereign immunity and statutory immunity...[110] implicate the court's subject matter jurisdiction"[111] and further stated that "the defense of statutory immunity can be raised for claims brought against state employees acting in their individual capacities."[112]

The state can be liable on the basis of the negligence of its employees "when operating a motor vehicle owned and insured by the state against personal injuries or property damage..."[113] A Connecticut court has ruled that an action against the state on the basis of the negligence of its employee is only authorized as a suit against the state.[114] The Connecticut Legislature has granted the state's Claims Commissioner authority to settle claims involving the state, its entities

106 *Id.* (citing *Struckman v. Burns*, 205 Conn. 542, 558, 534 A.2d 888 (Conn. 1987)).

107 Conn. Gen. Stat. §§4-141 *et seq.*

108 *Id.* at §4-165. This provision states: "No state officer or employee shall be personally liable for damage or injury, not wanton, reckless or malicious, caused in the discharge of his or her duties or within the scope of his or her employment. Any person having a complaint for such damage or injury shall present it as a claim against the state under the provisions of this chapter."

109 *Miller v. Egan*, 265 Conn. 301, 313, 828 A.2d 549 (Conn. 2003).

110 These are claims brought pursuant to Conn. Gen. Stat. §4-165.

111 *Mercer v. Strange*, 96 Conn. App. 123, 899 A.2d 683, 687 (2006) (quoting *Manifold v. Ragaglia*, 94 Conn. App. 103, 113-114, 891 A.2d 106 (2006)).

112 *Id.* The U.S. Supreme Court overturned the Connecticut Supreme Court regarding the question of whether tribal sovereign immunity barred a suit against a tribal employee to rule that if suit is brought against a tribal employee in the tribal employee's individual capacity, the employee is not entitled to the protection of sovereign immunity. *Lewis v. Clarke*, 137 S. Ct. 1285, 1286-87, 197 L. Ed. 2d 631 (2017). The U.S. Supreme Court stated: "'Officers sued in their personal capacity come to court as individuals,'" citing *Hafer v. Melo*, 502 U.S. 21, 27, 112 S. Ct. 358, 116 L Ed.2d 301 (1991).

113 Conn. Gen. Stat. §52-556.

114 *Cumberland Farms, Inc. v. Dubois*, 154 Conn. App. 448, 107 A.3d 995 (2014). The court ruled that because Conn. Gen. Stat. §52-556 only authorizes suit against the state and because the state employee was not sued in his individual capacity, the trial court lacked subject matter jurisdiction over the claim against the defendant.

and its employees.[115] The Claims Commissioner may authorize suit against the state on any claim,[116] but state officers and employees are not personally liable for damage if an injury causing the damage is not wanton, reckless or malicious within the scope of employment.[117]

H. DELAWARE

The Delaware Constitution[118] states: "All courts shall be open; and every person for an injury done him or her in his or her reputation, person, movable or immovable possessions, shall have remedy by the due course of law, and justice administered according to the very right of the case and the law of the land..." However, the Constitution also provides that suits brought against the State of Delaware must be pursuant to "regulations as shall be made by law;"[119] thus, the Delaware Supreme Court has stated that "the only way to limit or waive the state's sovereign immunity is by act of the General Assembly."[120] Lawsuits against the state will fail unless the Delaware General Assembly has waived the defense of sovereign immunity.[121]

The General Assembly enacted the Delaware Tort Claims Act[122] but "to reinstate a limited degree of sovereign immunity where the General Assembly thought the State had no immunity at all."[123] The Supreme Court[124] has ruled: "The purpose of the State Tort Claims Act, as stated in its synopsis, was to codify existing common law principles of sovereign immunity. In Delaware, this immunity is virtually absolute." The Supreme Court stated: "The act was further

---

115 Conn. Gen. Stat. §§4-142 and 160.

116 *Id.* at §4-160.

117 *Id.* at §4-165.

118 Delaware Constitution, Article I, §9.

119 *Id.*

120 *Doe v. Cates*, 499 A.2d 1175, 1176 (Del. 1985) (citing *Shellhorn & Hill, Inc. v. State*, 187 A.2d 71, 74-75 (Del. Supr. 1962)).

121 *Id.* at 1177.

122 Del. Code tit. 10, §§4001 *et. seq.*

123 *Doe v. Cates*, 499 A.2d at 1180.

124 *Id.*

intended to discourage law suits which might create a chilling effect on the ability of public officials or employees to exercise their discretionary authority."[125]

To bring a claim pursuant to the Tort Claims Act, a plaintiff must show the absence of good faith, that the act causing injury or damages was performed with gross or wanton negligence, or that performance did not arise out of an official duty requiring discretion of a public officer, employee or member of the State of Delaware.[126] A governmental entity can be liable for negligent acts involving a motor vehicle, construction of a public building and, discharge of fumes or liquids.[127]

I. DISTRICT OF COLUMBIA

"The principles of sovereign immunity are well established in the District." A court has ruled "the District is immune from suit in tort if the act complained of was committed in the exercise of a discretionary function."[128] Still, if the conduct complained of "arises out of the exercise of ministerial power," courts have ruled that "there is a duty to act in a reasonably safe and skillful manner"[129] and there is no immunity.

The mayor of the District of Columbia has the discretionary power to settle claims against the District.[130] A claim must arise from the negligence or wrongful act of an officer or employee of the District that would have caused a private

125 *Id.* at 1180-81.

126 *Id.* at §4001. Certain specific officials are given absolute immunity. Additionally, the Delaware Supreme Court has ruled that "the legislature did not intend by enacting 10 Del. C. 4001 to waive sovereign immunity in all cases where a ministerial act was performed with gross or wanton negligence or in bad faith." *Doe v. Cates*, 499 A.2d at 1180.

127 *Id.* at §4012.

128 *District of Columbia Housing Authority v. Pinkney*, 970 A.2d 854 (D.C App. 2009). See also *Chandler v. District of Columbia*, 404 A.2d 964, 965 (D.C. 1979).

129 *Id.*, distinguishing between a discretionary function of planning and design from negligence in maintaining a structure, which would not be barred by sovereign immunity. The court stated that "discretionary acts involve the formulation of policy, while ministerial acts involve the execution of policy."

130 D.C. Code §2-402. See statutes relating to claims against the District at D.C. Code §§1-401 to 2-416.

individual to be liable,[131] and the District is immune from liability for discretionary governmental functions that are based on policy considerations.[132]

J. FLORIDA

The Florida Constitution states: "Provision may be made by general law for bringing suit against the state as to all liabilities now existing or hereafter originating."[133] The Florida Legislature enacted a Sovereign Immunity Statute[134] that waives sovereign immunity for the state and its agencies for damages caused by negligent or wrongful conduct of public employees in the scope of their employment if a private person would be liable.[135] The Florida Supreme Court has ruled that there can be no governmental liability unless a common law or statutory duty of care existed that would have been applicable to an individual under similar circumstances; additionally, assuming a duty is owed, a court must determine whether sovereign immunity bars an action for an alleged breach of that duty.[136] The procedural requirements under this statute are strictly construed.[137] A municipality cannot waive immunity, only the legislature is authorized to waive immunity.[138]

Statutory law prohibits an officer, employee, or agent of the state, or of any of its subdivisions, from being held personally liable in tort, or named as a party defendant, in any action for any injury or damage suffered as a result of any act, event, or omission of action in the scope of employment or function, unless the officer, employee, or agent acted in bad faith, or with malicious purpose, or in a manner exhibiting wanton and willful disregard of human rights, safety, or

---

131 D.C. Code §2-402(a)

132 *Chandler v. District of Columbia*, 404 A.2d 964 (D. C. App. 1979).

133 Florida Constitution, Article X, §13.

134 F.S.A §768.28.

135 *Id.* at §768.28(1).

136 *Henderson v. Bowden*, 737 So. 2d 532 (Fla. 1999) (referring to the Florida Constitution, Article X, §13 and Fla. Stat. §768.28). See also *Breaux v. City of Miami Beach*, 899 S.2d 1059, 1063 (Fla.2005).

137 *Smart v. Monge*, 667 So. 2d 957 (Fla. 2nd DCA 1996) (finding that the trial court properly dismissed father's tort action for damages against sheriff for the wrongful death of his asthmatic son where the father's attorney failed to comply with the notice requirement of Fla. Stat. §768.28(6), which required the father to have presented his claim in writing to the sheriff prior to filing suit.)

138 *Donisi v. Trout*, 415 So. 2d 730 (Fla. 4th DCA 1981).

property.[139] A determination of immunity is subject to interlocutory review to protect immunity.[140]

Although government agencies are not immune for their actions or omissions if their activities involved broad policy or planning decisions, or operational activities,[141] government agencies are immune if an agency's actions or omissions of the agency are discretionary.[142] An action against the state must be brought within three years after a claim accrues or within two years for a wrongful death action. Additionally, a claim against the government must be brought within four years or the action is forever barred unless it is a claim for contribution or medical malpractice.[143] Prior to instituting an action against a state agency, a claimant must present the claim in writing to the agency and the Department of Financial Services within three years after the claim accrues and the agency or the department denies the claim in writing.[144]

---

139 F.S.A. §768.28(9).

140 *Keck v. Eminisor*, 104 So. 3d 359 (Fla. 2012).

141 *Commercial Carrier Corp. v. Indian River County*, 371 So. 2d 1010 (Fla. 1979). The Florida Supreme Court held "that caseworker activities were operational level for which there is a waiver or immunity." *Department of Health & Rehabilitative Servs. v. Yamuni*, 529 So. 2d 258 (Fla. 1988).

142 The Supreme Court held decisions concerning the installation of traffic control devices, the initial plan and alignment of roads, or the improvement or upgrading of roads or intersections are basic capital improvements and are judgmental, planning-level functions for which governmental immunity is not waived under Fla. Stat. §768.28. *Department of Transp. v. Neilson*, 419 So. 2d 1071 (Fla. 1982). Still, the Supreme Court found a county was not immune from liability for negligent operation of a county-owned park and swimming facility even though operating a swimming facility is a discretionary decision that assumes the common law duty to operate the facility safely would be immune. *Avallone v. Board of County Comm'rs*, 493 So. 2d 1002 (Fla. 1986).

143 F.S.A. §768.28(14). These time periods are strictly construed. *Levine v. Dade County School Bd.*, 442 So. 2d 210 (Fla. 1983); *Menendez v. North Broward Hospital Dist*, 537 So. 2d 258 (Fla. 1988) (Subsection 768.28(6) requires notice to the state agency prior to instituting an action or suit is to be dismissed). "[W]hen a prisoner files an action alleging that he suffered physical injury due to the negligent or wrongful acts or omissions of the employees of a government entity, the one-year statute of limitations period in Fla. Stat. §95.11(5)(g), intended to curb frivolous filings by prisoners, does not apply; instead, the four-year statute of limitations in Fla. Stat. §768.28(14) governs." *Green v. Cottrell*, 204 So. 3d 22 (Fla. 2016).

The limitations are tolled if a state agency had fraudulently concealed facts concerning its failure to supervise and monitor. *Fla. Dep't of Health & Rehabilitative Servs. v. S.A.P.*, 835 So. 2d 1091 (Fla. 2002).

144 *Menendez v. North Broward Hospital Dist.*, 537 So. 2d 89 (Fla. 1988) (referring to Fla. Stat. §768.28(6)).

K. GEORGIA

The Georgia Constitution provides that all state agencies, officers and employees, and the State of Georgia have sovereign immunity unless consent is given by the General Assembly.[145] "The applicability of sovereign immunity to claims brought against the State is a jurisdictional issue."[146] The question is whether "a case properly may come before a court at all."[147]

The Georgia General Assembly enacted the Georgia Tort Claims Act,[148] which waives its sovereign immunity if a tort is committed by state officers and employees while acting within the scope of their employment in instances in which a private individual would be liable.[149] The State of Georgia is not liable for exercising due care in enacting laws, for discretionary acts, for collecting taxes, for administrative acts, civil disturbance, intentional torts, inspections, licensing, planning, financing, and computer malfunctions.[150] Its state officers and employees can be liable for damages caused by their negligence, actual malice, or their actual intent to cause injury in the performance of their official duties.[151]

---

145 Georgia Constitution, Article I, §I, Para. IX. The Constitution provides that sovereign immunity can only be waived by an act of the state legislature.

The Supreme Court of Georgia ruled physicians could not sue the governor and many other state officials to perform abortions because sovereign immunity protects the State of Georgia, its entities and state employees and officers unless consent to sue is given by the Georgia General Assembly. *Lathrop v. Deal,* 801 S.E. 2d 867 (Ga. 2017).

146 *McConnell v. Dept. of Labor,* 302 Ga. 18, 805 S.E.2d 79 (Ga. 2017).

147 *Id.* at 19 (citing *Lathrop v. Deal,* 301 Ga. 408, 432, 801 S.E. 2d 867 (Ga. 2017)). The Supreme Court ruled that the "applicability of sovereign immunity is a threshold determination, and, if it does apply, a court lacks jurisdiction over the case and, concomitantly, lacks authority to decide the merits of a claim that is barred." *McConnell,* 302 Ga. at 19. Before deciding the merits of a case, a court must consider first whether the doctrine of sovereign immunity bars any of a plaintiff's allegations against the state. *Id.*

148 Official Code of Georgia, O.C.G, §§50-21-20 *et seq.*

149 *Id.* at § 50-21-23.

150 *Id.* at §50-21-24.

151 Constitution, Article I, §I, Para. IX(d).

L. HAWAII

Tort liability for the State of Hawaii is determined pursuant to the Hawaii State Tort Liability Act.[152] This Act waives the state's immunity from liability for the torts of its employees and makes the state "liable in the same manner and to the same extent as a private individual under like circumstances..."[153] "The basic principle of governmental tort liability in Hawaii ...is that the state and its political subdivisions shall be accountable for the torts of governmental employees in the same manner and to the same extent as a private individual under like circumstances."[154]

The Hawaiian Supreme Court has stated that, in determining whether there is a duty owed by the government to a plaintiff who suffers injury, "the task is to balance the policy considerations supporting recovery by the injured party against those favoring a limitation of the government's liability;" additionally, "[i]n deciding whether a duty exists or not," courts "must determine how far it is desirable and socially expedient to permit the loss distributing function of tort law to apply to governmental agencies, without thereby unduly interfering with the effective function of such agencies for their own socially approved ends."[155]

The Hawaiian State Tort Liability Act "includes several exceptions to its applicability, including claims based on 'the exercise or performance or the failure to exercise or perform a discretionary function or duty on the part of a state officer or employee, whether or not the discretion involved has been abused.'"[156] The Supreme Court has stated that this exception "is to 'protect the decision-making processes of state officials and employees which require evaluation of

152 Haw. Stat. §662.

153 *Id.*

154 *Cootey v. Sun Investment*, 718 P.2d 1086, 1087-88 (Haw. 1986). The Supreme Court stated: "The State Tort Liability Act did not create any causes of action where none existed before. The effect of the Act is to waive immunity from traditionally recognized common law causes of action in tort, other than those expressly excluded." *Id.* at 1088.

155 *Id.* at 1088.

156 *O'Grady v. State*, 398 P.3d 625 (Haw. 2017), (citing Haw. Stat. §662-15.) There are other exceptions in §661-5 which are "a retention of sovereign immunity over certain claims." "[C]onsequently, the exceptions do not operate to withdraw subject-matter jurisdiction from the courts." *O'Grady*, citing *Schwartz v. State*, 361 P.3d 1161, 1166 (Haw. 2015). The Court ruled in *O'Grady* that "subject-matter jurisdiction, which is fundamental to a court's power to act on the merits of a case from the outset of the action," can "be challenged at any time." 398 P. 3d at 642.

broad public policies.'"[157] "[T]he State bears the burden to assert and prove the application of the discretionary function exception to liability under the State Tort Liability Act."[158] Additionally, "[i]n determining whether a State action falls within the discretionary function exception," the Supreme Court has stated that it considers "whether the challenged conduct involves the 'effectuation of broad public policy' as opposed to 'routine,' 'operational level activity.'"[159]

M. IDAHO

Without a clearly expressed consent, an Idaho governmental organization can only be sued by permission from the state's Constitution or by a legislative mandate that waives sovereign immunity.[160] Idaho enacted the Idaho Tort Claims Act (ITCA)[161] to provide that governmental entities and employees, acting within the scope of employment, will be subject to liability for negligence or for wrongful acts if a private person or entity would be liable.[162] The liability applies whether the act or omission is a governmental or a proprietary function.[163] Still, a governmental entity or employee is not liable if acting without malice or criminal intent and when exercising ordinary care with respect to claims regarding several specified activities,[164] including acts or omissions in executing a discretionary duty.[165]

The Idaho Supreme Court has stated: "Idaho Code §6-904 is part of the ITCA which generally 'abrogates the doctrine of sovereign immunity' but preserves

157 *Id.*, citing *Nakahira v. State*, 799 P.2d 959, 961 (Haw. 1990).

158 *O'Grady*, 398 P.3d at 643, citing *U.S. Bank Nat'l Ass'n v. Castor*, 313 P.3d 717,730 (Haw. 2013).

159 *Id.*, quoting *Tseu ex rel. Hobbs v. Jeyte*, 962 P.2d 344, 347 (Haw. 1998) and stating: "The exercise of some discretion on the part of a State official is not necessarily indicative that the exception applies, and our cases have focused more on distinguishing broader policy decision from daily, operational ones." *Id.* at 644.

160 *Sanchez v. State*, 141 P.3d 1108 (Idaho 2006).

161 Idaho Code §6-901 *et seq.*

162 *Id.* at §6-903.

163 *Id.*

164 *Id.* at §§6-904, 6-904A, 6-904B.

165 *Id.* at §661-15.

immunity 'in certain specific situations.'"[166] The Supreme Court affirmed that the ITCA was "enacted to provide much needed relief to those suffering injury from the negligence of government employees" and that the Act 'is to be construed liberally" with liability as "the rule and immunity...the exception."[167]

N. ILLINOIS

The Illinois Constitution states:[168] "Except as the General Assembly may provide by law, sovereign immunity in this State is abolished." However, "[i]n accordance with this constitutional grant of authority, the General Assembly adopted the State Lawsuit Immunity Act,[169] reinstating the doctrine of sovereign immunity."[170] The Act provides that, except as provided in the Court of Claims Act[171] and other specified statutes, the State of Illinois cannot be made a defendant or party in any court.

Nonetheless, the Illinois Supreme Court[172] decided that state employees should not be protected by the doctrine of sovereign immunity "because the doctrine was not designed to shield state employees from being held accountable" for certain actions, particularly criminal acts. The General Assembly enacted the Court of Claims Act[173] "to create a forum for actions against the State."[174] The Act provides limited waiver of sovereign immunity because members of the legislature felt that maintaining limited sovereign immunity was extremely important,

166 *Teurlings. v. Larson*, 320 P.3d 1224 (Idaho 2014) (citing *Lawton v. City of Pocatello*, 886 P.2d 330, 334 (Idaho 1994)).

167 *Id.* The Supreme Court reiterated that exceptions to liability in §6-904 "apply to the state as a matter of right," but pointed out that "they are only applicable to an employee if the employee is within the scope of his or her employment at the time of the negligent act or occurrence," citing *Hoffer v. City of Boise*, 257 P.3d 1226, 1228-29 (Idaho 2011).

168 Illinois Constitution, Article XIII, §4.

169 745 I.L.C.S. 5/0.01 *et seq.*

170 *Parmar v. Madigan*, 2018 IL 122265, 106 N.E.3d 1004, 1008 (Ill. 2018) (citing Pub. Act 77-1776.)

171 745 I.L.C.S. §5/1. The Court of Claims Act is set out in 705 I.L.C.S. 505/1 *et seq.*

172 *State Bldg. Venture v. O'Donnell*, 940 N.E.2d 1122 (Ill. 2010).

173 705 I.L.C.S. §§505/1 *et seq.*

174 *Parmar, citing Healy v. Vaupel*, 549 N.E.2d 1240 (Ill. 1990).

and necessary to prevent litigation chaos.[175] The General Assembly granted the Court of Claims exclusive jurisdiction over contract and tort claims against the State.[176] Determination of whether or not the state is a party to a suit is not one of formal identification of the parties as they appear in the record, but instead depends upon the issues involved and the relief sought.[177]

A common-law 'public duty rule' in Illinois has provided "that local governmental entities owe no duty to individual members of the general public to provide adequate government services, such as police and fire protection.[178] This 'long-standing public duty rule was "grounded in the principle that the duty of the governmental entity to 'preserve the well-being of the community is owed to the public at large rather than to specific members of the community.'"[179] "While the public duty rule and sovereign immunity are both common-law concepts, the 'public duty rule' developed separately and exists independently of any constitutional, statutory or common-law concepts of 'sovereign immunity.'"[180]

The Supreme Court later decided that "the public duty rule and its special duty exception has proved difficult in its application when statutory immunity or limited statutory immunity applies"[181] and that application of the rule "is incompatible with the legislature's grant of limited immunity in cases of willful and wanton misconduct." That court noted: "When the public duty rule is applied...a plaintiff is precluded from pursuing a cause of action for willful and wanton misconduct, in contravention of the clear legislative decision to

---

175 *Schoeberlein v. Purdue University*, 544 N.E. 2d 283 (Ill. 1989).

176 705 I.L.C.S. 505/8. The Court of Claims consists of seven judges, *Id.* at §505/1, who have "exclusive jurisdiction to hear all claims against the State of Illinois concerning laws of the State of Illinois, contracts with the State of Illinois, unjust imprisonment, and tort actions against the State of Illinois if a like cause of action would lie against a private person." *Id.* at I.L.C.S §505/8. The Court of Claims limits benefits to $100,000 except for tort actions arising out of a state employee's operation of a motor vehicle. *Id.* at §505/8(d).

In *Fritz v. Johnston*, 807 N.E.2d 461 (Ill. 2004), the Illinois Supreme Court ruled that a veterinarian's duty arose independently of the veterinarian's employment of the State of Illinois and that he was not performing a uniquely governmental function when treating race horses; thus, the Court of Claims did not have exclusive jurisdiction to hear a claim against him.

177 *Sass v. Kramer*, 381 N.E.2d 975 (Ill. 1978).

178 *Coleman v. East Joliet Fire Protection Dist.*, 46 N.E. 3d 741 (Ill. 2016). The public duty rule prevented citizens from suing public employees when the public employee was providing governmental services.

179 *Id., quoting Schaffrath v. Village of Buffalo Grove*, 513 N.E.2d 1026 (Ill. 1987).

180 *Id.* at 752.

181 *Id.* at 757.

allow recovery against the public entity in certain cases involving willful and wanton misconduct" and stated that "application of the public duty rule to preclude recovery is incompatible with the legislature's grant of limited immunity;" accordingly, the Illinois Supreme Court abolished the public duty rule for local governmental employees in 2016.[182]

O. INDIANA

The Constitution of Indiana[183] reads: "Provision may be made, by general law, for bringing suit against the state; but no special law authorizing such suit to be brought or making compensation to any person claiming damages against the State, shall ever be passed." Still, the Indiana Tort Claims Act grants immunity from tort liability to the state and many of its governmental entities.[184]

Nonetheless, the Indiana Supreme Court has ruled that the state retains common-law sovereign immunity for non-tort statutes.[185] The Supreme Court stated that "what is construed narrowly is not the legislature's *grant* of immunity but its purposed *waiver* of it"[186] and that it will "find a waiver of sovereign immunity only when the statute at issue contains an unequivocal affirmative statement

182 *Id.* at 758. The Supreme Court decided that application of the public duty rule should not apply when a public employee acted with willful and wanton misconduct. The court opined that "the public policy behind the judicially created public duty rule and its special duty exception have largely been supplanted by the legislature's enactment of statutory immunities, rendering the public duty rule and its special duty exception obsolete." *Id.*

The Local Governmental and Governmental Employees Tort Immunity Act, 745 I.L.C.S. 10/1-101.1 *et seq,* states: "Any defense or immunity, common law or statutory, available to any private person shall likewise be available to local public entities and public employees. *Id.* at 10/1-101.1(b) The Act defines "willful and wanton conduct" as a course of action that demonstrates "an actual or deliberate intention to cause harm or which, if not intentional, shows an utter indifference to or conscious disregard for the safety of others or their property." 745 I.L.C.S. 10/1-210. This definition applies in any case where a "willful and wanton" exception is incorporated into any immunity under this Act.

A public employee is not liable for an injury resulting from a discretionary act or omission even if the discretion is abused. 745 I.L.C.S. Sec. 10/2-201.

183 Indiana Constitution, Article 4, §24.

184 Ind. Code §§34-13-3-1 *et seq.*

185 *Esserman v. Ind. Dep't of Envtl. Mgmt.,* 84 N.E.3d 1185, 1191 (Ind. 2017). The Indiana Supreme Court ruled in *Esserman* that "a statute does not waive immunity unless that intention is "clearly evince[d]", creating a presumption against waiver of sovereign immunity absent statutory language to the contrary." *Id.*

186 *Id.*

that clearly evinces the legislature's intention to subject the State to suit for the specific statutory claim asserted."[187]

The Indiana Tort Claims Act only applies to tort actions[188] but with many exceptions to waiver of immunity. An employee generally is not liable for damages for a discretionary act causing injury or damages occurred while the employee is acting within the scope of employment.[189] "Whether an act is discretionary is a question of law for the court's determination,"[190] but discretionary immunity is "narrowly construed because it is an exception to the general rule of liability."[191] The Supreme Court has adopted the "'planning/operational test' for addressing claims of discretionary function immunity" which insulates "only those significant policy and political decisions which cannot be assessed by customary tort standards."[192]

A suit against a governmental employee must allege that conduct occurred outside the scope of employment, that the alleged conduct involved a criminal

---

187 *Id.* at 1192. The court decided that the whistleblower act, Ind. Code §5-11-5.5-8, failed to evince a legislative intention to waive sovereign immunity. *Id.* The court noted that while the whistleblower act states that an employee may sue her employer, the act does not name the State or one of its agencies or officials as a permissible defendant. *Id.* The Supreme Court did not rule "that aggrieved state employees are without recourse under Indiana law." It noted that "[t]he State Personnel Act unambiguously affords a legal remedy to state-agency employees who face retaliatory discipline for having reported violations of state or federal law. See Ind. Code §§4-15-10-1, 4.

188 Ind. Code §34-13-3-1(a).

189 *Id.* at §34-13-3-3. The exceptions include a governmental entity or an employee acting within the scope of employment for a loss that results from the following, among others: the initiation of a judicial or an administrative proceeding, the performance of a discretionary function, the adoption or enforcement of or failure to adopt or enforce a law unless the act of enforcement constitutes false arrest or false imprisonment, an act or omission performed in good faith and without malice under apparent authority of a statute, and unintentional misrepresentation.

190 *City of Beech Grove v. Beloat*, 50 N.E.3d 135, 138 (Ind. 2016).

191 *Id.*

192 *Id.* The Supreme Court stated: "This assessment requires close consideration of the nature of the governmental actions and the decision-making process that was involved" and "[l]abeling an action as planning or operational, without more, is insufficient to determine whether immunity exists." The court noted: "Planning activities include acts or omissions 'in the exercise of a legislative, judicial, or executive or planning function which involves formulation of basic policy decisions characterized by official judgment or discretion in weighing alternatives and choosing public policy,'" citing *Marrek v. Cleveland Metroparks Bd. of Com'rs*, 459 NlE.3d 873 (Ind. 1984). The court opined that "the distinction between planning and operational functions is only a standard, not a precise rule" and that the "ultimate consideration is whether the action is one that was intended to be immune." *Id.* The court stated that a court "should look to the purposes of immunity to determine whether those purposes would be furthered by extending immunity to the act in question." *Id.*

act, was malicious, willful and wanton, or was calculated to benefit the employee personally.[193]

P. IOWA

Sovereign immunity in Iowa "is not absolute."[194] The Iowa Supreme Court has ruled that the state may constructively waive state sovereign immunity in certain circumstances by impliedly consenting to suit.[195] Additionally, the Iowa Legislature authorized suits against state employees under the Iowa Tort Claims Act.[196]

The Act states that governmental entities "shall be liable in respect to such claims to the same claimants, in the same manner, and to the same extent as a private individual under like circumstances."[197] A party has no claim against the state for, among others, discretionary functions and intentional torts.[198]

Q. KANSAS

Pursuant to the Kansas Tort Claims Act,[199] a Kansas governmental entity is liable for the tortious act(s) of a governmental employee who, when acting within the scope of employment, is negligent or commits a wrongful act or omission under circumstances where a private person would be liable;[200] municipalities may not exempt themselves from liability under the act.[201] The Act specifies that it does not authorize liability for damages for, among others, legislative or judicial functions, failure to enforce a law, adopting policy, collecting taxes, and

193 Ind. Code Sec. §34-13-5.

194 *Lee v. State & Polk Cnty. Clerk of Court*, 874 N.W.2d 631, 638 (Iowa 2016). The court stated: "On the contrary, it is subject to several implicit limits or exceptions." *Id.*

195 *Id.*

196 Iowa Code §669.1 *et seq.*

197 *Id.* at §669.4.

198 *Id.* at §669.14.

199 K.S.A. §§75-6101 *et seq.*

200 *Id.* at §75-6103.

201 *Id.* at §75-6101(c).

highway construction.[202] Additionally, the Act[203] does not apply to claims for services from a health care provider other than a charitable health care provider, a municipally owned hospital, a local health department, an indigent health care clinic, a coroner, or a community mental health center and its employees.

The Kansas Supreme Court has ruled that "qualified immunity shields public officials from personal liability unless their conduct violates clearly established constitutional rights."[204]

R. KENTUCKY

The Kentucky Constitution states that "the General Assembly may, by law, direct in what manner and in what courts suits may be brought against the Commonwealth."[205] Consequently, sovereign immunity "may be waived by the legislature," but the Kentucky Supreme Court has stated that the legislature must do so "by the most express language or by such overwhelming implications from the test as will leave no room for any other reasonable construction."[206] Additionally, the Supreme Court has further ruled that a claim for monetary relief violates sovereign immunity and the separation of powers set out in the Kentucky Constitution, unless a monetary fund is provided by the Kentucky General Assembly.[207]

The Kentucky General Assembly enacted the Board of Claims Act[208] to provide "a limited waiver for 'negligence claims for the negligent performance of ministerial acts' by 'any officers, agents, or employees' of the Commonwealth 'while acting within the scope of their employment by the Commonwealth.'"[209]

---

202 *Id.* at §75-6104.

203 *Id.* at §75-6115.

204 *Goldbarth v. Kansas State Bd. of Regents*, 9 P.3d 1251 (Kan. 2000).

205 Kentucky Constitution, §231. Section 230 provides that "[n]o money shall be drawn from the State Treasury, except in pursuant of appropriations made by law...."

206 *Gaither v. Justice & Public Safety Cabinet*, 447 S. W.3d 618 (Ken. 2014).

207 *Beshear v. Haydon Bridge Co.*, 416 S.W. 3d 280, 295-96 (Ky. 2013).

208 Ky. Rev. Stat. §§44.070 *et seq.*

209 *Gaither*, citing K.R.S. §44.073(2). In *Gaither*, the court described a ministerial act as "one that requires only obedience to the orders of others, or when the officer's duty is absolute, certain, and imperative, involving merely execution of a specific act arising from fixed and designated facts."

The legislative intent was to give a limited means to assert negligence claims against the Commonwealth of Kentucky but not to waive sovereign immunity.[210]

The Board of Claims has jurisdiction over claims against municipalities.[211] It has jurisdiction over all negligence claims of any Commonwealth offices, officers or employees acting within the scope of employment,[212] but, sovereign immunity is preserved for claims involving discretionary acts or decisions, executive decisions, actions in the performance of obligations running to the public as a whole, governmental performance of a self-imposed protective function to the public, and administrative acts.[213]

The Supreme Court has described discretionary acts "as those involving the exercise of discretion and judgment, or personal deliberation, decision and judgment."[214] It has defined discretionary acts or functions as those that necessarily require the exercise of reason in the adaptation of means to an end, and discretion in determining how or whether the act should be performed or a course pursued.

S. LOUISIANA

The Louisiana Constitution states that "neither the state, a state agency, nor a political subdivision shall be immune from suit and liability in contract or for injury to person or property."[215] The Louisiana Supreme Court has recognized this constitutional provision "as an 'unequivocal, self-executing waiver of sovereign immunity as to suit and liability in contract and tort cases.'"[216]

---

210 *Id.* at §49.060.

211 *Id.* at §44.070. The Claims Commission also is empowered to hear claims involving higher education. *Id.*

212 *Id.* at §49.020.

213 *Id.* at §44.070(13).

A claim against the state may not exceed $200,000 for a single claim or $350,000 for multiple claims and no claimant may receive more than $200,000. *Id.* at 44.070.

214 *Gaither*, citing *Yanero v. Davis*, 65 S.W.3d 510, 522 (Ky. 2001). The court stated: "Discretion in the manner of the performance of an act arises when the act may be performed in one or two or more ways, either of which would be lawful, and where it is left to the will or judgment of the performer to determine in which way it shall be performed."

215 Louisiana Constitution, Article XII, §10(A).

216 *Canal/Claiborne, Ltd. v. Stonehedge Dev., LLC*, 156 So. 3d 627 (La. 2014) (citing *Fulmer v. State, Dept.*

The Louisiana Legislature authorized suits in contract or in tort under the "Louisiana Governmental Claims Act."[217] The Louisiana Legislature does not impose liability on public entities nor their officers or employees for exercising or failing to exercise within the scope of their employment their policymaking or discretionary acts unless the acts were intentional misconduct or were criminal, or fraudulent,[218] and does not impose liability on boards or commissions of political subdivisions, [219] or on emergency personnel when acting within the scope of employment.[220] Additionally, the Louisiana Constitution provides that the state will not pay a judgment unless the legislature has appropriated funds.[221] Further, although the Legislature may authorize suits against the state or state agencies,[222] the Louisiana Supreme Court has ruled that granting a commission the power to sue or be sued is not a waiver of sovereign immunity.[223]

All suits against the state or its agencies must be maintained in a Louisiana state court.[224] Additionally, suits against state employees must be timely presented to the Attorney General to determine if the employee was acting within

of Wildlife and Fisheries, 68 So.3d 499, 503 (La. 2011)).

217 La. Rev.Stat. §§13:5101-5113.

218 *Id.* at §9.2798.1.

219 *Id.* at §2792.4.

220 *Id.* at §2793.1.

221 Louisiana Constitution Article XII, §10(C).

222 *Id.* at §10(B). Sections 10(A) and (B) retain sovereign immunity for suits other than those in contract or tort. See *Chamberlain v. State of Louisiana, Dept. of Transp. and Dev't,* 624 So.2d 874 (La. 1993) and discussion in *Canal/Claiborne,* 156 So. 3d at 636-40.

223 *Canal/Claiborne, Ltd.,* 156 So. 3d at 640. But see *Board of Commissioners v. Splendour Shipping & Enterprises Co.,* 273 So. 2d 19, 24-25 (La. 1973), wherein the Supreme Court found commissioners liable because the court then thought immunity was "unfair, irresponsible and unnecessary." The Supreme Court noted in *Canal* that its decision in *Splendour* found that "sovereign or governmental immunity was a judicially-created doctrine, which was outmoded and which was inconsistent with the state's policy of requiring that state agencies either 'act responsibly, or be subject to answer in court.'" *Canal,* 156 So. 3d at 636, citing *Splendour,* 273 So. 2d at 26.

To have a jury trial, a plaintiff must make demand in writing and must properly file a bond. La. Rev. Stat. §13:5105.

A political subdivision may obtain a jury trial only if public ordinance authorizes a jury trial. *Arshad v. City of Kenner,* 95 So. 3d 477 (La. 2012).

224 La. Rev. Stat. § 13:5106. Liability per person for wrongful death or personal injury is limited to $500,000. *Id.* at §5106(B).

the scope of employment and whether or not the Attorney General will defend the employee.[225]

T. MAINE

Maine has absolute immunity for claims against the state.[226] The Maine Tort Claims Act[227] "begins with a broad grant of governmental immunity from tort claims" but then enumerates some exceptions to immunity.[228] It limits the personal liability of a governmental employee for "negligent acts or omissions within the course and scope of employment...for any such claims arising out of a single occurrence."[229]

The Act states: "Except as otherwise expressly provided by statute, all governmental entities shall be immune from suit on any and all tort claims seeking recovery of damages."[230] Additionally, the Act provides that "[n]otwithstanding

225 *Id.* at §13.5108.1.

226 The State is never liable for specified claims, including, among others, any claim resulting from undertaking a legislative or judicial act, performing prosecutorial or discretionary functions or duties, activities of the state military forces when on duty, and leasing of governmental property. See Me. Rev. Stat. tit. 14, §8104-B. However, the Act enumerates several exceptions to immunity; it provides that the State has waived immunity for negligent acts or omissions (1) in its ownership or use of motor vehicles, machinery and equipment, (2) in the construction, operation, or maintenance of any public building, (3) in the sudden and accidental discharge, dispersal, release or escape of smoke, vapors, soot, toxic chemicals, contaminants or other pollutants into or upon land or water, and (4) in the performance of street cleaning or repair operations on highways and other such areas. Me. Rev. Stat. tit. 14, §8104-A.

227 Me. Rev. Stat. tit. 14, §§8101-08.

228 *Day's Auto Body, Inc. v. Town of Medway*, 145 A.3d 1030, 1034 (Me. 2016). The court considers the Maine Tort Claims Act (MTCA) as employing "an exception-to-immunity approach rather than an exception-to-liability approach." *Id.* at 1035. The court ruled "that the mere fact a vehicle or piece of equipment or machinery is involved in the conduct that allegedly caused harm does not, in itself, implicate the exception to immunity." *Id.* The court also considered the question of whether a town is an employee under the Act and decided "that it is possible for a legal entity to meet the MTCA's definition of 'employee.'" *Id.* at 1037.

229 Me. Re. Stat. tit. 14, §8104-D. The limit is $10,000. This provision states that "the employee is not liable for any amount in excess of that limit on any such claims."

230 *Id.* at 8103. In *Clifford v. MaineGeneral Medical Center*, 91 A.3d 567 (Me. 2014), the Maine Supreme Judicial Court ruled that the Torts Claims Act does not bar due process claims under the Maine Civil Rights Act (MCRA), 5 Me. Rev. Stat. §§4681-85. The court noted that while the MCRA does not address the issue of immunity, the court has determined that qualified immunity is available to governmental employees or actors for claims brought pursuant to the MCRA," citing *Jenness v. Nickerson*, 637 A.2d 1151, 1154, 1159 (Me. 1994).

any liability that may have existed at common law, employees of government shall be absolutely immune from personal civil liability" for legislative or quasi-legislative acts or failures to act, judicial or quasi-judicial acts or failures to act, discretionary functions or duties, prosecutorial functions, and intentional acts or omissions within the course and scope of employment unless performed in bad faith.[231]

"Exceptions to absolute immunity are narrowly construed,"[232] and "'a waiver of governmental immunity is not to be implied.'"[233] Additionally, "summary judgment is appropriate when a defendant is immune from liability."[234]

U. MARYLAND

The Maryland Legislature enacted the Maryland Torts Claims Act (MTCA)[235] to "ensure that an individual who is injured by the tortious conduct of the State or state employees has a remedy for his or her injury."[236] "Before the General Assembly enacted the MTCA, 'the State and its agencies could not be sued

231 *Id.* at §8111. Any claim or cause of action permitted by the Maine Tort Claims Act cannot be commenced against a governmental entity or employee unless the claimant gives notice to the governmental entity within 180 days after the claim or cause of action arose. *Id.* at 8107.

In *Deschenes v. City of Sanford,* 137 A.3d 198 (Me. 2016), the Supreme Judicial Court ruled that a personal injury action against a town was barred because of the plaintiff's failure to submit any written notice to a town within 180 days of the accrual of the claim.

232 *Lightfoot v. School Admin. Dist.,* 816 A.2d 63, 65 (Me. 2003) (quoting *Thompson v. Dep't of Inland Fisheries & Wildlife,* 796 Al1d 674, 676 (Me. 2002) and stating "the public building exception applies only to 'the State's acts in the care or operation of its buildings and property, not to the State's care or supervision of people in its charge'" (quoting *ABT & A Co. v. State,* 644 A.2d 460 (Me. 1994)). See also *Drake v. Smith,* 390 A.2d 541, 543 (Me. 1978).

233 *Perry v. Dean,* 156 A.3d 742 (Me. 2017) (quoting *Young v. Greater Portland Transit Dist.,* 535 A.2d 417,419 (Me. 1987)). The court ruled that because the Probate Code did not contain an express waiver of sovereign immunity from tort claims and because there was no evidence in the record that the Department of Health and Human Services had obtained liability insurance coverage that waived immunity pursuant to 14 Me. Rev. Stat. §8116, the Department was immune from breach of fiduciary duty claims.

234 *Day's Auto Body,* 145 A.3d at 1034 (quoting *Grossman v. Richards,* 722 A.2d 371 (Me. 1999)).

235 Md. Code, State Gov't, §§12-101 to 12-110.

236 *Proctor v. Wash. Metropolitan Area Transit Authority,* 412 Md. 691, 990 A.2d 1048 (Md. 2010). Section 12.102 of the Maryland Tort Claims Act states: "This subtitle shall be construed broadly, to ensure that injured parties have a remedy."

unless the General Assembly authorized suit and enabled State agencies to obtain funds necessary to satisfy judgments.'"[237]

In the MTCA, the Maryland General Assembly waived immunity with respect to the negligent actions or omission of State personnel within the scope of their public duties.[238] However, the waiver does not extend to actions or omissions of State personnel that are grossly negligent.[239] Additionally, because of then existing waivers of sovereign immunity for specific instrumentalities or agencies of the State, the Legislature, in enacting the MTCA, elected to limit its scope.[240] The Maryland Court of Appeals[241] stated that the MTCA serves "as a 'gap-filler' to waive the immunity of State agencies in tort when no other statute expressly waived the agency's immunity."[242]

The Local Government Tort Claims Act (LGTCA)[243] was enacted to "afford a remedy to those injured by the acts of local government officers and employees."[244] State personnel are immune from suit "and from liability in tort

237 Proctor, 412 Md. at 711 (quoting Condon v. State, 332 Md. 481, 492, 632 A.2d 753, 758 (1993)).

238 *Rodriguez v. Cooper*, 458 Md. 425, 430, 182 A.3d 853 (2018).

239 *Id.*

240 *Proctor*, 412 Md. at 711. Section 12-103 of the State Government Article states: "This subtitle does not (1) limit any other law that (i) waives the sovereign immunity of the State or the units of the State government in tort; or (ii) authorizes the State or its units to have insurance for tortious conduct; (2) waive any right or defense of the State or its units, officials, or employees in an action in a court of the United States or any other state, including any defense that is available under the 11th Amendment to the United States Constitution; or (3) apply to waive any immunity of a bicounty unit, county municipal corporation, or other political subdivision of any unit, official, or employee of any of those agencies or subdivisions."

The MTCA applies as a general waiver of immunity to tort actions against any agency for which there is no specific statute addressing waiver. However, pursuant to §12-104 of the State Government Article, the State's liability and its units may not exceed $400,000 to a singe claimant for injuries arising from a single incident or occurrence. Additionally, the Act states, §12-104(a)(2) that immunity is not waived as described under §5-522(a) of the Court and Judicial Proceedings Article. Section 5-522, Md Code, Courts and Judicial Proceedings, states that immunity of the State is not waived under §12-104 of the MTCA for punitive damages, a "claim that arises from the combatant activities of the State Militia during a state of emergency," and a "tortious act or omission of State personnel that...is not within the scope of the public duties of the State personnel... or... made with malice or gross negligence"...or a "cause of action that law specifically prohibits."

241 *Proctor*, 412 Md. at 712.

242 The Legislature has also established a cap on noneconomic damages, such as damages for mental anguish, pain and suffering, and loss of companionship or consortium, in all personal injury and wrongful death actions. Md. Code, Courts and Judicial Proceedings Article, §11-108.

243 Md. Code, Courts and Judicial Proceedings, §5-301 *et seq.*

244 See *Rios v. Montgomery Cnty*, 386 Md. 104, 125-26, 872 A.2d 1, 13 (2005). The LGTCA limits liability, provides for indemnification, and establishes procedural requirements relating to suits against offi-

for a tortious act or omission that is within the scope of the public duties of the State personnel and is made without malice or gross negligence."[245]

The General Assembly has also provided for representation of state officers and employees by the Attorney General when they are sued in their personal capacities for actions taken in the course of their public employment.[246]

The Attorney General has the sole discretion to determine whether to provide representation to an employee; if the Attorney General provides representation, the Attorney General and the employee enter into an agreement. The agreement will state explicitly that the state is not responsible for payment of a judgment against the employee and will advise the employee to apply to the Board of Public Works for payment of a judgment or settlement against the employee.[247]

The Maryland Court of Appeals pointed out in *Cooper v. Rodriguez*[248] that "[c]ommon law public official immunity is distinct from ...public duty doctrine." The court stated: "Under the public duty doctrine, where a statute or common law principle imposes upon a public entity a duty to the public as a whole, as opposed to a duty to a particular group of people, 'the duty is not...enforceable in tort.'"[249] "[C]ommon law public official immunity applies to 'public officials (as opposed to mere employees) who perform negligent acts during the course of their discretionary (as opposed to ministerial) duties.'"[250] The court in *Cooper* ruled that "gross negligence is an exception to common law public official immunity," this being "consistent with the reasoning underlying the MTCA."[251]

---

cials of local government employees." *Houghton v. Forrest,* 412 Md. 578, 591, 989 A.2d 223, 231 (2010). In *Espina v. Jackson*, 442 Md. 311, 112 A.3d 442 (Me. 2015), the court ruled that state constitutional claims are within the scope of the LGTCA damages cap.

The LGTCA provides specific limitations on a local government's liability. Section 5-303(a)-(c) provides for a limitation of liability and indemnification of $200,000 per an individual claim, and $500,000 per total claims that arise from the same occurrence for damages resulting from tortious acts or omissions.

245 *Id.* at §5-522(b). See *Cooper v. Rodriguez*, 443 Md. 680, 118 A.3d 829 (2015). The statute substitutes the liability of the State for the liability of the state employee committing the tort. *Menefee v. State,* 417 Md. 740, 752, 12 A.3d 153, 160 (2010).

246 Md. Code, State Government, Art.§12-304; *Rodriguez v. Cooper*, 458 Md. at 453-54.

247 Md. Code, SG at §§12-304 and 12-305. Representation by the Attorney General does not deprive a State officer, employee, or unit of sovereign immunity. SG §12-306(b).

248 *Cooper*, 118 A.3d at 849.

249 *Id.* citing *Muthukumarana v. Montgomery Cnty.*, 370 Md. 447, 468, 805 A.2d 372, 395 (2002).

250 *Id.* at 855, citing *Houghton v. Forrest*, 412 Md. 578, 585, 989 A.2d 223, 227 (2010).

251 *Id.*

The court stated: "One of the core principles of the MTCA is that it provides the State immunity for the gross negligence of State personnel, while allowing State personnel to be liable for gross negligence."[252]

V. MASSACHUSETTS

The Massachusetts Legislature enacted the Massachusetts Torts Claims Act (MTCA)[253] after the Supreme Judicial Court of Massachusetts had decided "that the underlying basis for common-law sovereign immunity for both the Commonwealth and municipalities was 'logically indefensible,' and stated [its] intention to abrogate the doctrine of municipal immunity.'"[254] That court has stated: "One of the major purposes of [the act] clearly is to allow plaintiffs with valid causes of action to recover in negligence against governmental entities in Massachusetts. A second, and equally important, purpose is to preserve the stability and effectiveness of government by providing a mechanism which will result in payment of only those claims against governmental entities which are valid, in amounts which are reasonable and not inflated."[255]

Section 2 of the MTCA states: "Public employers shall be liable for injury or loss of property or personal injury or death caused by the negligent or wrongful act or omission of any public employee while acting within the scope of his office or employment, in the same manner and to the same extent as a private individual under like circumstances."[256] "Although the act statutorily eliminates the

252 *Id.* at 856.

253 M.G.L.A. Ch. 258, §§2 to 14.

254 *Cormier v. City of Lynn*, 479 Mass. 35, 38, 91 N.E.3d 662, 665 (2018) (citing *Morash & Sons, Inc. v. Commonwealth*, 363 Mass. 612, 618-19, 296 N.E. 2d 461 (1973) and *Whitney v, Worcester*, 373 Mass 208, 210, 366 N.E. 2d 1210 (1977)).

255 *Acevedo v. Musterfield Place, LLC,* 479 Mass. 705, 98 N.E.3d 673 (2018) (quoting *Vasys v. Metropolitan Dist. Comm'n*, 387 Mass 51, 57, 438 NE.2d 836 (1982) and holding that a controlled affiliate of a housing authority was not entitled to sovereign immunity under the Tort Claims Act).

256 M.G.L.A, Ch. 258, §2. Section 2 excepts public employers from liability for the "levy of execution on any real and personal property to satisfy judgment" and limits liability for a public employer to $100,000 with no liability for interest prior to judgment or for punitive damages. In *Hallett v. Town of Wrentham,* 398 Mass. 550, 499 N.E.2d 1189 (1986), the court ruled that the $100,000 limitation cap in §2 on wrongful death recovery applied to the sum of recoveries and that it does not violate equal protection.

immunity that governmental bodies would ordinarily enjoy under common law, it sets forth several exceptions to that general waiver of sovereign immunity."[257]

Section 10 of the MTCA excepts from the general waiver of immunity, among others, intentional torts and claims based on a public employee's act or omission if the employee was exercising due care in the execution of any statute or regulation or the exercise or performance or the failure to exercise or perform a discretionary function or duty by a public employee acting within the scope of employment.[258] In deciding whether the discretionary function bars a plaintiff's claim, the Maryland Supreme Judicial Court[259] has ruled that a court must first determine whether a governmental employee had any discretion to perform the act that caused harm. If the governmental employee did not have discretion because a course of action was prescribed by a statute, regulation, or established agency practice, the "'discretionary function exception to governmental liability has no role to play in deciding the case.'"[260] The court stated that the "discretionary function is narrow, 'providing immunity only for discretionary conduct that involves policy making or planning.'"[261]

W. MICHIGAN

Under the governmental tort liability act,[262] the State of Michigan is immune from liability if a "governmental agency is engaged in the exercise or discharge

257 *Cormier*, 479 Mass. at 39.

258 In *Morrissey v. New England Deaconess Assoc.*, 458 Mass. 580, 940 N.E.2d 391 (2010, the Massachusetts Supreme Judicial Court ruled that a private nuisance claim fell within the exception in §10(e) to the waiver of sovereign immunity based on the issuance of a denial, suspension or revocation of a permit. In *Cormier*, 479 Mass. at 43, the court ruled that a school district and its employees had immunity under §10(j) for injuries to a student who was permanently injured when another student pushed him down the stairs. Section 10(j) eliminated government liability from the wrongful conduct of a third party "unless the condition was 'originally caused' by the public employee." *Cormier*, 479 Mass. at 40 (citing *Brum v. Dartmouth*, 428 Mass. 684, 692, 695, 702 N.E.2d 1147 (1999)).

259 *Greenwood v. Town of Easton*, 444 Mass. 457, 828 N.E.2d 945 (2005).

260 *Id.* at 469

261 *Id.* at 470. The court further stated: "If allegedly tortious conduct were to be immunized from causing liability simply because there was some element of discretion in that conduct, the discretionary function exception would go a long way toward restoring the governmental immunity that [the MCTA] was designed to eliminate." *Id.*

262 M.C.L. §§691.1401 to .1419.

of a governmental function."[263] In noting the statutory exceptions to governmental immunity in the Michigan tort liability act, the Michigan Supreme Court[264] stated: "The Legislature's refusal to abolish completely governmental immunity, evidences a clear legislative judgment that public and private tortfeasors are to be treated differently."

The Michigan Act provides for immunity for governmental officers, employees, and volunteers for acts caused by these persons while acting on behalf of a governmental agency if the person reasonably believed he or she was acting within the scope of authority, the conduct did not amount to gross negligence, and the governmental agency was engaged in the exercise or discharge of a governmental function.[265] The Act also provides immunity for judges, legislators and the elective or highest appointed executive official of all levels of government if these persons were acting within the scope of judicial, legislative, or executive authority.[266]

The Act does not provide for immunity for a governmental agency for "actions to recover for bodily injury or property damages arising out of the performance of a proprietary function," which is an "activity conducted primarily for the purpose of producing a pecuniary profit for the governmental agency" other than activities "normally supported by taxes or fees."[267]

---

263 M.C.L. §691.1407(1). In *Ross v. Consumers Power Co*, 420 Mich. 567, 618, 363 N.W.2d 641 (1984), the court stated: "Immunity from tort liability, as provided by M.C.L. 691.1407..., is expressed in the broadest possible language–it extends immunity to all governmental agencies for all tort liability whenever they are engaged in the exercise or discharge of a governmental function."

264 *Nawrocki v. Macomb County Road Com'n*, 463 Mich 143, 156, 615 N.W.2d 701 (2000). In quoting Ross, 420 Mich. at 618, the court stated: "Government cannot merely be liable as private persons are for public entities are fundamentally different from private persons. Private persons do not make laws... Moreover, in our system of government, decision-making has been allocated among three branches of government—legislative, executive and judicial—and in many cases decisions made by the legislative and executive branches should not be subject to review in tort suits for damages, for this would take the ultimate decision-making authority away from those who are responsible politically for making the decisions."

265 M.C.L. 691.1407(2).

266 *Id.* at .1407(5)

267 *Id.* at 1413. Claims are filed with the Clerk of the Court of Claims, which is the court having exclusive jurisdiction over claims against the State. *Id.* at §§600.6419 and .6431.

X. MINNESOTA

The Minnesota Tort Claims Act[268] waives "governmental tort immunity by creating a general rule of liability 'where the state, if a private person, would be liable to the claimant.'"[269] Still, the immunity waiver "is subject to the discretionary function exception, which provides that 'the state and its employees are not liable for...a loss caused by the performance or failure to perform a discretionary duty, whether or not the discretion is abused.'"[270]

The Supreme Court of Minnesota[271] has defined the purpose of statutory immunity as being "to protect the legislative and executive branches from judicial second-guessing of certain policy-making activities through the medium of tort actions," reasoning that "it is important for courts to focus on the idea that statutory immunity seeks to protect policy-based decisions and to prevent the impairment of effective government." The Supreme Court has stated: "Statutory immunity is extended when there has been a planning-level decision; that is, social, political, or economic considerations have been evaluated and weighed as part of the decision-making process" but that "[s]tatutory immunity does not extend to operational-level decisions, those involving day-to-day operations of government, the application of scientific and technical skills, or the exercise of professional judgment."[272]

The Minnesota Supreme Court has ruled that, in determining whether a local government is entitled to statutory immunity, a court must first "identify the precise government conduct being challenged" and must next consider whether

268 Minn. Stat. §3.736.

269 *Id* at §3.736(1). The Act provides: "The state will pay compensation for injury or loss of property or personal injury or death caused by an act or omission of an employee of the state while acting within the scope of office or employment or a peace officer who is not acting on behalf of a private employer and who is acting good faith... under circumstances where the state, if a private person, would be liable to the claimant, whether arising out of governmental or proprietary function."

The Act limits the total liability of the state and its employees acting within the scope of their employment to $1,500,000 for any number of claims arising out of a single occurrence.

270 *Rico v. State of Minnesota*, 472 N.W.2d 100 (Minn. 1991) (quoting Minn. Stat. §3.736(3)(b)).

In addition, the act does not waive "the defense of judicial, quasi-judicial, or legislative immunity...." Minn. Stat. §3.736(1).

271 *Schroeder v. St. Louis County*, 708 N.W.2d 497, 503 (Minn. 2006) (quoting *Husbaum v. County of Blue Earth*, 422 N.W.2d 713, 718, 719 (Minn. 1988) and Minn. Stat. §466.03(6)).

272 *Id.*

a governmental employee is "entitled to common law official immunity."[273] The Supreme Court has explained that "[a]lthough the discretionary function exception to the Tort Claims Act and the official immunity doctrine both protect discretionary acts, the discretionary acts protected by each are not identical."[274] It earlier pointed out that "[g]overnmental immunity under the discretionary function exception and official immunity serve different purposes: governmental immunity 'is designed to preserve the separation of powers,' whereas official immunity primarily is 'intended to insure that the threat of potential liability does not unduly inhibit the exercise of discretion required of public officers in the discharge of their duties.'"[275]

"The doctrine of official immunity protects from personal liability a public official charged by law with duties that call for the exercise of judgment or discretion unless the official is guilty of a willful or malicious wrong."[276] Although "[o]fficial immunity generally applies to prevent 'a public official charged by law with duties which call for the exercise of his judgment or discretion' from being held personally liable to an individual for damages...;'" immunity "does not extend to officials 'charged with the execution of ministerial, rather than discretionary, functions.'"[277] Still, "the mere existence of some degree of judgment or discretion will not necessarily confer common law official immunity; rather the focus is on the nature of the act at issue."[278]

---

273 *Id.* at 504.

274 *Rico v. State*, 472 N.W.2d at 107.

275 *Id.* The Minnesota Supreme Court determined that "discretion has a broader meaning in the context of official immunity," quoting *Elwood v. County of Rice*, 423 N.W.2d 671, 677 (Minn. 1988) and stating: "In defining the scope of official immunity, we have distinguished between the performance of discretionary duties—which is immunized, and ministerial duties–for which officers remain liable." *Id.* The Supreme Court "described an official's duty as ministerial 'when it is absolute, certain and imperative, involving merely execution of a specific duty arising from fixed and designated facts,'" *id*, quoting *Cook v. Trovatten*, 274 N.W.165, 167 (1937)). The Supreme Court stated: "Under these standards, the decision to remove an unclassified policy-making employee, who may be discharged at any time without reason, is discretionary rather than ministerial." *Id.*

276 *Id.* at 107, quoting Elwood, *id.*

277 *Schroeder,* 708 N.W.2d at 504 (quoting *Anderson v. Anoka Hennepin Indep. Sch. Dist. II*, 678 N.W.2d 651, 655 (Minn. 2004)).

278 *Id.* quoting *Anderson*, 678 N.W.2d at 655-56. "Official immunity does not apply: (1) when a ministerial duty is either not performed or is performed negligently, or (2) when a willful or malicious wrong is committed." *Anderson*, 678 N.W.2d at 662.

Y. MISSISSIPPI

The Mississippi Tort Claims Act[279] waives sovereign immunity for torts of its governmental entities and their employees while acting within the course and scope of their employment[280] and is the exclusive route for filing suits against a governmental entity and its employees.[281] However, the Act retains governmental immunity for a governmental entity and its employees acting within the course and scope of employment for a legislative or judicial action or inaction or for the exercise or performance or failure to exercise or perform a discretionary function or duty.[282]

In defining the "discretionary function or duty" exception, the Mississippi Supreme Court[283] has adopted the "public policy function test" set out in *United States v. Gaubert.*[284] In *Wilcher v. Lincoln County Bd. of Supervisors,*[285] the court stated: "Because discretionary-function immunity 'protects only governmental actions and decisions based on considerations of public policy,' when applying the discretionary-function exception, this Court must distinguish between

---

279 Miss. Code §§11-46-1 to 11-46-23.

280 *Id.* at §11-46-5. The Act states that it is "a rebuttable presumption that any act or omission of an employee within the time and at the place of his employment is within the course and scope of his employment." *Id.* at (3). The state's immunity from suit in federal courts guaranteed by the Eleventh Amendment to the United States Constitution is not waived. *Id.* at (4).

The state's liability is limited to $500,000 for all claims arising from a single occurrence, and there is no liability for punitive damages. *Id.* at §11-46-15.

281 *City of Jackson v. Sutton,* 797 So.2d 977 (Miss. 2001). Section 11-46-7(1) states: "The remedy provided by this chapter against a governmental entity or its employee is exclusive of any other civil action or civil proceeding...." The court ruled in *City of Jackson* that the Mississippi Tort Claims act does not violate the Mississippi Constitution, Article 3, §14.

Section 11-46-11 requires a notice of claim to be filed with the chief executive officer of the governmental entity within ninety days before instituting a lawsuit.

282 *Id.* at §11-46-9. This provision also sets out other exceptions wherein immunity is not waived. The Mississippi Supreme Court has stated that the state "'cannot be held liable for damages if the conduct falls within one of the exceptions found in Miss. Code Section 11-46-9." *Little v. Mississippi Depart. of Transp.,* 129 So.3d 132 (Miss. 2013) (quoting *State v Hinds County Bd. of Supervisors,* 635 So.2d 839, 842 (Miss. 1994)).

283 *Wilcher v. Lincoln County Bd. of Supervisors,* 243 So.3d 177 (Miss. 2018).

284 *Gaubert,* 499 US.315, 322, 111 S. Ct. 1267, 113 L. Ed.2d 335 (1991). (*Gaubert* is discussed in Chapter 4.) In *Wilcher,* the Supreme Court overruled *Brantley v. City of Horn Lake,* 152 So.3d 1106, 1112-14 (Miss. 2014), wherein the court had abandoned the two-part, public-policy function test in determining whether a function was discretionary or ministerial.

285 *Wilcher,* 243 So.3d at 188 (quoting *Gaubert,* 499 U.S. at 325).

real policy decisions implicating governmental functions and *simple acts of negligence,* which injure innocent citizens"[286] A governmental entity has no immunity for a "simple act of negligence." The court concluded: "Thus, '[w]hen reviewing whether a challenged action is afforded immunity, a court's focus is on the nature of the actions taken and whether they are susceptible to policy analysis.'"[287]

Z. MISSOURI

The Missouri Tort Claims Act[288] waives sovereign immunity only (1) for injuries directly resulting from the negligent acts or omissions by public employees arising out of the operation of motor vehicles within the scope of their employment and (2) injuries caused by state property that was in a dangerous condition at the time of the injury, the injury directly resulted from the dangerous condition, the dangerous condition created a reasonably foreseeable risk of harm of the kind of injury that was incurred, and either a negligent or wrongful act of omission of a government employee within the course of employment created the dangerous condition.[289] As the court pointed out in *Hale v. City of Jefferson,*[290] the legislature reinstated sovereign immunity after the Supreme Court had abrogated the doctrine.[291]

286 *Id.*

287 *Id.*

288 Mo. Stat. §§537.600-650.

289 *Id.* at §537.600. The waiver of sovereign immunity in §537.600 is an absolute waiver whether or not the public entity was functioning in a governmental or proprietary capacity and whether or not the public entity was covered by a liability insurance tort policy. Liability is limited to $2,000,000 for all claims arising out of a single accident or occurrent and to $300,000 for any person in a single accident or occurrence. *Id.* at §537.610. The state is not liable for punitive damages. *Id.*

The Missouri Supreme has upheld the constitutionality of §537.610. Discussion in *Hodges v. City of St. Louis,* 217 S.W.3d 278 (Mo. 2007).

290 *Hale,* 6 S.W.3d 187, 192 (Mo. Ct. App. 1999).

The Supreme Court ruled in *State v. Grate,* 490 S.W.3d 368, 372 (Mo. 2016), that a city's purchase of insurance coverage did not waive the city's sovereign immunity. The Supreme Court ruled in *Newsome v. Kansas City, Missouri School District,* 520 S.W.3d 769, 781 (Mo. 2017), that a school district's purchase of an insurance policy could not waive the school district's liability above the amount of its liability coverage in §537.610.

291 *Id.* See *Jones v. State Highway Comm'n,* 557 S.W.2d 225 (Mo. 1977).

The Missouri Supreme Court[292] has ruled that, because "]t]he general rule regarding sovereign immunity is that the sovereign cannot be sued without its consent," a court must strictly construe "statutory provisions that waive sovereign immunity."

AA. MONTANA

The Montana Tort Claims Act[293] provides for waiver of governmental immunity for torts of the state and "its employees acting within the scope of their employment or duties whether arising out of a governmental or proprietary function except as specifically provided by the legislature under Article II, section 18, of the Constitution of the State of Montana."[294]

Still, a governmental entity is immune from suit for a legislative, judicial, or gubernatorial act or omission.[295] Additionally, a "public duty doctrine" provides immunity "for an individual plaintiff's injury resulting from a governmental officer's breach of a duty owed to the general public rather than to the individual plaintiff."[296]

---

292 *McNeill Trucking Co., Inc. v. Missouri State Highway and Transp. Comm'n,* 35 S.W.3d 846 (Mo. 2001).

293 Mont. Stat. §§2-9-101 to 114.

294 *Id.* at §2-9-102. Article II, §18 of the 1972 Montana Constitution provides: "The state, counties, cities, towns, and all other local governmental entities shall have no immunity from suit for injury to a person or property, except as may be specifically provided by law by a 2/3 vote of each house of the legislature."

In §2-9-101(1), the legislature defined what constituted a "claim" against a governmental entity. It states: "Claim' means any claim against a governmental entity, for money damages only, that any person is legally entitled to recover as damages because of personal injury or property damage caused by a negligent or wrongful act or omission committed by any employee of the governmental entity while acting within the scope of employment, under circumstances where the governmental entity, if a private person, would be liable to the claimant for the damages under the laws of the state." Discussion in *Kent v. City of Columbia Falls,* 350 P.3d 9 (Mont. 2015).

295 *Id.* at §§2-9-111 to 113. Additionally, tort claims against the state are limited to $750,000 for each claim and $1,500,000 for each occurrence, and the state is not liable for punitive damages. *Id.* at §§2-9-105 and 108.

The Missouri Supreme Court pointed out in *Eklund v. Trost,* 151 P.3d 870, 882 (Mont. 2006) that governmental agencies and officers have immunity tort liability when they commit torts while performing quasi-judicial functions and defined a "quasi-judicial function" as "an adjudicatory function exercised by an agency, involving the exercise of judgment and discretion in making determinations in controversies," citing §2-15-102(9). The Supreme Court noted that its "cases have further defined quasi-judicial function by noting the difference between quasi-judicial and ministerial or administrative functions for which immunity is not provided," citing *Trout v. Bennett,* 830 P. 2d 81, 87 (Mont. 1992).

296 *Kent,* 350 P.3d 9. The Missouri Supreme Court stated in *Kent* that "where a municipality owes a duty to the general public, that duty is not owned to any particular individual," quoting *Prosser v. Kennedy*

BB. NEBRASKA

The Nebraska State Tort Claims Act (STCA)[297] "operates as a limited waiver of the State's tort immunity."[298] The State is "liable in the same manner and to the same extent as a private individual under like circumstances."[299] "[W]hether a plaintiff has sued a state officer or employee in his or her individual capacity is irrelevant to whether the STCA bars a tort claim against that officer or employee."[300] Plaintiffs are limited to suing state officers and employees in their official capacities under the STCA.[301]

"[S]tatutes that purport to waive the State's protection of sovereign immunity are strictly construed in favor of the sovereign and against the waiver" and the Supreme Court will "broadly read exemptions from a waiver of sovereign

Enters. Inc., 179 P.3d 1178 (Mont. 2008).

297 Neb. Rev. Stat. §§81-8,209 to 81-8,239.11. Section 81-8,209 states: "The State of Nebraska shall not be liable for the torts of its officers, agents, or employees, and no suit shall be maintained against the state, any state agency, or any employee of the state on any tort claim except to the extent, and only to the extent provided by the State Tort Claims Act. The Legislature further declares that it is its "intent and purpose through such act to provide uniform procedures for the bringing of tort claims against the state or an employee of the state and that the procedures provided by such act shall be used to the exclusion of all others."

298 *Davis v. State of Nebraska,* 902 N.W.2d 165 (Mont. 2017). The court pointed out: "The exceptions to the waiver of the State's tort immunity include claims based on the exercise or performance of a discretionary function by a state officer or employee." *Id.* at 166, 180-81. Section 81-8,219 states that the STCA does not apply to, among others, claims "based upon an act or omission of an employee of the state, exercising due care, in the execution of a statute, rule, or regulation...or based upon the exercise or performance or the failure to exercise or perform a discretionary function or duty on the part of a state agency or an employee of the state, whether or not the discretion is abused," as well as all intentional torts.

299 Neb. Rev. Stat. §81-8,215.

300 *Davis,* 902 N.W.2d at 181.

301 *Id.* The court stated in *Davis* that "if an officer or employee was acting within the scope of his or her office or employment and the alleged tortious conduct falls within an exception to the State's waiver of tort immunity, the STCA bars a tort claim against the officer or employee, regardless of the capacity in which he or she was purportedly sued." *Id.* The court further stated that "only when the officer or employee was *not* acting within the scope of his or her office or employment can a plaintiff pursue a tort claim against the officer or employee individually." *Id.*

immunity."[302] Additionally, the State can raise for the first time on appeal an exception to the State's waiver of immunity under the STCA.[303]

CC. NEVADA

"Nevada has waived traditional sovereign immunity from tort liability, with some exceptions."[304] The Nevada Tort Claims Act[305] does not waive immunity for "an act or omission of an officer, employee or immune contractor, exercising due care, in the execution of a statute or regulation...or "[b]ased upon the exercise or performance or the failure to exercise or perform a discretionary function or duty on the part of the State or any of its agencies or political subdivisions or of any officer, employee or immune contractor of any of these, whether or not the discretion involved is abused."[306]

The Nevada Supreme Court has explained that discretionary-function immunity "is grounded in separation of powers concerns and is designed to preclude the judicial branch from 'second-guessing,' in a tort action, legislative and executive branch decisions that are based on 'social, economic, and political policy.'"[307] The Supreme Court[308] has adopted the federal two-part test for determining the applicability of discretionary-function immunity as set out in *United States v. Gaubert*.[309]

---

302 *Amend v. Nebraska Public Service Comm'n*, 905 N.W. 2d 551 (Mont. 2018). The Supreme Court stated: "A waiver of sovereign immunity is found only where stated by the most express language of a statute or by such overwhelming implication from the text as will allow no other reasonable construction."

303 *Id.* The court ruled that a claim "arising out of false imprisonment, which is a claim barred by sovereign immunity, can be raised for the first on appeal and considered by a court sua sponte."

304 *Franchise Tax Board v. Hyatt*, 407 P.3d 717 (Nev. 2017), citing N.R.S. §41.031.

305 N.R.S. §§41.031 to 41.0337.

306 *Id.* at §41.032. The State does not waive its immunity from suit conferred by the Eleventh Amendment to the United States Constitution. *Id.* at §41.031(3). Additionally, an award for damages is limited to $100,000 and may not include punitive damages. *Id.* at §41.035. The State and any local government may provide insurance for tort liability. *Id.* at §41.038.

307 *Franchise Tax Board*, 407 P.3d at 728 (citing *Martinez v. Maruszczak*, 168 P.3d 710, 719 (Nev. 2007)).

308 *Id.* at 729.

309 *Gaubert*, 499 U.S. 315, 111 S. Ct. 127, 113 L. Ed.2d 335 (1991), discussed in Chapter 4. The Nevada Supreme Court noted in *Franchise Tax Board* that the discretionary -function immunity doctrine does not include immunity for intentional torts and bad-faith conduct.

DD. NEW HAMPSHIRE

The doctrine of sovereign immunity has been "deeply entrenched" in New Hampshire.[310] Still, the Supreme Court has noted that the Legislature addressed criticism of the sovereign immunity doctrine by waiving immunities "for claims by persons injured by negligent acts of State employees, subject to certain exceptions and restrictions...and by limiting the damages recoverable against the State."[311] The Claims Against the State[312] requires that "when a claim is brought against the state or its agent, official, or employee, a court must determine whether the state is responsible for the act and, if so, must dismiss the action against the agent, official, or employee and permit the plaintiff to proceed solely against the state."[313] The Act does not waive immunity for any claim "based upon the exercise of a legislative or judicial function," or for a "claim based upon the exercise or performance or the failure to exercise or perform a discretionary executive or planning function or duty on the part of the state or any state agency or a state officer, employee, or official acting within the scope of his office or employment," or for an intentional tort.[314]

310 *Opinion of the Justices*, 493 A.2d 1182, 1185 (N. H. 1985) (citing *Krzysztalowski v. Fortin*, 230 A.2d 750, 751 (1967).

311 *Opinion*, 493 A.2d at 1185. Section 541-B:14 limits damages arising out of a single incident to "$475,000 per claimant and $3,750,000 per any single incident, or the proceeds from an insurance policy procured pursuant to RSA 9:17, whichever amount is greater; except that no claim for punitive damages may be awarded...." A claim must be brought within three years of the injury or property damage and notice must be given the state agency within 180 days of the time of the injury or damage. The lack of written notice does "not bar a claim unless the agency can show by a preponderance of the evidence that its ability to defend against the action was substantially prejudiced thereby." *Id.*

In addressing the question of whether the limitation of liability in the Act violated the Open Courts Provision of the State Constitution, Part I, Article 14, which states "that all citizens have a right to the redress of their actionable injuries," the New Hampshire Supreme Court decided the legislature could constitutionally limit damages recoverable from the state and that the only issue was whether the limit was a reasonable exercise of the legislature's authority. The court decided the limit was not "so severe as to be 'very wide of any reasonable line of demarcation,'" citing *Estate of Cargill v.City of Rochester*, 406 A.2d 704, 708 (1979). *Opinion*, 493 A.1d at 1193, which addressed the limit at that time being $2,000,000.

312 N.H. Rev. Stat. §§541-B:1 to 541-B:23.

313 *Id.* at §541-B:9-a.

314 *Id.* at §541-B:19. The New Hampshire Supreme Court has stated: "Despite the firmly established position of the sovereign immunity," the New Hampshire Supreme Court "significantly altered the common law immunity of municipalities by abolishing the governmental-proprietary function distinction." Opinion, 493 A.2d at 1185.

The Supreme Court of New Hampshire has ruled:[315] "Under official immunity, government officials are protected from personal liability for those decisions, acts or omissions that are: (1) made within the scope of their official duties while in the course of their employment; (2) discretionary rather than ministerial; and (3) not made in a wanton or reckless manner."

The Supreme Court defines a discretionary decision, act, or omission as one that "involves the exercise of personal deliberation and individual professional judgment that necessarily reflects the facts of the situation and the professional goal" and has noted that there are "no hard and fast rules as to the course of conduct that must be followed and those acts requiring the exercise of judgment involving what is just and proper under the circumstances."[316] "By contrast, 'an official's decision, act or omission is ministerial when it is absolute, certain and imperative, involving merely execution of a specific duty arising from fixed and designated facts.'"[317] The Supreme Court "'[r]ecognized that discretionary function immunity was necessary to protect 'certain essential, fundamental activities of government...so that our government can govern.'"[318]

EE. NEW JERSEY

The New Jersey Tort Claims Act (TCA)[319] "effectuates the Legislature's intent to establish immunity for government action as the rule and liability as the exception."[320] The New Jersey Supreme Court stated that the "legislative design" in the TCA "insulates government suit based on a violation 'attributable to someone else's wrongful acts, when the government's conduct is only an indirect contributing cause of the harm.'"[321] The State Legislature has declared:[322]

315 *Frost v. Delaney*, 118 A.3d 663, 672 (N.H. 2015).

316 *Id.* at 672-73.

317 *Id.* at 673 (citing *Everitt v. Gen. Elec. Co.*, 156 N.H. 202, 220,, 932 A.2d 831 (N.H. 2007)).

318 *Maryea v. Velardi*, 135 A.3d 121 (N.H. 2016) (citing *Everitt*, 15 N.H. at 210.)

319 N.J.S. §§59:1-1 to 59:12-3.

320 *Lee v. Brown*, 178 A.3d 701, 709 (N.J. 2018)

321 *Lee*, 178 A.3d at 709.

322 *Id.* at §59:1-2.

> The Legislature recognizes the inherently unfair and inequitable results which occur in the strict application of the traditional doctrine of sovereign immunity. On the other hand, the Legislature recognizes that while a private entrepreneur may readily be held liable for negligence within the chosen ambit of his activity, the area within which government has the power to act for the public good is almost without limit and therefore government should not have the duty to do everything that might be done. Consequently, it is hereby declared to be the public policy of this State that public entities shall only be liable for their negligence within the limitations of this act and in accordance with the fair and uniform principles established herein. All of the provisions of this act should be construed with a view to carry out the above legislative declaration.

The TCA states that "a public entity is not liable for an injury, whether such injury arises out of an act or omission of the public entity or a public employee or any other person" except as provided in the Act.[323] It provides that "[a] public entity is not liable for an injury resulting from the exercise of judgment or discretion vested in the entity" nor for "legislative or judicial action or inaction, or administrative action nor inaction of a legislative or judicial nature"[324] and specifically excludes "liability based on contract or the right to obtain relief other than damages against the public entity or one of its employees."[325] Further, failure to meet the ninety-day deadline for notice of a claim[326] can cause a denial of remedial relief.[327]

FF. NEW MEXICO

The New Mexico Tort Claims Act[328] states that "[a] governmental entity and any public employee while acting within the scope of duty are granted immunity

323 *Id.* at §59:2-1.

324 *Id.* at §59:2-3. This section sets out other exclusions from liability.

325 *Id.* at §59:1-4.

326 *Id.* at§ 59:8-9.

327 *McDade v. Siazon*, 32 A.3d 1122 (N.J. 2011). The Supreme Court stated the grant or denial or remedial relief, if a motion is filed, is left to the "sound discretion of the trial court and will be sustained on appeal in the absence of a showing of an abuse thereof."

328 N.M.S.A. §§41-4-1 to 41-4-30.

from liability..."[329] Still, the Act provides for waiver of immunity, among others, for negligence in the use of motor vehicles and in the operation and maintenance of buildings and equipment.[330]

The Act permits a state entity to recover from a public employee the costs of litigation and damages if the employee acted fraudulently or with actual malice.[331]

In *Flores v. Herrera*,[332] the New Mexico Supreme Court addressed the question of whether the New Mexico Whistleblower Protection Act (WPA)[333] permits a state employee to assert a claim against a state officer in the officer's individual capacity. The court noted the WPA "creates an official-capacity suit against state officers that creates two kinds of remedies–...monetary damages and injunctive relief of reinstatement of a public employee...." and that, because reinstatement can "only be effectuated by an officer acting in his or her official capacity," the act created an "action against state officers only in their official capacities."[334] Additionally, the court determined that the Legislature had "made it plain that a

---

329 *Id.* at §41-4-4.

330 Waiver of immunity is set out in §§41-4-5 to 4-4-12. It includes liability for damages and injury "caused by the negligence of public employees while acting within the scope of their duties in the operation of maintenance of any motor vehicle, aircraft or watercraft, *id.* at §41-4-5, negligence of public employees within the scope of their duties in the operation or maintenance of buildings, machinery, and equipment, id at §41-4-6; and for intentional torts "caused by law enforcement officers while acting within the scope of their duties," *id.* at §41-4-12.

Section 41-4-19 sets out the maximum liability of a governmental entity or a public employee while acting within the scope of duties to be $200,000 for property damage arising out of a single occurrence, $300,000 for medical expenses arising out of a single occurrence; $400,000 to any person arising out of a single occurrence other than real property damage and medical expenses; and a total liability of $750,000 for all claims arising out of a single occurrence.

In considering the question of whether the damages cap in the New Mexico Torts Claims Act violated New Mexico's guarantee of access to the courts under Article II, §18 of the New Mexico Constitution, the New Mexico Supreme Court ruled in *Trujillo v. City of Albuquerque*, 965 P.2d 305, 311 (N. Mex.1998), that "the right of access to the courts does not create a right to unlimited government tort liability." The court concluded that "[a]ccess to the courts encompasses the ability of a party to have access to the judiciary to resolve legal claims" and that "such access is not boundless," citing *Jiron v. Mahlab*, 659 P.2d 311, 312 (N. Mex.1983). The court pointed to sovereign immunity having been "recognized for many years as a common law defense to claims against government entities in New Mexico." *Id.* at 312. The court adopted a "rational basis scrutiny" for deciding future challenges to a tort claims damage cap. *Id.* at 318.

331 N.M.S.A. §41-4-4(E)

332 *Flores*, 384 P.3d 1070 (N. Mex. 2016).

333 N.M.S.A. §§10-16C-1 to -6.

334 Flores, 384 P.3d at 1074.

plaintiff may seek recovery directly from the State," and thus the act should not be interpreted as implicitly authorizing personal-capacity suits.[335]

GG. NEW YORK

The State of New York does not waive immunity for torts of its agents unless the New York Legislature so provides.[336] However, the New York Legislature did waive immunity from liability for certain tort claims under the New York Court of Claims Act.[337] New York waives its immunity, assumes liability, and consents to being sued with the same rules of law as applied to actions against individuals or corporations provided a plaintiff follows the Act's requirements.[338]

The waiver of sovereign immunity by New York Court of Claims Act for the state is not applicable to municipalities, which are liable equally as individuals and private corporations for their torts.[339]

The State of New York has given exclusive jurisdiction over claims against the State of New York to the Court of Claims,[340] but that court lacks jurisdiction over claims not involving the State of New York.[341] A person who has a claim against the State of New York must give written notice to the Attorney General within ninety days after accrual of a negligence claim[342] and within six months of the accrual of a breach of contract claim.[343]

---

335 *Id.*

336 *Green v. State*, 176 N.Y.S. 81 (N.Y.Ct.Cl.1919).

337 N.Y.Ct.Cl. Act §§8-12.

338 *Id.*, §8.

339 *Steitz v. Beacon*, 295 N.Y.S. 51 (N.Y.1945). In *Connolly v. Long Island Power Authority*, 30 N.Y.3d 719, 726-27, 70 N.Y.S. 3d 909, 94 N.E.3d 471 (2018), the court stated: "It is well settled that '"[d]espite the sovereign's own statutory surrender of common-law tort immunity for the misfeasance of its employees, governmental entities somewhat incongruously claim–and unquestionably continue to enjoy–a significant measure of immunity fashioned for their protection by the courts'" (citing *Haddock v. City of New York*, 75 N.Y.2d 478, 484, 554 N.Y,S.2d 439, 553 N.E.2d 987 (1990)).

340 *Lowth v. Town of Cheektowaga*, 82 F.3d 563 (2d Cir. N.Y. 1996) (Supreme Court had no jurisdiction in suit against New York Higher Education Services Corporation because it was a suit against a state agency.) *Bell v. New York Higher Education Assistance Corp.*, 526 N.Y.S. 2d 316 (N.Y.Sup.Ct. 1987).

341 *Amato v. State*, 502 N.Y.S 2d 928 (N.Y.Ct.Cl.1986).

342 N.Y.Ct.Cl. Act §10(3).

343 *Id.* at §10(4).

In order to overcome an immunity challenge in New York, a plaintiff must plead a special duty that applies to the plaintiff.[344] In *Valdez v. City of New York,*[345] the Court of Appeals of New York found there was not sufficient evidence to establish a special duty between the police and the plaintiff in the case. The Court of Appeals stated "under the public duty rule, although a municipality owes a general duty to the public at large to furnish police protection, this does not create a duty of care running to a specific individual sufficient to support a negligence claim, unless the facts demonstrate that a special duty was created."[346]

The New York court discussed the general law in New York that the state is not liable for discretionary acts taken during the performance of governmental functions[347] and that the state is liable for ministerial acts only if they violate a special duty owed to the public in general.[348] In *Valdez,* the New York Court of Appeals held that the plaintiff must show (1) an affirmative duty to act for the injured party; (2) the municipality's agent knew that harm could occur; (3) direct contact between plaintiff and municipality; and (4) plaintiff's justifiable reliance on the municipality's undertaking of the function to establish the special relationship.[349]

---

344 See *Connolly v. Long Island Power Authority,* 94 N.E.2d at 475. The New York Court of Appeals stated in *Connolly* that "if the action challenged in the litigation is governmental, the existence of a special duty is an element of the plaintiff's negligence cause of action, citing *Lauer v. City of New York,* 95 N.Y.2d 95, 722N.YS.2d 112, 733 N.E.2d 184 (2000). The court explained in *Connolly,* 94 N.E.3d at 475-76: "A government entity performs a purely proprietary role when its activities essentially substitute for or supplement traditionally private enterprises. In contrast, a [government entity] will be deemed to have been engaged in a governmental function when its acts are undertaken for the protection and safety of the public pursuant to the general police powers" (citing *Turturro v. City of New York,* 28 N.Y.3d 469, 477-78, 45 N.Y.S.3d 874, 69 N.E.3d 693 (2016)). The court in *Connolly* further stated: "If the plaintiff establishes the elements of the cause of action, including special duty, the government entity can avoid liability under the governmental function immunity defense by proving the challenged actions were discretionary in nature and that discretion was, in fact, exercised.... However, because the governmental immunity defense protects government entities from liability only for discretionary actions taken during the performance of governmental functions, the...defense has no applicability where the '[entity] has acted in a proprietary capacity, even if the acts of the [entity] may be characterized as discretionary'" (citing *Turturro,* 28 N.Y.3d at 479)).

345 *Valdez,* 18 N.Y. 3d 69, 960 N.E.2d 356 (N.Y. 2011).

346 *Id.*

347 *Id.*

348 *Id.* The court stated that the doctrine of governmental function immunity "reflects separation of powers principles and is intended to ensure that public servants are free to exercise their decision-making authority without interference from the courts." *Id.* at 76.

349 *Id.*

HH. NORTH CAROLINA

Pursuant to the "doctrine of sovereign immunity, the State is immune from suit 'absent waiver of immunity.'"[350] Additionally, "statutes waiving this immunity, being in derogation of the sovereign right to immunity, must be strictly construed."[351]

In *Ray v. North Carolina Dept. Of Transp*,[352] the North Carolina Supreme Court stated: "This Court has long recognized the common law doctrine of sovereign immunity, acknowledging that '[i]t is an established principle of jurisprudence... that a state may not be sued...unless by statute it has consented to be sued or has otherwise waived its immunity from suit.'"

The North Carolina Torts Claims Act does provide a limited waiver of immunity; it authorizes recovery against the state for the negligent acts of its officers, employees, involuntary servants or agents while acting within the scope of employment under circumstances where a private person would be liable.[353] The Act constitutes the North Carolina Industrial Commission as a court "for the purpose of hearing and passing upon tort claims against...departments, institutions and agencies of the State."[354]

Still, a "public duty doctrine is a common law negligence doctrine that exists apart from the doctrine of sovereign immunity" and that may limit tort liability even though the state has waived sovereign immunity.[355] This doctrine was codified in the state's tort claims act with the "intent to limit the public duty doctrine's application...."[356]

Intentional acts of state employees "are not compensable" and, because a suit against a public official in that person's official capacity "is a suit against

350 *White v. Trew*, 736 S.E.2d 166, 167 (N.C. 2013) (quoting *Meyer v. Walls*, 489 S.E. 2d 880, 884 (N.C. 1997)).

351 *Irving v. Charlotte-Mechlenburg Bd. of Educ.*, 781 S.E.2d 282 (N.C. 2016) (citing *Guthrie v. N.C. State Ports Auth.*, 299 S.E.2d 618, 627 (N.C. 1983)).

352 *Ray*, 727 S.E.2d 675, 678 (N.C. 2012) (quoting *Smith v. Hefner*, 68 S .E.2d 783, 787 (N.C. 1952)).

353 *White v. Trew*, 736 S.E.2d at 167; North Carolina Tort Claims Act at N.C.G.S.A. §143-291.

354 N.C.G.S.A. §143-291(a). If a state agency purchases an insurance policy providing coverage in an amount at least equal to the limits of the state's tort claims act, the insurance coverage "shall be in lieu of the State's obligation for payment...." *Id.* at §143-291(b).

355 Discussion in *Ray v. North Carolina Dept. of Transp.*, 727 S.E.2d at 678-79.

356 *Id.* at 681. See N.C.G.S. 143-299.1A, which clarifies and limits the doctrine as an affirmative defense.

the State," "sovereign immunity bars an intentional tort claim against a public official in his official capacity."[357]

II. NORTH DAKOTA

Article I, §9 of the North Dakota Constitution states: "Suits may be brought against the state in such manner, in such courts, and in such cases, as the legislative assembly may, by law, direct." In *Bulman v. Hulstrand Constr. Co., Inc.*[358] the North Dakota Supreme Court ruled this article provides "a constitutional basis for sovereign immunity, which can only be modified or waived by the Legislature."[359]

In *Kitto v. Minot Park Dist*,[360] the Supreme Court abolished governmental immunity from tort liability for political subdivisions but did not "touch" sovereign immunity of the state." After *Kitto*, the state's Legislative Assembly enacted legislation, titled "Claims Against the State," that addressed tort liability for political subdivisions and permitted money damages "for an injury proximately caused by the negligence or wrongful act or omission of a state employee acting within the employee's scope of employment under circumstances in which the employee would be personally liable to a claimant...."[361] Under the Act, neither the state nor a state employee can be held liable for a "claim based upon a decision to exercise or perform or a failure to exercise or perform a discretionary function or duty on the part of the state or its employees..." or a claim "resulting from the decision to undertake or the refusal to undertake any legislative or quasi-legislative act...or any judicial or quasi-judicial act...."[362]

In *Bulman*, the court decided *Kitto* "intimated that the doctrine of sovereign immunity was constitutionally mandated" and that subsequent decisions

357 *White v. Trew*, 736 S.E.2d at 167.

358 *Bulman*, 521 N.W.2d 632 (N.D. 1994).

359 Article I, §9 is also an Open Courts provision; it states: "All courts shall be open, and every man for any injury done him in his lands, goods, person or reputation shall have remedy by due process of law, and right and justice administered without sale, denial or delay."

360 *Kitto*, 224 N.W.2d 795, 797 (N.D. 1974).

361 Claims against the State, N.D.C.C. §§ 32-12.2.01 et seq., specifically §32-12.2-02. The act set caps limitations that currently limit liability to the state to $250,000 per person and $1,000,000 for 'any number of claims arising from any single occurrence." *Id.*

362 *Id.* at §32-12.2-02(3). The act sets out additional claims for which neither the state nor a state employee can be held liable.

construed Article I, §9 as entrusting "the matter of sovereign immunity to the Legislative Assembly."[363] The court overruled these decisions, concluding that Article I, §9 of the Constitution "does not preclude this Court from judicially abolishing the common-law doctrine of sovereign immunity, if appropriate."[364]

In abrogating the state's immunity in *Bulman*, the Supreme Court decided:[365] "Whatever justifications initially existed for sovereign immunity, they are no longer valid in today's society. Few principles of modern law have been so uniformly and soundly criticized." While abolishing the state's sovereign immunity from tort liability, the Supreme Court did not impose "tort liability on the state for the exercise of discretionary acts in its official capacity, including legislative, judicial, quasi-legislative, and quasi-judicial functions."[366]

In *Larimore Public School Dist. v. Aamodt*,[367] the North Dakota Supreme Court considered whether the damage cap in the Claims Against the State act violates Article I, §9 of the North Dakota Constitution. In ruling it does not, the court stated: "The legislature has the power to place limits on access to courts, and to create immunities without violating Article I, Section 9."[368] The court held that the constitutional provision "is not an absolute right and does not guarantee a complete remedy for every claimed wrong." It noted that the "damage cap for tort claims against political subdivisions is not an absolute bar to a money damages remedy" and decided it does not "set a limit so arbitrarily low as to be the functional equivalent of an absolute bar."[369]

---

363 *Bulman*, 521 N.W.2d. at 636 (quoting *Senger v. Hulstrand Const., Inc.*, 329 N.W.2d 507, 509-510 (N.D. 1982)).

364 *Bulman*, 521 N.W.2d at 638.

365 *Id.* The court stated that "sovereign immunity from tort liability, like the governmental immunity for political subdivision at issue in *Kitto*, perpetuates injustice by barring recovery for tortious conduct merely because of the status of the wrongdoer." It further stated: "We do not believe it requires laborious analysis to assert that the harshness and inequity of the doctrine of sovereign immunity are counterintuitive to any ordinary person's sense of justice." The court commented that "even under the earliest common law of England, sovereign immunity did not produce the harsh results it does today and only rarely did it completely deny relief." The court decided that stare decisis also does not "justify the perpetuation of an outdated, unforgiving common-law doctrine." *Id.* at 639.

366 *Id.* at 640.

367 *Larimore*, 908 N.W.2d 442, 450 (N.D. 2018).

368 *Id.*

369 *Id.* at 453.

JJ. OHIO

The State of Ohio has waived its immunity from liability "and consents to be sued, and have its liability determined, in the court of claims" which was created in Chapter 2743 of the Ohio Code. Section 2744.02 of the Ohio Code provides that except as for defenses and immunities set out in that section "a political subdivision is not liable in damages in a civil action for injury, death, or loss to person or property allegedly caused by any act or omission of the political subdivision or an employee of the political subdivision in connection with a governmental or proprietary function." Filing an action in the Court of Claims "results in a complete waiver of any cause of action, based on the same act or omission, that the filing party has against any officer or employee."[370]

A political subdivision is immune from liability, among others (1) if its involved employee "was engaged in the performance of a judicial, quasi-judicial, prosecutorial, legislative, or quasi-legislative function;" (2) if the employee's conduct was required by law or authorized by law, or if the conduct was "necessary or essential to the exercise of the political subdivision's powers;" (3) if the action or failure to act was within the discretion of the employee with respect to policy-making, plan, or enforcement powers by virtue of the duties and responsibilities of the employees office or position; and (4) "if the injury, death, or loss to person or property resulted from the exercise of judgment or discretion ...unless the judgment or discretion was exercised with malicious purpose, in bad faith, or in a wanton or reckless manner."[371]

A governmental employee is immune from liability unless, among others, "[t]he employee's acts or omission were manifestly outside the scope of the employee's employment or official responsibilities" or "were with malicious purpose, in bad faith, or in a wanton or reckless manner."[372]

---

370 Ohio Rev. Stat. §2743.02. The waiver is void if the court determines the act or omission "was manifestly outside the scope of the officer's or employee's office or employment or that the officer or employee acted with malicious purpose, in bad faith, or in a wanton or reckless manner." *Id.* at §2743.02(A)(1).

There is no jury trial in the Court of Claims for actions brought against the state. Ohio Code §2743.11.

371 Ohio Code 2744.03(A).

372 *Id.* Any immunity or defense conferred upon an employee "does not affect or limit any liability of a political subdivision for an act or omission of the employee as provided in section 2744.02 of the Revised Code."

KK. OKLAHOMA

In 1983, in its decision in *Vanderpool v. State of Oklahoma*,[373] the Oklahoma Supreme Court abrogated the common-law doctrine of sovereign immunity. Still, in response to *Vanderpool*, the Legislature enacted a form of sovereign immunity into the body of statutory law through the Governmental Tort Claims Act (GTCA).[374]

The Oklahoma Torts Claims Act states: "The State of Oklahoma does hereby adopt the doctrine of sovereign immunity. The state, its political subdivisions, and all of their employees acting within the scope of their employment, whether performing governmental or proprietary functions, shall be immune from liability for torts."[375]

The Supreme court acknowledged in *Gowens v. Barstow* that "[t]he GTCA is the exclusive remedy to recover against a governmental entity in tort."[376] The GTCA "generally extends governmental accountability to all torts for which a private person or entity would be liable, subject only to the GTCA's specific limitations and exceptions."[377] Governmental immunity for Oklahoma and its

---

373 *Vanderpool*, 672 P.2d 1153, 1154, 1157 (Okla. 1983). See also *Salazar v. City of Oklahoma City*, 976 P.2d 1056 (Okla. 1999).

374 51 O.S. §151 et seq. The Legislature "kept in force certain forms of immunity from liability by providing in §155 thirty carefully circumscribed exemptions." *Salazar*, 976 p.2d at 1066.

375 Section 152.1. Section 153 of the OTCA states: "The state or a political subdivision shall be liable for loss resulting from its torts or the torts of its employees acting within the scope of their employment subject to the limitations and exceptions specified in The Government Tort Claims Act and only where the state or political subdivision, if a private person or entity, would be liable for money damages under the laws of this state. The state or a political subdivision shall not be liable under the provisions of The Governmental Tort Claims Act for any act or omission of an employee acting outside the scope of the employee's employment."

The Oklahoma Supreme Court ruled in *Gowens v. Barstow*, 364 P.3d 644 (Okla. 2015), that acts performed by governmental employees with reckless disregard do not automatically rise to the level of constituting malice or bad faith to result in those acts being outside the scope of employment under the GTCA. In *Barstow*, the court overruled *Fehring v. State Ins. Fund*, 19 P.3d 276 (Okla. 2001), which some courts thought "had the unintended effect of granting complete immunity to a GTCA entity from *respondeat superior* liability for its emergency vehicle drivers' torts based on ordinary negligence and reckless disregard."

376 *Barstow*, 364 P.3d at 650.

Section 153 of the GTCA states: The liability of the state or political subdivision under The Governmental Tort Claims act shall be exclusive and shall constitute the extent of tort liability of the state, a political subdivision or employee arising from common law, statute, the Oklahoma Constitution, or otherwise. If a court of competent jurisdiction finds tort liability on the part of the state or political subdivision of the state based on a provision of the Oklahoma Constitution or state law other than The Governmental Tort Claims Act, the limits of liability provided for in The Governmental Tort Claims Act shall apply."

377 *Marianai v. State of Oklahoma*, 348 P.3d 194, 197-98 (Okla. 2015), citing *McCathern v. City of Okla-*

political subdivisions is waived only to the extent and in the manner provided in the Tort Claims Act.[378]

LL. OREGON

Prior to enactment of the Oregon Tort Claims Act,[379] Oregon "public bodies" were immune from tort liability.[380] However, the Oregon Tort Claims Act made "every public body subject to civil action for its torts and those of its officers, employees and agents acting within the scope of their employment or duties, whether arising out of a governmental or proprietary function…."[381] Nonetheless §30.265(l) of the Act states: "The sole cause of action for any tort of officers, employees or agents of a public body acting within the scope of their employment or duties and eligible for representation and indemnification under ORS 30.285 or 30.287 shall be an action against the public body only." It further provides: "If an action or suit is filed against an officer, employer or agent of a public body, on appropriate motion the public body shall be substituted as the only defendant." Further, §30.270(1) of the act substantially limits damages recoverable against a public body.

In *Clarke v. Oregon Health Sciences Univ.*,[382] the Oregon Supreme Court addressed the question of whether §30.265(l) and 30.270(l) violates Article I, §10, the Remedy Clause of the Oregon Constitution.[383] The court pointed to Article IV, §24 of the Oregon Constitution that states: "Provision may be made by general law, for bringing suit against the State, as to all liabilities originating after,

homa City, 95 P.3d 1090 (Okla. 2004). In *McCathern*, the Oklahoma Supreme Court referred to the "central principle embodied by the GTCA" being "that private tort law is neither abridged nor enlarged by that act."

378 *Salazar*, 976 P.2d at 1066. Section 151.1(B) states: "The state, only to the extent and in the manner provided in this act, waives its immunity and that of its political subdivisions. In so waiving immunity, it is not the intent of the state to waive any rights under the Eleventh Amendment to the United States Constitution."

379 O.R.S. §§30.260-.300.

380 Discussion in *Clarke v. Oregon Health Sciences Univ.*, 175 P.3d 418, 420-21 (Ore. 2007). The Oregon Tort Claims Act partially waived immunity for public bodies.

381 O.R.S. at 265.

382 *Clarke*, 175 P.3d at 420.

383 Article I, §10, which states: "No court shall be secret, but justice shall be administered, openly and without purchase, completely and without delay, and every man shall have remedy by due course of law for injury done him in his person, property, or reputation.

or existing at the time of the adoption of this Constitution." The court decided this provision "presumes that the 'State' is immune from liability," although not specifying " what entities are encompassed by that term."[384] The court concluded a public body would have been entitled to sovereign immunity at common law and thus the plaintiff would have had no common protection under Article I, §10, deciding the legislature can limit damages against a public body "to any amount it chooses", but also concluding that elimination of a cause of action against public employees would violate Article I, §10.[385]

After *Clarke*, the Legislature increased the damages cap.[386] The Supreme Court ruled in *Horton v. Oregon Health and Science Univ.*[387] that the Legislature could extend the "assurance of benefits to some while limiting it to others."

MM. PENNSYLVANIA

In referring to suits brought against the state, Pennsylvania's Constitutional Open Courts provision[388] states: "Suits may be brought against the Commonwealth in such manner, in such courts and in such cases as the Legislature may by law direct." Pursuant to this constitutional provision, the Legislature enacted a statute[389] declaring "that the Commonwealth, and its officials and employees acting

384 *Clarke*, 175 P.3d at 425-26.

385 *Id.* at 434. In *Clarke*, the Oregon Supreme court focused on whether capped damages were a substantial remedy in light of the plaintiff's 12 million dollars economic damages and held that it was not.

386 See O.R.S. §30.272.

387 *Horton*, 387 P. 3d 998, 1030 (Ore. 2016).

388 Pennsylvania Constitution, Article I, §11. Article 1, §11 states: "All courts shall be open; and every man for an injury done him in his lands, goods, person or reputation shall have remedy by due course of law...."

389 1 P.C.S.A. §2310. The statute states: "When the General Assembly specifically waives sovereign immunity, a claim against the Commonwealth and its officials and employees shall be brought only in such manner and in such courts and in such cases as directed by the provisions of Title 42 (relating to judiciary and judicial procedure) or 62 (relating to procurement)...." A statute in Chapter 42, 42 Pa. C.S.A. §8521, states: "Except as otherwise provided in this subchapter, no provision of this title shall constitute a waiver of sovereign immunity for the purpose of 1 Pa. C.S. §2310 (relating to sovereign immunity reaffirmed; specific waiver) or otherwise." This statute also states: "Nothing in this subchapter shall be construed to waive the immunity of the Commonwealth from suit in Federal courts guaranteed by the Eleventh Amendment to the Constitution of the United States." Another statute in Chapter 42, 41 Pa. C.S.A. §8522, sets out nine acts wherein the General Assembly has waived sovereign immunity and that may impose liability on the Commonwealth. Section 8541 in Chapter 42, relating to governmental immunity, provides that local agencies are not liable "for any damages on account of any injury to a person or property caused by any act of the local agency or an employee thereof or any other person."

within the scope of their duties, shall continue to enjoy sovereign immunity and official immunity and remain immune from suit except as the General Assembly shall specifically waive the immunity." The Supreme Court of Pennsylvania has ruled that "statutes in derogation of sovereignty should be construed strictly in favor of the sovereign.[390]

The doctrine of sovereign immunity in Pennsylvania "has been tempered to recognize the rights and interests of those who may have been harmed by government actors, and/or, in the contract arena, to remove a substantial disincentive for private individuals to pursue government contracts."[391] The Supreme Court has stated: "Understandably, some immunity applications may be distasteful to those who may discern government wrongdoing, or at least unremediated collateral injury to private concerns resulting from governmental policy changes" but decided that, because "the area implicates the separation of powers among the branches of government...courts are not free to circumvent the Legislature's statutory immunity directives pertaining to the sovereign."[392]

NN. RHODE ISLAND

In enacting the Governmental Liability Act,[393] the Rhode Island Legislature waived "a major portion of the state's common-law sovereign immunity."[394]

---

390 *Clipper Pipe & Service, Inc. v. Ohio Cas. Ins. Co.*, 115 A.3d 1278, 1282 (Pa. 2015). The court stated that a rule "exempting the sovereign from the operation of the general provisions of a statute is premised on a policy of preserving for the public the efficient, unimpaired functioning of government" and also is "grounded on the assumption that non-specific statutes are most often directed to the affairs of the citizenry." *Id.* at 1282-83. The court reasoned that "most statutes are intended and understood to apply to members of the public instead of the government itself." *Id.* at 1283.

391 *Scientific Games Intern., Inc. v. Commonwealth,* 66 A.3d 740, 199-200 (Pa. 2013).

392 *Id.* at 200. The court further stated that a claim arising from a contract entered into by a Commonwealth agency under the Procurement Code (Chapter 62), is either within the exclusive jurisdiction of the Board of Claims or it is barred by sovereign immunity.

393 R.I.G.L. §§9-31-1 *et seq.* Section 9-31-1 of the act states: "The state of Rhode Island and any political subdivision thereof, including all cities and towns, shall be, subject to the period of limitations set forth in §9-1-25, hereby liable in all actions of tort in the same manner as a private individual or corporation; provided, however, that any recovery in any action shall not exceed the monetary limitations thereof set forth in this chapter."

The money limitations are set out in §9-31-2. Damages against the state may not exceed $100,000. However, "in all instances in which the state was engaged in a proprietary function in the commission of [a] tort, or in any situation whereby the state has agreed to indemnify the federal government or any agency thereof for any tort liability, the limitation on damages set forth [in §9-31-2] shall not apply."

394 Discussion in *Laird v. Chrysler Corp.*, 460 A. 2d 425 (R.I. 1983). The court stated §9-31-1 "is, on its face, a blanket waiver of sovereign immunity." *Id.* at 428.

In referring to the state's torts claims act in *Laird v. Chrysler Corp.*, the Rhode Island Supreme Court stated:[395] "The statute clearly waives the state's immunity from tort actions in Rhode Island courts." The Supreme Court also decided the Legislature intended to waive the state's Eleventh Amendment immunity to suit in federal court.[396] Still, the Supreme Court did "demarcate an exception to the... liability imposition," recognizing "'a zone of governmental operation" the court thought "should be insulated from tort claims, even in the absence of sovereign immunity.'"[397]

The exception to state liability is "known as the public-duty doctrine."[398] The Supreme Court has stated that this doctrine "does not resurrect the concept of sovereign immunity but it does take into account the unquestionable fact that many activities performed by government could not and would not in the ordinary course of events be performed by a private person at all."[399] The court referred to the public-duty doctrine as immunizing "the state from 'tort liability arising out of discretionary governmental actions that by their nature are not ordinarily performed by private persons.'"[400]

The Supreme Court has carved out exceptions that may impose state liability, including when a governmental entity owes a 'special duty' to the plaintiff and "when an alleged act or omission on the part of a governmental entity is egregious."[401] The court stated that "under our analysis of the public-duty doctrine, we differentiate between 'discretionary' governmental activities and acts capable of performance by private citizens."[402]

---

395 *Id.* at 427. The court addressed in *Laird* the question "of first impression before [the] court whether the Legislature also intended to waive the state's Eleventh Amendment immunity from suit in federal court."

396 *Id.* at 429. The Supreme Court noted that the Tort Claims Act "did not abolish the personal immunity of certain government officials, specifically judges and prosecutors," stating: "These officials are deemed immune from suit for the benefit of the public in whose interest it is that they remain free to perform their functions without fear of consequences." *Id.*

397 *Roach v. State of Rhode Island*, 157 A.3d 1042, 1050 (R.L. 2017) (quoting *Calhoun v. City of Providence*, 390 A.2d 350, 353, 355 (R.I. 1978)).

398 *Roach*, 157 A.3d at 1050.

399 *Id.*

400 *Id.* quoting *Morales v. Town of Johnston*, 895 A.2d 721, 730 (R.I. 2006).

401 *Id.* quoting *Schultz v. Foster-Glocester Regional School Dist.*, 755 A.2d 153, 155 (R.I. 2000).

402 *Id.* at 1051.

OO. SOUTH CAROLINA

South Carolina has abolished sovereign immunity for the most part.[403] It eliminated the state's immunity from suit based on contractual obligations as an example.[404] In "expressly" urging the legislature to address the doctrine, the Supreme Court of South Carolina stated:[405] "More than twenty years ago this Court noted that the doctrine had come under fire as being 'archaic and outmoded.'" The South Carolina Supreme Court[406] referred to the decision of the Wisconsin Supreme Court in *Holytz v. Milwaukee*[407] that criticized the doctrine and stated: "Sovereign immunity can no longer be tolerated in this State."[408]

Still, the South Carolina Legislature decided that "total immunity from liability on the part of the government is not desirable" and enacted the South Carolina Tort Claims Act to provide limited immunity for the state's tortious actions.[409] The South Carolina Tort Claims Act,[410] is "the exclusive civil remedy available for any tort committed by a governmental entity, its employee, or its agents."[411]

---

403 See South Carolina Tort Claims Act, S.C. Code §§15-78-20 *et seq.*, specifically §15-78-20. See also *McCall by Andrews v. Batson,* 329 S.E.2d 741 (S.C. 1985).

404 See *Kinsey Constr. Co., Inc. v. S.C. Department of Mental Health,* 249 S.E.2d 900 (1978).

405 *McCall by Andrews,* 329 S.E.2d. at 742.

406 *Id.*

407 *Holytz,* 115 N.W.2d 618 (Wis. 1962). Decision is discussed *infra.*

408 329 S.E.2d at 742. The court decided that "abrogation of the rule will not extend to legislative, judicial and executive acts by individuals acting in their official capacity," stating: "These discretionary activities cannot be controlled by threat of tort liability by members of the public who take issue with the decisions made by public officials. We expressly decline to allow tort liability for these discretionary acts. The exercise of discretion includes the right to be wrong." *Id.*

409 See S.C. Code 15-78-20.

410 S.C. Code §§15-78-20 *et seq.* Section 15-78-20 states: "The General Assembly recognizes the potential problems and hardships each governmental entity may face being subjected to unlimited and unqualified liability for its actions." Section 15-78-20 further states: The General Assembly...intends to grant the State, its political subdivisions, and employees, while acting within the scope of official duty, immunity from liability and suit for any tort except as waived by this chapter. The General Assembly additionally intends to provide for liability on the part of the State, its political subdivisions, and employees, while acting within the scope of official duty, only to the extent provided herein. All other immunities applicable to a governmental entity, its employees, and agents are expressly preserved. The remedy provided by this chapter is the exclusive civil remedy available for any tort committed by a governmental entity, its employees, or its agents except as provided in §15-78-70(b).

Section 15-78-60 sets out forty exceptions to the waiver of sovereign immunity.

411 Section 15-78-20(f) provides that the provisions of the South Carolina Torts Claims Act "establishing

PP. SOUTH DAKOTA

South Dakota's Constitution establishes sovereign immunity in South Dakota;[412] it states: "The Legislature shall direct by law in what manner and in what courts suits may be brought against the state." Still, the South Dakota Supreme Court has noted "that sovereign immunity arises in part from the common law"[413] and has stated: "Sovereign immunity is limited in that it only exists in the absence of consent to be sued."[414] An express waiver of sovereign immunity is required unless an "aggrieved party can establish that the acts complained of are ministerial rather than discretionary."[415]

A state statute[416] permits suit against the state for "all actions to determine adverse claims to real or personal property, or involving the possession of real or personal property, or to foreclose mortgages or other liens upon real or personal property, or to partition the same;" in these suits, the statute provides that the State of South Dakota may be "made defendant in the courts of this state." Additionally, to the extent liability insurance is purchased, "the state shall be deemed to have waived the common law of sovereign immunity and consent to suit in the same manner that any other party may be sued."[417]

---

limitations on and exemptions to the liability of the State, its political subdivision, and employees, while acting within the scope of official duty, must be liberally construed in favor of limiting the liability of the State."

The act does not waive the state's immunity from suit in federal court under the Eleventh Amendment to the Constitution of the United States nor does the act provide "consent to be sued in any state court beyond the boundaries of the State of South Carolina." *Id.* at §20(e).

412 Article 3, §27.

413 *Unruh v. Davison County*, 744 N.W.2d 839, 841-42 (S. D. 2008) (quoting *Sioux Falls Constr. Co. v. City of Sioux Falls*, 297 N.W.2d 454, 457 (S. D. 1980)).

414 *Id.* quoting *Alden v. Maine*, 527 U.S. 706, 754, 119 S. Ct. 2240, 144 L. Ed. 2d 636 (1999).

415 *Adrian v. Vonk*, 807 N.W.2d 119 (S.D. 2011) (quoting *Hanson v. S.D. Dept. of Transp.*, 584 N.W.2d 881, 886-87 (S.D. 1998)).

416 S. D. C. L. §21-32-8. The act established the Office of Commissioner of Claims to consider contract and tort claims against the state and requires that a claim must be commended within one year. See §§21-32-1 and 2.

417 *Id.* at §21-32-16. The court commented in *Unruh*, 744 N.W.2d at 842: "In 1981, the Legislature authorized the State of South Dakota to obtain liability insurance for the purpose in insuring the State, its officers, agents, and employees." See S.D.C.L. §21-32-15. The court noted that in 1986, the Legislature extended sovereign immunity and the waiver provisions of SDCL chapter 21-32 to all public entities, including counties, with the enactment of SDCL chapter 21-32A. *Unruh*, 744 N.W. 2d at 843.

QQ. TENNESSEE

"The sovereign State of Tennessee is immune from lawsuit 'except as it consents to be sued.'"[418] Sovereign immunity in the state "originated in the common law, but the doctrine is now embodied both in a state constitutional provision and in a statute."[419] Article I, §7 of the Tennessee Constitution states that "[s]uits may be brought against the State in such manner and in such courts as the Legislature may by law direct." A statute[420] provides: "No court in the state shall have any power, jurisdiction or authority to entertain any suit against the state, or against any officer of the state acting by authority of the state, with a view to reach the state, its treasury, funds or property, and all such suits shall be dismissed as to the state...." The state's General Assembly has the exclusive power to prescribe the terms and conditions under which the state may be sued.[421]

A waiver of sovereign immunity must be explicit; statutes waiving sovereign immunity must "clearly and unmistakably express the General Assembly's intent to permit claims against the State."[422]

RR. TEXAS

Sovereign immunity is absolute in Texas. Although courts in Texas have recognized sovereign immunity is "a common-law doctrine that initially developed without any legislative or constitutional enactment,"[423] nonetheless, in *Harris County Hosp. Dist. v. Tomball Regional Hosp.*,[424] the Texas Supreme Court referred to the sovereign immunity doctrine as having been established in Texas for over one hundred years and presumably thought that a reason to continue to sustain

418 *Smith v. Tennessee National Guard*, 551 S.W.3d 702, 708 (Tenn.2018) (quoting Stewart v. State, 33 S.W.3d 785, 790 (Tenn. 2000)).

419 *Mullins v. State*, 320 S.W.3d 273, 278 (Tenn. 2010).

420 Tenn. Code §20-13-102(a).

421 *Smith v. Tennessee National Guard*, 551 S.W.3d at 709.

422 *Id.*

423 *Reata Const. Corp. v. City of Dallas*, 197 S.W.3d 371, 374 (Tex. 2006), citing *Cohens v. Virginia*, 6 Wheat 264, 19 U.S. 264, 293, 5 L. Ed. 257 (1821) and *Hosner v. De Young*, 1 Tex. 764, 769 (1847) (recognizing the doctrine was without statutory or constitutional authority).

424 *Harris County*, 283 S. W. 3d 838, 844 (Tex. 2009).

it.[425] In *Tooke v. City of Mexia,*[426] the Supreme Court observed that immunity "shields the public from the costs and consequences of improvident actions of their government."[427] In *City of El Paso v. Heinrich,*[428] the Texas Supreme Court commented that "a lack of immunity may hamper governmental functions by requiring tax resources to be used for defending lawsuits" rather than "using those resources for their intended purposes."

The Texas Supreme Court concluded in *Heinrich,*[429] that the purpose of sovereign immunity is to protect the State from lawsuits for money damages;[430] however, the Supreme Court also acknowledged "an action to determine or protect a private party's rights against a state official who has acted without legal or statutory authority is not a suit against the State that sovereign immunity bars."[431] Assessing "the intersection of these two rules," the court concluded that "while governmental immunity generally bars suits for retrospective monetary relief, it does not preclude *prospective injunctive remedies* in official-capacity suits against government actors who violate statutory or constitutional provisions."[432]

---

425 *Id.* See *Hosner v. DeYoung,* 1 Tex. at 769, wherein the court ruled in 1847 that a state cannot be sued in her own courts.

426 *Tooke,* 197 S.W.3d 325, 331-32 (Tex. 2006).

427 *Id.* quoting *Federal Sign v. Texas Southern University,* 951 S.W.2d 401, 417 (Tex. 1997).

428 *Heinrich,* 284 S.W.3d 366, 373 (Tex. 2009).

429 *Id.* at 368.

430 *Id.* See also *Tex. Natural Res. Conservation Comm'n v. IT-Davy,* 74 S.W.3d 849, 853 (Tex. 2002) and *Reata Const. Corp.,* 197 S.W.3d at 374.

431 *Id.* quoting *Federal Sign v. Texas Southern Univ.,* 951 S.W.2d at 405, *superseded in part by statute,* Act of May 30, 1999, 76th Leg. R.S., ch. 1352 §9, 1999 Tex. Gen. Laws 4578, 4583-87, as recognized in *Gen. Servs. Comm'n v. Little-Tex Insulation Co.,* 39 S.W.3d 591 (Tex. 2001).

432 *Heinrich,* 284 S.W.3d at 368-69 In *Wichita Falls State Hospital v. Taylor,* 106 S.W.2d 692, 693 (Tex. 2003), the Supreme Court noted that courts often use the terms "sovereign immunity" and "governmental immunity" interchangeably. However, the court pointed out that they involve two distinct concepts. Sovereign immunity refers to the State's immunity from suit and liability. Governmental immunity protects political subdivision of the State, including counties, cities, and school districts. Second, as the Texas Supreme Court long ago propounded in in *W. D. Haden Co. v. Dodgen,* 308 S.W.2d 838, 840 (Tex. 1958), private parties may seek declaratory relief against state officials who allegedly act without legal or statutory authority. These suits are not "suits against the State." That is, "suits to compel state officers to act with their official capacity do not attempt to subject the State to liability." *Tex. Natural Res. Conservation Comm's v. IT-Davy,* 74 S.W.3d at 855. In contrast, declaratory judgment actions brought against state officials "to establish the validity of a contract of the state, or to enforce...the performance of a contract of the state, or to require act to be performed...which impose contractual liability upon the state," do constitute suits against the State. Moreover, as the court stressed in *Heinrich,* there is a "well settled" rule that "private parties cannot circumvent the State's sovereign immunity from suit by characterizing a suit for money damages...as a declaratory-

Because the Supreme Court decided a state official's illegal or unauthorized actions are not acts of the State, it ruled an action to determine or protect a private party's rights against a state official who has acted without legal or statutory authority is not a suit against the state that sovereign immunity bars.[433] The Supreme Court subsequently explained that while the *Heinrich* decision held "a claim for prospective declaratory and injunctive relief against government actors in their official capacities but acting *ultra vires* is not barred by immunity even if the requested relief compels the governmental entity to make monetary payments," the rule of sovereign immunity still "bars suits against governmental entities for prospective monetary relief."[434] In *Hall v. McRaven*,[435] the Texas Supreme Court defined an *ultra vires* action, which it decided should not be barred by sovereign immunity, as a "claim based on actions taken 'without legal authority'" and stated it "has two fundamental components: (1) authority giving

---

judgment claim." *Heinrich*, 284 S.W.3d at 371 (quoting *IT-Davy*, 74 S.W.3d at 856). According to the Supreme Court in *IT-Davy*, such suits cannot be maintained without legislative permission. 74 S.W.2d 3d at 856.

433 *Heinrich*, 284 S.W.3d at 368-9. The court opined in *Heinrich*, 284 S.W.3d at 371, that private parties cannot circumvent the State's sovereign immunity from suit by characterizing a suit for money damages as a declaratory-judgment claim. See also *Tex. Dep't of Parks & Wildlife v. Miranda*, 133 S.W.3d 217, 225-26 (Tex. 2004).

434 *Harris Cnty. Hosp.*, 283 S.W.3d at 849 n. 6 (citing *Heinrich*, 284 S.W.3d at 369). The court ruled in *Heinrich* that, "where statutory or constitutional provisions create an entitlement to payment, suits seeking to require state officers to comply with the law are not barred by immunity merely because they compel the state to make those payments." *Id.* at 371-2. Yet, "to fall within this [ultra vires] exception, a suit must not complain of a government officer's exercise of discretion, but rather must allege, and ultimately prove, that the officer acted without legal authority or failed to perform a purely ministerial act." *Id.* at 372. In addition, the court confirmed that, "as a technical matter, the governmental entities themselves–as opposed to their officers in their official capacity–remain immune from suit" on such claims. *Id.* at 372-73. Accordingly, such *ultra vires* suits "cannot be brought against the State, which retains immunity, but must be brought against the state actors in their official capacity. *Id.* at 373. The court decided this rule derives from the premise that acts of officials not lawfully authorized are not acts of the State. *Id.* at 373 (quoting *Cobb v. Harrington*, 190 S.W.2d 709, 712 (Tex. 1945). In a suit complaining of *ultra vires* action brought against the responsible governmental officer in the officer's official capacity, the extent, if any, to which the complainant can obtain damages from the state for the officer's *ultra vires* action remains unclear.

435 *McRaven*, 508 S.W.3d 232, 239 (Tex. 2017). The court referred to its statement in *Heinrich*, 284 S.W.3d at 372, that "clarified two general means of proving an *ultra vires* claim: (1) an action 'without legal authority' or (2) failure to 'perform a purely ministerial act." *McRaven*, 508 S.W.3d at 240.

In *Texas Transp. Comm'n v. City of New Jersey Village*, 478 S.W.3d 869, 879 (Tex. 2015), the court affirmed that a state agency is immune from *ultra vires* suits and such suits "must be brought against the state actors in their official capacity," citing *Heinrich*, 284 S.W.3d at 372-73. The court stated in *Texas Transp. Comm'n* that a determination of whether a state actor's conduct "falls within the *ultra vires* exception to sovereign immunity depends on what actions" were required.

the official some (but not absolute) discretion to act and (2) conduct outside of that authority."[436]

The Texas Supreme Court has stated that Texas courts traditionally defer to the Legislature to waive sovereign immunity because, as it explained, the Legislature is better suited to address the conflicting policy issues.[437] Still, its recent decisions, discussed in detail in Chapter 4, illustrate that the Supreme Court fails to defer to the Legislature's waiver of sovereign immunity in almost all circumstances. The Texas Supreme Court has ruled that to be effective to waive sovereign immunity "a statute or resolution must contain a clear and unambiguous expression" of the state's waiver.[438] Additionally, although the Supreme Court has stated it should have little difficulty in recognizing the Legislature's intent to waive immunity from suit when a statute provides that a state entity may be sued or that "sovereign immunity to suit is waived,"[439] recent Texas Supreme Court decisions, discussed in more detail in Chapter 4, present questions regarding the Court's position that it recognizes the intent of the Legislature.

The Texas Supreme Court has ruled that a plaintiff must demonstrate affirmatively a court's subject-matter jurisdiction by alleging a valid waiver of immunity.[440] In statutes in which immunity from suit is waived to the extent of liability, the Supreme Court has ruled that "immunity from suit and liability are co-extensive."[441] The Texas Court has ruled that it will consider facts alleged by the plaintiff and, to the extent it is relevant to the jurisdictional issue, the

436 *McRaven*, 508 S.W. 3d at 239, quoting *Houston Belt & Terminal Ry. Co. v. City of Houston*, 487 S.W.3d 154, 158 (Tex. 2016). The court described an *ultra vires* action as one in which "the higher authority has created a *ministerial* (nondiscretionary) duty for the subordinate official to engage in conduct the plaintiff claims is wrongful." The court stated in *McRaven*: "Only when...improvident actions are *unauthorized* does an official shed the cloak of the sovereign and act *ultra vires*." 508 S.W.3d at 243.

437 See discussion in *Wasson Interests, Ltd. v. City of Jacksonville*, 489 S.W. 3d 427, 439 (Tex. 2016).

438 *Wichita Falls State Hospital*, 106 S.W.3d at 696. As the Texas Supreme Court pointed out, the Texas Legislature ratified this approach by adding §311.034 to the Texas Government Code. Section 311.034 of the Texas Government Code states: "In order to preserve the legislature's interest in managing state fiscal matters through the appropriate process, a statute shall not be construed as a waiver of sovereign immunity unless the waiver is effected by clear and unambiguous language." See also *Tex. Dep't of Trans. v. City of Sunset Valley*, 146 S.W.3d 637, 641 (Tex. 2004).

439 See statement of the Texas Supreme Court in *Wichita Falls State Hospital*, 106 S.W.3d at 696-97.

440 *Dallas Area Rapid Transit v. Whitley*, 104 S.W.3d 540, 542 (Tex. 2003).

441 *Id.*

evidence submitted by the parties.[442] Still, the Supreme Court has approved a trial court from preventing a plaintiff obtaining discovery to obtain required documents and evidence and has held that if pleadings affirmatively negate the existence of jurisdiction, this often being the case when a plaintiff is precluded from obtaining sufficient evidence because of being denied discovery, it will grant an immediate plea to the jurisdiction without permitting a plaintiff the opportunity to amend.[443]

The Texas Supreme Court did not address in *Heinrich* a means by which victims solve the problem they encounter in bringing an *ultra vires* suit against a governmental official when the court has ruled that even if a *ultra vires* claim is brought, "the remedy may implicate immunity."[444] That court referred to what it characterized as federal immunity law, that while an *ultra vires* suit may be brought "if the defendant is a state officer, sovereign immunity bars the recovery of damages from the state treasury in a private suit" generally prospectively as well as retrospectively.[445] Thus, according to the Supreme Court, while

---

442 *Id.*

443 *County of Cameron v. Brown,* 80 S.W.3d 549, 555 (Tex. 2002).

In a case of first impression, *Nazari v. State of Texas,* 2018 WL 3077659 (Tex. 2018), the Texas Supreme Court ruled that sovereign immunity precluded a defendant from asserting a counterclaim against the State even though the State had brought the action against the defendant. A concerned justice that concurred in part and dissented in part, quoted a concurring opinion in *Reata Construction Corp. v. City of Dallas,* 197 S.W.3d 371, 383 (Tex. 2006), wherein the concurring justice had stated that "preventing all offsetting claims...looks less like sovereign immunity than sovereign inequity."2018 WL 3077659 at 19.

444 *Heinrich,* 284 S.W.3d at 373. Although the court stated in *Heinrich,* 284 S.W.3d at 372, that "suits to require state officials to comply with statutory or constitutional provisions are not prohibited by sovereign immunity, even if a declaration to that effect compels the payment of money," the court ruled that to fall within the *ultra vires* exception, "a suit must not complain of a government officer's exercise of discretion, but rather must allege, and ultimately prove, that the officer acted without legal authority or failed to perform a purely ministerial act." *Id.* This, of course, even though the Supreme Court approves a trial court denying a plaintiff any discovery so that no "public" funds are used to defend lawsuits against the government. Discussion in *Heinrich,* id. at 368.

445 *Id.* at 374. In *Texas Dep't of Insurance v. Reconvenance Services, Inc.,* 306 S.W.3d 256, 257, 259 (Tex. 2010), the Supreme Court reversed the court of appeals' decision and rendered judgment dismissing the plaintiff's suit for lack of subject-matter jurisdiction. The court of appeals had held the trial court had jurisdiction because the plaintiff's pleading sufficiently alleged an *ultra vires* action, i.e., that the Department of Insurance had acted beyond its statutory authority in purporting to prohibit title companies and agents from charging a separate fee for plaintiff's services. *Id.* at 258. Because the plaintiff sued only the Texas Department of Insurance rather than its officials acting in their official capacities, the Supreme Court ruled the Department retained its sovereign immunity and the Texas courts were without subject-matter jurisdiction to entertain the plaintiff's suit as pleaded. *Id.* at 259. It then rendered judgment dismissing the suit without providing the plaintiff the opportunity to replead. *Id.*

governmental officials in their official capacities are not immune from an *ultra vires* suit, governmental entities remain immune from suit.[446]

Although the Supreme Court acknowledged it should distinguish suits to determine a party's rights against the State and a party can maintain a suit to determine its rights without legislative permission,[447] the court left open the question how victims harmed by state action can assert effectively their rights against the government when courts preclude them from monetary relief from the State. Additionally, when the Supreme Court dismisses claims against governmental employees when they act within the scope of employment even if the employee 'is motivated by ulterior motives or personal animus,"[448] victims of governmental misconduct generally have no recourse for injuries or damages caused by governmental tortious actions as well as its illegal conduct.

For example, in *Goodyear Tire & Rubber Co. v. Mayes,*[449] the Texas Supreme Court ruled that "even if the employee performs negligently or is motivated by ulterior motives or personal animus," there may be "a connection between the employee's job duties and the alleged tortious conduct."[450] Additionally, in *University of Texas Health Science Center v. Rios,* [451] the Texas Supreme Court held that government employees are not required to prove their subjective intent to be dismissed from a suit pursuant to the election-of-remedies provision in the Texas Tort Claims Act.[452] The court stated there may be a connection between an employee's job duties and an alleged tortious conduct "even if the employee performs negligently or is motivated by ulterior motives or personal animus so long as the conduct itself was pursuant to her job responsibilities."[453]

Sovereign immunity in Texas embraces two principles: immunity from suit and immunity from liability.[454] In considering immunity in Texas, courts look to

---

446 *Id.* See also *Heinrich,* 284 S.W.3d at 372-3.

447 *Heinrich,* 284 S.W.3d at 370.

448 See discussion in *Univ. of Texas Health Science Center v. Rios,* 542 S.W.3d 530, 535 (Tex. 2017).

449 *Mayes,* 236 S.W.3d 754, 757 (Tex. 2007).

450 *Id.*

451 *Rios,* 542 S.W.3d at 535.

452 Tex. Civ. Prac. & Rem. Code §101.106, discussed *infra* and in Chapter in 4.

453 *Id.*

454 *Mo. Pac. R.R. Co. v. Brownswille Navigation Dist.,* 453 S.W.2d 812, 813 (Tex. 1970). See also *Texas Dept. of Parks and Wildlife v. Miranda,* 133 S.W.3d at 224 and *Tooke v. City of Mexia,* 197 S.W. 3d 325, 332 (Tex. 2006). The Texas Torts Claims Act waives both components of governmental immunity--Tex.

whether the State has consented to suit, but also whether the State has accepted liability.[455] The Texas Supreme Court has ruled that immunity from suit prohibits suits against the state unless the state expressly consents to the suit.[456] Thus, even if the state acknowledges liability on a claim, immunity from suit bars a remedy until the Legislature consents to suit.[457] If a plaintiff who sues the state of Texas does not establish the state's consent to sue, sovereign immunity from suit defeats a trial court's subject-matter jurisdiction.[458]

The state may assert sovereign immunity from suit in a plea to the jurisdiction, which is a dilatory plea that seeks dismissal of a case for lack of subject-matter jurisdiction and defeats a cause of action without regard to whether the claims asserted have merit.[459] When the state in a plea to the jurisdiction challenges the pleadings, a trial court must determine if the pleadings contain facts that "affirmatively demonstrate" a Texas trial court's jurisdiction to hear the case.[460] Immunity from liability, on the other hand, is an affirmative defense that cannot be raised by a plea to the jurisdiction.[461] When facts underlying the merits and subject-matter jurisdiction are intertwined, "the state may assert

---

Civ. Prac. & Rem Code §101.021 (waiving immunity from liability), §101.025 (waiving immunity from suit).

455 See discussion in *Wichita Falls State Hospital v. Taylor*, 106 S.W.3d 692 (Tex. 2003).

456 *Id.* at 696. Texas has long recognized that sovereign immunity, unless waived, protects the State of Texas, its agencies, and its officials from lawsuits for damages, absent legislative consent to sue the State. See *Hosner v. DeYoung*, 1 Tex. at 769. In *Tex. Dep't of Parks & Wildlife v. Miranda*, 113 S.W.3d at 224, the Supreme Court noted that a statute waives immunity from suit, immunity from liability, or both. The Court stated that immunity from suit is a jurisdictional question of whether the State has expressly consented to suit whereas immunity from liability determines whether the State has accepted liability even after it has consented to suit.

457 *Miranda*, 133 S.W.3d at 224. The Tex. Civ. Prac. & Rem. Code § 107.002(b) states that a resolution granting permission to sue the state "does not waive to any extent immunity from liability." The Texas Supreme Court has stated that even if the Legislature has authorized a claimant to sue, the State's immunity is retained until the State acknowledges liability. In *Federal Sign v. Texas Southern University*, 951 S.W.2d at 405, the Texas Supreme Court commented that the state neither creates nor admits liability by granting permission to be sued, citing Tex. Civ. Prac. & Rem. Code § 107.002. *Federal Sign*, 951 S.W.2d at 405.

The Texas Supreme Court has ruled that immunity from liability, unlike immunity from suit, does not affect a court's jurisdiction to hear a case and cannot be raised in a plea to the jurisdiction. *See Tex. Dep't of Trans. v. Jones*, 8 S.W.3d 636, 638-9 (Tex. 1999).

458 *Tex. Dep't of Trans. v. Jones*, 8 S.W. 3d at 638.

459 *Bland Indep. Sch. Dist. v. Blue*, 34 S.W.3d 547, 554 (Tex. 2000). Subject-matter jurisdiction is essential to the authority of a court to decide a case.

460 *Id.*

461 *State v. Lueck*, 290 S.W.3d 876, 880 (Tex. 2009).

immunity from suit by a plea to the jurisdiction, even when the trial court must consider evidence 'necessary to resolve the jurisdictional issues raised.'"[462]

In *Harris County Hospital District v. Tomball Regional Hospital*,[463] the Texas Supreme Court referred to "a heavy presumption" in favor of sovereign immunity derived, according to the Court, from principles related to separation of powers and from "practical concerns." The Texas Supreme Court ruled in *Harris County Hospital District* that a hospital district was immune from suit by a hospital authority, which sought to recover the cost of medical care the hospital authority rendered to indigent patients.[464]

The Texas Legislature enacted the Texas Tort Claims Act[465] to waive sovereign immunity for some tortious governmental conduct but only "to the extent of liability" created by that Act.[466] A person having a claim under the Act may sue a governmental unit for damages permitted by the Act[467] only for: (1) wrongful acts or omissions or negligence of an employee acting within the scope of employment when operating a motor-driven vehicle or motor-driven equipment if the employee would be personally liable to the claimant[468] and (2) per-

---

462 *Lueck*, 290 S.W.3d at 880, citing *Bland Indep. Sch. Dist. v. Blue*, 34 S.W.3d at 555.

463 *Harris County*, 283 S.W.3d at 848.

464 *Id.*

465 Texas Tort Claims Act, 69th Leg., R.S., ch. 959 §1, §§. 101.101-.109, 1985 Tex. Gen. Laws. 3301 (codified as amended at Tex. Civ. Prac. & Rem. Code §§101.001-.109).

The Texas Tort Claims Act is discussed in more detail in Chapter 4.

466 Tex. Civ. Prac. & Rem. Code, §101.025.

467 Section 101.025 states: "(a) Sovereign immunity to suit is waived and abolished to the extent of liability created by this chapter. (b) A person having a claim under this chapter may sue a governmental unit for damages allowed by this chapter."

468 Tex. Civ. Prac. & Rem. Code §101.021(1)(A). However, liability from this waiver of immunity is limited to a maximum amount of $100,000 money damages for each person. Id. §101.023(b). Because "a regional transportation authority might delegate some or all of the operation of its public transportation system to one or more independent contractors," the Texas Supreme Court pointed out in *Fort Worth Transportation Authority v. Rodriguez*, 547 S.W.3d 830 (Tex. 2018) that "the Legislature contemplated liability for such a situation" and provided that an independent contractor of the authority that performs a function of the authority is subject to the same liability cap. Tex. Transp. Code §452.056(d). In *Rodriguez*, a plaintiff sued three such independent contractors, seeking the statutory maximum of $100,000 from each entity. The court, however, ruled that "the liability of any number of independent contractors performing essential governmental functions for an authority under chapter 452 is limited to a single damages cap..." It held that the three entities were "cumulatively liable up to a single $100,000 damages cap."

Interestingly, the court in *Rodriguez* also ruled that the bus driver was protected by governmental immunity, ruling the election-of-remedies provision, discussed *infra*, which provides absolute immunity to governmental employees who act within the scope of employment when they perform tortious acts, ap-

sonal injury and death caused by a condition or use of tangible personal or real property if the governmental unit would be liable to the claimant if it were a private person.[469] Additionally, the Texas Tort Claims Act requires that a party who asserts a tort claim against a governmental unit must give the governmental unit formal notice of the claim within six months after the incident that gave rise to the claim.[470] However, the notice-of-claim requirements does "not apply if the governmental unit has actual notice" of the injury or that the claimant's property was damaged.[471]

In *City of San Antonio v. Tenorio*,[472] the Texas Supreme Court "tilted the scales" in favor of the government in dismissing a case brought by a motorcyclist against a city arising from a collision caused by city officers pursuing a suspect in an armed robbery. The Texas Court ruled that the city did not have "actual" notice that it was at fault in causing the collision as the court stated was required for waiver of governmental immunity. In response to the plaintiffs' contention that the city was aware of its role in contributing to the injuries, the Texas Supreme Court interpreted the "actual notice" requirement to mean that "a governmental unit must have the same knowledge it is entitled to receive under the written notice provisions" of the Texas Tort Claims Act.[473]

The Texas Legislature enacted a "comprehensive election-of-remedies provision to the Texas Tort Claims Act in 2003."[474] In *Mission Consolidated Indep. Sch. Dist. v. Garcia*,[475] the Texas Supreme Court stated that the purpose of the election-of-remedies provisions, Texas Practice and Remedies Code §101.106,

---

plied to the bus driver as well even though she was working for a private entity, the independent contractor, rather than for the state. The court held that an employee of an independent contractor that performs an essential governmental function under the Transportation Code chapter 452, who is acting within the scope of employment, is afforded protection under the Tort Claims election-of-remedies provision as if she were an employee of the government.

469 Tex. Civ. Prac. & Rem. Code §101.021. These exceptions have been referred to as three areas: use of publicly owned automobiles, premises defects, and injuries arising out of conditions or use of property. See *Tex. Dep't of Trans. v. Able*, 35 S.W.3d 608, 611 (Tex. 2000). Section 101.058 of the Tort Claims Act further modifies a governmental unit's waiver of immunity from suit by imposing limitations of liability articulated in the recreational use statute.

470 *Id.* at §101.101(a).

471 *Id.* at §101.101(c).

472 *City of San Antonio v. Tenorio*, 543 S.W.3d 772, 774 (Tex. 2018).

473 *Id.* at 775.

474 *Id.*

475 *Garcia*, 253 S.W.3d 653 (Tex. 2008).

"was to force a plaintiff to decide at the outset whether an employee acted independently and is thus solely liable, or acted within the general scope of his or her employment such that the governmental unit is vicariously liable."[476] As the Court of Appeals for the Fifth Circuit declared in *Wilkerson v. University of North Texas*,[477] the election-of-remedies provision, §101.106 "mandates plaintiffs to pursue lawsuits against governmental units rather than their employees"[478] and "entitles" a governmental "employee 'to dismissal' of the relevant tort claim."[479]

The problem for victims of government misconduct is that the Texas Supreme Court's interpretation of §101.106 prevents any suits against the government for the intentional torts of its employees. The state is substituted as the defendant in a tort claims suit against a governmental employee, and the state has absolute immunity for intentional torts.[480]

As discussed in Chapter 4, the Texas Tort Claims Act does not waive immunity for any actions against the government except, as noted above, for the use of publicly owned automobiles, premises defects, and injuries arising out of conditions or use of property. Further, the election-of-remedies provision, Texas Civil Practice and Remedies Code §101.106, effectively negates any tort claims against governmental employees. Section 101.106(a) states that, if a claimant files a tort claim against a governmental unit, the claimant cannot also sue the governmental employee regarding the same subject matter.[481] While a public employee can be liable individually for the employee's tortious conduct outside

476 *Id.* at 657.

477 *Wilkerson*, 878 F.3d 147, 159 (5th Cir. 2017).

478 *Id.* citing *Tex. Adjutant Gen.'s Office v. Ngakoue*, 408 S. W.3d 350, 352 (Tex. 2013).

479 *Id.* citing *Laverie v. Wetherbe*, 517 S.W.3d 748, 752 (Tex. 2017). See, however, *Lewis v. Clarke*, 137 S. Ct. 1285, 1287-89, 197 L. Ed. 2d 631 (2017), wherein the U.S. Supreme Court ruled a tribal governmental employee sued in the employee's individual capacity is not entitled to sovereign immunity and reversed a decision of the Connecticut Supreme Court that had granted the employee immunity. Additionally, the Supreme Court ruled in *Lewis v. Clarke,* 137 S. Ct. At 1292, that an indemnification statute for governmental employees does not make the government the real party in interest to support state sovereign immunity.

480 Further discussion in Chapter 4.

481 Tex. Civ. Prac. & Rem. Code §101.106(a). Thus, as to *same subject matter* suits, a plaintiff must elect to file suit against the employee individually or against the governmental unit. Section 101.106(b) states: "The filing of a suit against any employee of a governmental unit constitutes an *irrevocable election* by the plaintiff and immediately and *forever bars any suit or recovery by the plaintiff against the governmental unit regarding the same subject matter* unless the governmental unit consents." (Emphasis added.) If a suit is filed against both the governmental unit and any of its employees, the governmental unit can file a motion to dismiss the suit against the individual employees. *Id.* at §101.106(e).

the general scope of employment, §101.106(b) of the Act requires a plaintiff to make an irrevocable election at the time suit is filed between suing the governmental unit under the Act or proceeding against the employee alone.[482] If a plaintiff sues both the government unit and any of its employees, §101.106(e) requires the suit against the employee to be dismissed on the governmental unit's motion. Further, §101.106(f) provides that, if a suit is filed against a governmental employee based on conduct within the general scope of that person's employment and the suit could have been brought against the governmental unit, the suit is considered to be against the employee in the employee's official capacity only.[483] If the employee files a motion to dismiss the suit, the plaintiff must amend the pleading to instead name the governmental unit as the defendant.[484] However, the Texas Tort Claims Act retains absolute immunity for the governmental unit for intentional tort claims, such as, among others, claims of assault, libel, false imprisonment, false arrest, malicious prosecution, abuse of process, libel, slander, misrepresentation, deceit, and interference with contract rights.[485]

Although a governmental employee can be held liable for tortious wrongdoing if the employee is sued in his or her individual capacity and the wrongdoing occurred outside the scope of employment, Texas courts have interpreted government employee's actions that occur "within the scope of employment" very expansively to protect further governmental employees at expense of their victims. As noted *supra*, in *University of Texas Health Science Center v. Rios*,[486] the Texas Supreme Court ruled that there may be a connection between an employee's job duties and an alleged tortious conduct "even if the employee performs

482 *University of Texas Health Science Center v. Rios*, 542 S.W.3d 530 (Tex. 2017) (noting that if a "plaintiff nevertheless sues both employer and employee, section 101.106(e) requires that the employee 'immediately be dismissed'" and ruling that the government's "statutory right to dismissal accrues when the motion is filed and is not impaired by later amendments to the pleadings or motions").

483 Section 101.106(f), Tex. Civ. Prac. & Rem. Code, states: "If a suit is filed against an employee of a governmental unit b*ased on conduct within the general scope of that employee's employment and if it could have been brought under this chapter against the governmental unit,* the suit is considered to be against the employee in the employee's official capacity only." (Emphasis added.)

484 *Id.*

485 Further discussion of the Texas Torts Claims Act and Texas cases interpreting the Act in Chapter 4.

486 Rios, 542 S.W.3d 530, 535 (Tex. 2017).

negligently or is motivated by ulterior motives or personal animus so long as the conduct itself was pursuant to her job responsibilities."[487]

In 1993, the Texas legislature enacted the Texas Whistleblowers Act,[488] which prohibits a governmental entity from retaliating against "a public employee who in good faith reports a violation of law by the employing governmental entity or another public employee to an appropriate law enforcement authority."[489] In Texas *Department of Assistive and Rehabilitative Services v. Howard*,[490] the Third Court of Appeals stated the Texas Whistleblowers' Act "is designed to enhance openness in government and compel the State's compliance with law by protecting those who inform authorities of wrongdoing."[491] The court viewed "whistleblowing by a public employee as a courageous act of loyalty to a larger community"[492] and further stressed that, because "the Act is remedial in nature," the Act "should be liberally construed to effect its purpose."[493] Nevertheless, the Texas Supreme Court has reversed judgments of several Texas courts of appeal wherein the courts of appeal, in liberally construing the Act, had denied the state's plea to the jurisdiction.[494]

In *State v. Lueck*,[495] the Texas Supreme Court imposed a "jurisdictional hurdle" that despite language in the Whistleblowers Act has erected a significant immunity bar in a whistleblower case.[496] In *Lueck*, the Texas Supreme Court reversed

---

487 *Id.*

488 Act of May 4, 1993, 73d Leg., R.S., ch. 268, §1, 1993 Tex. Gen. Laws 583, 609-11 (codified as amended at Tex. Gov't Code §§554.002-.010).

489 Tex. Gov't Code §554.002(a). See *Serna v. City of San Antonio*, 244 F.3d 479, 482 (5th Cir. 2001).

490 *Howard*, 182 S. W.3d 393 (Tex. App.–Austin 2005, pet. denied),

491 *Id.* at 399 (citing *City of New Braunfels v. Allen*, 132 S.W.3d 157, 161 (Tex. App.–Austin 2004, no pet.)

492 *Id.* at 396. The Third Court of Appeals also commented that "[t]he State of Texas elevates public employees who report legal wrongdoing to a protected status as a matter of fundamental policy." *Id.*

493 *Id.* at 399, citing *Hill v. Burnet County Sheriff's Dep't*, 96 S.W.3d 436, 440 (Tex. App.– Austin 2002, pet. denied) and *Allen*, 132 S.W.3d at 161.

494 See, e. g., *Univ. of Tex. Sw. Med. Ctr. at Dallas v. Gentilello*, 260 S.W.3d 221, 224 (Tex. App.–Dallas 2008) (recounting how the plaintiff, a tenured professor medicine, was stripped of faculty chair positions after internally reporting what he believed were violations of federal regulations), *rev'd*, 300 S.W.3d 753 (Tex. 2009); *see also Tex. Dep't of Human Servs. v. Okoli*, 263 S.W.3d 275, 277 (Tex. App.–Houston [lst Dist.] 2007) (describing how the plaintiff, a former state employee, had his employment terminated after reporting alleged illegal activity to two supervisors and a manager), *rev'd sub. nom. Tex. Dep't of Health & Human Servs. v. Okoli*, 295 S.W. 3d 667 (Tex. 2009).

495 *Lueck*, 290 S.W.3d 876 (Tex. 2009).

496 *Id.* at 884. In confusing language in *Lueck*, the Texas Supreme Court interpreted the first sentence of

the Third Court of Appeals, which had affirmed a district court's dismissal of the State's plea to the jurisdiction in a suit against the state under the Texas Whistleblowers' Act.[497] The Texas Supreme Court ruled as a matter of law that Lueck, a public employee, did not allege a violation of the Texas Whistleblowers' Act and dismissed his case for lack of subject-matter jurisdiction.[498] Although Lueck had attached to his petition a copy of an e-mail report he sent to his supervisor warning of regulatory non-compliance by a state agency, the court reasoned that the e-mail did not report "a violation of law...within the meaning of the Whistleblower Act."[499] In addition, the court determined that an agency supervisor "is not an appropriate law enforcement authority to whom a report should be made."[500] For these two reasons, the court held that "Lueck's allegation affirmatively negate[d] the court's subject-matter jurisdiction over the cause."[501]

In *Lueck*, the court referred to the general principle that "clear and unambiguous language" is necessary to waive sovereign immunity[502] and ruled[503] that, for a waiver of immunity from suit, the language in §554.0035 of the Whistleblowers' Act requires a plaintiff actually to allege a violation of the Act with facts supporting the elements of §554.002(a).[504] Lueck contended that "sec-

---

the whistleblower act to mean that the Act waives sovereign immunity from suit, but decided the second sentence of §554.0035 "simply limits judgments against the State to "the extent of liability for the relief allowed under [the Act] for a violation of [the Act]" and that the "second sentence not only waives immunity from liability, but confines the scope of the State's consent to suit that was established in the first sentence." 290 S.W.3d at 882. The court concluded that, "like the Texas Tort Claims Act, the Whistleblower Act imposes a limited waiver of immunity that allows consideration of the section 554.002(a) elements, to the extent necessary in determining whether the claim falls within the jurisdictional confines of section 554.0035." *Id.* The court held that the Whistleblower Act, like the Texas Tort Claims Act, creates a statutory scheme in which the dual immunity system in Texas is co-extensive. Thus, the Texas Supreme court concluded in *Lueck* that "it necessarily follows" from language of §554.0035 that a plaintiff "must actually allege a violation of the Act for there to be a waiver from suit." It ruled that the elements of §554.002(a) "can be considered as jurisdictional facts when it is necessary to resolve whether a plaintiff has alleged a violation under the Act." *Id.* at 881.

497 *Lueck*, 290 S.W.3d at 878-80.

498 *Id.* at 886.

499 *Id.* at 885.

500 *Id.*

501 *Id.* at 878.

502 *Id.* at 880 (quoting Tex. Gov't Code §311.034) (noting that state agencies "are immune from suit and liability in Texas unless the Legislature expressly waives sovereign immunity").

503 *Id.* at 881.

504 Section 554.002(a) provides that a "governmental entity may not... take [any] adverse personnel

tion 554.002(a) contains non-jurisdictional elements that speak to the underlying merits of the claim and, therefore, [could not] be considered when determining jurisdiction."[505] However, the Supreme Court explained that, because §554.0035 directs the immunity inquiry to §554.002(a),[506] holding those elements as jurisdictional facts was consistent with the principle that mere reference to the Act "does not establish the state's consent to be sued and thus is not enough to confer jurisdiction on the trial court."[507]

In sum, the Supreme Court announced that a public employee must be able initially to show that the employee reported a violation of law to an *undefined* "appropriate law enforcement authority" to even file a whistleblower suit against the state and, if the plaintiff's pleadings "affirmatively negate the existence of those jurisdictional facts, the court must dismiss without an opportunity to amend."[508] Additionally, while the Texas Supreme Court has announced it defers to the Legislature to waive sovereign immunity because "the Legislature is better suited to address the conflicting policy issues,"[509] and even though the state's whistleblowing statute has been heralded as protecting "courageous acts of loyalty to a larger community" and that public employees who report legal wrongdoing should be elevated to "a protected status as a matter of fundamental policy,"[510] the Texas Supreme Court construes that Act strictly against the whistleblower.

In *University of Texas Southwestern Medical Center at Dallas v. Gentilello*,[511] the Texas Supreme Court failed to protect a professor from retaliatory acts

action against a public employee who in good faith reports a violation of law by the employing governmental unit or another public employee to an appropriate law enforcement authority."

505 *Id.*

506 *Id.* at 882.

507 *Id.* at 881-82 (quoting *Tex. Dep't of Criminal Justice v. Miller*, 51 S.W.3d 583, 587 (Tex. 2001).

508 *Id.* at 884-86 (dismissing the case for lack of subject-matter jurisdiction because "Luecks's pleadings affirmatively demonstrate[d] that he did not allege a violation under the Whistleblower Act"); see also *Tex. Dep't of Parks & Wildlife v. Miranda*, 133 S.W.3d at 227 ("If the pleadings affirmatively negate the existence of jurisdiction, then a plea to the jurisdiction may be granted without allowing the plaintiff's an opportunity to amend.").

Further discussion of the Texas Whistleblowers Act and cases construing it in Chapter 4.

509 *Wasson Interest, Ltd. v. City of Jacksonville*, 489 S.W.3d 427, 439 (Tex. 2016).

510 *Texas Dep't of Assistive and Rehabilitative Services v. Howard*, 182 S.W.3d 393, 396 (Tex. App.–Austin, 2005, pet denied).

511 *Gentilello*, 300 S.W.3d 753 (Tex. 2009).

for reporting violations of Medicare and Medicaid regulations. In *Galveston Independent School District v. Jaco*,[512] the Supreme Court would not protect an athletic director from retaliation for reporting of a high school player's violations of league rules and regulations. That court also did not protect a professor from retaliation by university officials for reporting to a university chief financial officer, general counsel, and internal auditor a college dean's statutory violations that included alleged violations of state civil and criminal action.[513] In *Texas Department of Health and Human Services v. Okoli*,[514] the Supreme Court would not protect a plaintiff for reporting internal falsification of dates and documents. In *Texas Comn's on Environmental Quality v. Resendez*,[515] the Supreme Court failed to protect a governmental employee for retaliation after reporting possible fraud in the distribution of assets in a governmental agency, and in *Office of the Attorney General v. Weatherspoon*,[516] did not protect an assistant attorney general after her supervisor, in the Office of the Attorney General, demanded she sign a false affidavit and then terminated her for her refusal to sign the affidavit. By the importance and the jurisdictional requirement the Texas Supreme Court has placed on a claimant properly reporting to an ill-defined "appropriate law enforcement authority" to sustain a whistleblower claim, the Texas Supreme Court has endorsed a technicality that is "particularly inappropriate in a statutory scheme in which laymen, unassisted by trained lawyers, initiate the process."[517]

Rulings of the Texas Supreme Court with respect to the state's whistleblowers act and its interpretation of the election of remedies provision in the Texas Tort Claims Act[518] may preclude claimants from having any recourse against the state government. A victim should contend there is a total bar to such claims that is a violation of the Open Courts Provision in the Texas Constitution[519]

512 *Jaco*, 303 S.W.3d 699 (Tex. 2010).

513 *University of Houston v. Barth*, 403 S.W.3d 852 (Tex. 2013).

514 *Okoli*, 440 S.W.3d 611 (Tex. 2014).

515 *Resendez*, 450 S.W.3d 520 (Tex. 2014).

516 *Weatherspoon*, 470 S.W.3d 280 (Tex. 2015).

517 See *Love v. Pullman Company*, 404 U.S. 522, 527, 92 S. Ct. 616, 30 L. Ed. 2d 679 (1972).

518 Tex. Prac. & Rem. Code §101.106.

519 Texas Constitution, Article 1, §13.

and the Due Process Clause of the Fourteenth Amendment to the United States Constitution.

As noted previously, the Texas Supreme Court has ruled that it will consider facts alleged by a plaintiff against the state and, to the extent it is relevant to the jurisdictional issue, the evidence submitted by the parties.[520] Further, the court has held that if pleadings affirmatively negate the existence of jurisdiction, it will grant a plea to the jurisdiction without permitting a plaintiff the opportunity to amend.[521] These procedural impediments require a victim of improvident governmental conduct to obtain documents and other evidence to prove a claim against the government prior to filing a lawsuit. Although a litigant is precluded from discovery in a suit against the government, governmental documents can be obtained pursuant to the Public Information Act.[522] Should the government refuse to provide documents, a litigant can file a mandamus suit to obtain needed and relevant documentation. Section 552.321(a) of the Texas Government Code reads as follows:

> A requestor or the attorney general may file suit for a writ of mandamus compelling a governmental body to make information available for public inspection if the governmental body refuses to request an attorney general's decision as provided by Subchapter G *or refuses to supply public information or* information that the attorney general has determined is public information that is not excepted from disclosure under Subchapter C." (Emphasis added.)

There then are *three* avenues available to a requestor to seek mandamus relief pursuant to the Public Information Act[523]–(1) a governmental body fails to request an opinion from the Open Records Division of the Office of the Attorney General (OAG) on whether information withheld is public, (2) a governmental body refuses to supply public information, *or* (3) a governmental body refuses to supply information the attorney general has determined is public information and, according to the OAG, not excepted from disclosure.

---

520 *Dallas Area Rapid Transit v. Whitley*, 104 S.W.3d 540, 542 (Tex. 2003).

521 *County of Cameron v. Brown*, 80 S.W.3d 549, 555 (Tex. 2002).

522 Texas Government Code, chapter 552.

523 *Id.* at §552.321(a).

In *Tex. Dept. of Pub. Safety v. Gilbreath*,[524] the Third Court of Appeals referred to the "three" instances in which a trial court has authority to issue a writ of mandamus and ruled in *Thomas v. Cornyn*[525] that a requestor may bring a mandamus action despite the issuance of an adverse attorney general's opinion that favors the withholding of information. In addition, that court ruled that an opinion of the attorney general is not binding on the courts. Additionally, the Texas Supreme Court recently discussed the interplay of the requirements[526] for a requestor to petition for a writ of mandamus. In *Kallinen v. City of Houston*,[527] the Supreme Court affirmed:

> The Texas Public Information Act ("PIA"), Chapter 552 of the Texas Government Code, guarantees access to public information subject to certain exceptions....
>
> The PIA provides that when a governmental body receives a written request for information for which it wishes to claim an exception, it must timely seek a ruling from the Attorney General if the exception's applicability to the requested information has not previously been determined. But the PIA also provides that a requestor may sue to compel disclosure of the information.

The Supreme Court then cited the provisions of §552.321(a) as follows to enunciate the provisions of that section:

> A requestor or the attorney general may file suit for a writ of mandamus compelling a governmental body to make information available for public inspection if the governmental body [A] refuses to request an attorney general's decision... or [B] refused to supply [1] public information or [2] information that the attorney general has determined is public information that is not excepted from disclosure.

The Supreme Court stated: "The parties agree that conditions A and B2 do not apply," but the Court disagreed with the City of Houston's position that B1 could not apply when a governmental body was challenging whether an exception to

524 *Gilbreath*, 842 S.W.2d 408, 411 (Tex. App.– Austin 1992, no writ).

525 *Cornyn*, 71 S.W..3d 473, 483 (Tex. App.–Austin 2001, no pet.)

526 Pursuant to Tex. Gov't Code §552.321(a).

527 *Kallinen*, 462 S.W.3d 25, 26-27 (Tex. 2015).

disclosure applied, until the Attorney General had determined the information was public. The Supreme Court decided the City's position was flawed for several reasons.[528] First, the Supreme Court stated that the City's position "equates information that is public with information that has been determined by the Attorney General to be public, so that condition B2 swallows up condition B1." The Supreme Court expressed concern that "[T]his violates a duty of statutory interpretation to 'give effect to all the words of a statute and not treat any statutory language as surplusage if possible.'" The Supreme Court was also concerned that the City's view of §552.321(a) "would relegate mandamus relief to compelling a governmental body to request an Attorney General's decision and then comply with it." The Supreme Court ruled that the requirement that a governmental body seek a ruling from the OAG when withholding requested information "is a check on the governmental body, not a remedy for the requestor to exhaust." The Court stated that the City's view of §552.321(a) "would make the Attorney General's ruling unreviewable." Thus, a requestor is not required to obtain a ruling from the OAG prior to filing a mandamus action.

SS. UTAH

The Governmental Immunity Act of Utah[529] provides for governmental immunity from suit for "each governmental entity and each employee of a governmental entity...for any injury that results from the exercise of a governmental function."[530] The Supreme Court of Utah[531] referred to sovereign immunity as being "a well-settled principle of American common law at the time Utah became a state" to rule that the sovereign immunity principle was not unconstitutional under the Utah Constitution.[532] The Utah Supreme Court also ruled that the text of the Utah Governmental Immunity Act "significantly altered the common law

528 *Id.* at 28.

529 U.C.A. §§63G-7-201-.904.

530 *Id.* at §63G-7-201. "A governmental entity and an employee of a governmental entity retain immunity from suit unless that immunity has been expressly waived" pursuant to the Governmental Immunity Act. *Id.* at §63G-7-101.

531 *Madsen v. Borthick*, 658 P.2d 627, 629 (Utah 1983).

532 Utah Constitution, Article I, §11. In *Cook v. City of Moroni*, 107 P.3d 713 (Utah, 2005), the court found no merit in the plaintiffs' argument that dismissal of their property owner's claim against the city on immunity grounds violated the Open Courts Clause of the Utah Constitution.

of sovereign immunity and substituted a statutory framework that totally abandoned "the old distinction between governmental and proprietary."[533]

In *Bingham v. Roosevelt City Corporation*,[534] the Utah Supreme Court stated: "Determining whether a government entity's action is immune from suit requires a three-step analysis: first, we must determine whether the activity performed was a government function; second, if so, we must determine whether the Act waives immunity for that conduct; and third, if immunity is waived, we must determine whether the Act contains any exception to that waiver that would result in a retention of immunity."[535]

TT. VERMONT

The law is "well settled" in Vermont that "[l]awsuits against the State are barred unless the State waives its sovereign immunity."[536] However, under the Vermont Tort Claims Act,[537] the state waived its immunity "for injury to persons or property or loss of life caused by the negligent act or wrongful act or omission of an employee of the State while acting within the scope of employment, under the same circumstances, in the same manner, and to the same extent as a private person would be liable to the claimant...."[538] Still, an exception to the waiver of immunity under the state's tort claims act is a claim "based upon the exercise or performance or failure to exercise or perform a discretionary function or duty

533 Madson, 658 P.2d at 629-30. The Supreme Court stated: "Having abandoned that distinction..., we decline to give the governmental-proprietary distinction new life in the interpretation of sovereign immunity." *Id.* at 630.

534 *Bingham*, 235 P.3d 730, 748 (Utah, 2010). The Utah Supreme Court found that a landowners' claim was not barred by the Utah Governmental Immunity Act. The Supreme Court also referred to Article I, §22 of the Utah Constitution that provides protection against a government taking of private property. The court noted that in determining whether, in any substantial degree, governmental action violated this constitutional provision, it also inquired whether there had been any substantial interference with private property that would destroy or materially lessen its value, or the owner's right to is use and enjoyment. *Id.* at 734-35.

535 *Id.* The court stated that in "the second step in the analysis, the Act contains several waivers of governmental immunity, including one section that waives immunity for 'injury proximately caused by a negligent act or omission of an employee committed within the scope of employment.'" U.C.A. §63G-7-301.

536 *Estate of Gage v. State*, 882 A.2d 1157 (Vt. 2005), citing *Denis Bail Bonds, Inc. v. State*, 622 A.2d 495, 497 (Vt. 1993).

537 12 V.S.A. §§5601-06.

538 *Id.* at §5601(a).

on the part of a state agency or an employee of the state, whether or not the discretion involved is abused."[539]

The Vermont Supreme Court stated in *Searles v. Agency of Transp.*,[540] that the purpose of the discretionary function in the Tort Claims Act[541] "'is to assure that the courts do not invade the province of coordinate branches of government by passing judgment on legislative or administrative policy decisions through tort law."[542]

UU. VIRGINIA

"The doctrine of sovereign immunity is 'alive and well' in Virginia."[543] The Virginia Supreme Court has stated: "'It is an established principle of sovereignty, in all civilized nations, that a sovereign State cannot be sued in its own

---

539 *Id.* at §5601(e)(1).

In *Johnson v. Agency of Transp.*, 904 A.2d 1060 (Vt. 2006), the Vermont Supreme Court ruled that a governmental employee's choice of temporary traffic controls was a discretionary function, and thus the Vermont Tort Claims Act's discretionary-function exception shielded the Agency of Transportation from liability. In *Vanderbloom v. State of Vermont,* 129 A.3d 665 (Vt. 2015), the Supreme Court ruled that the state was immune from liability for allegedly negligently designing and constructing a state highway, but the court stated that the discretionary-function exception "does not preserve the State's sovereign immunity in cases in which the State intends to follow particular design standards but then negligently fails to design to those chosen standards," citing *McMurphy v. State,* 757 A.2d 1043, 1046 (2000).

540 762 A.2d 812, 813 (Vt. 2000), citing *Sabia v. State,* 669 A.2d 1187, 1196-97 (Vt. 1995).

541 §5601(e)(1).

542 The Vermont Court also referred to the decision of the U.S. Supreme Court in *United States v. Gaubert,* 499 U.S. 315, 322, 111 S. Ct. 1267, 113 L. Ed. 21d 335 (1991), discussed in Chapter 4, wherein the Court set forth a two-part test for determining whether a plaintiff's claim is barred by the discretionary function exemption–whether the challenged act involves an element of judgment or choice or whether a law prescribes a course of action for an employee to follow. The Vermont Supreme Court noted that its tort claims act is "nearly identical" to the Federal Tort Claims Act. 762 A.2d at 816, n. 1. The Vermont Supreme Court ruled in *Estate of Gage,* 882 A.2d at 1159, that the State's decision not to place a guardrail around a hazardous brook fell "squarely within the discretionary-function exception" and therefore the State was immunized from suit. The Vermont Court decided that "the conduct at issue was not the State's implementation of a specific pre-existing policy for removal of roadside hazards, but its identification of such hazards for removal, balancing safety, cost, and environmental factors" and stated that the purpose of the discretionary function was "to prevent judicial second-guessing of administrative decisions 'grounded in social, economic, and political policy'" (quoting *United States v. Varig Airlines,* 467 U.S. 797, 814, 104 S. Ct. 2755, 81 L. Ed. 2d 660 (1984)). The Vermont Court stated, 882 A.2d at 1160, n. 6: "Because the discretionary function exception to the Vermont Tort Claims Act is nearly identical to that of the Federal Tort Claims Act, '[t]his Court therefore looks to case law interpreting the federal provision to guide us in analyzing 12 V.S.A. §5601(e)'" (quoting *Lane v. State,* 811 A.2d 190, 192, n. 2 (Vt. 2002)).

543 *Gray v. Va. Sec. of Transp.* 662 S.E.3d 66, 70 (Va. 2008); *City of Va. Beach v. Carmichael,* 527 S.W.3d 778, 782 (Va. 2000), *Messina v. Burden,* 321 S.E.2d 657, 659-60 (Va. 1984).

courts...without its consent and permission."[544] If an entity is not an agency or arm of the Commonwealth of Virginia and, thus, entitled to absolute immunity, it nonetheless is entitled to immunity for its governmental, as opposed to proprietary, functions. The Virginia Court has recognized that "because the Commonwealth can act only through individuals, the doctrine applies not only to the state, but also to certain government officials"[545] and has stated a "more important question" is "under what circumstances an employee of a governmental body is entitled to the protection of sovereign immunity."[546]

The Virginia Tort Claims Act[547] provides that "the Commonwealth of Virginia is liable for damages to or loss of property or personal injury or death caused by the negligent or wrongful act or omission of any employee while acting within the scope of his employment under circumstances where the Commonwealth..., if a private person would be liable to the claimant for such damage, loss, injury, or death."[548]

---

544 *Gray*, 662 S.E.2d. at 70 (citing *Board of Public Works v. Gant*, 76 Va. 455, 461 (1882)).

545 *Id.* at 70-71. The Virginia Supreme Court stated: "The Commonwealth, however, can waive sovereign immunity and consent to being sued in its own courts" but that "only the General Assembly, acting in its capacity of making social policy, can abrogate the Commonwealth's sovereign immunity" (citing *Alliance to Save the Mattaponi v. Commonwealth*, 621 S.E.3d 78, 96 (Va. 2005)). Further, "[a] waiver of sovereign immunity will not be implied from general statutory language but must be explicitly and expressly stated in the statute," citing *Hinchey v. Ogden*, 307 S.W.3d 891, 895 (Va. 1983). The Supreme Court did rule in *Gray* that Articles I, §§5 (Bill of Rights) and 11 (taking of property for a public purpose); III, §1 (prohibiting certain conduct), and IV, §1 (General Assembly is vested with legislative power of the Commonwealth), of the Virginia Constitution "are self-executing constitutional provisions and thereby waive the Commonwealth's sovereign immunity." 662 S.E. 2d at 73-74.

546 *Messina*, 321 S.E.2d at 660. The court stated that while "protection of the public purse" is a basis for the doctrine, "another equally important purpose of the rule is the orderly administration of government." The court reasoned the doctrine "serves a multitude of purposes, including but not limited to protecting the public purse, providing for smooth operation of government, eliminating public inconvenience and danger that might spring from officials being fearful to act, assuring that citizens will be willing to take public jobs, and preventing citizens from improperly influencing the conduct of governmental affairs through the threat or use of vexatious litigation. The court referred to the doctrine "as a rule of social policy, which protects the state from burdensome interference with the performance of its governmental functions and preserves its control over state funds, property and instrumentalities." It stated: "Given the several purposes of the doctrine, it follows that in order to fulfill those purposes, the protection afforded by the doctrine cannot be limited solely to the sovereign." The court decided: "Unless the protection of the doctrine extends to some of the people who help run the government, the majority of the purposes for the doctrine will remain unaddressed." *Id.* at 660-61.

547 Va. St. §§8.01-195.1-.9.

548 *Id.* at §§8.01-195-3. The Act does provide a cap on the amount of liability. The Commonwealth's liability for negligent acts of governmental employees generally is limited to $100,000 or the maximum limits of a liability policy, whichever is greater, exclusive of interest and costs. *Id.*

In *Ligon v. County of Goochland*,[549] the Virginia Supreme Court addressed a question of first impression as to whether the doctrine of sovereign immunity barred a retaliatory discharge claim against a county filed under the "whistleblower protection" provision in the Virginia Fraud Against Taxpayers Act (VFATA).[550] The court ruled that sovereign immunity did bar the claim of retaliatory discharge, stating that courts in Virginia generally do not recognize a common law tort claim for retaliatory discharge and that the "whistleblower protection" provision in the Virginia Code "provides a limited cause of action unknown at common law."[551] It further stated that the General Assembly did not announce a waiver in the VFATA.[552]

In another "matter of first impression," the Virginia Supreme Court ruled that municipal corporations performing governmental functions have immunity from a breach of contract claim.[553]

VV. WASHINGTON

The State of Washington has abolished state sovereign immunity for the tortious conduct of its governmental employees.[554] In *Kelso v. City of Tacoma*,[555] the Washington Supreme Court expressed concerns about the sovereign immunity doctrine that led to its abolition, stating: "The doctrine of governmental immunity springs from the archaic concept that 'The King can Do No Wrong.'" It confirmed: "Many courts and text writers have branded the doctrine a creator of injustice, asserting that the entire burden of damage resulting from the wrongful acts of the government has been imposed upon the single individual who suf-

549 *Ligon*, 689 S.W.2d 666, 314 (Va. 2010).

550 Va. Code §§8.01-216.1-.19, specifically §8.02-216.8.

551 *Ligon*, 689 S.E.2d at 669.

552 *Id.*

553 *Jean Moreau & Associates, Inc. v. Health Center Com'n*, 720 S.E.2d 105, 111 (Va. 2012). The Virginia Supreme Court thought there was no reason to differentiate a municipal's immunity for tort claims from "quasi-contractual claims." *Id.* It stated: "If municipal corporations act as arms or agencies of the State when they exercise governmental functions, then they should be protected—like the Commonwealth—from both tort and quasi-contractual claims," limiting, however, recovery from municipal corporations to proprietary functions. *Id.*

554 The Revised Code of Washington, 4.92.090, enacted in 1961, states: "The state of Washington, whether acting in its governmental or proprietary capacity, shall be liable for damages arising out of its tortious conduct to the same extent as if it were a private person or corporation."

555 *Kelso*, 63 Wash. 2d 913, 914, 390 P. 2d 1, 4 (1964).

fers the injury, rather than distributed among the entire community constituting the government, where it could be borne without hardship upon any single individual, and where it properly belongs."[556] The Washington Supreme Court further stated: "There are probably few tenets of American jurisprudence which have been so unanimously berated as the governmental immunity doctrine. This court and the highest courts of numerous other states have been unusually articulate in castigating the existing rule; text writers of law reviews have joined the chorus of denunciators."[557]

In *Washburn v. City of Federal Way*,[558] the Washington Supreme Court referred to the legislature's abolition of state sovereign immunity after "vigorous attacks"[559] on its immunity and explained that the abolition "extended to local governmental entities such as municipalities."[560]

All claims against the State of Washington or its officers, employees, or volunteers, acting in such capacity, for damages arising out of tortious conduct, must be presented to the office of risk management."[561] The State of Washington has established "a liability account in the custody of the treasurer... as a nonappropriated account to be used solely and exclusively for the payment of liability settlements and judgments against the state...for the tortious conduct of its officers, employees, and volunteers and all related legal defense costs."[562] The purpose of the account is stated to be: "(a) Expeditiously pay legal liabilities and defense costs of the state resulting from tortious conduct; (b) promote risk con-

---

556 *Id* at 5.

557 *Id.*, citing *Holytz v. City of Milwaukee*, 115 N.W.2d 618 (Wis. 1962).

558 *City of Federal Way*, 178 Wash. 2d 732, 310 P.3d 1275 (Wash. 2013).

559 *Id.* at 738, citing *Kelso v. City of Tacoma*, 63 Wash.2d at 914.

560 *Id.*, citing Laws of 1967, ch. 164, §1.

561 *Id.* at 4.92.100. A claim must be presented on a standard tort claim form that is maintained by the office of risk management. The claim form requires at a minimum a description of the conduct and circumstances that brought about an alleged injury or damage; a description of the injury or damage; a statement of the time and place the injury or damage occurred; a listing of the names of all persons involved and contact information, if known; and a statement of the amount damages claimed. No action can be commenced "against the state, or a state officer, employee, or volunteer, acting in such capacity..." until sixty days after a claim is presented to the office of risk management. *Id.* at 4.92.110.

562 Rev. Code of Wash. 4.92.130. Disbursements are made from the account to a "claimant, or to the clerk of the court for judgments, upon written request to the state treasurer from the risk manager." "The director may direct agencies to transfer moneys from other funds and accounts to the liability account if premiums are delinquent." The account cannot "exceed fifty percent of the actuarial value of the outstanding liability as determined annually by the office of risk management."

trol through a cost allocation system which recognizes agency loss experience, levels of self-retention, and levels of risk exposure; and (c) establish an actuarially sound system to pay incurred losses, within defined limits."[563]

If a state officer, employee, or volunteer has been represented by the attorney general "and the body presiding over the action or proceeding has found that the officer, employee, or volunteer was acting within the scope of his or her official duties, and a judgment has been entered against the officer, employee, or volunteer...a judgment creditor must seek satisfaction only from the state, and the judgment [cannot]...become a lien upon any property of such officer, employee, or volunteer."[564]

WW. WEST VIRGINIA

The Constitution for the State of West Virginia states: "The state of West Virginia shall never be made defendant in any court of law or equity...."[565] Additionally, the Governmental Tort Claims and Insurance Reform Act[566] states:

> The Legislature finds and declares that the political subdivisions of this state are unable to procure adequate liability insurance coverage at a reasonable cost due to: The high cost of defending such claims, the risk of liability beyond the affordable coverage, and the inability of political subdivisions to raise sufficient revenues for the procurement of such coverage without reducing the quantity and quality of traditional governmental services. Therefore, it is necessary to establish certain immunities and limitations with regard to the liability of political subdivisions and their employees..., to...permit such political subdivisions to provide necessary and needed governmental services to its citizens within the limits of their available revenues.[567]

563 *Id.* The account is "financed through annual premiums assessed to state agencies, based on sound actuarial principles" with annual premium levels being determined by the risk manager. This requires an actuarial study "conducted to assist in determining the appropriate level of funding."

564 *Id.* at 4.92.075. If the attorney general finds that the acts or omissions of a state officer, employee, or volunteer "were purported to be in good faith, within the scope of that person's official duties..."a request for representation "shall be granted, in which event the necessary expenses of the defense" of the action is paid as provided in R.C.W. 4.92.130. *Id.* at 4.92.070. The attorney general appears and defends the defense of the suit against the officer, employee, or volunteer. *Id.*

565 West Virginia Constitution, Article 6, §35.

566 W. Va. Code §§29-12A-1 to 29-12A-18.

567 *Id.* at §29-12A-2.

As the West Virginia Supreme Court noted,[568] "the legislature specified seventeen instances in which political subdivisions have immunity from tort liability."[569] The state maintains its immunity in most circumstances, and governmental officials performing discretionary functions have immunity from liability for civil damages if "their conduct does not violate clearly established statutory or constitutional rights of which a reasonable person would have known."[570] The Supreme Court has stated that "immunities must be assessed on a case-by-case basis in light of the governmental entities and/or officials named and the nature of the actions and allegations giving rise to the claim."[571]

"In the absence of an insurance contract waiving the defense, *the doctrine of qualified or official immunity bars a claim of mere negligence against a State agency* not within the purview of the West Virginia Governmental Tort Claims and Insurance Reform Act...and against an officer of that department acting within the scope of his or her employment, *with respect to the discretionary judgments, decisions, and actions of the officer*."[572] Nonetheless, "an official is not immune from a discretionary action that "violate[s] clearly established laws of which a reasonable official would have known."[573]

XX. WISCONSIN

The Wisconsin Constitution[574] provides: "The legislature shall direct by law in what manner and in which courts suits may be brought against the state."

568 *Standard Distributing, Inc. v. City of Charleston*, 625 S.E.2d 305, 310 (W.Va. 2005).

569 See W.Va. Code 29-12A-5(a). A political subdivision is immune from liability if a loss or claim results from legislative or quasi-legislative functions. *Id.* A political subdivision has immunity "regardless of whether the loss or claim is caused by negligence on the part of the subdivision's employees while acting within the scope of employment." *Standard Distributing*, 625 S.E. 2d at 311.

570 *Hess v. West Virginia Div. of Corrections*, 705 S.E.2d 125 (W. Va. 2010) (quoting *Bennett v. Coffman*, 361 S.W.3d 465 (W.Va. 1987)).

571 *West Virginia Dep't of Health and Human Resources v. Payne*, 746 S.E.2d 554 (V. Va. 2013).

572 *Id.* at 563, quoting *Clark v. Dunn*, 465 S.E.2d 374 (1995) (and emphasis added by the court.). The court commented that the purpose of official immunity "is not to protect an erring official, but to insulate the decisionmaking process from the harassment of prospective litigation." The court reasoned that "immunity rests on the view that the threat of liability will make officials unduly timid in carrying out their official duties." *Id.*

573 *Id.* citing *State v. Chase Securities*, 424 S.E. 2d 591 (1992).

574 Wisconsin Constitution, Article IV, §27.

Courts interpreted the language in the Wisconsin Constitution to mean that the state could be sued only with its consent.[575]

The Wisconsin Supreme Court expressed a condemnation of governmental immunity in *Holytz v. City of Milwaukee*,[576] stating: 'There are probably few tenets of American jurisprudence which have been so unanimously berated as the governmental immunity doctrine. This court and the highest courts of numerous other states have been unusually articulate in castigating the existing rule; text writers and law reviews have joined the chorus of denunciators." Although the Wisconsin Supreme Court eliminated governmental immunity in *Holytz*, removing the state's defense of nonliability for torts, the court stated that its decision had no effect upon the state's sovereign right under the Constitution to be sued only upon its consent.[577]

Currently, a governmental entity has immunity from liability for acts done "'in the exercise of its legislative or judicial or quasi-legislative or quasi-judicial functions.'"[578] The Wisconsin Supreme Court has noted that an entity the state creates "independent from the state, which acts as neither its arm nor its agent... falls outside the protection of sovereign immunity;" these such entities, referred to as "independent going concerns," do not have immunity.[579]

The Wisconsin Supreme Court[580] has rejected an argument that the application of sovereign immunity violates an Open Court provision of the Wisconsin Constitution.[581]

---

575 *See., e. g., Holytz v. City of Milwaukee,* 115 N. W. 2d 618, 626 (Wis. 1962)

576 *Id.* at 621-22. The Supreme Court referred to its decision in *Smith v. Congregation of St. Rose,* 61 N.W.2d 896, 898 (Wis. 1953), wherein it stated: "this court has long felt that the reasons for granting such immunity...are archaic."

577 Holztz, 115 N.W. 2d at 623.

578 *Melchert v. Pro Electric Contractors,* 892 N.W.3d 710, 718 (Wis. 2017) (citing *Holytz*). This is codified in Wis. Stat. §893.80(4). The court stated: "Legislative and quasi-legislative functions generally refer to those policy choices made in an official capacity....," *id* at 719, citing *Estate of Lyons v. CNA Ins.,* 558 N.W.2d 758 (Wis. Ct. App. 1996).

579 *Mayhugh v. State of Wisconsin,* 867 N.W.2d 754, 758 (Wis. 2015). Wis. Stat. §893.80(4) ("[I]n determining whether a state entity is an independent going concern, courts...consider both the character and breadth of the statutory powers granted to the entity.") *Id.* at 759. When an entity's powers "weigh in favor of independence," they are ineligible for sovereign immunity. *Id.* at 760.

580 *Id.* at 764.

581 Article I, §9 of the Wisconsin Constitution states that "[e]very person is entitled to a certain remedy in the laws for all injuries, or wrongs which he may receive in his person, property, or character...." The Wisconsin Supreme Court, id, agreed with precedent, from which it declined to diverge, that "[t]here is no 'right' of a citizen to hold his sovereign substantively liable for a tort," citing *Apfel-*

YY. WYOMING

Following the Wyoming Supreme Court abolishing the doctrine of municipal immunity in 1978,[582] the Wyoming legislature enacted the Wyoming Governmental Claims Act (WGCA),[583] "recognizing the 'inherently unfair and inequitable results which occur in the strict application of the doctrine of government immunity,' yet seeking 'to balance the respective equities between persons injured by governmental actions and the state of Wyoming whose revenues are utilized by governmental entities on behalf of those taxpayers.'"[584] The Wyoming Supreme Court[585] stated: "That balance was struck by a general grant of immunity to 'a governmental entity and its public employees while acting within the scope of duties....'"[586]

The WGCA states:[587] "A governmental entity and its public employees while acting within the scope of duties are granted immunity from liability for any tort except as provided by [statute]."[588] As the Wyoming Supreme Court noted in *Whitham v. Feller*,[589] the definition of "governmental entity" includes "local government," and the definition of "local government" includes "school districts." Thus, the court granted immunity to a school district defendant and dismissed claims that the school district employees were acting outside the scope of their duties, "as was required for [plaintiffs] to allege that the school district and its employees were not entitled to immunity under the Act."[590]

---

bacher v. State, 152 N.W.144 (1915) and *Forseth v. Sweet*, 158 N.W.2d 370 (Wis. 1968), among others.

582 *Oroz v. Bd. of Cty. Comm'rs of Carbon Cty.*, 575 P.2d 1155, 1158 (Wyo. 1978) (declaring that "[h]enceforth, the rule is liability and the exception is immunity....")

583 Wyo. Stat. Ann. §§1-39-101 to 121.

584 *Archer v. State of Wyoming*, 413 P.3d 142, 145 (Wyo. 2018) (citing Wyo. Stat. Ann. §1-39-102(a)).

585 *Id.* at 146, quoting Wyo. Stat. Ann. §1-39-104(a).

586 Except as provided by Wyo. Stat. §§1-39-105 through 1-39-112.

587 Section 1-39-104(a).

588 Wyo. Stat. §§1-39-105 through 1-39-112.

589 *Feller*, 415 P. 3d 1264, 1267 (Wyo. 2018).

590 *Id.* The court stated: "It is not this Court's prerogative to expand the exceptions to immunity beyond that provided by the legislature in the WGCA" and rejected the plaintiffs' "request to recognize an exception to immunity for violation of school policy and/or criminal conduct." *Id* at 1269-70.

The Wyoming statute provides:[591] "In the case of the state, this act abolishes all judicially created categories such as 'governmental' or 'proprietary' functions and 'discretionary' or 'ministerial' acts previously used by the courts to determine immunity or liability. This act does not impose nor allow the imposition of strict liability for acts of governmental entities or public employees." The Wyoming statute[592] waives governmental immunity "to the extent a governmental entity has insurance coverage either exceeding the limits of liability...or covering liability which is not authorized by" the WGCA.[593]

591 Wyo. Stat. §1-39-102(b).

592 Wyo. Stat. §1-39-118(b)(I).

593 In *Archer,* 413 P.3d at 184, the court disregarded plaintiffs' claims they had no opportunity to conduct discovery on the existence of insurance coverage before their case was dismissed. The Supreme Court stated that its "standard of review requires us to accept the facts stated in the amended complaint as true, and there are no allegations regarding insurance coverage." *Id.*

CHAPTER 7. A SUMMATION OF SOVEREIGN IMMUNITY PRINCIPLES WITH A CHECKLIST OF PROCEDURAL GUIDELINES FOR SUITS AGAINST THE STATE

This chapter presents a review of principles relating to the doctrine of sovereign immunity as discussed in the book chapters. It sets out a summary analysis of the sovereign immunity doctrine and provides the reader with a suggested checklist of steps to follow prior to filing legal claims against the government.

A. REVIEW OF SOVEREIGN IMMUNITY PRINCIPLES

The following is a checklist of the major points in the chapters.

1. The doctrine of sovereign immunity bars private lawsuits against the government without its consent with few exceptions.

2. The sovereign immunity doctrine was initially, and is historically, based on court decisions, not on statutory law.

3. Courts have upheld the sovereign immunity judicial doctrine based on another doctrine--the doctrine of *stare decisis*; however, courts have departed from precedent when there is sound reason to do so, such as a necessity to vindicate principles of law and to remedy continued injustice founded on present case law.

4. The Eleventh Amendment guarantees that an unconsenting state is immune from suits brought in federal courts by the state's citizens as well as by citizens of another state.

5. If properly raised, the Eleventh Amendment bars actions in federal court against a state, state agencies, and state officials acting in their official capacities.

6. Unlike other affirmative defenses, the Eleventh Amendment defense sufficiently partakes of the nature of a jurisdictional bar that may be raised at any point in proceedings, including on appeals.

7. A suit in federal court against a state official or state employee should be brought in that person's individual capacity, not the person's official capacity, to avoid an Eleventh Amendment bar.

8. District court decisions rejecting state claims of sovereign immunity under the Eleventh Amendment are reviewable immediately under 28 U.S.C. §1291 as final decisions pursuant to the collateral order doctrine. An appellate court reviews a district court's legal conclusions *de novo*, its findings of fact for clear error, and its balance of the equities for abuse of discretion. The denial of state sovereign immunity is a legal conclusion the appellate court reviews *de novo.*

9. In limited circumstances, a private party may bring suit without a valid abrogation or waiver of immunity. Pursuant to the doctrine of *Ex parte Young* and the Administrative Procedure Act that replaced *Ex parte Young* as the doctrinal basis for a claim for prospective relief, a state official sued in the official's official capacity may be enjoined from taking action that violates federal law.

10. Because an unconstitutional legislative enactment is "void," a state official who enforces such a law comes into conflict with the superior authority of the Constitution and therefore is stripped of the person's official or representative character and should be subjected to the consequences of the official's individual conduct.

11. Most suits against state officials and employees for violations of constitutional rights generally are brought pursuant to 42 U.S.C. §1983, which makes deprivation of constitutional rights actionable independent of state law. State immunities are not applicable to these actions. Nonetheless, suits must be brought in an official's individual capacity because the Supreme Court has ruled that neither states nor officials acting within their official capacities are "persons" within the meaning of §1983.

12. Congress has recognized an implied damages action against federal officials and employees for violations of constitutional rights that is similar to an action against state officials under 42 U.S.C. §1983. Although some courts express reluctance to extend this type of action, originally called a *Bivens* action, the action has statutory recognition at 28 U.S.C. §2679(b)(2)(A).

13. Congress may abrogate sovereign immunity in some cases.

14. A party may bring suit against the government in circumstances wherein Congress has abrogated validly the state's immunity.

15. Congress cannot abrogate the state's immunity under its Article I powers.

16. Section Five of the Fourteenth Amendment empowers Congress to abrogate state immunity through legislation that enforces substantive provisions of the Fourteenth Amendment.

17. Title VII of the Civil Rights Act constituted a proper abrogation of Eleventh Amendment immunity.

18. The Equal Pay Act was a proper exercise of Congress' power under Section Five of the Fourteenth Amendment; Congress' abrogation of states' immunity was therefore proper.

19. The Age Discrimination in Employment Act's abrogation of Eleventh Amendment immunity exceeded Congress' authority under Section Five of the Fourteenth Amendment.

20. Congress validly abrogated Eleventh Amendment with respect to Title II of the Americans with Disabilities Act but not as to Title I of that Act.

21. Courts have ruled that when the states ratified the Bankruptcy Clause in the United States Constitution, the states acquiesced in a subordination of whatever sovereign immunity they might otherwise have asserted in proceedings necessary to effectuate the *in rem* jurisdiction of bankruptcy courts. The following facets of the exercise of *in rem* jurisdiction rejects a state's sovereign immunity defense--exercise of jurisdiction over the estate of the debtor, equitable distribution of the estate's property among creditors, and discharge. A waiver of immunity aligns with the primary goal of federal bankruptcy law–collecting and preserving a debtor's assets for equitable distribution among all creditors.

22. The Fifth Amendment permits suits against the federal government for a taking of private property for a public use without just compensation. A litigant is not required to establish a waiver of sovereign immunity because the Fifth Amendment explicitly grants a right to sue the government.

23. State constitutions generally include takings clauses similar to the Fifth Amendment that permits a property owner to bring suit against the state for just compensation, including in an inverse condemnation lawsuit.

24. There is no state immunity from jurisdiction with respect to actions relating to a government's immovable property.

25. Political subdivisions of the state are provided "governmental" immunity to preclude suits against these lesser state entities for acts involving discretionary duties of governmental employees performed in good faith within the scope of an employee's authority.

26. Both Congress and state legislatures can waive sovereign and governmental immunity, but most states require waivers to be clear and construe ambiguities in favor of immunity.

27. The federal government permits breach-of-contract claims. Claims are brought to the United States Court of Federal Claims.

28. Some states have not waived sovereign or governmental immunity for breach-of-contract claims.

29. The federal government has absolute immunity from liability for intentional torts of its employees. Further, as a general rule, its employees also have absolute immunity for their tortious acts if they were acting within the scope of employment when the acts occurred.

30. The Federal Whistleblower Act mandates that federal employees not suffer adverse consequences as a result of disclosing evidences of violations of federal laws or regulations. Still, victims have had limited protection under the Act. A federal whistleblower complaint is filed with the Office of Special Counsel.

31. Some states have whistleblower acts, but state courts may limit protection for whistleblowers by imposing technicalities as prerequisites to filing claims under the acts.

32. Many states have open court provisions that may provide some redress to victims being denied access to courts based on sovereign and governmental principles. Additionally, victims have protection under the Due Process Clause of the Fourteenth Amendment to the United States Constitution when they are denied access to the courts.

33. Tribal nations exercise "inherent sovereign authority," but courts have held that tribal employees do not have sovereign immunity when they are sued in their individual capacities.

34. An indemnification statute does not make a tribe the party in interest to support tribal sovereign immunity for tribal employees sued in their individual capacities.

35. While the Alien Torts Statute has provided limited access to courts in the United States for victims of violations of international law, that act does not waive immunity for foreign States.

36. The Foreign Sovereign Immunities Act is the sole basis for obtaining jurisdiction over a foreign State in United States courts. Although that Act establishes immunity for foreign States in most instances, the Act sets out some exceptions to immunity that permit courts in the United States to exercise

jurisdiction over claims against foreign sovereigns in specific cases, such as, among others, foreign states' commercial activities in the United States, their ownership of immovable property in the United States, and their violations of international law.

37. Courts are divided as to whether victims must exhaust remedies in a foreign State prior to filing a claim against a foreign State or its officials in a court in the United States.

38. The Foreign Sovereign Immunities Act does not grant foreign State officials immunity when they are sued in their individual capacities nor for acts committed outside the scope of their duties. Courts are divided as to whether these officials have immunity under the common law.

B. SUMMARY CRITIQUE OF SOVEREIGN IMMUNITY DOCTRINE

The book chapters establish that many courts in the United States consider themselves "self-constituted guardians of the Treasury,"[1] and, as such, seek to protect the public fisc through a strict interpretation of the doctrine of sovereign immunity. Nonetheless the chapters have also set out the opinions of several justices that protection of the public fisc is not a legitimate reason to perpetuate a perceived antiquated doctrine of sovereign immunity that has the ultimate effect of protecting governmental wrongdoing at the expense of the public. Rather than having a purpose "to shield the public from the costs and consequences of improvident actions of their governments,"[2] as one court suggested, a continued endorsement of the sovereign immunity doctrine can have the counter effect of increasing governmental costs due to the concealment and protection of illegal governmental activity. Additionally, a rigid application of sovereign and governmental principles discounts an impartial and independent judicial system.

In the United States, the sovereign is the *people*, not the state. However, when a state's constitution specifically provides that a state cannot be named as a defendant, when its laws deny its citizens' access to the courts to challenge egregious

1 *Indian Towing Co. v. United States*, 350 U.S. 61,69 (1955) (emphasizing that the Court "as a self-constituted guardian of the Treasury" should not "import immunity back into a statute designed to limit it."

2 *Tooke v. City of Mexia*, 197 S.W.3d 325, 332 (Tex. 2006).

governmental acts, the state has made it the sovereign, rather than the people. A review of the history of the doctrine of sovereign immunity informs that the doctrine's purpose may have been to remove sovereignty from the people. Such a purpose cannot be in conformity with the purposes of a democracy.

At a minimum, the need to hold governmental officials accountable for their improvident acts and societal demands for honest and ethical conduct on the part of governmental officials should mandate a reassessment of the doctrine of sovereign immunity. The position that governmental operations would be halted if citizens can sue the government may no longer justify retaining a "manifestation merely of power."[3] Governments and their officials, like all other entities and individuals, must be subject to the rule of law, must be bound to obey it, and must be accountable if they do not. To the extent the doctrine of sovereign immunity places governments and their officials above the law, the doctrine may indeed be "more a relic of medieval thought than anything else."[4]

In evaluating the doctrine of sovereign immunity, and considering both pros and cons, the reader is referred to earlier decisions from the Supreme Courts of Virginia and North Dakota that were set out in Chapter 6.

In *Messina v. Burden*,[5] the Supreme Court of Virginia reasoned that while "protection of the public purse" is a basis for the doctrine, "another equally important purpose of the rule is the orderly administration of government." The court concluded the doctrine "serves a multitude of purposes, including but not limited to protecting the public purse, providing for smooth operation of government, eliminating public inconvenience and danger that might spring from officials being fearful to act, assuring that citizens will be willing to take public jobs, and preventing citizens from improperly influencing the conduct of governmental affairs through the threat or use of vexatious litigation." The court referred to the doctrine "as a rule of social policy, which protects the state from burdensome interference with the performance of its governmental functions and preserves its control over state funds, property and instrumentalities."[6] It stated: "Given the several purposes of the doctrine, it follows that in order to fulfill those purposes, the protection afforded by the doctrine cannot be limited solely to the sovereign." The court decided: "Unless the protection of the doc-

3 *Pennhurst State Sch. & Hosp. v. Halderman*, 465 U.S. 89, 164 n. 48 (1984) (Stevens, J., dissenting).

4 *Id.*

5 321 S.E.2d 657 (Va. 1984).

6 *Id.* at 659-60.

trine extends to some of the people who help run the government, the majority of the purposes for the doctrine will remain unaddressed."[7]

As the Virginia Court pointed out, there can be some justification to provide immunity for certain governmental officials, particularly when they perform judicial, legislative, or administrative functions. However, Congress and the states can address a governmental need to protect the public fisc by placing limits on amounts litigants can obtain in suits against the government. Further, governmental entities, like all others, can obtain insurance to protect against the financial burden of civil suits brought by victims of improvident governmental conduct.

In abrogating immunity for the State of North Dakota, the North Dakota Supreme Court expressed its concern in *Bulman v. Hulstrand Constr. Co., Inc.*[8] that "[w]hatever justifications initially existed for sovereign immunity, they are no longer valid in today's society," noting that "[f]ew principles of modern law have been so uniformly and soundly criticized." The North Dakota Supreme Court decided that "sovereign immunity from tort liability... perpetuates injustice by barring recovery for tortious conduct merely because of the status of the wrongdoer," commenting "that the harshness and inequity of the doctrine of sovereign immunity are counterintuitive to any ordinary person's sense of justice," and declaring that stare decisis also does not "justify the perpetuation of an outdated, unforgiving common-law doctrine."[9]

C. STEPS IN FILING LEGAL ACTION AGAINST THE GOVERNMENT

Accepting though that sovereign immunity may remain a "part of the fabric of our law" indefinitely and that victims of governmental wrongdoing must have some means to counter the procedural hurdles that deny them redress for their

7 *Id.* at 61.

8 521 N.W.2d 632 (N.D. 1994).

9 *Id.* at 639. The court commented that "even under the earliest common law of England, sovereign immunity did not produce the harsh results it does today and only rarely did it completely deny relief." *Id.* Still, while abolishing the state's sovereign immunity from tort liability, the North Dakota Supreme Court did not impose "tort liability on the state for the exercise of discretionary acts in its official capacity, including legislative, judicial, quasi-legislative, and quasi-judicial functions." *Id.* at 640.

injuries and damages, a summary follows of procedural rules and guidelines for victims of abuse by an authoritative government and court system.

To prevent an assertion of sovereign immunity from defeating a trial court's subject-matter jurisdiction, a citizen suing the government must establish the sovereign's consent to suit. Some statutes waive a government's immunity from suits involving express or implied contracts, constitutional claims, and claims founded on statutory provisions. A consent to sue the government can consist of statutory waivers of sovereign immunity, but courts in states that maintain sovereignty require waivers to be unequivocally clear and strictly construe ambiguities in favor of the sovereign.

Prior to filing a lawsuit in a federal court against a state or a state employee in that person's official capacity, victims must consider that the state generally will invoke Eleventh Amendment immunity to allege a jurisdictional bar to suit. Still, Congress may have abrogated immunity by congressional legislation intended to enforce substantive provisions of the Fourteenth Amendment. Additionally, if a state moves to Federal court a claim filed against it in a state court, the voluntarily removal of the case should waive that state's Eleventh Amendment immunity.

For suits charging governmental officials with unconstitutional conduct, sovereign immunity will apply if the government is the "real, substantial party in interest." Similarly, claims for monetary damages brought against state officials in their official capacities are considered to be suits against the state. Thus, victims are limited to obtaining only injunctive relief against future conduct unless the victims sue governmental officials in their individual capacities. Still, officials sued in their individual capacities can still assert qualified immunity as an affirmative defense in a federal court. State law should be perused to determine liability of governmental employees under that state's immunity laws, and additionally, whether the state deems suit against a government official or employee in that person's individual capacity nevertheless to be a suit against the state.

Qualified immunity for federal officials can be defeated in several ways, including proof of an official's knowledge or intent with respect to actions that violate constitutional rights, or through a statutory implied cause of action for damages resulting from constitutional tort violations of federal officials and employees, i. e., a *Bivens* action.

A §1983 action brought against a state official in the official's *individual* capacity is actionable independent of state law if the state official deprived a victim of the victim's constitutional rights while acting under the color of state statute, regulation, or custom. Section 1983 claims must be brought against a state employee in that person's individual capacity; the Supreme Court has ruled that neither the state nor a governmental employee acting within an official capacity is a "person" for purposes of a §1983 action.

The Federal and most state Tort Claims Acts waive sovereign immunity for limited types of tortious acts or injuries. Additionally, whistleblower acts waive sovereign immunity in limited circumstances. A court's interpretation of these acts in the context of limiting or overriding sovereign immunity to the extent of denying a claimant access to courts can be a violation of a state's open courts provisions and/or a violation of the Due Process Clause of the Fourteenth Amendment to the United States Constitution.

Prior to filing a legal action against the federal or a state government and/or their officials and employees, a claimant should recall the following procedural guidelines.

1. Obtain needed documentation prior to following a claim against the government or its employees. This can be accomplished by requesting and procuring documents through a state's public information act or from the federal government through the Freedom of Information Act.[10] A request for documents should be made prior to bringing a claim against the government to have sufficient facts and evidence to avoid a trial court dismissing the complaint based on a sovereign immunity jurisdictional bar.

2. Draft a petition carefully, making certain it meets a state or federal jurisdictional challenge, and should the petition have been filed without proper documentation, request a trial court to defer ruling on a government's summary judgment motion or plea to the jurisdiction until the litigant can develop the case more fully.

3. In response to a state court's granting of a state's summary judgment motion or plea to the jurisdiction that would prevent a claimant from even pursuing a remedy against the state, preserve error regarding the state's denial of the claimant's right to access to the courts by an allegation in the response to that motion or plea. The due process clause of the Fourteenth Amendment to the

10 5 U.S.C. §552.

United States Constitution requires a state to afford civil litigants a "meaningful opportunity to be heard" by removing obstacles and providing for their "full participation in judicial proceedings.[11] The claimant should challenge a possible dismissal of a claim against the state or its officials or employees as being a violation of the (a) a state's open courts provision, if any, and (b) additionally, a Fourteenth Amendment due process allegation that will preserve the claimant pursuing a writ of certiorari to the United States Supreme Court if the state trial court grants the motion or plea and the appellate courts affirm.[12] The allegation must be preserved throughout the proceedings.

4. Consider bringing a tort action claim against a governmental employee in the employee's individual capacity to avoid dismissal of the claim based on it being a claim against the federal or a state government that is barred by absolute sovereign immunity. Any damages possibly assessed against the employee may be paid by the government; the United States Supreme Court has ruled that an indemnification statute for governmental employees does not make the government the real party in interest to support state sovereign immunity. (A few states have provisions that an action against a governmental employee in that person's individual capacity is nonetheless an action against the state.)

5. Prior to bringing a tort claim against the State of Texas or its officials or employees, review in depth the election of remedies provision that was an amendment to the Texas Tort Claim Act. The election of remedies provision is discussed in Chapter 4 under "Tort Claims Act" and in Chapter 6 in the discussion of sovereign immunity law in Texas. The election of remedies provision, as interpreted by the Texas Supreme Court, precludes almost all tort actions against the state as well as its officials and employees. A tort claim against the

11 *Boddie v. Connecticut*, 401 U.S. 371, 91 S. Ct. 789, 82 L. Ed. 2d 113 (1971).

12 Rule 14(g) of the Rules of the Supreme Court of the United States (2017) require that if review of a state-court judgment is sought, a petitioner must specify "the stage in the proceedings, both in the court of first instance and in the appellate courts, when the federal questions sought to be reviewed were raised; the method or manner of raising them and the way in which they were passed on by those courts; and pertinent quotations of specific portions of the record or summary thereof, with specific reference to the places in the record where the matter appears (e. g., court opinion, ruling on exception, portion of court's charge and exception thereto, assignment of error), so as to show that the federal question was timely and properly raised and that ... [the] Court has jurisdiction to review the judgment on a writ of certiorari."

state, its officials, or employees should include allegations of Open Courts and Due Process Fourteenth Amendment violations.

6. Prior to filing a whistleblowers' action against the state of Texas or its officials, bring the whistleblower claim to an "outward-looking-law-enforcement authority" and obtain complete documentation of having brought the claim. (See discussion in Chapter 4 regarding an "outward-looking-law-enforcement authority.")

7. If suit is brought against a public university or a similar state agency and the university or agency seeks dismissal of the claim based on governmental immunity, challenge the defense of governmental agency status if the university or other state agency obtains substantial funds from contributions from the public, generally in the form of donations to their foundations.[13]

8. For a victim of a federal official's unconstitutional conduct, consider bringing a special cause of action called a *Bivens* action for damages resulting from the official's unconstitutional conduct despite the fact that some courts have been reluctant to extend that action. The theory of a *Bivens* action, which now is statutorily based, is that federal officials lose their sovereign immunity shield when they are involved in constitutional torts. A lawsuit brought against a federal official in a *Bivens* action should be brought against the official in the official's individual capacity.

9. If a state official deprives a plaintiff of the plaintiff's constitutional rights, consider a §1983 action against the state official, which is actionable independent of state law. Most suits against state officials are brought pursuant to §1983, which provides that a "person" who, under color of state statute, regulation, or custom, deprives another of any rights, privileges or immunities

---

13 In *Savage v. Glendale Union High School, Dist. No. 205, Maricopa County*, 343 F.3d 1036 (9th Cir. 2003), cert. denied, 124 S. Ct. 2067 (2004), the Court of Appeals for the Ninth Circuit ruled that a school district in Arizona was not an arm of the state, deciding that the Arizona State treasury would not be vulnerable to a money judgment against the school district because its school district could generate funds in addition to those provided by the state.

Additionally, in *Mariono v. Lenoir*, 526 S.W.3d 403 (Tex. 2017), the Texas Supreme Court denied governmental immunity to an employee of a public university's foundation, determining that the physician was not an employee of a governmental unit. (In some instances, university officials and personnel are paid completely by a university's foundation funds.)

"secured by the Constitution and laws" shall be liable to the injured party. Although state immunities are not applicable in a §1983 suit, the Supreme Court has sustained sovereign immunity for the states despite the language in §1983 by ruling that neither States nor state officials acting in their official capacities are "persons" within the meaning of §1983. Further, the Eleventh Amendment prevents states from bringing a suit against the state in a federal court. Thus, to obtain damages, bring the lawsuit against the state official in the official's individual capacity.

10. File breach-of-contract claims against the federal government, including a governmental taking of the property for which the Fifth Amendment provides compensation, and claims founded on acts of Congress or regulations of executive departments, with the United States Court of Federal Claims. The Tucker Act waived immunity for suits arising out of express or implied contracts to which the federal government was a party.

11. In filing a claim against a foreign government, review the immunity exceptions set out in the Foreign Sovereign Immunity Act and draft a petition accordingly to obtain waiver of immunity. Here again, obtain sufficient documentation prior to filing a petition.

www.ingramcontent.com/pod-product-compliance
Lightning Source LLC
LaVergne TN
LVHW052304200926
848481LV00002B/464